Organizational Change

Organizational Change

Edited by

Linda J. Hayes

John A. Austin

Ramona Houmanfar

Michael C. Clayton

CONTEXT PRESS
Reno, Nevada

Publisher's Note

This publication is designed to provide accurate and authoritative information in regard to the subject matter covered. It is sold with the understanding that the publisher is not engaged in rendering psychological, financial, legal, or other professional services. If expert assistance or counseling is needed, the services of a competent professional should be sought.

Distributed in Canada by Raincoast Books

© 2001 Context Press

Context Press is an imprint of New Harbinger Publications, Inc.
5674 Shattuck Ave.
Oakland, CA 94609
www.newharbinger.com

Printed in the United States of America

Library of Congress Cataloging-in-Publication Data
Organizational Change / edited by Linda J. Hayes ... [et al.].
    p. cm.
    Includes bibliographical references
    ISBN-13: 978-1-878978-39-4
    ISBN-10: 1-878978-39-X
    1. Organiztional change. I. Hayes, Linda J.

    HD58.8 .O7286 2001
    658.4'06--dc21
    2001028009

Table of Contents

Section 3: Methodological Innovations

Section 4: Applications in Public and Private Sectors

Section 5: Theoretical Issues

Using Institutional Effectiveness Assessment to Plan, Implement, and Evaluate Organizational Change in Higher Education: Great Promise Largely Unfulfilled

Reid Johnson
Institutional Effectiveness Assessment Consulting Services

Introduction to IEA

At the risk of understatement, it is safe to say that Institutional Effectiveness Assessment (IEA) is one of the most important and pressing issues in American higher education in the 1990's. Today, over 80% of the 50 United States and all six regional accreditation agencies require in only slightly varying language that colleges and universities answer what I call the Four Cardinal Questions of Effectiveness (Johnson & Seymour, 1996):

1. What goals is the higher education institution trying to accomplish?
2. How is the institution trying to accomplish its goals?
3. How well is the institution accomplishing its goals?
4. How is the institution using its assessment results to insure continuous effectiveness improvement into the future?

For private or independent colleges and universities, both *regional accreditation* (which governs their eligibility for governmental loans and grants, and on which transferability of their course credits is based) and *specialized accreditation* (which paves the way into entry level jobs or more advanced education in many fields, and on which many credentialing - i.e., certification and licensure - exams are based), depend on the college or academic program's ability to demonstrate at least adequate IEA. The same two IEA challenges also apply to public colleges and universities, but most of them also face IEA-related *assessment mandates* from state higher education agencies and even IEA-based *performance funding* from state governments, as well. In short, IEA is both a very salient academic integrity and economic issue for most colleges and universities in this country. Thus, a thorough understanding of IEA and the strengths and weaknesses of the many available IEA models, methods, and materials is vital to successfully performing higher education roles today, whether one's job description is primarily administrative, faculty, or staff.

The basic idea of all these external IEA mandates is simple: Every higher educator should ask those four Cardinal Questions of their particular area of responsibility - be that at the course, program, office, division, institutional, or system level - and use good IEA practices to comprehensively and systematically answer each question as accurately as possible. The results of such evaluations, in turn, should be integrated into each institution's routine management, planning, budgeting, and resource allocation policies and procedures in a way that ensures continuous effectiveness improvement from that point on. Granting that full implementation of an IEA system can take up to one to three years to accomplish, even the most ineffective or recalcitrant school should have a good IEA system up and running within three years of receiving its mandate or deciding to do so on its own.

In 1998, IEA is clearly not a new concern or recent higher education phenomenon. The first regional accreditation IEA mandate was passed in 1984, the first state assessment mandate was enacted in 1979, and some specialized accreditors' IEA requirements predate those by decades (Ewell, 1993). Given IEA's import and long history, it would therefore be reasonable to expect that all conscientious higher educators have a good working knowledge of IEA principles and procedures, and are routinely using them to the benefit of their academic programs, administrative and support offices, institutions, and higher education systems. It would be reasonable, but it would also be wrong.

Based on annual *Campus Trends* surveys conducted by the American Council on Education (ACE) (El-Khawas, 1995), and on annual reports from regional accrediting agencies such as the IEA-pioneering Southern Association of Colleges and Schools' Commission on Colleges (SACS COC) and America's largest regional accreditor, the North Central Association (NCA), as well as my own professional experience consulting on IEA with over 50 colleges, universities and systems in 20 states and five of the six accreditation regions, the majority of higher education administrators - and the *large* majority of faculty and staff - still have little or no accurate knowledge of good IEA principles and practices, and are doing as little IEA using as "quick and dirty" IEA methods as they possibly can. (I call such just-try-to-get-by tactics "IEA Minimalism".)

For many reasons which will hopefully become apparent throughout this paper, the present state of affairs is nothing less than a recipe for disaster when it comes to higher education effectiveness and effectiveness improvement. I also believe those in public higher education are courting even potentially greater calamities - such as increased under-funding and possible loss of educator-control over higher education operations and curricula - by our failure to respond quickly and constructively to external IEA demands. But a more detailed explication of those perils can await a later treatment. For now, let's get back to the basics.

Key Terms and Concepts

One of the litany of excuses higher educators have used for not embracing IEA and not giving it the same level of "good faith effort" they devote to their other higher education responsibilities - such as instruction, scholarship, and/or service - is that

IEA involves difficult to understand terms and concepts, and difficult to implement methods and procedures. In an effort to assure that we are speaking the same language for purposes of this paper, herewith a primer of basic IEA terms and concepts. (Please advise if you find a difficult one!)

Institution. A college or university granting associate, baccalaureate, masters, and/or doctoral degrees, and performing a higher education mission.

Mission. A college or university's core purpose and goals, reflecting its distinctive mixture and priorities of instruction, scholarship, and service, and utilizing its resources to best serve its tradition, students, community, and/or consumers. (For virtually all higher education institutions, their primary mission priority is *instruction*.)

Effectiveness. Quality and efficiency.

Quality. Meeting or exceeding internal and external standards of excellence.

Efficiency. (Productivity - Cost) Meeting or exceeding internal and external standards of productivity, timeliness or speed, and cost.

Assessment. Any evaluative measurement.

Evaluation. Judging the goodness/badness - or positiveness/negativeness, desirability/undesirability, satisfactoriness/unsatisfactoriness, success/failure, etc. - of something.

Measurement. The quantification - which needn't mean *enumeration* - of some natural phenomenon. (Examples of non-numerative measurements in higher education are pass/fail, admitted/rejected, graduated/not graduated, hired/not hired, etc.)

Outcomes Assessment. Basing an evaluative assessment on the measurement of the actual products/outputs/results of an effort, rather than only on the intentions, resources, or processes that went into that effort.

Validity. A technical attribute of an assessment, meaning that its measurements are specific, accurate, and relevant for its purpose.

Institutional Effectiveness Assessment (IEA). *Evaluating* the *quality* and *efficiency* of a college or university - or any of its constituent programs and offices - by *validly* measuring the *results* of its instructional, scholarship, and service efforts, with an emphasis on *instructional outcomes.*

Continuous Effectiveness Improvement (CEI). Using the results of IEA to analyze and prioritize evaluations, plans, budgets, and resource allocations, for the purpose of ensuring a higher quality and efficiency of institutional policies and procedures in the future.

Now what was so difficult about that? Without intending to be unduly critical or cynical toward many of my higher educator colleagues, I think it is safe to say that difficulty of understanding is not the real reason most faculty, administrators, and staff have not given IEA a fair chance to prove its worth on their campuses. I'll explore some more probable alternative reasons in a later section, but first let's look back at how IEA has evolved - or perhaps de-evolved - in American higher education thus far.

A Brief History of the "Higher Education Assessment Movement" and IEA

The first two American colleges to attempt to systematically assess the achievement of their students as a primary indicator of the quality of their educational efforts did so in 1972. Alverno College was a small Catholic women's college in Milwaukee, Wisconsin facing possible demise due to decreased enrollments and funding, which was all too common of similar schools of that day. Instead of resigning themselves to their fate and going quietly, new leadership at Alverno decided to gamble that their school was doing a good enough job to survive if they could just demonstrate their effectiveness in a new and dramatic way. Thus, Alverno converted to an entirely performance-based (*a la competency-based*) curriculum, where its students were continuously assessed throughout their course of studies, and their progress and even graduation depended not just on course grades but on demonstration of competencies compared to pre-set performance criteria. Students were recruited, and faculty and administrators were hired and fired based on this new performance-based education system. It was risky, it was dramatically different from traditional higher education, and it worked. Not only did Alverno not fold, it thrived, and has become a model of performance-based higher education and assessment for institutions everywhere.

At the same time, new leadership at one of the University of Missouri's regional campuses, Northeast Missouri State University (NESU - now Truman State), was also looking to assessment as a possible renaissance tool for enhancing its own image and curriculum. By systematically administering norm-referenced standardized tests to its students every year, and using those externally benchmarked results as more objective bases for student and curriculum evaluation and intervention, NESU began touting its "education with integrity" as being more accountable and credible than those of its peer institutions. As with Alverno, its assessment strategy worked; i.e., NESU became a much higher profile institution, began attracting more and better students, received higher funding levels, and became a model for other schools interested in such uses of standardized testing.

This began what for over two decades has been called the "Higher Education Assessment Movement" in America. Two schools interested in improving their evidence for quality - and to some extent their economic efficiency - had shown comprehensive systematic student assessment to be an effective tool for both those vital purposes.

Throughout the next decade, a few "second wave" colleges and universities - such as Kings College (PA), Keane College (NJ), Clayton State (GA), Miami-Dade Community College (FL), and the University of Tennessee - began to launch major assessment initiatives on their campuses, with some based on the Alverno or NESU models and some exploring new assessment avenues of their own. Most U. S. colleges and universities at this time, however, were paying little or no attention to higher education assessment, or were only launching experimental assessment projects on a very limited basis.

The whole tenor of the higher education assessment movement changed in 1979, when based on very limited empirical experience with NESU-like standardized testing, the Tennessee Higher Education Commission (T-HEC) sought and received state legislation requiring some public colleges and universities to use one standardized test to assess the achievement of their students, and using those test results to determine part of those institutions' state funding. Tennessee's "Performance Funding Law" constituted the first *external higher education assessment mandate* in this country, and launched a new era of "one step forward and two steps back" in what was to soon become IEA. Now higher education assessment was becoming an externally mandated accountability tool, rather than an internally motivated self-improvement tool as it had originally begun. As news of the Tennessee law spread, most higher educators heard about assessment for the first time. Many questions began to be raised about what higher education assessment really was, and how it would affect higher educators, their students, and their institutions.

By the mid-1980's, new developments in the evolution of higher education assessment were coming thick and fast. Perhaps most importantly, in 1984, the Southern Association of Colleges and Schools' Commission on Colleges (SACS COC) promulgated the first regional accreditation assessment requirement, making all colleges and universities in eleven states - large, small, two-year, four-year, doctoral, public, private, prestigious, open-door, and proprietary alike - subject to serious sanctions for not implementing comprehensive assessment programs. The SACS COC also changed higher education assessment's lexicon, shifting from an emphasis on methodology - i.e., *assessment*, to an emphasis on the desired outcome of the methodology - i.e., *institutional effectiveness*. Thus, because of the extreme importance of regional accreditation to all higher education institutions, and because the SACS COC was a constituent body of higher educators - mostly college presidents - instead of outsiders, and because of their clear emphasis on assessment-for-self-improvement, higher education assessment took on a much higher level of import and legitimacy, and became a primary issue on most campuses in the southeast. It was also during this time that publishing higher education assessment instruments - especially surveys and tests - became a growth industry.

By the end of the 1980's, the majority of campuses were reporting at least some assessment efforts, higher education assessment was a staple topic in the *Chronicle of Higher Education* and was being found in most disciplines' professional literature as well, the American Association for Higher Education (AAHE) had begun holding annual higher education assessment conferences, over 40 states were considering or had passed assessment mandate laws, and all six regional accreditation agencies were headed toward requiring outcomes assessment for initial accreditation and reaffirmation (Johnson et al., 1991). Since the early 1990's, all accredited U.S. colleges and universities have been under one or more external mandates to do IEA; i.e., define their institutional mission and goals, describe how they are trying to attain those goals, assess how well goal attainment is being accomplished, and use the assessment results to plan, implement, and evaluate continuous effectiveness improvement efforts. Institutional responses have been very diverse, with some making good faith efforts toward IEA - including some that have been exemplary - but with most adopting a minimalistic stance, or even doing nothing in a self-defeating "this too shall pass" stratagem.

Thus, in the last decade, it is difficult to find an issue which has had a greater impact on the course of higher education in America than institutional effectiveness assessment (IEA), nor one which as offered greater studies in contrast and controversy.

Hindsight from 1998 affords a perspective on the evolution - or de-evolution - of IEA which has been difficult to see as events have unfolded. (Since the two decades of the higher education assessment movement had essentially the same models and methods as IEA, I will henceforth refer to the whole period since the early 1970's as IEA, as well.) Let me use that perspective to cite a few patterns and elucidate some key issues - especially problems - which I think characterize the status of IEA today. It could be subtitled, "A Study in *De*-Evolution".

IEA Today

The Impetuses for IEA. As was noted briefly above, the initial impetuses for IEA came from within the institutions, i.e., *internal improvements* in quality and *efficiency*. Subsequently, college administrators naturally added a third impetus, *internal accountability*, i.e., using assessment results to guide internal evaluations and policy-making decisions. But since 1979, the greatest pressures for assessment have come from outside agencies and regulators such as state legislatures and commissions on higher education, and regional and specialized accreditors, initially in the form of *external effectiveness improvement* mandates - i.e., offering positive and negative incentives for assessment-based self improvements in quality and/or efficiency, and eventually in the form of *external accountability mandates* - i.e., much more invasive and predominantly negative incentives for *efficiency* improvements, which usually work to the detriment of quality. Worse still, many of the external efficiency-based mandates - particularly those under the heading of "Performance Funding" laws or regulations, are masquerading as "quality improvement" efforts while they actually undermine most internally and externally motivated quality improvement efforts. So many of the higher educators working in IEA today are doing it because they *have to* - *not* because they *want to* or are good at it - and they're having to do it for the wrong reasons - external accountability vs. effectiveness improvement. Thus, on many campuses, the real pressure is to do the assessments that produce the most favorable report, not to do the best or most accurate assessments for effectiveness improvement purposes.

The "IEA Methodology Paradox". Without getting off on a tangent with too many technical details, the scientifically-based measurements which constitute the methodological integrity of IEA are subject to a built-in dilemma which I call "The Quality:Efficiency Validity Seesaw". Simply put, the more valid a measurement technique, the more costly it tends to be in time, effort, and expense; conversely, any measurement that is quick, easy, and inexpensive is unlikely to be very valid for IEA purposes (i.e., quality and efficiency improvement and accountability). IEA in the 1970's and 1980's, although a distinctly minority enterprise, was marked by relatively high quality/validity assessment models and methods, such as systematic behavioral and performance appraisals, the better standardized tests, and other locally standardized measures. The 1990's have produced a boom market for higher education assessment instruments, but the large majority of IEA measures today are of the "quicker and dirtier" variety, like surveys, unsystematic observations, subjective opinions, and multiple-choice or unstandardized tests. Because these less valid measures produce questionable or invalid results, the database of IEA results on which institutional evaluations and interventions are supposed to be based is corrupted, which makes all IEA-based evaluations, plans, and actions tainted as well. This all too common pattern defeats the purposes for which IEA should be done in the first place.

IEA as "Add-On" Responsibility. Even in schools who say they are doing a lot of IEA, it is most often perceived and performed as an *extra* task - above and beyond higher educators' routine functions in teaching, scholarship, service, or administration. But that is not IEA's proper role. Done correctly, IEA becomes a new and better *way* of perceiving and performing one's teaching, scholarship, service, and administrative roles and functions, not a separate, add-on task. Until IEA becomes completely embedded in the fabric of higher education institutions' routines, its effects will be but a shadow of its potential.

IEA's "Ownership". In the early decades of IEA, close cooperation and collaboration between higher education administrators and faculty was critical to getting any significant IEA accomplished, much less accomplished well. Thus, while IEA projects and programs may have been administrator-driven, the faculty - and occasionally staff persons - *owned* IEA; i.e., they primarily decided what was to be assessed and why, how, when, and where it would be assessed, administered the assessments, and had first crack at analyzing and interpreting the results, and making recommendations on how the results should be used. Today the primary impetuses and ownership of IEA are external, in the form of regional and specialized accreditation standards, and legal regulations and mandates from state commissions on higher education or legislatures. Functionally, this means that the people deciding why to assess, what to assess, how to assess, when to assess, and what will be done with the results are administrators (through regional accreditors) and politicians, business people, and bureaucrats (through commissions and legislatures). In addition to the obvious de-motivating factors this loss of ownership brings for the faculty and staff "front line troops" who are actually doing the assessments, today's IEA owners are much less knowledgeable and concerned about higher education effectiveness in general, and instructional outcomes and measurement quality in particular, and much more attuned to accountability issues, cost efficiency, and whatever local educational and political issues might be hot at the time. The worst of these external mandates, the so-called Performance Funding Laws that are currently so popular among state legislators, are often anti-intellectual, anti-higher education and anti-quality in nature, and some even directly pay colleges and universities to *lower* their quality in the name of short-term cost efficiency. Just as with any other enterprise - in business, sports, or government - bad owner decisions can drive even the best-intentioned institution right into the ground.

    The "Defaulted *Quid Pro Quos*". Lest the reader think that I too conveniently blame educationally naïve outsiders and politicians for all of higher education's IEA woes, some of us within the academy have been largely responsible for empowering external forces to corrupt IEA in the first place. As the brief history above noted, most of the initial regional accreditation and state IEA mandates were promulgated in the 1980's. On the whole, those initial IEA standards - such as those adopted by the SACS COC and NCA (which govern colleges and universities in over 30 states), and the state assessment mandates in South Carolina, Georgia, and Virginia (not Tennessee, Florida, or Texas) - were relatively good. They basically required higher education institutions to address the Four Cardinal IEA questions, specified timelines and reporting information, and demanded accountable evidence of effectiveness improvement, but left the "what, how, when, where, and how to use" IEA largely up to the institutions themselves. Implicit in these early, "constructive" IEA mandates was a *quid pro quo*; i.e., if all the higher education institutions under their authority would do IEA *and do it right*, the institutions could retain ownership of the IEA process and have input on the standards and uses of IEA results. But the large majority of colleges and universities did *not* take this opportunity to design a legitimate IEA system and use it constructively on their campuses. Some openly resisted and railed against perceived "threats to institutional autonomy" and "loss of academic freedom". Most took what I've referred to as a "minimalist" approach, consisting of passive resistance, just doing enough IEA to approach the bare minimum letter of the law, or thinking and hoping that "this too shall pass". Only a few colleges and universities gave IEA a good faith effort. Most of us *defaulted* the *quid pro quo* without ever giving IEA a fair chance to prove itself as a fair and functional effectiveness improvement tool. The results of these defaults have been twofold: much more prescriptive, proscriptive, and counterproductive state assessment mandates for public colleges and universities, such as the so-called Performance Funding laws; and widespread ineffectiveness in the application of regional and specialized IEA accreditation requirements for both public and private schools, often taking the form of administrators or faculty accreditors who take a "live and let live" attitude regarding IEA standards: i.e., "My school's not doing much in IEA, either. Why should I penalize the college I'm visiting for not doing something we don't want to do ourselves?!" In both cases, the original good intentions and sound models and methods of IEA are being subverted, bureaucratized, and corrupted for other less noble political purposes. And at most schools, we have no one to blame but our leaders and ourselves.

Thus, what we have going on in American higher education today is a "sham IEA" masquerading fairly successfully as IEA. We have an enormous amount of campus activities being conducted in the name of IEA, with most failing to meet even the most minimal standards of educational and measurement integrity. We have faculty, staff, and administrators "massaging" assessment data to fit whatever the IEA *mandate du jour* happens to demand, and above all, trying to cover up the very weaknesses real IEA is intended to identify and help ameliorate. We have elaborate IEA reporting and accountability systems manned primarily by bureaucrats and run by people who know and care little about real higher educational IEA. Meanwhile, the quality of American higher education and its public image and funding base continue to erode.

I don't know which is worse: the ironic fact that an excellent effectiveness improvement tool like IEA has been corrupted into anti-effectiveness exercises in futility just at the time the critically important enterprise of higher education needs it most; or the enormous loss of higher educational effectiveness improvements we suffer every year IEA continues to be predominantly performed as a sham. For purposes of this paper, I am going to concentrate on the second choice, particularly the losses of improvements in higher education organizational structures, policies, and procedures.

The remainder of this chapter is based primarily on my professional experiences over the past twelve years with IEA in higher education. So that the reader can be better informed of my frame(s) of reference and understand my point(s) of view, let me briefly summarize my relevant training and experience with IEA. My higher education included double majors in Mathematics and Psychology (at the University of North Carolina-Asheville) and an M.A. and Ph.D. in Psychology (at the University of South Carolina), with a specialization in school psychology and educational measurement. In 1986, I was an Associate Professor of Psychology at Winthrop University, South Carolina specializing in the assessment of individuals, programs, and systems in K-12 education. After three years experience as a School Psychologist, three years as an educational researcher, and 14 years in higher education which included 11 years as founding director of an exemplary competency-based school psychology graduate program, I was the acknowledged "assessment expert" on my campus. That year I was given an additional duty by the Winthrop administration to study and evaluate the implications of this new thing they'd heard of called "higher education assessment", and prepare a report on how Winthrop should deal with it. I read all the pertinent literature (which wasn't much), attended the second AAHE National Higher Education Assessment Conference in Denver, and communicated with the dozen or so leaders in the field at that time. I concluded that higher education assessment was - or could be - essentially the same as "program evaluation", and "management by objectives", and "strategic planning" and other proven K-12 assessment models, just transposed to the post secondary level, and that Winthrop would be well served to embrace this "new" approach to evaluating and planning for its quality improvement.

Since that time I have largely devoted my professional career to higher education assessment, now IEA, serving my institution as program-level, department-level, college-level, and university-level assessment director at Winthrop and another university. I have also served as Founding Director of a 50-institution higher education assessment consortium, published some dozen papers, monographs, and book chapters on higher education assessment, and given over 100 presentations and workshops to state, regional, national, and international professional audiences on IEA-related topics. I was also chosen as a regional accreditation evaluator for IEA by the SACS COC, a specialized accreditor by National Association of School Psychologists and the National Council on the Accreditation of Teacher Education, and a higher education Evaluator for the Malcolm Baldridge National Quality Award. Finally, in the past ten years I have consulted with over 50 colleges, universities, and higher education systems in 20 states and in five of the six accreditation regions.

That training and experience has taught me many things about IEA and higher education, but especially the following six points: (1) IEA *can and should* be the most powerful and successful tool for improving the effectiveness of higher education ever developed. (2) The success of IEA is based largely on the scientific integrity and *validity of its assessment methodology*. (3) IEA *can be done validly* and feasibly by any higher education institution willing to give it a good faith effort. (4) To be successful, especially into the future, IEA *must become an integral part* of the institution's evaluation, planning, budgeting, and resource allocation processes, and be followed through in the future with a conscientious continuous effectiveness improvement effort. (5) Politics and personal/professional defensiveness can damage and destroy even a well-intentioned, otherwise functional IEA system, and can even become a force for *anti-effectiveness*. (6) What passes for IEA in American higher education today is often a sham, due in large part to ill-conceived resistance and minimalism on the campuses, and ill-informed and ill-motivated controls by non-educators in state governments.

Unfortunately, as of this point in the summer of 1998, IEA's considerable promise remains largely unfulfilled.

IEA and Organizational Change in Higher Education

IEA is, at its heart, a change agent; i.e., systematically and accurately identifying the strengths and weaknesses of present practices, and suggesting options for improvements. When IEA is properly planned, designed, implemented, analyzed, interpreted, and evaluated, it constitutes the most objective and accurate basis available to higher education decision-makers for evaluating present practices, implementing ameliorative interventions, and improving planning, budgeting, and resource allocation processes to assure continuous effectiveness improvements into the future. And directly or indirectly, valid IEA results can almost always be used for positive - i.e., more effective - organizational changes.

The basic IEA model is a simple one, based on addressing the Four Cardinal IEA Questions (CQs) with models and methods that are valid and practical for the dual purposes of effectiveness improvement and accountability. (For a more detailed step-by-step IEA system, see the appendices for the author's Comprehensive Institutional Effectiveness Assessment System [CIEAS) for Higher Education Academic Programs and Administrative and Support Offices.)

CQ 1. What goals is the higher education institution trying to accomplish?

CIEAS Phase I. State the college or university's most important institutional mission goals, translated into assessable outcomes. Then state the core goals for each constituent unit - school, division, program, and office - derived from the institutional mission goals and translated into assessable outcomes. State effectiveness criteria (satisfactory levels of quality and efficiency) for each institutional and unit goal.

CQ 2. How is the institution trying to accomplish its goals?

CIEAS Phase II. Describe the primary strategies (policies and procedures) the institution and each of its constituent units use to attain each core goal.

CQ 3. How well is the institution attaining its goals?

CIEAS Phase III. Validly assess the degree of effectiveness (quality and efficiency) of each unit and institutional goal attainment by measuring actual outcomes and comparing the results to each goal's effectiveness criteria (from Phase I). In addition to each goal's degree of attainment, identify each strategy's strengths and weaknesses and costs re goal attainment.

CQ 4. How is the institution using its assessment results to assure continuous effectiveness improvement in the future?

CIEAS Phase IV. Based on the valid outcome assessment results, identify each goal's need for improvement, and prioritize those needs. (NOTE: I recommend six prioritization criteria. In descending order of importance they are Centrality to Mission, Quality, Quality Improvement, Consumer Demand, Customer Need, and Efficiency.) Base unit and institutional planning, budgeting, and resource allocation decisions on those need priorities. Allocation of IEA-based resources begins the next annual IEA cycle, and next year's assessment results will evaluate the effectiveness of those decisions. This also constitutes a continuous effectiveness improvement system for the future.

IEA can and should be used to generate evaluative data on policies and procedures at all levels of higher educational operations, from an individual academic course or office procedure all the way up through a multi-institutional higher education system. The following are some common examples of the types of organizational and strategic changes generated by a good IEA system at each level of a typical higher education institution, first considering academic programs, then administrative and support offices. (NOTE: The order will generally be from the bottom up, but not strictly hierarchical since we will begin at the *academic program and support office levels* - the two levels which have proved to be the linchpins of a successful IEA system - and work downwards and upwards from there.)

An **Academic Program** is the functional unit of a higher education experience, where most of the teaching, learning, and student development occurs. It is defined as *a required course of study awarding some form of recognition or qualification for successful completion, and the faculty and students responsible for its effectiveness.* An academic program should routinely generate data on all three types of IEA goals; results on goal attainment in instruction, in scholarship, and in service.

But first, the program faculty - usually with technical assistance from IEA experts among the faculty and/or staff - must translate institutional academic goal statements - which are often vague, general, and/or not outcomes-oriented - into operationalized, assessable instructional, scholarship, and service *core outcomes*. For example, the instructional goals of any academic program can be operationalized into some type(s) and level(s) of student *competency outcomes* (i.e., *knowledge and skills*) and/or student *development outcomes* (i.e., *attitudes and behaviors*). Once the program's core outcomes have been so defined, it becomes a relatively simple task to choose appropriate outcomes measures which are valid and feasible for program effectiveness assessment purposes.

Instructional outcomes typically assessed are student achievement at the end of the program, success in more advanced educational programs or employment, success on more advanced assessments (like qualifying or credentialing exams), and student, alumni, faculty, and consumer opinions on program effectiveness. These results can and should routinely lead to changes/ improvements in such strategies as program curricula, program degree/completion requirements, course sequences and prerequisites, instructional assignments and methods, course offerings and schedules, and program administration policies, as well as program goals and priorities, and program effectiveness assessment processes. *Scholarship and service outcomes* - primarily for faculty but also potentially for students - are typically assessed by comparing scholarly products (publications, papers, presentations, consultations, grants, etc.) and service products (benefits to and satisfaction of service recipients) to program target criteria for those two types of goals. Assessment results can be used to modify scholarship and service strategies, modify/eliminate/ generate goals, and change program/department/school/institutional policies and procedures regarding scholarship and service activities to enhance effectiveness.

Academic Courses are the primary vehicle for attaining academic programs' *instructional goals*, in addition to less direct strategies like advising, tutoring, counseling, and academically-related employment and volunteer services. A course's objectives, evaluation criteria, instructional strategies, instructor assignments, schedules, etc., should be driven by that course's role(s) in the academic program(s) it serves. Thus, course-level instructor and student performances generate databases for program evaluation, and program-level evaluations and intervention and planning decisions determine each course's role(s) and function(s) in the future.

Academic Departments have traditionally constituted the basic structural unit in higher education for such organizational purposes as personnel assignments, course designations, administrative reporting, evaluation, planning, and budgeting. But for IEA purposes, virtually all departments are too complex and multi-purposed to serve as the basic organizational unit since even relatively small departments usually serve several related but different sets of program goals (e.g., majors, minors, general education, remedial education, honors, graduate programs, service to other programs, etc.). Thus, in the CIEAS, departments are treated primarily as *aggregates* of their constituent programs, and department goals, strategies, and assessments are superordinate compilations of their constituent programs' goals, strategies, and assessments for instruction, scholarship, and service. IEA databases at this level can be used to modify/eliminate/generate academic programs, plan/budget equipment and facilities requests, modify/eliminate/generate scholarship and/or service policies, and do personnel planning and assignments. In cases where there are distinctive department-level goals which are not subsumed in one or more constituent program goals, separate goal attainment strategies and assessments must be developed and implemented to cover those.

Just as departments are primarily considered aggregates of their constituent academic programs for IEA purposes, intermediate administrative units in higher education such as **academic divisions/schools/colleges** are primarily considered to be aggregates of their constituent departments, and therefore programs. And just as with departments, academic schools' primary IEA goals, strategies, and assessments for instructional, scholarship, and service goals are those of their constituent programs. IEA databases at this level can be used to modify/eliminate/generate academic departments and their planning and budgeting needs. If there are unique school-level goals not subsumed under one or more academic program and department goals, a separate set of goals, strategies and their appropriate assessments would again be needed.

Next to the academic program, the institutional level is probably the most important unit of IEA measurement. All but the smallest colleges and universities have a fifth level of organizational structure for their academic programs; e.g., an institutional-level division of **Academic Affairs**. Schools which are part of university systems or other administrative consortia may even have a sixth system-level division of **Academic Administration**. Both of these, too, would be primarily considered aggregates of their constituent schools, colleges, or institutions, and for IEA purposes would be treated the same as departments and intermediate units above. At these levels, IEA databases can be used for even broader and more far reaching academic programming decisions, such as modifying/eliminating/ generating academically-related mission goals and institutional-level or system-level restructuring. The higher the level of academic hierarchy, the more likely that there are unique goals not subsumed under constituent programs, and thus the greater the need for supplemental IEA goals, strategies, and assessments at each ascending level.

For both internally motivated effectiveness improvement and externally motivated accountability reasons - particularly newly promulgated regional accreditation standards - many higher education institutions are now considering how to expand IEA principles and methods developed primarily for academic programs to their **administrative and support offices**, as well. This is a new area of concern with very little track record, since most institutions are just now developing or experimenting with IEA for their non-academic operations.

I have adapted my CIEAS for application to higher education administrative and support offices, incorporating the same core principles and functional methodologies that have proven successful for academic operations. That version, too, is intended to be a primary tool for identifying and facilitating effective organizational changes.

The administration and support sides of college and university operations are primarily devoted to the *service goals* of the institution's mission. That is, while qualified administrators and staff can certainly make direct contributions to the institution's instructional and scholarship goals, their routine functions in higher education are primarily in the area of supporting the school's educational and student development efforts and managing the institution effectively, as any other commercial enterprise.

Just as the program is the basic functional unit for a college's academic operations, so too is the **office** the basic functional unit for administrative and support operations. For conceptualization purposes, I have divided all possible non-academic offices into *four categories* based on their primary roles and functions: *educational support offices* (e.g., libraries, tutoring centers, and computer centers); *student support offices* (e.g., student affairs, student activities, student life, counseling centers, admissions, athletics, financial aid, placement services, etc.); *administrative support offices* (e.g., all administrative officers, information systems, office services, etc.); and *institutional support offices* (whose services could apply to any comparable commercial enterprise, e.g., the physical plant, accounting, receiving, payroll, human resources, food services, etc.). For IEA purposes, offices are to the other levels of non-academic operations as programs are to the other levels of academic operations.

As with academic programs, each administrative and support office should derive from the institutional and/or division mission its own core goals and set criteria for satisfactory goal attainment, translate those goals into assessable outcomes, describe the primary strategies it uses to attain those outcomes now, assess the effectiveness of those outcomes' attainment, and use the results to evaluate the effectiveness of its services and plan improvement interventions. Routine office-level IEA data would include objective measures of the quality, speed, and cost of each of its primary services, plus service recipient satisfaction and suggestions for improvements. Assessment results would then be benchmarked to both internal (the preset goal attainment criteria and previous effectiveness levels) and external (best-in-field, model, or peer effectiveness levels of comparable operations) to determine strategic strengths and weaknesses. Strengths would then become planning resources and weaknesses would become planning needs, and feed into the institution's planning, budgeting, and resource allocation process, using the same six Prioritization Criteria as for academic programs (i.e., Centrality to Mission, Quality, Quality Improvement, Consumer Demand, Customer Need, and Efficiency). IEA data would thus become the primary basis on which to plan and implement interventions intended to improve the quality, speed, cost, and/or satisfaction levels of that office's services, and the primary internal benchmark for effectiveness improvement in the future.

As with academic programs, administrative and support offices often have higher levels of organizational structures, such as **departments, divisions, institutional, or systems-level management offices.** And just as with academic programs, those superordinate levels would be primarily considered aggregates of their constituent offices for IEA purposes. Thus, the effectiveness of the Student Affairs Division would be primarily judged by the levels of effectiveness in goal attainment demonstrated by its constituent offices (e.g., Student Life, Student Activities, Health Services, Foreign Student Services, etc.), and the Central Administration would be judged primarily by the goal attainments of the President, Vice Presidents, Board of Trustees, etc. Any unique roles and functions performed by an upper-level office which was not assessed by a lower-level office would need to develop its own corresponding series of goals, strategies, and assessments.

Administrative and support office organization and reporting lines are generally well established on most college campuses, but IEA brings new tools and procedures to the task, including *outcomes assessments* (rather than the process-only assessments most offices have relied on in the past), "360 degree" satisfaction evaluation and suggestions for improvement (from an office's service recipients, peers, and supervisors), and a more open and objective databased decision-making procedure. For these reasons, IEA offers as dramatic an opportunity for attaining new heights of effectiveness for administrative and support offices as it does for academic programs.

In summary then, the implementation of a valid comprehensive IEA system provides higher education institutions with more powerful and accurate evaluative information which can be used to improve the effectiveness of any level of college operation today, tomorrow, and into the future. Because of its increased openness, accuracy, objectivity, and comprehensiveness, IEA can revolutionize the way we evaluate and do strategic planning for our academic courses, programs, departments, schools and colleges, and bring comparable benefits to all levels of our administrative and support offices as well. If we in higher education are serious about wanting classes which are better attended, more educational, and more cost efficient, and programs which are more successful at educating more of its students to higher standards at minimum costs, and schools and colleges which are more responsive to student and faculty needs, and administrative and support offices which provide better services at faster rates and more satisfaction at minimum costs, IEA is simply the best means available for attaining those goals.

Summary Conclusions and Recommendations

The college or university that commits to a comprehensive IEA system undertakes substantial changes in the ways it has traditionally made decisions about the effectiveness of its academic programs and administrative affairs in at least two ways. First, it commits to a more databased decision-making and administration model, which is more objective, systematic, comprehensive, open, and collaborative than traditional approaches. Second, it is bound to more accountable decision-making based on data generated primarily from the bottom-up, rather than the top-down, and it is committed to prioritize evaluations and planning, budgeting, and resource allocation decisions primarily on the basis of *how effective each course/program/ department/division is in serving the institution's core mission goals*, rather than the primarily secretive, subjective, and sociopolitical decision-making bases of the past. *If* - and today that is a very big if - a higher education institution does a good job of defining its mission goals, translating its mission-derived unit goals into assessable outcomes, accurately describing its primary strategies at each level, and validly assessing all its most important outcomes, then IEA will provide program directors, department chairs, deans, vice presidents of academic affairs, and administrative and support office heads with the best and most accurate basis for decision-making in the history of their school. Furthermore, assuming valid data, IEA databased decision-making is self-correcting in the long run, so long-term effectiveness improvement at all levels of the institution is virtually assured.

Given these overwhelmingly positive attributes of IEA, why then have most college and university faculty and administrators chosen to resist, minimalize, and even sabotage their institutions' IEA efforts? Based on my extensive experience, one must separate the excuses given from their underlying motives in order to find the true answer. IEA is, first and foremost, a more objective, accurate, systematic, comprehensive, and open data-gathering and decision-making model than most faculty and administrators are used to, and therein lie the primary problems in gaining widespread functional support for a valid IEA effort on most campuses. At least 90% of the faculty and administrators with whom I have worked pay lip service to the ideals of IEA, but when it comes to actually implementing a valid IEA system on their campuses, or worse still, to subject that faculty member's own courses or academic program or that administrator's own office to IEA evaluation, an avalanche of potential problems and excuses - most of which fit under the heading of *"they"* would never go along with it" - ensues. (*They* are usually administrators when you talk to faculty, faculty when you talk to administrators, and the board and/or students when you're talking to both at the same time.) Other common excuses for not giving IEA a fair chance are the aforementioned *ignorance* ("I don't understand IEA."), *cost* ("It sounds too expensive."), *distrust of assessment* ("You can't measure what

I do."), *work load* ("I already have more than I can do without adding IEA to the list."), *logistics* ("We're too disorganized around here to ever make it work."), *morale* ("It would threaten the collegial atmosphere of our campus."), *politics* ("I'd like to do it but the powers-that-be would never stand for it."), and *paranoia* ("Even if we do IEA and do it well, the _____ [administration, faculty, board, commission, state government, etc.] would just screw it up and use the results against us."). These arguments, of course, tend to be either spurious (e.g., IEA's excess costs are moderate and short-lived; We *can* measure what any higher educator does), or within the purview of the administrators and faculty to change if they want to (e.g., the political climate, morale, work load).

These excuse themes are so consistent across the entire range of institutions in American higher education that I have developed a list of "Higher Educators Who *Should* Really Be Afraid of IEA" to rebut those arguments. They are:

1. Those who don't care about the quality and efficiency of what they do.
2. Those who don't care about the quality and efficiency of their programs or offices.
3. Those who aren't willing to work to make their programs or offices more effective.
4. Those who are not effective at what they do.
5. Those who teach in academic programs for which there is little or no interest from prospective students and/or demand from prospective employers.
6. Those who work in an office for which there is little or no interest or demand from prospective service recipients.
7. Those who don't trust "the system" below and/or above them to perform tasks and make decisions according to IEA principles.

With the exception of Group 7, those higher educators' fears of IEA are entirely justified, because if IEA works the way it is supposed to it will expose the weaknesses of their operations and perhaps even threaten their job security! (And if a higher educator is *not* in these first six groups, he or she should embrace IEA as an excellent tool for educational, professional, and personal effectiveness improvement!)

On the other hand, if 7 is a justified fear - as it often appears to be these days- it poses a real dilemma, since IEA can be a consistently effective tool and self-correct *only* if its methods and principles are adhered to in a conscientious and professional manner up and down the line. If some system components - especially those at the top - are unprincipled enough to corrupt the IEA process for ulterior purposes, that can be very difficult, and time consuming, problem to correct.

Wherever I produce this list, I am almost unanimously criticized for being too hard on the quality of higher education and/or too cynical toward higher educators today. But the facts regarding higher education's overall lack of quantity and quality of IEA efforts - even 9-14 years after they were mandated, in some cases - speak for themselves, and my experiences with higher educators from hundreds of institutions and their regulators are remarkably consistent in portraying the sham I have alluded to above. Believe me, if there were a brighter picture that I could honestly report, I would gladly do so.

At this point near the middle of 1998, my conclusions and recommendations are that:

- American higher education is not nearly as bad as some of our critics would have us believe, but not nearly as good as we would like to believe.
- IEA is the most powerful and successful tool available to improve the effectiveness of higher education, and its use is supported by evidence of successes in many programs, offices, and schools, and is mandated by all regional and specialized accreditors and most states.
- Today's IEA mandates and institutional efforts are triumphs of form over substance - i.e., IEA shams, enabling unprincipled or naïve higher educators to do little or nothing or even "anti-IEA" in the name of IEA compliance.
- All higher educators who *don't* fall in the first six of my categories of "Higher Educators Who Should Fear IEA" should do everything within their power to see that IEA is given a fair chance to succeed on their campuses, and give it their best "good faith effort" in their own programs and offices, as well.
- If we don't - i.e., we keep doing what we're doing and not doing valid IEA - non-educators - particularly in the state and federal governments - with anti-intellectual, anti-higher educational, anti-effectiveness personal and political agendas will take greater and greater control of higher education and do it substantial, perhaps even catastrophic harm, beginning with the public colleges and universities but eventually extending to private institutions via federal interventions, as well.
- I see no impetus for such a groundswell of conscientious higher educator, administrator, or regulator support for real IEA, and thus no reason to be optimistic about IEA fulfilling its potential as a facilitator of beneficial organization change in higher education, today or in the near future.

References

El-Khawas, E. (1995). *Campus Trends*. Washington, DC: American Council on Education.

Ewell, P. (1993). Pocketbooks, promises, and politics: Rethinking higher education assessment in the 1990s. In *South Carolina Higher Education Assessment (SCHEA) Network Xchange*. Rock Hill, SC: Winthrop University.

Johnson, R., Prus, J., Andersen, C., & El-Khawas, E. (1991). *Assessing assessment: An in-depth status report on the higher education assessment movement in 1990*. Washington, DC: American Council on Education.

Johnson, R., & Seymour, D. (1996). The Baldridge as an award and assessment instrument for higher education. In D. Seymour (Ed.), *High Performing Colleges* (pp. 54-71). Maryville, MO: Prescott.

Appendix A

The Comprensive Institutional Effectiveness Assessment System (CIEAS): Twelve Steps in Four Phases

Phase I: Define Effectiveness Goals

Step 1.A.   Define core institutional outcome goals (and set planning prioritization criteria[1])

Step 1.B.   Derive core unit outcome goals

Step 2.   Define/derive core program outcome goals

Step 3.   Operationalize program's assessable outcomes

Phase II: Identify Current Strategies

Step 4.   Describe primary program/unit effectiveness strategies

Phase III: Assess Goal Attainment

Step 5.   Select appropriate outcomes (et al) measures

Step 6.   Plan assessment logistics

Step 7.   Implement assessment plan (= Steps 1-6)

Step 8.   Analyze for efficacy, internal validity, and external validity; then diagnose program effectiveness strengths & weaknesses (i.e., goals, indicators, strategies, msrs).

Phase IV: Report Results & Plan Improvements

Step 9.   Write PERIPs, including improvement planning needs and resources for immediate interventions, short-term planning, and long-term planning

Step 10.   Unit heads aggregate and evaluate ERIPs and recommend planning and budgeting prioritization[1]

Step 11.   Institutional leaders aggregate and evaluate ERIPs and decide budget priorities[1]

Step 12.   When the next year's budget is "finalized", make resource allocations to fund unit/program effectiveness improvement plans, beginning the next annual IEA cycle

[1] Recommended effectiveness priorities = Centrality to mission, quality, quality improvement, consumer demand, customer need, and cost efficiency.

Comprehensive Institutional Effectiveness Assessment System (CIEAS)

1. [2] Define the institution's educational mission and core outcome goals. Derive division/unit/department educational mission and core outcome goals from those core institutional goals.

2. Define/derive academic program mission and core outcome goals (incl. goals for instruction, scholarship, and service), and addressing the priorities of centrality to institutional mission, quality, improvement, consumer demand, customer needs, and efficiency (= productivity - costs).

3. [2] For each outcome goal - at all levels - select at least one effectiveness indicator which is an operationalized, assessable core outcome/result/product of instruction, scholarship, and/or service which objectively shows the degree of success or failure in goal attainment.

4. For each effectiveness indicator, describe the primary program strategies currently used to try to assure goal attainment (i.e., curriculum methods and requirements, scholarship activities and support, service methods and policies, institutional/unit policies and procedures, etc.).

5. [2] For each effectiveness indicator, select at least two outcomes assessment measures which will evaluate the degree of goal attainment and strategic strengths and weaknesses (i.e., will diagnose how effective each of the program's strategies is in attaining its core goals).

6. Finalize an effectiveness assessment plan, including the logistics of which outcomes measures will be admisinstered to which assessees, by whom, how, when, and to whom, and how those effectiveness assessment results will then be used.

7. Implement the battery of effectiveness measures (using the first use of any particular measure as a "pilot" assessment, testing its validity for IEA purposes).

8. Analyze and interpret the assessment results in three ways: first, for its content validity and efficacy for IEA; second, for diagnosing the program's strategic strengths and weaknesses (= internal validity); and third, for internal and external accountability purposes (= external validity). When valid, use results to guide effectiveness improvement planning, budgeting, and resource allocation decisions for the next fiscal period.

9. [2] Each academic program summarizes and reports their annual effectiveness assessment results annually in a Program Effectiveness Report and Improvement Plan (PERIP), where documented weaknesses become planning needs/justifications and documented strengths become strategic resources. PERIPs address three levels of planning needs: immediate interventions which can be accomlished at the program level without higher administrative funding or policy changes; short-term planning requests which require higher level funding and/or policy changes within the next year; and long-range planning requests which require higher level funding and/or policy changes in the next one-to-five years, or longer. (Immediate program-level improvement efforts - and/or accountability reports and/or planning requests - can be generated at any point in the IEAS cycle. In fact, it is typical for improvement activities to begin as early as Steps 1-5, even before the first outcomes assessment results are even obtained!)

10. Chairs/Deans/VPs/Unit Heads aggregate and evaluate PERIPs, prioritize planning and budget requests (using the same six prioritization criteria in Step 3), add their own unit-level planning and budget requests and IEA documentation/justification, and send the program and unit(s) requests - with recommendations - on to the institutional-level administration.

11. Institutional leaders (and budget or finance committees) aggregate and evaluate unit-level ERIPs, prioritize planning and budget requests (using the same six prioritization criteria in Steps 3 & 11), add their own institutional-level planning and budget requests and IEA documentation/justification, and recommend resource allocations to the final authorities (e.g., Board of Trustees +/- Budget Review Group representing the institution's constituencies and stakeholders).

12. [2] After revenue information is received and "final" budgetary decisions are made, resources are allocated, cascading through units to the programs to fund requested effectiveness improvement or maintenence activities at all levels - i.e., in goals, indicators, strategies, measures, and/or planning activities - for next year's instruction, scholarship, and service improvement efforts, starting the next annual cycle of effectiveness improvement plans, efforts, and assessments.)

[2] In my experience, the five most difficult steps for many higher educators.

Discussion of Johnson

Institutional Effectiveness Assessment in Higher Education

Mark A. Adams
ABC School

Reid Johnson's contribution to this volume "Using Institutional Effectiveness Assessment To Plan, Implement, and Evaluate Organizational Change in Higher Education: Great Promise Largely Unfulfilled", provides an excellent historical account and current status of a trend in Higher Education toward assessment and accountability assessment. More specifically, institutions of higher learning, since the mid 1970's have increasingly began to measure (at least in some manner or fashion) their activities as an institution (Teaching, Scholarship, and Service). This has been more formally referred to as Higher Education Assessment. There is considerable debate about what institutions of higher education should assess, or in other words, what content should be the aim of assessment activities? In addition, there is considerable debate about How we should go about assessment in higher education, or in other words, how will assessment take form, or what should our method(s) be?

Reid Johnson's chapter addresses both the What and the How of Higher Education Assessment, provides a revealing and important history of the movement toward assessment and accountability in higher education, and concludes with a system for implementing IEA which he has termed the "Comprehensive Institutional Effectiveness Assessment System (CIEAS)".

Before continuing with a discussion of this chapter, it might be helpful for the reader if I provide a brief history of my relevant experience, training, and current administrative faculty position, in order to provide a context for the points of discussion addressed later. As a doctoral student in the Behavior Analysis program at the University of Nevada, one of the core aspects of my training was the objective methodology by which behavior analysts systematically measure, evaluate, and intervene on the behavior of man and animal. In addition, the interventions or "agents of change" are accomplished by manipulations (by the experimenter) of antecedent and consequent events, ideally immediately before (antecedent) and after (consequent) the behavior in question. This methodology has been applied to many populations to bring about significant changes in their behavior. Examples of populations that I have worked with include developmentally disabled, children with autistic behavior, psychiatric patients, "normal" adolescents and children, to name a few. I mention my background with this much detail because of the importance and influence this training has had with respect to my views on assessment in higher education. In 1996, I was hired at the Research Analyst for the Assessment Office, at UNR. It was in this position that I first learned of Institutional Effectiveness Assessment (IEA) at an American Association of Higher Education (AAHE) Conference. After meeting Reid at another AAHE conference and reading some of his materials (Johnson, 1992a; Johnson, 1992b; Johnson, 1997; Prus & Johnson, 1994), our office was able to convince him to come to UNR and provide consultation to the university on IEA, for all different levels of faculty and administration. I am currently the Assistant Coordinator of the Assessment Office at UNR. Our office has almost two years experience with attempting to support and implement IEA efforts across the UNR campus.

When compared to Johnson, I have a limited experience in higher education assessment, however, I would like to reiterate various points made in the chapter, and follow with some suggestions and insights from my own experience. In order to accomplish this as systematically and parsimoniously as possible, I will go through the points I would like to comment on in the order they appear in the chapter.

Knowledge of IEA at Institutions of Higher Education

I agree that the majority of faculty and staff at institutions of higher education know very little about the principles and practices of IEA. In addition, very few academic departments or administrative/support offices even attempt IEA, and those that do often use "quick and dirty" methods.

What can be done to alleviate the lack of knowledge? I would recommend providing workshops that educate the faculty and administration about the principles and practices of IEA. The specific topics and titles can take many forms, and can exemplify the principles and practices of IEA, without even specifically referring to them. For example, a workshop on designing effective assignments, how to construct an effective syllabus, how to develop exams and test, to name a few, could easily demonstrate sound IEA. Many of the points of departure articulated by Johnson can be remedied through discussions in these workshops. Workshops on similar topics have been well attended by teaching faculty and administrators at UNR. Many faculty, both beginning and tenured, are genuinely interested in becoming better teachers, and jump at the opportunity to learn something new, sharpen skills, and improve teaching strategies. What other alternative is there, besides educating faculty and administrators about IEA?

The Motivation for IEA: Internal vs. External

Johnson's historical account of the "Higher Education Assessment Movement" describes the development of an initially "well-intended", internally motivated assessment of higher education to an externally driven, mandated accountability of higher education.

Why did this happen? Johnson states that the reason is mainly due to the unfortunate circumstance whereby higher education "thumbed its nose" at assessment, even when it reached the level of requirements for accreditation by the various

Commissions on Colleges (COC). I have also encountered many universities that are only now beginning to attempt assessment activities on their campuses, and many that claim to "do assessment" that quickly reveals itself as a "sham", to use Johnson's terms. However, I am not as convinced as Johnson that IEA could have "saved" higher education from the familiar situation Alverno College and Truman State found themselves in the 1970's. Without pressures that Alverno, Truman, and many other institutions faced (such as decreased enrollments, decreased funding), external mandates, and perhaps the unfortunate extreme "performance funding law", I am not sure assessment in higher education and IEA would ever passed the stage of the "next wave in education". Some examples of these waves Johnson mentions, such as management by objectives, strategic planning, etc. In addition, at some of the larger more bureaucratic institutions of higher education, change almost always occurs via mandates. These mandates usually come from Deans, Vice Presidents, and Presidents, as opposed to State Legislatures. Survival for higher education institutions ultimately comes down to money. It is the issue of funding that drives most assessment mandates. Federal funding is decreasing rapidly for public higher education, and enrollments not as predictable as in the past. This will bring inevitable change, even if all institutions conducted sound IEA.

Accreditation and IEA

Accreditation by the Northwest Association of Schools and Colleges, Commission on Colleges (NASC COC) for the University of Nevada, Reno has probably been the most significant influence on assessment activities on our. The most recent guidelines for accreditation demand assessment plans, implementation of assessment plans, collection and analysis of outcome measures, and improvement strategies to be implemented throughout the entire university campus (NASC Commission on Colleges Accreditation Handbook, 1996 Edition). This is precisely the type of external mandate that Johnson refers to in his chapter. It will be vitally important that institutions are not allowed to escape or "sham" regional accreditors with "quick and dirty" IEA or even "anti-IEA" efforts. In addition, as Johnson points out, the application of IEA accreditation requirements must not be allowed to drift.

Balancing External Accountability with Internal Effectiveness Improvement

With the advent of many misguided assessment mandates in higher education, how can institutions balance the need to provide assessment information for external purposes, and also use assessment information for internal effectiveness improvement. The latter being what Johnson might call "the right reason for doing IEA". I would agree, however I might temper my agreement by stating the motivation to conduct IEA in the 70's and 80's, without mandates, was simply inadequate, and most sound IEA efforts were motivated by termination of the institution, not a "desire" to improve higher education.

UNR has the beginnings of an institutional assessment system that could balance the need for external and internal assessment strategies. UNR currently conducts internal program reviews of all academic departments. These reviews basically consist of departmental self-studies documents generated by academic departments, external review team visits and reports, and concludes with academic affairs and the academic department reviewing the self-study and the external review team report. Planning, budgeting, and resource allocation are influenced by this program review process. This process has great potential for developing into a more systematic IEA. In addition, the university conducts satisfaction measures and surveys at the institutional level from freshman, academic experiences of all students, graduating seniors, alumni, and employers. This information, in conjunction with standardized assessments (Johnson refers to these as more valid and costly) and locally developed measures of student learning gain can be the main database for meeting external mandates and generating reports on institutional effectiveness.

A quick comment on Johnson's "IEA Methodology Paradox". The costs of these standardized instruments can be decreased significantly, if sampling techniques are utilized. Therefore, institutions can have the benefit of standardized, norm-referenced tests, without the expense and saving the time necessary to develop a similar test locally.

Summary and Recommendations

Institutions of Higher Education are at a crossroads. One path, leads to the same methods and outcomes, wrapped in a different package. The other path (the IEA path) leads to a re-evaluation of the mission and goals of higher education, at a level that will allow at least some level of objective, systematic, assessment and evaluation. This understandably, disturbs many in higher education but also gives others some hope for the integrity of their discipline. Johnson ends his chapter with a rather dismal picture of higher education and IEA efforts, "...no reason to be optimistic about IEA fulfilling its potential as a facilitator of beneficial organization change in higher education, today or in the near future". Perhaps the distant future will reveal a conscientious system of higher education in the United States.

I will conclude by providing some comments that have helped me confront the difficult task of IEA, and that might help IEA sustain the test of time in higher education and/or provide useful for anyone interested in or engaged in assessment activities.

First, the long list of excuses for not conducting good faith IEA efforts can be eliminated. However, this is not easy, nor perhaps necessary. Here is where I think mandates are good procedures. If you mandate that all academic departments answer the 4 Cardinal Questions and provide positive consequences for those who comply and negative consequences for those who do not, a significant part of the battle has been won. You can argue points of departure, but while engaged in assessment and IEA, not when trying to convince someone to start. In my experience, once a program or department gets started with assessment and IEA, they get nothing but more interested and motivated. However, this will quickly fade if the behavior of IEA is not positively consequated. Herein lies a set of issues beyond the scope of this discussion, namely the maintenance of IEA activity, once you get it started. The mandate to answer the 4 Cardinal Questions will suffer unless support for academic programs and departments is not provided. This can be done at a minimal cost, in terms of resources, salaries, and indirect expenses. UNR has an Assessment Office, many other institutions have established a similar office on their campus and many are in the process of doing so.

Second, provide educational opportunities for faculty and administrators with respect to IEA principles and practices. Some suggestions provided earlier include workshops on designing effective assignments, how to construct an effective syllabus, how to develop exams and test, to name a few that can educate and demonstrate sound IEA, especially at the individual course and instructor levels.

Third, I would try and integrate the necessity and original intent of IEA and Higher Education Assessment, namely internal effectiveness improvement and evaluation and the inevitable external accountability mandate within the same system of IEA. The only real difference is the aim of the assessment instrument being used. Some assessments in IEA are interested in measuring student learning within a particular course, and others at the other end of a continuum, interested in measuring employer satisfaction with employees that graduated from the institution. With extreme changes in the financial climate of higher education (Breneman, Leslie, & Anderson, 1996), the nature of external mandates is unpredictable, and institutions with assessment and IEA strategies that can be modified to accommodate external mandate changes, yet maintain systematic internal improvement will thrive.

References

Breneman, D. W., Leslie, L. L., & Anderson, R. E. (1996). *ASHE reader on Finance in Higher Education*. Simon & Schuster Custom Publishing.

Johnson, R. (1992a). *South Carolina higher education assessment (SCHEA) project. Final report*. South Carolina Higher Education Assessment Network, Rock Hill.

Johnson, R. (1992b). *Using assessment to improve teaching effectiveness*. Workshop presented at the School of Social Work, East Carolina University.

Johnson, R. (1997). *A comprehensive system for assessment the effectiveness of academic programs*. Paper presented at the 1997 AAHE Conference on Assessment and Quality.

Northwest Association of Schools and Colleges, Commission on Colleges. Accreditation Handbook, 1996 Edition. 11130 NE 33rd Place, Suite 120, Bellevue, WA 98004.

Prus, J., & Johnson, R. (1994). A critical review of student assessment options. *New Directions for Community Colleges, 22*(4), 69-83.

Herding Cats and Spinning Plates: A Case History of Managing Change in Academia

Philip N. Chase
West Virginia University

When I first told people that I had accepted my dean's appointment as chair of my department, many offered their condolences, especially former chairs. "It's like that position between a rock and hard place you've always heard about," they would say, or my favorite, "managing faculty is like herding cats." I accepted their expressions of doom and gloom with as much humor as I could muster, but I was scared; had I really just failed a one question IQ test by agreeing to be an academic chair?

A few years into the job I decided they were only partially right. I was watching a television special about The Ed Sullivan Show that showed one of those circus acts with some guy spinning plates on wobbly sticks. "Spinning plates", I thought, "that's really what chairing is like." The demands on departments in research I universities of teaching, research, and service are extensive. The explosion of administrative initiatives including issues of public relations, alumni development, diversity, the Americans with Disabilities Act, technology enhancement, students as consumers, on-campus parking, and accountability adds to the task. There are too many plates to keep up, one or more of the plates will eventually topple over, and if you are not careful, they will all fall to the floor. Chairing an academic department involves figuring out how many plates you can keep spinning and making sure you are spinning the right plates.

This view of chairing an academic department might get a few laughs, but it is not really helpful, so for the purposes of this chapter I began to think about generalizations that could be culled from my experience that others might find useful. The generalizations that most readily occurred to me are those from behavioral systems analysis, organizational behavior management, and performance management [I will use the term, performance management (Daniels, 1989) throughout the rest of the chapter as it seems to be the most current term]. I will use the occasion of this book, therefore, to describe these generalizations with examples of them from the events that have occurred in the Department of Psychology at West Virginia University.

I warn the reader, though, that this is a simple case history. I can offer data to help describe the history, but I did not conduct an experiment. Therefore, I cannot claim with assurance that the generalizations will hold, but I think they are consistent with the generalizations that appear in many of the chapters in this book and elsewhere.

This is also just a snippet of history from the long and complex history that West Virginia's Department of Psychology has enjoyed. The specific successes that I will describe would not have been possible without the events that other chairs helped shaped. Some of these chairs also identified their work with performance management: Roger Maley and John Krapfl were pioneers in the field of performance management. Andy Lattal is an extraordinary behavior analyst. Others were data driven practitioners like Quin Curtis, K. Warner Schaie, Kathleen McClusky, William Fremouw, and Barry Edelstein. Making data driven decisions is a critical feature of performance management. Examples of their achievements that allowed subsequent successes to occur are too numerous to mention, but it was clear to me and I should make clear to you that I inherited a very healthy organization. The generalizations from performance management that follow, therefore, may only hold in such a healthy organization.

Generalizations from Performance Management

A pithy way of describing performance management is that it involves:
- determining what you want to accomplish,
- communicating to others what you want to accomplish,
- measuring whether it has been accomplished, and
- giving credit to those responsible for the accomplishments.

Each of these phrases can be subdivided into a number of different procedures, tools, and rules of thumb that can be used to help achieve the general outcome of managing others.
- Determining what needs to be done is divided into:
    - Performing systems analysis of both physical and social systems to determine who and what is affected by actions
    - Gathering information from representative individuals and groups
    - Analyzing and comparing the short and long term consequences of actions
    - Using 80/20 analysis (Pareto's Law)
    - Following the money
    - Keeping it simple.
- Communicating what needs to be done involves:
    - Proposing actions to individuals/teams
    - Asking for advice, comments, and feedback
    - Assuring individual/team "buy-in" to the proposed actions
    - Assigning and delegating actions
    - Giving individuals/teams the tools to complete the actions
    - Writing actions in plain English
    - Saying it again and again and again (redundancy).
- Measuring whether it was done includes:
    - Turning the customers' definitions of success into precise outcome measures

   - Measuring individual performance, unit performance, and
     organizational performance
   - Evaluating measures in the context of systematic changes in practice
     or intervention.
 - Giving credit to those who get it done involves:
   - Reinforcing, rewarding, and recognizing performance.

Although these components of performance management can be specified in
a logical outline as above, in actual practice they are highly iterative and nonlinear.
Like most complex interventions, a chronological analysis of performance management is not possible. One example is the process of goal setting. As described above,
goal setting is part of determining what you want to accomplish. Goal setting,
though, includes communication, especially obtaining input and getting buy-in
from critical people in the organization. Goal setting also includes measurement
because specific goals are always tied to how you will measure whether they have
been successfully accomplished. Goal setting also involves rewarding, recognizing,
and hopefully reinforcing the behavior of those involved in setting the goals.
Further, determining what you want to accomplish may be the first step in
implementing performance management, but because of the iterative process of
systems analysis the actual goals selected will change as one begins to communicate
them to others. Thus, my examples of these features of performance management
will be neither chronological nor exhaustive, but rather illustrative.

Determining What You Want to Accomplish-Goal Setting

Often the most difficult part of performance management is determining what
you want. This difficulty starts with recognizing that in a democratically run
department dedicated to sharing its governance among administrators, faculty, and
students, "you" is clearly not any one individual. Determining what "you" want
translates into determining what the department, college, university, students,
community, parents, and the discipline want. And the "wants" of these various
constituencies often conflict. For example, one of the biggest issues in academia
today is to determine for whom the faculty work. Do they work for the discipline or
do they work for the university? They technically work for both, but the relative
emphasis and the interaction of that emphasis with the changes that are occurring
in universities across the United States is a critical management issue.

In order to resolve the potential discrepancies in what different constituencies
want, performance management suggests conducting a systems analysis to determine the representative individuals and groups affected by the system. In simple
terms a systems analysis involves looking at the inputs, outputs, and feedback
mechanisms of any action. For more complex and thorough views on systems
analysis applied to performance I recommend reading the chapters in this book by
Brethower and by Rummler. Performance systems analysis suggested that I ask the
following questions to determine representative individuals for the department:
Who has input into the decisions of a department? Who is affected by these

decisions? And how do we know they are affected? Fortunately, in many regards the college and department had already established mechanisms for gathering such information. These mechanisms started with frequent conversations with the dean.

My discussions about departmental goals with our dean, Gerald Lang, occurred over the period of time from when I accepted the appointment of chairing the department to acceptance of our formal goals by the faculty and students. The dean accepted our goals and emphasized the necessity of improving our administrative efficiencies and increasing our financial independence, especially through increased grant support and alumni development. He also suggested that although the department's reputation was strong outside the university, not everyone in the university was aware of its strength. Objectively, the department performed well, but the department had not done enough to publicize its accomplishments. Similar, informal conversations with other chairs, and with administrators at other levels of the organization confirmed most of what the dean told me.

In order to continue to gather input from the dean, I scheduled regular meetings with Dean Lang and his successors, Rudy Almasy and Duane Nellis. These meetings always had a purpose, for example, asking advice on handling a problem, but I tried not to pack the agenda too tight so that we had time to talk plainly about ourselves, the college, and the university. These meetings provided frequent opportunity to interact on specific decisions, but also helped me gauge what was important from the dean's perspective, to understand the dean as an individual, and to keep him informed about the department. A key generalization here is that frequency counts. Performance management uses the tools of science and one of those tools is to increase the frequency of observation. A systems analysis suggested that I needed to observe what the dean considered important and to do that effectively required frequent interaction with him.

On the other side of me in this system was the department. To gather frequent information from the department I met twice a month with an Executive Committee that represented various aspects of the department. The Executive Committee consisted of the Associate Chair, the Director of Curriculum and Instruction, the Director of Clinical Training, a faculty member elected as a representative of the faculty, and a graduate student elected as representative of the students. One of our foci in our initial meetings was to devise the departmental goals for my five year term. Discussions with the executive committee covered a range of issues and I attempted to pinpoint our efforts by using the performance management criteria for prioritizing the various and possibly conflicting "wants". Pareto's Law was used to pinpoint those goals that would have the biggest impact on the department. The long term and short term consequences of any actions proposed were discussed. How the proposed actions affected the finances of the department and how to keep the resolution as simple as possible were kept at the forefront of our decisions. After many meetings we agreed on the following goals:

- Enhance the administrative efficiency of the department
- Improve the physical plant through significant renovations or obtaining a new building
- Improve the financial state of the department
- Develop another graduate program for the department
- Enhance the effectiveness of our graduate training programs
- Enhance the effectiveness of our undergraduate program
- Enhance the distribution of resources across faculty and programs
- Upgrade the departmental computing with higher percentage of state of the art computers, software, and peripherals
- Improve public relations
- Maintain high faculty and student moral and collegiality
- Maintain high quality and quantity of research, teaching, and service

Each goal was analyzed into more specific objectives that indicated how they would be measured. As an example of a set of more or less qualitative measures, the first goal was analyzed into the following specifics:

- Decrease the number of administrative positions in the department
- Rearrange the functions of the administrators
- Change the locations of the administrative offices
- Begin annual evaluations of administrative functions
- Begin performance appraisals with staff
- Hire a Director of Clinical Training

As an example with more quantitative types of measures, improving the financial state of the department was divided into the following:

- Increase grant support
- Increase royalties for texts, workbooks, course guides, and media used in courses while keeping costs to the students as low as possible
- Increase support from alumni and friends
- Increase money from lab fees
- Decrease inefficiencies in overhead costs of copying, telephone, and computer use
- Increase revenues from the Quin Curtis Center for Psychological Services (QCC)
(A full list of these original objectives is provided in Appendix A).

To emphasize representativeness further and to gain more input and buy-in from those most affected by these goals, they were then discussed with the faculty and student representatives at two departmental meetings. All goals met agreement except the goal to develop a new graduate program. The department rejected this by stating firmly that we needed to concentrate on maintaining and strengthening the existing graduate programs. Further discussion of this goal in other meetings also led to the conclusion that no faculty saw this as a sufficiently important task to champion it. It was then dropped as an explicit goal. The elimination of this goal as a priority is an example of the importance of buy-in. Even though I thought a new graduate program was important, without someone other than the chair to champion it, I knew that it would not happen in a democratically run organization (This idea of championing came from Nick Cavoti, Chair of Psychology at Washington and Jefferson College, during an informal discussion in St. Petersburg, Florida 1994).

The process of goal setting did not stop with agreement from the dean and the department; the goals continued to shift depending on more proximal influences and changes in the organization. As an illustration of how determining what to accomplish works, however, I will end this description here and move on to communication.

Communicating What You Want to Accomplish

Although communication is critical to goal setting, further attention to communication is needed once agreement on the goals has been reached. One of the first communication steps in managing performance involves deciding who is best suited for carrying out the procedures and describing to them what you want to accomplish. Others describe this as selection and delegation. Common sense says "you are the company you keep" and "good leaders surround themselves with good people". In my case, this was relatively easy, a "no brainer", as people told me. The good people for each of the main jobs in our department were obvious. Maybe so, but the selection and delegation process is a good example of some communication tools that helped us accomplish what we specified in our goals.

Changes in administrative positions and their functions. Before meeting with the Executive Committee to discuss goals, my discussions with Dean Lang had indicated that the department should change the structure of its administration. These changes began with my appointment of administrators for the department. I appointed Michael Perone as Associate Chair, Katherine Karraker as Director of Curriculum and Instruction, and asked Georg Eifert and Robert Hawkins to continue as Co-directors of Clinical Training and Coordinators of our Adult and Child Clinical Programs. Kennon (Andy) Lattal and Hayne Reese were asked to continue as the Coordinators of our Behavior Analysis and Life-Span Developmental Programs respectively. Each of these individuals were able to trade administrative duties for teaching to allow them the time to do their job. The Associate Chair and Director of Curriculum and Instruction each reduced their formal teaching by two courses and the graduate training program coordinators reduced their formal teaching by one course each.

The Associate Chair was asked to coordinate tasks related to our building, departmental communications, and equipment, especially computer technology. This was a clear choice of matching skills to jobs that needed to be done. Michael Perone was one of the most technically sophisticated psychologists I knew and had superb communication skills. Mike also shared my concern for building technology from the ground up. We both believed that it was easy to get carried away with all the choices that technology offers, but we thought it was important for our department to spend money on a strong foundation. We wanted to select technology that had proven value and make it available to as many people as possible. Mike also conducted basic research with animals and, therefore, represented that critical aspect of our department during Executive Committee discussions.

The Director of Curriculum and Instruction was assigned all the tasks of two previous positions, the Director of the Graduate Program and the Director of the Undergraduate Program. Katherine Karraker had established her reputation with student programs by coordinating the undergraduate program successfully for the past four years. As we already had an explicit written statement of the duties of both positions in our Graduate Handbook (a critical communication tool established by a previous chair, Barry Edelstein), Katherine and I were able to negotiate how she could spend her time so that the two jobs could be managed by one individual. Some of this required delegating tasks to the two staff assigned to work with her. I also agreed to assign one of our teaching assistants to work with her. Katherine also was a member of the Life-Span Developmental Program and represented those whose research concerned children, families, older adults and others who visited the department from the community.

The Co-directors of Clinical Training split the tasks described in our Graduate Handbook for the clinical programs. Although the original choice of these individuals was made in order to represent the child and adult specialties in our clinical program, with Rob representing child clinical and Georg representing adult clinical, we decided to divide their duties more on their strengths and preferences. This was explicitly a temporary arrangement, however, as we agreed that we needed to hire a permanent Director of Clinical Training. During the first year of my administration the department hired Daniel McNeil as Director of Clinical Training. His duties subsumed the duties of the co-directors and coordinators of all the clinical training programs. Frequent meeting with him allowed me to keep in touch with the concerns of the clinical programs.

Andy Lattal and Hayne Reese were also obvious choices for continuing to coordinate their respective graduate programs. As distinguished scholars, teachers, and leaders, they provided critical academic leadership and international reputations to our graduate programs. They, along with the Rob, Georg (later, Dan) and a student representative, met twice a month with Katherine to discuss issues related to graduate training. They also met separately with the individual graduate training programs to discuss curriculum, recruitment, student evaluation, and other graduate training issues. Information from these programs flowed through them to Katherine and then to the Executive Committee as the formal means of communicating our research and graduate education needs. Katherine also met regularly with a committee of faculty and students concerning issues related to our undergraduate program. Their issues were also then discussed by the Executive Committee.

These assignments not only met the objective of matching the best people to some of the critical jobs in the department, but the changes in administration also helped us meet one of our goals, one that was especially important to the Dean. We reduced the number of faculty involved in (burdened with) administrative work by two. The former positions of Director of Graduate and Undergraduate Programs were subsumed under the Director of Curriculum and Instruction, and the duties of the two Co-Director's of Clinical Training were subsumed under the position of Director of Clinical Training.

Changes in staff positions and their functions. At the beginning of my administration the department also had substantial turn-over in staff. One secretary/receptionist, Barbara Michniac, had left the department earlier in 1993 and was not replaced. Her duties, however, were assigned to Francis Sine, who also switched from a nine month to twelve month position. A short time later, Ms. Sine left the department and was replaced by Imogene Kelley, who worked as a temporary secretary prior to being hired full-time. The departmental Office Manager, Janet Stalewski, left the department when she married and moved from the area. Tammy McPherson replaced her. Tammy also assumed the duties of directly supervising the other staff. The Chair's administrative secretary, Michelle Howard, left the department because she was promoted to Office Manager in another department. She was replaced by Eileen Thomson. In my fourth year as chair, the Office Manager position was eliminated from the department and Tammy McPherson was transferred to the college's Expert Business Office. This position was replaced in November, 1997 with an Information Systems Technician, Mark Aronhalt. In addition, another secretary, Joyce Williams, retired from the university during my fourth year as chair. Joyce was not replaced because her retirement was part of the university's 1996-97 severance plan to reduce the number of faculty and staff. The changes in staff decreased the number of staff assigned to the department by two, but allowed the department to hand pick individuals who could accomplish what were now the department's staff priorities. This illustrates another generalization of managing performance: creating opportunities out of potential losses.

Committee Structure. Other examples of communication processes can be seen in the structure of departmental committees and meetings. The committees and meetings were used to discuss progress on various projects, to gather input, to gain buy-in to decisions, and to provide frequent opportunities for fine-tuning the descriptions of what needed to be done. These processes had worked so well in the past that I changed little that previous chairs, in their wisdom, had established. We maintained our Executive Committee and our committees for Faculty Evaluation, Undergraduate Training, Graduate Training, Alumni Development, and our twice a month departmental meetings. These committees and meetings were run more like team meetings. They were frequent, but short in duration. They had agenda and were canceled when there were no agenda. The agenda were accomplishment oriented. Humor and informality were encouraged.

We also established or revised some structures to help with communication. We began monthly staff meetings to better communicate with the staff and represent their needs. We developed electronic databases to provide us with better access to the data and information we collected on the department. We assured that every proposal that went to the department for a vote was in "close to final draft form" before it was discussed. This meant that all proposals came to the Executive Committee for discussion first. Then they were written in plain English to be distributed to the faculty and student representatives either before or at the departmental meetings. We revised the composition of our faculty search committees to be more representative of the department. We established a diversity committee to coordinate our efforts to recruit more diverse faculty and students to our department. I encouraged faculty to be on college and university committees. I volunteered for some key college and university committees. We also convinced Michael Perone to become a Faculty Senator for the university. Having a member of our faculty on the Faculty Senate and others on important committees helped the department be connected better to the issues of the university and improve our public relations within the university.

Redundancy. Before I begin discussing measurement I want to make one last point about communication: the importance of redundancy. Effective performance managers cannot rely on saying what they want just once, they have to say it over and over in many different ways. The best example of this during my term as chair was related to our efforts to improve our physical plant. I used every opportunity, no matter how loosely associated with the building, to point out the inadequacies of Oglebay Hall. Every budget report, every questionnaire filled out on the department, and many conversations with alumni, presidents, provosts, deans, and their associates had some reference to the deplorable conditions of the building. Eileen Thomson, the administrative Secretary to the Chair set up a systematic program to gather information and report the problems with the building. I tried as much as possible to mix humor into our complaints and even so I probably developed a reputation as a whiner, but I made sure that everyone knew that our building needed attention. I also arranged tours of the building with both university presidents who were in office during those five years, with the Chancellor of the university system in the state, and with members of the board of trustees for the university. These tours focused on the atrocious conditions of the building by starting with our only wet laboratory, which one member of a president's party referred to as "Igor's lab" because it looked like something out of monster movie. The tours also highlighted our only elevator, a 1917 vintage freight elevator, and emphasized the one hundred plus window air conditioners. These and other problems areas were interspersed with tours of spaces that had been renovated to show potential. As with the rest of this case history, I do not know whether these efforts were critical to our success. When the university hired an architectural firm to perform a campus master plan, however, everyone agreed our building was a top priority for change. As I write this, our new building is well under development.

Measuring What You Have Accomplished

Because there are so many possible measures representing the performance of an academic department, generalizations from performance management provide a helpful focus. One of the hallmarks of performance management is pinpointing measures at the individual level that can be aggregated at the departmental level in ways that define success for the "customers" of the department. In other words, a performance manager tries to determine what measures of individual performance would be most useful to those who were most affected by the accomplishments of the department. I tried to answer the questions: What do the members of the department want to know about the department? What are the most important ways that the administration, both at the university level and the college level, look at success? What does the community, especially the students' parents, want to know about what we do?

Much of the latter concern was precipitated by the current movement for university accountability and the apparent conflict between the goals of educating undergraduates and the goals of scholarship. People believe that undergraduate education is being shortchanged at the larger universities in the United States. Strong departments, however, have found ways to integrate quality undergraduate education with the goals for scholarship. Communicating the ways in which this integration affects undergraduates is important and reporting these effects critical.

The measures that the department uses have evolved over the years. In order to keep things simple we started with existing data. One source was the information collected in our annual faculty activity reports. The reports are organized around three general themes: research, teaching, and service. The reports provide the opportunity for faculty to describe just about any activity or accomplishment that might be relevant to the department, college and university. The reports are then checked and validated by the Faculty Evaluation Committee and the Chair. Because the department had been using faculty activity reports for a number of years, they provided a good source of data to examine. This helped to determine what categories might be useful to track over time. Accomplishments from these reports that could be aggregated at the departmental level that were also important for administrators, parents, and others included: the number of peer reviewed publications, the number of students taught, the number of bachelor's, master's, and doctoral degrees conferred, student evaluations of courses and other learning experiences, and the number of hours of community service provided. As an example, Figure 1 shows the number of publications per full time equivalent faculty (FTE) over the years 1993-1997. Each bar represents data from one full year of faculty activity. Of critical importance are the increasing trend in peer reviewed publications (darkest shaded bars) and the overall increase in productive scholarship.

Other measures were obtained by looking at our goals and the various reports the department completes for the university. Some of the accomplishments in the last five years are listed below. This is not an exhaustive list, simply illustrative of some accomplishments consistent with three of our overall goals:

Enhance the Administrative Efficiency of the Department:

- Streamlined administration by eliminating two administrative positions
- Streamlined staff by eliminating two staff positions

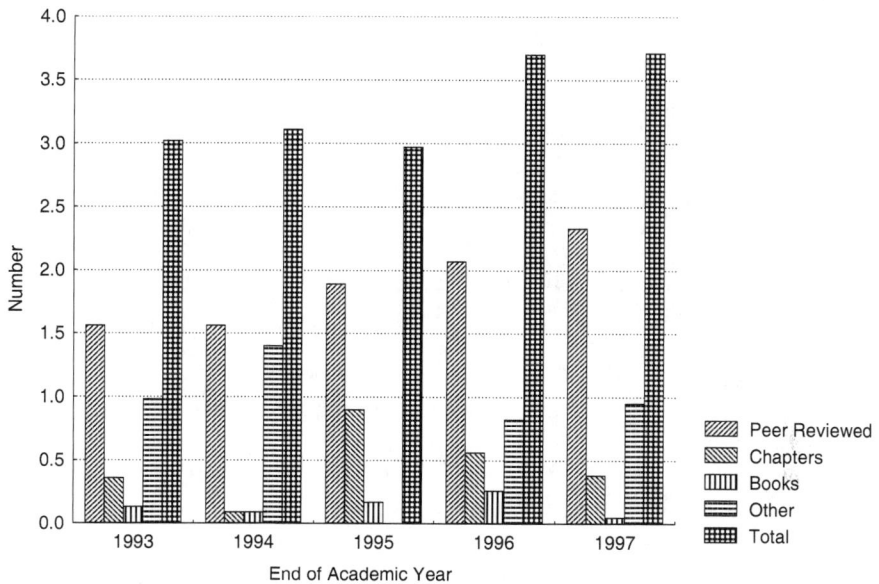

Figure 1. Number of publications per full time equivalent faculty (FTE) as reported in verified faculty activity reports for each academic year. Data from 1995 did not distinguish chapters from other publications.

- Designed a computerized accounting system for departmental budget
- Adopted a voice mail system to improve communications
- Brought fiber optics into the building to improve Internet access
- Began monthly staff meetings
- Replaced mimeograph duplication with Risograph for more efficient and effective large copying orders for courses and research
- Instituted performance evaluation procedures with all staff
- Designed a new staff position, Information Systems Technician, that allowed us to change the emphasis of the Associate Chair's position to supervising technology rather then hands-on implementation, problem-solving etc.

Improve the Physical Plant Through Significant Renovations or Obtaining a New Building:

- Completed the renovation of a psychophysiology laboratory
- Renovated and refurnished a new Main Office
- Renovated and refurnished a new Student Records Office
- Air conditioned, refurnished, and computerized the Introductory Psychology (Psych 1) Testing Center

- Air conditioned two large classrooms
- Renovated a large classroom as a multimedia classroom
- Renovated a laboratory classroom
- Approved final plans for the new elevator and handicapped accessible restrooms.
- Began planning our new building with architectural firm

Improve the Financial State Of the Department:

- Training Grants and Contracts
    - Undergraduate Training-Over $120,000 in Internal grants
    - Graduate Training-Over $200,000 per year in
        clinical and organizational practica and internships
- Quin Curtis Center- $20,000 in revenue per year
- Research (See Figure 2 Research Grant Awards and Figure 3. Overhead Accounts)
- Foundation Accounts (See Figure 4. Foundation Accounts)
- Lab Fees (see Figure 5. Lab Fee Account)

Figures 2-5 show the data measuring our financial state. Each demonstrates improvements across either five or six years. Figure 2 shows that the amount of funding obtained per year from externally funded research grants grew from $42,600 in 1993-94 to $340,152 in 1997-98. These are approximate amounts obtained by dividing each grant obtained by the number of years of funding. For a psychology department with 21-23 FTE's we need to continue to improve the amount of federally funded grants we obtain, but these changes were significant, involved seven

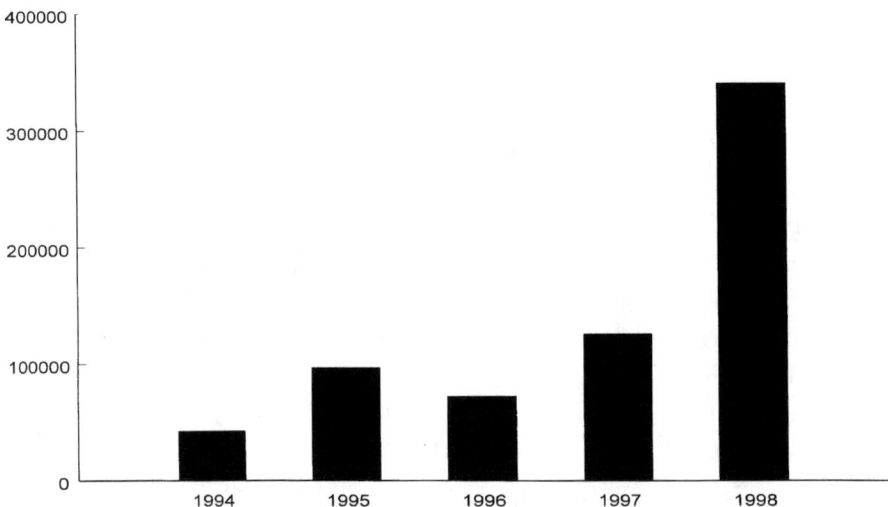

Figure 2. Number of dollars obtained in each year from external grant agencies for research only. Grant awards divided by the number of years of support and distributed evenly across years.

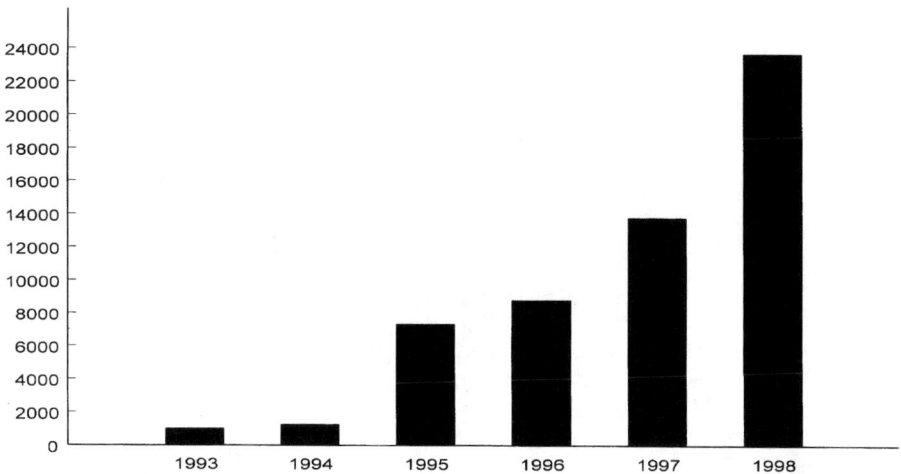

Figure 3. Number of dollars reported by the university accounting system for the end of the year balance of our overhead account.

faculty, and showed that the department could compete at the national level for research funding.

Improving the number of research grants funded also improved our overhead account. Figure 3 shows the systematic and dramatic growth in the overhead funding returned to the department by the university. By the end of 1992-93 we had a balance of $1,000 in our overhead account. In 1997-98 we had accumulated close to $24,000. Throughout this period the university returned 12% of the indirect costs of each external grant to the department. The department in turn developed a policy to distribute these monies according to a formula that gave 1/4 of the departmental overhead back to the principal investigator, 1/4 was used to support student research and travel, 1/4 was used to support faculty research and travel, and 1/4 was spent at the discretion of the Chair.

Figure 4 shows the end of each year balances as reported by the university foundation for the Chair's Foundation Account and Alumni Fund Account. These accounts hold the revenue from royalties on books used by faculty in their classes, contributions to the department as a whole by alumni and friends, and contributions earmarked for student research and travel. Again, a steady increase is shown except for 1996-97 when the department decided to buy new furniture for our main office, our student records office, the chair's office, and approximately two-thirds of the faculty. Right after this furniture was bought we discovered that the university intended to move us to a new building. After discussions with the dean, provost, and others we decided to save as much of this money as possible for use in the new building.

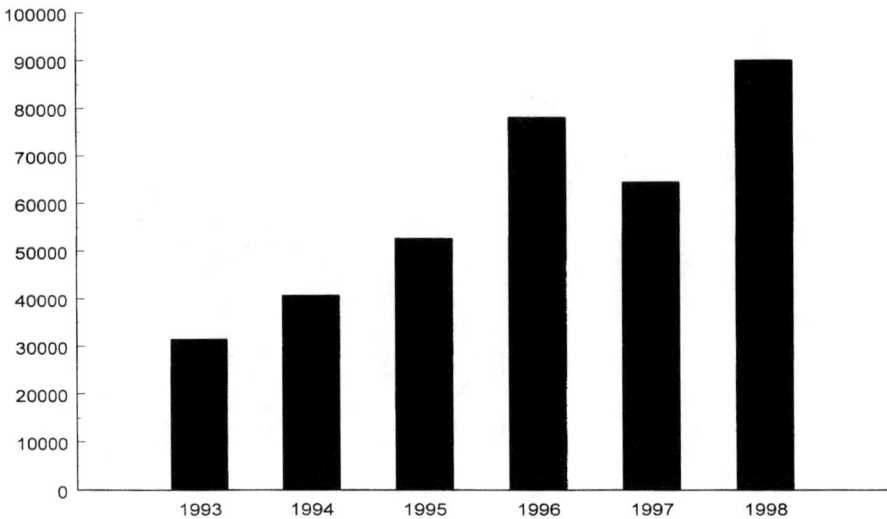

Figure 4. Number of dollars reported by the university foundation for the end of the year balance of the Chair's Foundation Account and Alumni Fund Account.

Figure 5 shows the end of each year balances as reported by department's annual Lab Fee Report. A previous chair, Barry Edelstein, had petitioned the university to allow us to charge a lab fee for two of our courses, Research Methods (Psychology 102) and Behavior Principles (Psychology 171). We began to collect these lab fees in 1994-94 and Figure 5 shows how the account has grown. Some of the increase can be accounted for by the three increases in lab fees charged by the university over these years. These lab fees have allowed us to spend substantial amounts on computers, electronic equipment, and supplies for both of these courses. They have also been allowed to accumulate because we anticipate spending a great deal of money on equipping the classrooms for these courses in the new building.

The data from figures 2-5 illustrate the follow the money principle. Even with the small amounts of money that a department handles, it is critical to manage performance that improves the net worth of the department. Within days of accepting the appointment of chair, it was obvious that our financial situation had to improve. The dean said it, the former chairs said it, faculty said it, and our students said it. What was equally clear was that in the current climate of a state supported institution like WVU, we were not going to get an increase in our base budget. Therefore, we needed to be entrepreneurial, we needed to find alternate sources of funding, we needed to keep looking for sources of funding that would support our goals, in general, we needed to increase our financial independence. In addition, these figures show the end of the year balances rather than separate measures of revenue and expenditures. Changes in university procedures for tracking revenue and expenditures across years made it difficult to obtain comparable figures. Moreover, the end of the year balances seem to reflect our goal to be more

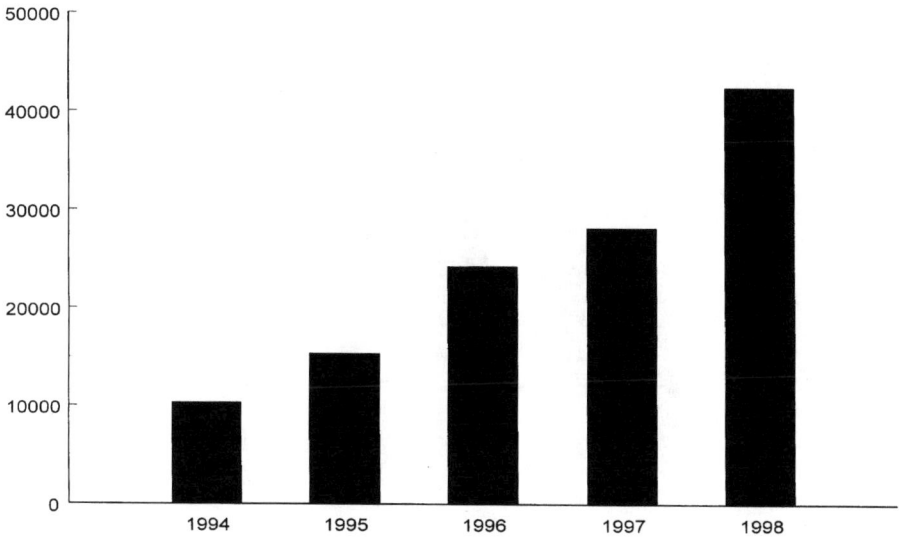

Figure 5. Number of dollars reported by the department's annual Lab Fee Report.

independent, to have enough money at the end of each year to plan for the next. These figures show that this goal was met.

What these figures do not show are the opportunities provided when performances related to money are managed carefully. In our case it allowed us to accomplish some other goals that we considered important, for example, upgrading departmental computing. Although we have not bought every new high technological gadget that has come out on the market we have:

- Brought fiber optics into the department ahead of the university schedule
- Replaced all faculty and staff computers twice in five years
- Replaced computers used in Psych 1 twice in last five years
- Established Psych 1 as one of the leading technology based courses at the university
- Bought multimedia systems for one classroom and two portable multimedia carts
- Replaced computers used in Research Methods Teaching Lab twice in five years
- Replaced computers used in Behavior Principles Teaching Lab once in five years
- Replaced computers in our student Microcomputer Lab twice in five years

Other work is also likely to be effected by having more money available. For example, Figure 6 shows that our student satisfaction ratings, although always high, have improved steadily. The data for 1997 are missing because the Director of Curriculum and Instruction was on sabbatical and the results of our annual student

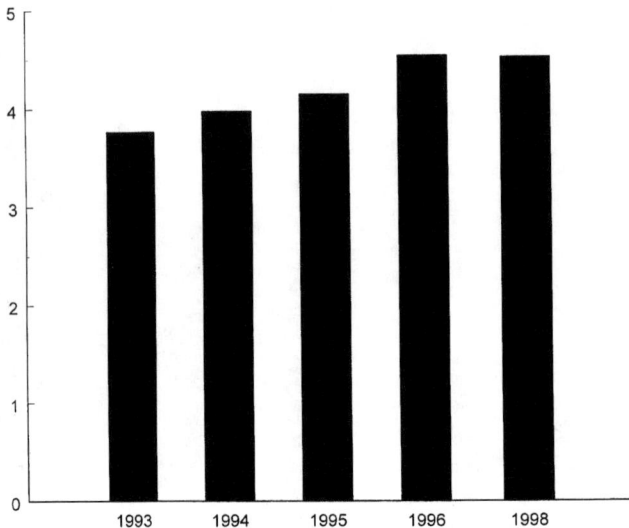

Figure 6. Mean rating by graduate students on an item asking for overall satisfaction with program in April of each year. A five point scale was used where 1 indicated very dissatisfied and 5 indicated very satisfied.

survey were not analyzed. Our research productivity as measured by peer reviewed publications has also steadily increased even though our FTE's have decreased from a high of 23.25 faculty in 1997 to a 21 faculty in 1998. (See Figure 1. Publications per FTE).

The department keeps track of other statistics that are used in various reports requested from the college, the university, and national organizations like the American Psychological Association. All of these data support the conclusion that the department is doing well and shows us where improvements could be made. I will stop here, however, to describe examples of the final set of generalizations.

Giving Credit to Those Who Get it Done

As outlined earlier in the presentation, this area of performance management involves potentially reinforcing behavior that is consistent with the goals of the department. For a behavior analyst, this should be the most straightforward and easiest of the general principles of performance management to achieve. Because the department had a long standing behavior analytic tradition, there were many built-in features that helped us give credit where credit was due.

First, as part of delegating most jobs that had to be accomplished, individuals in charge of various projects made periodic announcements and updates at our twice monthly departmental meetings. Whenever there was a proposal to discuss at these meetings, the person in charge also managed that part of the meeting. This put the person who was responsible for the work in the limelight making it clear who was accomplishing what for the department. As a related technique, I continued the tradition of using the faculty meetings to announce major accomplishments for faculty and students and to formally thank people for their efforts.

Second, as part of an overall plan to communicate the accomplishments of the department both internally and externally, we began to report at least once a year a list of highlights of the department. The structure of these highlights varied across the years. Often the highlights were distributed in a form that was dictated by some questionnaire I had to fill out for the college or the university, but they always reflected the goals of the department. They also most often named names-who was responsible for these highlights. This year's list is fairly typical (see Appendix B) and below I have reproduced the part related to student accomplishments:

Awards to Students:

- Oliver Wirth and Kurt Freeman received the William E. Vehse Travel Awards from the Eberly College of Arts and Sciences.
- Cindy Anderson, Kurt Freeman, Jane Kogan, Amy Odum, Tim Shahan, and Oliver Wirth received the Don Hake Award for Outstanding Graduate Careers in 1998.
- Tim Shahan received the Philip Comer Award for the Outstanding Graduate Teaching Assistant in 1998.
- Adam Doughty and Julie Wolfgang received Quin Curtis Awards for the Outstanding Undergraduate Students in 1998.
- Chad Galuska received the Outstanding Senior in Psychology Award from the Eberly College in 1998.
- Suling Chen won the Outstanding Graduate Teaching Assistant Award in the Eberly College in 1998.
- Peter Gleason, Rainer Diriwaechter, Adam Doughty, Brian Tolka, Michelle Heffner, Gwendolyn Bennett, Sandra Lee Annan, and Julie Sadler received Eberly College of Arts and Sciences Enrichment Awards in 1997-98 to support their research.
- Angela Lau and Aline Rabalais were awarded University Minority Fellowships for the summer of 1998.
- Marietou Mantane and Dana Brinton were awarded Global Educational Opportunities (GEO) Grants in the Spring of 1998. Marietou will study Rural Health in Senegal and Dana will conduct archeological research in France.
- Carin McKosky, Waynnie Mok, and Gwendolyn Bennett were Eberly Family Arts and Sciences Scholars in 1997-98.

By keeping track of these kinds of accomplishments throughout the year, we were also able to provide them for a variety of different purposes that served to recognize those responsible. For example, when I thought that any of these highlights was news worthy, I called the university news service. This led to a number of articles both in the university's publications as well in local media on faculty and student achievements. Usually if the news service was interested they would contact individuals, interview them, and then write the article or record the interview for broadcasting. This, of course, helped to publicize the strengths of the department. I also used the highlights as a standard part of our annual Alumni Newsletter. The Alumni Newsletter became another vehicle for bragging about the accomplishments of individuals in the department.

Third, we continued the departmental tradition of having frequent departmental gatherings, parties, and hospitality. The department officially sponsors a fall picnic to welcome everyone, a winter holiday party, a chili party in February to get us through the dark days of winter, an interview weekend party to celebrate applicants to our graduate program, and a pre-graduation ceremony in May. The department also has an active colloquium series that is tied to receptions and dinners and a number of special events to celebrate retirements, faculty awards, and other honors. These social events provide us with an active social life, which is important in a small town, but they also build departmental cohesiveness and help us recognize individual accomplishments.

Probably the most important mechanisms for recognizing and rewarding individual performance stem from annual faculty, staff, and student evaluations. Our systems for evaluating faculty and students have been in place for years and required only maintenance and minor changes. Both our faculty and student evaluation programs were detailed, designed with lots of input from the various constituencies of the department, and were tied to rewards. While I was chair, the university reinstituted a merit raise system and our policy on merit, which had been hammered out prior to our having merit raises in place, was simply implemented with a few adjustments. The policy is described in Appendix C. Note that the policy is tied to the annual faculty evaluations and that it rewards all excellent performance not just the top performers. The ratings that it refers to are those provided by an eight person committee made up of two full professors, two associate professors, two assistant professors and two graduate students. A full description of how this committee operates and its relations to annual evaluations from the chair and the dean can be obtained from the department.

Staff evaluations, however, had never been conducted systematically in our department even though the long term advantages of designing and implementing a performance evaluation program were clear. Thus, a staff performance system became one of our subgoals for improving administrative efficiencies. One of the criteria for hiring a new office manager was someone who had the experience to supervise the other staff using a sound performance based system. My interviews with applicants for this position emphasized this area of the Office Manager's performance. My initial conversations with the individual hired, Tammy McPherson, discussed how we would conduct staff evaluations, and staff evaluation were frequently discussed at subsequent meetings. But because Tammy had to get our financial data-base in order, had to meet explicit deadlines throughout the year for managing our finances, and had to deal with more immediate staff problems, like office assignments, vacations, sick leave policies, assignments to courses and faculty, hiring, etc., the performance evaluation program did not get off the ground in the first three years of my tenure.

Then things got worse. The university decided to establish a system of centralized financial management that was implemented in our college by pulling the office managers out of the large departments into what became known as an Expert Business Office. By the Fall of 1996 we no longer had an Office Manager to supervise the staff. After a year of trying and failing to convince the university that we needed to hire a senior staff person to take care of staff supervision, I began the process of setting up a staff supervision system.

The first step was to decide on the forms we would use for communicating to the staff what was expected of them. After discussing various options with the Dean, our former Office Manager, the staff, and the university's human resources department, we decided to use the university's standard position descriptions as a starting point. Instead of having to go through all the red tape of having human resources approve our own descriptions, which I would have set-up along the lines of a performance objectives matrix (Riggs & Felix, 1983; Daniels, 1989; Chase & Smith, 1994), we simply adopted the university's system for descriptions, but rewrote them in terms that would facilitate performance management.

Critical for the purposes of performance evaluation, the standard position description divided each position into five to ten essential functions. Previous versions of these descriptions varied in terms of how descriptive and oriented toward accomplishments they were. Thus, we focused on updating the descriptions with specific accomplishments for each staff member. The university's standard descriptions had a method of weighting the functions of the positions. The weights were simply a description of the percentage of time spent on each function, which does not necessarily translate into the differential importance of each function, like the weights assigned to objectives in a performance objectives matrix. The staff, however, found weighting in terms of time easy to implement and the weights gave us an estimate of the relative importance of the tasks. The staff wrote the position descriptions, I edited them, and the faculty and other staff checked them.

To provide systematic feedback on performance we also adopted a performance appraisal form that the dean's office was using. This form had been previously approved by human resources. This form also allowed staff to be evaluated on the basis of each essential function and on more global professional performance criteria like quality of work and interpersonal relations. It also included a comment section for both supervisors and incumbents.

The procedure I adopted for conducting the performance evaluations also included features that were consistent with a democratically run department. Prior to meeting with individual staff I asked them who they thought would be in the best position to comment on each of their essential functions. I also suggested individuals if I thought the staff member had missed a key individual. I then called a representative sample from this list to discuss the essential functions and the global performance criteria. For example, if a secretary worked with eight faculty, I called at least two of these faculty to ask them questions related to secretarial work. I also asked them to rate the secretary on the global performance criteria. I included the faculty and co-worker comments, examples, and ratings in my summary evaluation of the staff's performance. I then scheduled a meeting with staff member and we discussed the evaluation. These discussions were open ended and gave the staff plenty of opportunity to discuss the comments, examples, and ratings. In some cases the input from the staff required gathering more information before the evaluation was finalized. The meetings also provided me with the opportunity to provide specific praise to the staff and to discuss problems that they had with their work. I wrote a final version of the evaluation, the staff member read, commented on, and sign it, and it was copied to the staff, the dean, my staff files, and to human resources. Human resources reviewed both the revised position descriptions and the evaluations, and used them as part of the basis for providing upgrades and promotions.

I cannot claim that these evaluations went without a hitch. For example, one of the staff was extremely upset by the comments that I had gathered about her performance even though the majority of the comments were positive. In general, however, staff claimed they appreciated the department taking their jobs as seriously as the faculty's and finally differentiating levels of performance among the staff. Although it is too early to evaluate whether the staff evaluation system will result in better performance over the long term, it is consistent with the general tenets of performance management. The system was relatively simple to set-up and implement, was not time consuming, and therefore should benefit the department as a whole. As part of our overall program to recognize, reward, and possibly reinforce performance, I think the staff evaluation program illustrates what we have tried to accomplish.

Conclusion

My goal in writing this chapter was to describe aspects of performance management that I found useful while I was chair of an academic department. I started with some general rules for conducting performance management and tried to illustrate these generalizations through examples that occurred primarily during my tenure as chair. Along the way I bragged a little about the accomplishments of our department, but my purpose in doing so was simply to illustrate the utility of viewing this position from a performance management perspective. I also hope this chapter augments an already substantial literature on chairing academic departments. I have not mentioned this literature yet, but there are a number of publications that chairs with a penchant for performance management will find useful. Tucker (1984) describes particularly useful information on faculty evaluation, assignments, and merit pay. Creswell, Wheeler, Seagren, Egly, and Beyer (1990) also uses a systems perspective to describe chairing. Kimble (1979) provides a specific description of chairing a psychology department that may be pertinent especially to personal time management for chairs of any department. I recommend all of these.

I will end now by saying one last thing about goals. I really had one goal, to stop being chair after my five year contract was up and know that the department would continue to be a place where I wanted to work. By hook or by crook, accident of time, or just one more person failing the one question IQ test about taking on the responsibility of being chair, this goal was accomplished; Michael Perone agreed to accept the dean's appointment as our next chair. As Associate Chair, Mike has been one of those individuals who made significant and substantial contributions to running the department over my term as chair. His ability to blend big picture ideas, attention to detail, and humor will go a long way to continuing to improve the department. I know that he will achieve great things for the department and I step back to a full-time faculty position knowing the department is in good hands. My only concern is that Mike will do a better job as chair then I did, that he will not attribute his success to performance management, and then I will look really foolish.

References

Chase, P. N., & Smith, P. N. (1994). *Performance analysis: Understanding behavior in organizations.* Morgantown, WV: Envisions Development Group.

Creswell, J. W., Wheeler, D. W., Seagren, A. T., Egly, N. J., & Beyer, K. D. (1990). *The academic chairperson's handbook.* Lincoln, NE: University of Nebraska Press.

Daniels, A. (1989). *Performance management: Improving quality productivity through positive reinforcement* (3rd Edition). Tucker, GA: Performance Management.

Hayes, S. C., & Grundt, A. M. (1996). The top 50 researchers and institutions in behavior analysis and therapy, 1974-1994. *The Behavior Therapist, 19,* 141-142.

Kimble, G. A. (1979). *A departmental chairperson's survival manual.* New York: John Wiley & Sons.

Richards, E. D., Cox, B. J., & Norton, R. (1998). Leading researchers and institutions in behavior analysis and therapy in the 1990's. *The Behavior Therapist, 21,* 113-115.

Riggs, J. L., & Felix, G. H. (1983). *Productivity by objectives: Results oriented solutions to the productivity puzzle.* Englewood Cliffs, NJ: Prentice-Hall.

Tucker, A. (1984). *Chairing the academic department: Leadership among peers* (2nd edition). New York: Macmillan.

Appendix A

Complete Set of Original Goals and Objectives

A. Enhance the administrative efficiency of the department:
   1. Decrease the number of administrative positions in the department
   2. Rearrange functions of the administrators
   3. Change the locations of the administrative offices
   4. Begin annual evaluations of administrative functions
   5. Begin performance appraisals with staff
   6. Hire a Director of Clinical Training.
B. Improve the physical plant through significant renovations or obtaining a new building:
   1. Replace HVAC, including windows
   2. Replace elevator
   3 Improve handicapped access
   4. Redo Floors
   5. Gain access to whole building for Psychology
   6. Create new computer labs for experimental courses.
   7. Evaluate Graduate Student office needs
   8. Renovate space to replace Annex.
C. Improve the financial state of the department:
   1. Increase grant support
   2. Increase royalties for texts, workbooks, course guides, and media used in courses while keeping costs to the students as low as possible.
   3. Increase support from alumni and friends
   4. Increase money from lab fees
   5. Decrease inefficiencies in overhead costs of copying, telephone, computer use
   6. Increase revenues from the Quin Curtis Center for Psychological Services (QCC).
D. Develop another graduate program area for the department as measured by the percent of activities completed toward new program:
   1. Conduct needs assessment
   2. Bring hiring back to the department level (not current graduate program level)
   3. Obtain position(s) from the dean.
E. Enhance the effectiveness of our graduate training program areas as measured by the cost per student credit hour (sch), satisfaction data from former and current students, and other measures derived from the graduate training data base:
   1. Improve practicum supervision
   2. Increase use of the Quin Curtis Center
   3. Increase research productivity
   4. Increase minority representation

    5.   Increase graduate teaching assistantships

    6.   Decrease variability in graduate research assistantships especially from practica sites.

F.   Enhance the effectiveness of our undergraduate program as measured by the percentage of the following completed:

    1.   Enhance graduate student and faculty quality of instruction as measured by student evaluations and peer(?) evaluations

    2.   Enhance communication with pre-majors and majors about opportunities in psychology, registration, and requirements for graduation

    3.   Enhance advising

    4.   Develop databases for student records, course evaluations, advising assignments, independent study grades and evaluations

    5.   Improve efficiency of office procedures-registrations, course adjustment, advising, evaluations

    6.   Enhance curriculum by enforcing sequencing of courses, adding more lab courses, maintaining 200 level courses as specialized courses for majors, maintain functions of service courses, reduce waitlists

    7.   Evaluate and possibly enhance writing instruction

    8.   Monitor and possibly improve graduate school acceptance rate

    9.   Increase minority representation

    10. Increase high GPA (honors) students.

G. Enhance distribution of money and resources (enhance quality of life) as measured by faculty and staff satisfaction and thepercentage of the following tasks completed:

    1.   Establish rewards, awards, perks for each individual and tie distribution to merit system for faculty, performance appraisal for staff

    2.   Reinvest money from grants, royalties, and Quin Curtis Center in faculty who generate it

    3.   Set up two endowed chairs, one in developmental and one in behavior analysis to match the Eberly Chair in clinical

    4.   Distribute equipment, travel, copying, postage, office supplies, and telephone according to the merit system.

    5.   Get faculty to work at the university and state level on changing the funding mechanisms for faculty including merit pay and significant pay raises

    6.   Increase grant support

    7.   Maintain general support for faculty and staff

    8.   Maintain general perks (social events, lounge, lunch room etc.).

H. Upgrade the departmental computing as measured by percentage of state of the art computers, software and peripherals in department:

    1.   Establish plan for yearly upgrades (assume we can't do it all at once)

      2.   Get each upgrade funded
      3.   Establish and maintain task force for Graduate Computer Use
      4.   Develop database on paper/supply use in Graduate Computer Lab.

I.   Improve public relations as measured by increased number of positive reports on the department, its faculty, staff and students and the percentage of the following tasks completed.

      1.   Develop a press release system for the university's Daily Athenaeum, Morgantown's Dominion Post, the Charleston Gazette, the APA Monitor, and the APS Observer
      2.   Develop a Psychology Awareness Program
      3.   Develop a marketing and advertising plan for the Curtis Center
      4.   Develop a faculty activity database
      5.   Develop an annual report
      6.   Increase grant support
      7.   Unify publications from the department
      8.   Increase communication with parents and alumni.

J.   Maintain high faculty and student moral and collegiality in department.

K.   Maintain high quality and quantity of research, teaching, and service.

Appendix B

Some Examples of Goal Related Accomplishments from 1997-98

Enhance the effectiveness of our graduate training program areas:

- Oliver Wirth and Kurt Freeman received the William E. Vehse Travel Awards for the Eberly College of Arts and Sciences
- John Forsyth, currently an Assistant Professor at SUNY/Albany, was named a Guest Editor for an issue of *Behavior Therapy*.
- Steve Hayes, currently Foundation Professor and Chair of Psychology at the University of Nevada/Reno, was ranked as the 34th most productive author in behavior analysis and therapy journals in 1990-96 (Richards, Cox & Norton 1998).
- Cindy Anderson, Kurt Freeman, Jane Kogan, Amy Odum, Tim Shahan, and Oliver Wirth received the Don Hake Award for Outstanding Graduate Careers in 1998.
- Tim Shahan received the Philip Comer Award for the Outstanding Graduate Teaching Assistant in 1998.
- Suling Chen won the Outstanding Graduate Teaching Assistant Award in the Eberly College in 1998.
- Angela Lau and Aline Rabalais were awarded University Minority Fellowships for the summer of 1998.
- Seven percent of our graduate student population in 1997-98 were non-Caucasian minorities. One of these students was supported on an APA Minority Fellowship

- Twenty-two students received clinical training in the QCC by 6 faculty.
- Twenty-seven graduate students provided over 27,000 hours of community service through their practica and departmental internships in 1997-98.
- 9 psychology students received Ph.D.'s in August 1997, 4 received Ph.D.'s in December of 1997, and 2 received Ph.D.'s in May 1998.
- 7 psychology students were on APA approved internships in 1997-98.
- "Psychos", a group of students from psychology captained by Colleen Kennedy, were WVU's intermural soccer league champions in the Spring of 1998.

Enhance the effectiveness of our undergraduate program:

- Adam Doughty and Julie Wolfgang received Quin Curtis Awards for the Outstanding Undergraduate Students in 1998.
- Chad Galuska received the Outstanding Senior in Psychology Award from the Eberly College in 1998.
- Peter Gleason, Rainer Diriwaechter, Adam Doughty, Brian Tolka, Michelle Heffner, Gwendolyn Bennett, Sandra Lee Annan, and Julie Sadler received Eberly College of Arts and Sciences Enrichment Awards in 1997-98 to support their research.
- Marietou Mantane and Dana Brinton were awarded Global Educational Opportunities (GEO) Grants in the Spring of 1998. Marietou will study Rural Health in Senegal and Dana will conduct archeological research in France.
- Carin McKosky, Waynnie Mok, and Gwendolyn Bennett were Eberly Family Arts and Sciences Scholars in 1997-98.
- Students Graduating with Honors in May 1998:
      Summa Cum Laude: 7
      Magna Cum Laude: 5
      Cum Laude: 10.
- 26 psychology students were named to the Golden Key National Honor Society in 1997.
- 8 psychology students were named to the Phi Beta Kappa National Honor Society in 1997.
- 9 psychology students conducted honor's theses in the department in 1997-98.
- 78 psychology students made the Dean's list in the Fall 1997.
- The department had 303 majors and 342 premajors in 1997-98.
- The department taught 8217 students from Spring 1997-Fall 1997.
- Approximately 70 undergraduates provided over 30,000 hours of community service through their field experiences in the 1997-98.

Enhance distribution of money and resources (enhance quality of life).

- Implemented a Departmental Faculty Research Fund to award seed money to faculty developing grant proposals.
- Implemented Individual Faculty Accounts, account transfers, and purchasing procedures with the Expert Business Office to improve the efficiency of faculty purchasing.
- Implemented plan to allow 24 hour accessibility to copying on departmental copy machines.
- Implemented new Overhead policy to distribute overhead money to Principal Investigators, Alumni Fund, Faculty Research Fund, and Chair's Fund.

Improve public relations:

- Published the Alumni Newsletter. Sent to both graduate and undergraduate alumni.
- Continued efforts to report faculty and student news to media both inside and outside the university. Articles appeared on treating eating disorders, faculty book signing, treating depression, anxiety disorders, Alan Poling- a Western Michigan University's Distinguished Faculty and former student of WVU, retirements, and faculty awards.
- Continued efforts to communicate departmental highlights to Dean, Provost, President, and Board of Trustees.
- Continued efforts to describe our admission criteria and the national competitiveness of our programs to individuals in state who wrote references for students applying to our graduate programs.

Maintain high quality and quantity of research, teaching, and service:

- Phil Comer was named the Most Loyal Faculty and Staff Mountaineer in 1997.
- Andy Lattal received the J. R. Kantor Fellowship from the Archives of the History of American Psychology for 1997-98.
- Phil Chase was appointed Editor-elect of *The Behavior Analyst*. His term of office is from July 1998- June 2001.
- Georg Eifert was ranked as the 23rd most productive author in behavior analysis and therapy journals from 1990-96 (Richards, Cox & Norton, 1998).
- Two former faculty, Trevor Stokes and Frank Collins, were listed in the top 50 most productive scholars publishing in applied behavioral periodicals between 1974-94 (they were both faculty here during a significant part of that time period).

- Our department was ranked 4th internationally in publishing productivity in behavior analysis and therapy journals from 1990-96 (Richards, Cox & Norton, 1998).
- Our department was ranked 7th in the top 50 most productive institutions publishing in applied behavioral periodicals 1974-94 (Hayes & Grundt, 1996).
- The research of one former faculty, Paul Baltes, and one former student, Laura L. Cartensen, was highlighted in a **Science News** article by Bruce Bower on remembering and aging.
- Faculty provided 2904 hours of direct service to the community and many additional hours of indirect service as the supervisors of students on practica, internships and field experiences.

Grants and Contracts 1997-98:

Teaching and training

Joseph Scotti, Christina Adams, Tracy Morris, and Kevin Larkin- $7,500 for Psych 1 from West Virginia University.

Joseph Scotti, Christina Adams, Tracy Morris, and Kevin Larkin- $79,980 for Psych 1 from the State College and University System of West Virginia.

Michael Perone- $2500 for Psych 171 from the Eberly College of Arts and Sciences.

JoNell Strough- $7500 for Psych 151 from the Eberly College of Arts and Sciences and West Virginia University.

Jerry Richards (through Katherine Karraker)- $8,280 for Psychology 102 from West Virginia University and Eberly College of Arts and Sciences.

Stan Cohen- $4213 for Psychology 19 from West Virginia University and the Eberly College of Arts and Sciences.

Dan McNeil- $105,825 for practicum contracts

Phil Chase- $4,500 for a practicum contract

Stan Cohen- $5,065 for development of a statistics program from the Eberly College of Arts and Sciences and West Virginia University.

Research

John Crosbie–	$251,068 from NIMH (First of three years)
Cheryl McNeil–	$102,391 from NIMH (Second of three years)
David Schaal–	$277,363 from NIDA (Fourth of five year FIRST Award)
Joseph Scotti–	$35,750 from NIMH (one year B/Start)
Jerry Richards–	$320,584 from NIDA (First of three years)
Irv Goodman–	$60,000 from WVU Biomedical Research Team
Anne O'Reilly–	$3,000 from the Eberly College of Arts and Sciences
Christina Adams–	$5,000 from the WVU Faculty Senate

Publications (July 1, 1996- June 31, 1997):

Peer reviewed: 49
Invited Chapters- 8
Books- 1
Other- 20

- The QCC continued to increase its service to the community by conducting 99 new client intakes, serving clients from 9 different counties with all but 17 of these clients coming from outside the university (July 1, 1997- October 1, 1998).
- Instituted a more equitable course assignment structure in the department additional courses by the chair.
- Increased use of instructional technology. Six faculty have developed multimedia presentations that affect over 5,000 students per year. Three faculty have developed computer based testing and learning projects that affect over 4,000 students. Most other faculty are using multimedia equipment and/or Internet assignments in their classes.
- QCC provided 577 hours of clinical service in 1997.
- Department was ranked 7th in the top 50 most productive institutions publishing in applied behavioral periodicals 1974-94.
- Department ranked 89th in two different rankings of 167 graduate programs in psychology that produced doctorates during the evaluation period. These rankings placed us ahead of 15 SREB peer institution's psychology departments.
- Implemented a more thorough teaching evaluation procedure that includes three components: course structure and content, student evaluations, and student performance or outcomes.

Appendix C

Faculty Merit Policy

"Merit funds will be distributed by summing the "excellent" ratings of each faculty member since merit funds were distributed last (a period not to exceed three years). In the case of first year faculty, the sum of their excellent ratings will be divided by 2 to reflect a half year of service to the university. The total of all meritorious faculty ratings will then be divided into the amount of money available for merit distribution, yielding a "dollars per point" figure. This figure will then be multiplied by the number of points earned by each "meritorious" faculty member to yield the individual faculty member merit distribution."

Discussion of Chase

Management and Academia

William N. Cathey
University of Nevada

Herding Cats and Spinning Plates is certainly an appropriate description for Philip Chase's article on applying performance management techniques to an academic department in a university. While this is a case history for a particular department in a large state-funded teaching and research university, it should be recognized that this is a structure that is representative of a significant number of organizations in which the leadership comes from within the departmental group and the leader returns to the group after a few years. This is typically the case in educational institutions.

The challenge faced by an academic department chair is to develop an agenda that will move the group forward at the same time that the individuals within the group are also growing as researchers and teachers. Chase points out the faculty member's dilemma of whether their allegiance is to the discipline or to the department of the university. Dealing with this is also the department chair's dilemma. Chase started out with an advantage, however, because he had a theoretical framework in performance management that he used to develop an approach to his term as department chair. In most cases in academia, the chair has no training in management and must learn on the job; on the job training is not always the most effective method, in this situation.

One of Chase's accomplishments is to provide a guide for new academic department chairs. The situation described is typical of many academic departments, with the possible exception of Chase not having mentioned dealing with the enormous egos sometimes found in highly successful faculty. The organization of the paper was such that one could imagine going through the steps Chase described and developing a plan for ones own department. The emphasis on measuring outcomes is particularly good for those unfamiliar with the advantages of keeping track of accomplishments. Chase describes how the goals were developed, implemented, and assessed.

In the conclusion, Chase mentioned two additional goals: "to stop being chair after five years and to know that the department would continue to be a place where I wanted to work." These could have been mentioned at the beginning as well as in the conclusion. One of the unique characteristics of an academic department is for the chair to willingly relinquish leadership and return to the faculty. This places unusual stress on the chair when making many decisions related to planning and evaluation, since the decisions will have an impact on how the former chair is viewed when he returns to the faculty. Similarly, new chairs must decide how to blend their own plans and dreams into the work that was done by their predecessors. Having an operating philosophy such as Chase describes enables the organization to progress in spite of the leadership being periodically reabsorbed back into the organization. Chase suggests that this is indeed the case for the department he chaired.

To make a case history interesting, there needs to be enough detail in the description to define what the author is talking about. Chase does provide enough of the necessary detail, occasionally more than enough, so that the reader can connect the concepts with something concrete. While the quantitative measures were not particularly exotic, their inclusion was useful in order to describe how performance can be measured in simple ways. One additional piece of useful information would have been an analysis of the extent to which the administrative workload actually went down when the number of administrators was reduced.

This case history is helpful to the potential academic department chair; it is also helpful to the non-academic who wants to learn more about the culture of academia. It may be that this second, non-academic reader is the more important one since there is a need for higher education to be better understood as an entity that has great impact on the progress of our society. The fact that performance management techniques can be successfully applied to higher education is important in terms of convincing a broader community that higher education can be accountable as well as influential and valued.

As a concluding observation, Case and his colleagues are encouraged to follow the extent to which this approach has provided the groundwork for continued success. The first phase has been interesting and informative; the next stage will contain answers as to whether the approach is successful.

Deconstructing Performance Management Processes

Jon S. Bailey
Florida State University
John Austin
Western Michigan University

Performance Management is a complex process of analyzing human behavior in the workplace and subsequently implementing changes to the work environment that are designed to improve some aspect of productivity. It is, by nature, an applied science and in this case the scientific basis for Performance Management is operant conditioning as established first by Skinner (1938, 1953) and his colleagues. Yet, the principles of operant conditioning as applied to human behavior have been greatly expanded over the past 60 years. In it's simplest form, Performance Management might resemble operant conditioning to a considerable degree. In the same way that a rat or pigeon could be trained to press a lever or peck a key at a higher rate, employee behavior might be reinforced when the person accomplishes more work in a shorter period of time.

This apparent simplicity has been a major selling point of PM since it's first appearance in 1971 ("New tool", 1971). The magazine article described Ed Feeney's work in which employees in a package delivery company were prompted and then reinforced for putting more small packages in containers and preparing them for shipment. Feeney reported significant results from this simple application of operant conditioning and soon many others were beginning to follow suit. In the years that followed, consultants and researchers began tackling more and more complex performance problems in increasingly diverse and intricate organizations and it became necessary to train the next generation of practitioners.

Unfortunately, there are limited training materials available for this purpose. Most of the current books (e.g., Daniels, 1989; Rummler & Brache, 1995) are designed for consultants in Performance Management or those employed by companies in that capacity. The primary journal of the field, the *Journal of Organizational Behavior Management*, is designed to advance the knowledge of applied behavior analysis in work and organizational settings and is written for and by researchers in the field to share their findings. As such, the journal is generally not intended for teaching purposes, especially for undergraduate students at universities.

One program (Ackley & Bailey, 1995) at Florida State University (FSU) prepares undergraduate students in the fundamentals of Performance Management and has as a core requirement of the two semester sequence that they complete a PM project with a local business. Another, at Western Michigan University, has essentially replicated the FSU program. In these cases, students take on what initially appear to be modest and manageable performance problems, but these often turn out to be extremely involved and complex. The purpose of the PM project requirement is to allow students to practice their new skills and learn project management through their involvement in an actual application. This process of students' discovering the complexity of organizational performance problems not apparent in the PM texts or literature and our feeling the need to prepare students for such problems has prompted the current paper. Basically, to properly train students to successfully carry out Performance Management projects it is necessary to "deconstruct" Performance Management processes, that is, to analyze in close detail the steps necessary to carry out Performance Management and then to determine what skills and competencies are necessary for each step (see Brethower & Smalley, 1998 for details on this approach). Sequencing the steps and preparing, testing and revising the learning modules is the final step in this process. In this paper we propose to outline the necessary steps for training students to carry out Performance Management projects.

Ten Steps to Successful Performance Management Projects

The analysis of PM steps that is proposed here is somewhat similar to that which may be found in several other sources (Brown & Presbie, 1976; Daniels, 1989; Luthans, 1982) but is also significantly different in several respects. First, the steps have been derived from practice in supervising well over 300 PM projects in the past 10 years. In teaching these classes repeatedly, it has become abundantly clear when steps were left out or not adequately emphasized to students. Second, the steps have now been further validated through a multi-year project in a large mental health facility. In this project, program managers and supervisors were taught Performance Management skills and encouraged to improve fiscal accountability, client care, medical treatment, and administrative support (Bailey, Riordan, Coleman, Hutchison, & Oswald, 1998). Several hundred individual performance improvement projects have now been carried out successfully using the model at this facility. Many of these projects have been recognized as worthy by an independent non-profit agency (i.e., Florida TaxWatch) which supports improved productivity in public sector organizations. In the remainder of this paper, we will discuss the steps in the PM process. The ten steps we will discuss are shown in Figure 1.

Step 1: Selecting the performance problem. In order for students or supervisors to be successful in carrying out a PM project, for the purpose of demonstration and/ or development of their skills, it is important that they select the setting and the problem carefully. Experience has shown that it is all too easy to select a problem that is beyond the capabilities and resources of a student or front-line supervisor. Those making referrals and suggestions too may be unaware of the level of complexity in what appear to be simple organization and behavior problems.

"Lack of initiative" was referred as a serious problem in need of a solution in a small sandwich shop on the edge of campus. As we soon discovered, however, the owner/manager never mentioned this as a desirable trait and did not train new employees on this skill (perhaps, in part, because the manager had not behaviorally defined "initiative"). Finding opportunities for "initiative" turned out to be

The 10 Step PM Process

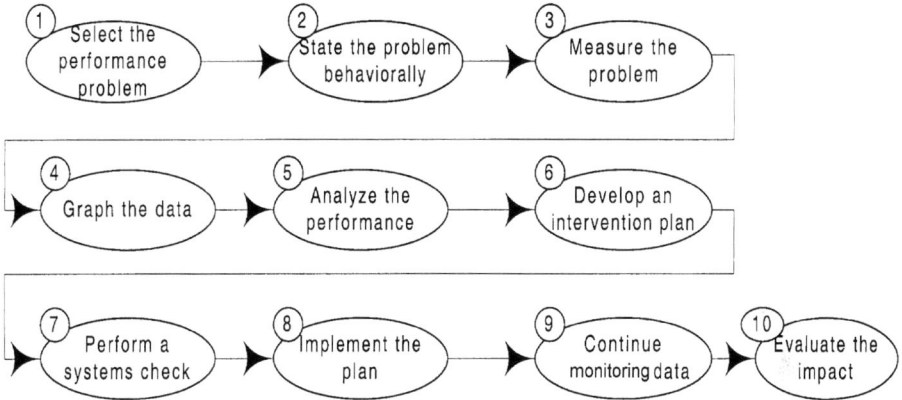

Figure 1.

extremely difficult and ultimately they were low in frequency and when the behavior did occur it was often out of sight of management and other employees.

In another project, the objective was to reduce the disappearance of towels and wash cloths in a state hospital setting. Thousands of new replacement items were purchased each year and the cost savings could have been significant. However, determining the exact location of the disappearance in a long chain of delivery-storage-dispensing-use-disposal-return turned out to be impossible given the size of the case.

The administrator of a local "dial-a-ride" service for elderly and handicapped persons alleged that "service was pitiful" and that it needed improvement immediately. When no hard data were forthcoming to support the charge, a customized phone interview with customers was initiated. Over a one-week period every customer was contacted; not a single complaint was heard and many compliments were offered.

In other cases, we have discovered that some "performance" problems are really due to manpower or resource shortages, a lack of customers, or to political conflict within the organization. In addition, managers are reluctant to allow focus on some more socially (or legally) sensitive problems. In one case, a local (non-profit) resale shop refused to allow a student to measure the safety of items donated and shelved, apparently for fear of the legal implications.

For the student or front-line supervisor to be successful, they must essentially select a problem that is obvious to everyone, that is not due to a failure of management to provide sufficient resources or to some political conflict within the company, and that is not a result of some structural deficit, supply problem or a lack of customers. This is an area of concern and critical importance for inexperienced practitioners of PM. It is critical because much time and energy can be wasted by focusing for weeks on problems that are essentially impossible to solve for practitioners without access to the appropriate level of the organization (i.e., to those with the resources, for example, to fix the problem). In other words, the concern in this case is that the inexperienced practitioner needs to be able to quickly determine if the likely solutions to the problem are potentially within their span of control or if they should de-select the problem and find a more suitable one to examine.

Students, of course, must be able to determine if the performance problem is of such a magnitude that they will not be overwhelmed by the sheer size and complexity of it all. One key point often overlooked by students and supervisors is the amount of time it will take to collect and analyze the data each day. Students simply have no frame of reference for this essential feature of Performance Management. In our experience, this can require 30-min to an hour per day and, of course, must be done with great consistency and immediacy. In addition, they must have impeccable social skills and operate with professionalism at all times. Again, most students have little experience with such requirements.

One of the more difficult concepts for students to grasp is that of identifying a problem that, if solved, would be of quantifiable value to the organization. Supervisors have more experience with this, but they too can have trouble with this essential feature of pinpointing. One of the goals of PM is to help organizations and their members achieve more of their strategic objectives. For this reason, finding a pinpoint that *adds value* is a necessary step in the PM process. Another reason for selecting valued pinpoints is that these give the practitioner a better chance at garnering both financial and political support for the project. The rule we tend to use is, if the contact person in the organization finds the problem important, the practitioner increases his or her chances of success. And, initial success is important in encouraging inexperienced practitioners' continued use of PM techniques.

Step 2: Stating the problem behaviorally. During this step (also known as pinpointing; see Daniels, 1989), our objective is to teach students to reframe a referred problem in behavioral terms. Often referrals at this point are vague problems such as "improving morale". As a result, students need to be able to recognize that the contact person sees some need for improvement, and at the same time, try to determine to what sorts of behavioral effects the contact person is referring. Other presenting problems are troublesome for inexperienced practitioners. "I'd like to improve my customer service" is a frequent request from managers, to which the student must respond by aiding in the behavioral definition of "customer service". What we need for adequate pinpointing are specifics.

Students are instructed that basically human performance can be defined in one of two ways: an actual observable behavior, or a result (i.e., an outcome of behavior). For now, it is sufficient to point out that it is desirable to define behaviors in such a way that an outcome is produced. "Cleanliness" is desired in most restaurants, for example, and managers are constantly worried about meeting not only the health code but also customer expectations for a clean establishment. A supervisor could state the goals for cleanliness behaviorally either by listing a number of "cleaning behaviors" such as sweeping, mopping, wiping, polishing, etc. or, by specifying outcomes. "No spots on the sink", and "No debris or water on the floor", would be examples of the results of cleaning.

When the inexperienced practitioner is faced with problems stated in vague terms, we instruct them to talk to the manager about what the problem "looks like", and/or about what outcomes are not being produced as a result of the existence of the problem. We instruct them that their goal as the PM consultant is to work with their contact person to precisely define the actual behaviors or results in such a way that a second, independent observer, working only from written descriptions, could detect the same behavioral events. Students are told to have the contact person then begin to list a series of examples of behavior that they are thinking of when they use words such as "poor attitude". When they have the specifics down, that is, they have a list of measurable outcomes or a list of behaviors, they are ready to tackle the measurement issues.

Step 3: Measuring the behavior. This is a most difficult step for new students of PM. Our experience is that students have little relevant background in applied measurement and that working through the conceptual issues of determining a target behavior and determining how to measure it reliably is a major barrier. We recommend students use outcome measures whenever possible, since these are easier than behavioral measures to define and reliably collect. Often, organizations have relevant performance data collected by computers so students can simply use printouts to summarize data. We point out that in a restaurant, for example, suggestive selling of "add-ons" can often be measured through cash register printouts of item-specific sales. Most restaurants want their servers to promote special drinks, appetizers, soups, salads, and desserts, all of which can be tracked via computer to determine sales per person per hour.

Other outcome measures include inventory in stock, sales, cost savings or administrative overhead. In another project, a student monitored the extent to which computer lab employees checked online messages. In that case, the computer lab already collected the timeliness data and the student was able to have these data sent to him directly every day via email. Some behaviors might have to be observed directly via trained observers or perhaps managers or supervisors in the setting in which case students will have to learn about time-sampling, frequency and interval observation and other occurrence measurement techniques. This can become extremely complex and the decision making matrix for choosing the right measurement system is not well defined.

An additional issue that arises for some projects is how to manage the collection and posting of several (3 or more) measures of performance. In these cases, students are advised to use a performance matrix (Daniels, 1989) whereby the frequencies, timeliness, cost, and/or ratings of several measures can be combined in a weighted fashion, not unlike that used in balanced scorecards (Kaplan & Norton, 1996). In one example of such a study, a student used a performance matrix to improve customer service at the local site of an international department store chain

(Eikenhout & Austin, 2000). The student measured five customer service behaviors in three departments, and trained employees to understand the matrix, which was subsequently posted on a weekly basis.

Another method of data collection we will point out to students involves using customer, supervisor, or peer subjective evaluations to rate employee performance. Many organizations already use "mystery shoppers" to get some idea of how employees actually perform their functions. Data collected in this manner are often done by way of a rating, e.g. a 1-5 scale, of certain services. There may also be a number of "yes-no" questions where the data are tabulated as a percentage of positive or negative responses. Students are instructed that the collection of these data should be considered carefully, as they often can be misleading or biased in various ways. Daniels (1989) refers to several ways to collect subjective data, including rating and ranking scales, and recommends using behaviorally anchored rating scales (BARS) when possible.

A final consideration in measurement is deciding on an evaluation design. We encourage students to use multiple baseline designs whenever possible. However, it is essential that students have a backup plan in case the intervention, when applied to the first baseline, generalizes to other baselines. As an alternate plan, we advise students to attempt a multiple baseline both across behaviors and employees, or across employees and departments. In this way, if something goes wrong during the first attempt, the student can revert to a backup plan rather than settling for an AB design.

Step 4: Graphing the behavior. We do our best to emphasize to students the data-based nature of applied behavior analysis. As the reader knows, decisions regarding when to intervene can not be made in advance. Rather, in the vast majority of cases, decisions to intervene are based on the appearance of baseline data. Students are advised to graph the data using Microsoft Excel (see Carr & Burkholder, 1998 for instructions on how to create graphs using this program), print out graphs, and bring these data to class every week so that they may be discussed and viewed publicly. Over years of teaching graphing it has become clear that what is needed most is for students to have considerable practice in preparing graphs according to this set of guidelines and to learn to critique graphs that do not meet the standard. For this latter purpose we have selected a set of figures from published studies and sequenced them from easy to difficult in terms of their deviance from the accepted standard. As an educational tool, using published studies appears to have motiva-tional value for students in that they seem to enjoy being able to find fault in the existing establishment. When discussing the data, we view the graphs according to the guidelines of visual inspection derived by applied behavior analysts (e.g., Parsonson & Baer, 1978).

After examining the details of how the graphs are constructed (i.e., conditions and axes labeling and orientation of the graph on the page), we discuss trend and variability and their impact on decisions to intervene. The novice PM practitioner learns that, ideally, one should intervene only after achieving a stable baseline. When stability is not a reasonable criterion, students are encouraged to intervene only when the data are trending in the opposite direction of the expected effect and that variability has not recently changed significantly. In addition, students learn that one should not intervene immediately after a significant break in data collection (as in after Spring Break or after semester start at the university), but rather, they are counseled to collect data after such a break until stability is again achieved.

Preparing and interpreting graphs also presents an opportunity to teach students about the demonstration of experimental control. The value of a reversal design over an AB for example, can be illustrated in the process of having students critique the stability of data or the failure of the study to include a replication of an intervention.

Step 5: Analyzing the performance problem. Before developing an intervention, we insist that data have to meet certain stability criteria as described above, and adequate diagnosis must be conducted. In our experience, students benefit greatly from a detailed and thoughtful assessment. Furthermore, some behavior analysts have argued that intervening before analysis is akin to the behavior modification of the 1960's, as opposed to modern applied behavior analysis (Mace, 1994). Obviously, we wish to teach students to practice the latter. We firmly believe that assessment and analysis make the necessary intervention more clear to the inexperienced practitioner. We advise our students that they should not even "begin to think" about intervention before conducting an analysis.

The analysis we suggest has several forms; each derived from other behavioral models of assessment, such as Gilbert's (1982) PROBE model and Daniels' (1989) ABC analysis. These models and others, as well as the basic model that we recommend, are explained in detail by Austin (2000) and Austin, Carr and Agnew (1999). The basic model we recommend has students ask specific questions in each of four categories: antecedents; equipment and processes; knowledge and skills; and consequences.

In the simplest and most informal assessments, students meet with key personnel in the organization and attempt to gain information about the performance deficiency through asking interview-style questions. Others have been able to append direct observation and actual data collection to support or refute hypotheses of variables maintaining and/or hindering performance. The purpose and result of analyzing the performance problem is to develop plausible hypotheses about why the problem is occurring, so that interventions may be created that address the source(s) of the problem.

Basically students learn to ask a series of questions (see Figure 2; and see Austin, 2000 for a similar but more lengthy question list) about conditions surrounding the target behavior and other related, possibly competing or replacement, behaviors. Usually scenarios have to be created to teach this since an examination of the research literature is not very enlightening in this respect. The majority of studies we have reviewed for this purpose do not shed any light on why certain interventions were chosen. While we were initially surprised at this finding it made all the more clear the need to develop job aids to assist students in developing this relatively sophisticated repertoire. A sample of the questions and likely interventions follows:

The 12 Diagnostic Questions

estion	Less intrusive	More intrusive
1. Does the person understand what behavior is expected?		
2. Is there a specific prompt for the behavior?		
3. Is the supervisor present?		
4. Does the employee have a personal problem that requires counseling or clinical treatment?		
5. Does the equipment work? Is it in good repair? Is the environment conducive to high performance?		
6. Does the person actually have the skill? Has it been demonstrated in the past?		
7. Is the task designed to be carried out in an efficient fashion? Can it be streamlined or eliminated?		
8. Is there any response cost or other punisher associated with performing the task?		
9. Does the behavior produce an observable effect?		
10. Does the person receive any feedback of any kind from peers customers or supervisors for their performance?		
11. Is there any intrinsic or tangible extrinsic reinforcement for the behavior?		
12. Is a competing behavior being reinforced?		

Figure 2.

Does the person understand what behavior is expected? If no, the intervention might be fairly simple: through some procedure internal to the company make arrangements for the individual to see his/her job description. In some cases we have discovered that there is no job description and that the employee was trained by a previous employee who also had never seen a job description.

Is there a specific prompt for the behavior? This question is aimed at the issue of the precision of stimulus control. 'Treat our customers well,' 'Always try to meet the customer's needs,' and other imprecise prompts for behavior abound in businesses. At first students do not see the need to be more specific but when we begin to describe the number of possible behaviors not covered in such platitudes they will usually get the point. For businesses it is far easier to issue general mandates than take the time to specify the precise behaviors they are looking for. For example, almost every retail (i.e., food, clothing) establishment has a closing routine that includes putting products away, cleaning, counting out the cash drawer, and locking up the establishment; very few have this procedure written out in detail enough that it can be determined if each step was completed to criterion. Indeed there is usually no assignment of duties and there are normally no criteria specified.

Does the person have the skill? This type of question was first raised by Mager and Pipe (1970) and of course is still relevant. By asking this question we sensitize the students to the issue of training, how complete it is, and how successful it was in actually generating behavior in the workplace. Ordinarily the students will ask this question of the direct supervisor and along with the follow-up question, 'Has it been demonstrated in the past?' they begin to understand that target behaviors may be a problem because everyone assumed that the critical skill was already a part of the person's repertoire.

Does the behavior produce an observable effect? Having students ask this question helps them raise an important point with their contact person. When someone engages in the correct behavior, does it produce any difference in the environment? Unfortunately the answer is almost always 'no'. Our experience frequently supports a vast gap in the 'expectation ... outcome' equation. That is, it would appear that many, and perhaps the majority of workers on a new job, attempt to properly carry out their duties only to discover that there are no differential consequences. They observe their colleagues being less compulsive about details, completing less work, and not following directions and yet getting the same hourly wage. Not completing all the steps in a cleaning routine does not result in any less business, employees do not come down with infectious diseases and at least at first glance the work environment does not appear to be greatly different. As Performance Managers, of course, if we are to generate stable and reliable performances, we must discover ways of adding some differential consequences to the environment.

In the best case, an observable effect reveals the existence of natural consequences. That is, consequences are automatically produced when the task is completed. These are desirable because they need no one to deliver them and yet they maintain the desired behavior. The recommended intervention of changing the task so that it creates an observable effect is not always possible, but when it is, it is usually highly effective.

Step 6: Develop the intervention and maintenance plan. Next, students are required to develop and clearly outline the potential interventions and list them on an intervention planning sheet. The intervention planning sheet simply has three columns: the first column is a list of all deficiencies identified during the assessment; and the second and third columns list the corresponding least and most intrusive interventions, respectively. That is, the intervention planning sheet lists, on a single page, all deficiencies and the corrective action needed to remedy them.

Depending on the answers to the 12 Diagnostic Questions, and a review of the relevant literature, the intervention should be readily apparent. We have divided the interventions into less intrusive and more intrusive since in some cases companies and organizations will initially answer yes to a question and then begin to hedge their answers. In a review of the literature students will often see interventions they would like to try but which are impractical in their situation. Part of their training, which we have not discussed in detail here, is reading journal (i.e., JOBM and JABA) articles that demonstrate the types of interventions typically used in Performance Management. In many cases, the study did not try a 'less intrusive' intervention but went straight to some elaborate and complex token economy or other motivational system. In the following pages, we will review 12 examples of what the two levels of intervention intrusiveness might look like, given the existence of certain organizational/environmental deficiencies. In normal practice, these deficiencies would have been uncovered during the course of the assessment (described in the preceding section).

Example 1

Deficiency: The person does not understand what behavior is expected.

Less intrusive intervention: The person is informed verbally and in writing.

More intrusive intervention: The person is trained and given a test over the job requirements. They must pass the test at some high criterion (e.g., 100 percent) and/or the person must complete a role-playing exercise where explaining what is expected to a new associate is part of the scenario.

Example 2

Deficiency: No prompt for the behavior.

Less intrusive intervention: The supervisor or manager determines when, where, and how a less intrusive prompt might be added to the environment, e.g. a small sign on the cash register that says, "Ask the customer to 'Come again and shop with us.'" as an attempt to promote specific customer friendliness behavior in a grocery store chain.

More intrusive intervention: Someone must prompt employees regularly. Managers, other employees, and/or customers have been effective prompting agents. In addition, the person could construct the prompt, each day, and place it in a prominent place. Perhaps even have them construct several of the prompts and apply to each of the cash registers each day and tie these into regularly occurring consequences.

Example 3

Deficiency: No supervisor present.

Less intrusive intervention: The manager informs the supervisor of the need to 'be where the action is', i.e., near his/her employees.

More intrusive intervention: The manager physically walks the supervisor to the proper area and stands nearby to observe that the supervisor stays in place. Note: having a supervisor 'present' does not guarantee that the person will give good feedback to employees, and therefore considerable training may be in order for supervisors expected to deliver feedback and reinforcement (which represents an even more intrusive intervention). See Question 10 for more detail on delivering feedback.

Example 4

Deficiency: The employee has a personal problem that requires counseling or clinical treatment.

This topic is included since there are increasing reports that many employees are having personal problems such as drug and alcohol abuse, or have chronic family problems (e.g., divorce, disagreements over custody of children) that can create problems at work. It would be inappropriate for the PM practitioner to either try to counsel with the person or to apply the standard PM interventions. The most prudent action is to be sensitive to this possibility and then do the following.

Less intrusive intervention: Meet with the person and suggest that if they are having personal problems they should seek some assistance. Give them a brochure that outlines the company policy on such issues. If this has been done or does not work, then try the more intrusive approach.

More intrusive intervention: Inform the manager of the work unit of the problem, outline your concerns and the less intrusive steps that have been taken.

Example 5

Deficiency: The equipment does not work, is not in good repair, or the environment is not conducive to high performance.

These topics are included to remind PM professionals that there are mechanical and environmental constraints and requirements to many tasks. Making errors in attention-demanding tasks, for example, may be most appropriately corrected by adding dividers between workstations or installing sound absorbing curtains. Any time a task is heavily dependent on some piece of equipment it should always be checked to see if it the performance deficit is due to equipment breakdown or failure. If the environment cannot be improved then other modifications may need to be made. If errors in placing orders was the target behavior, and if it was observed that the environment was noisy so that it was difficult to hear, one alternative would be to have orders placed in writing, or entered via computer keyboard or touch screen.

Less intrusive intervention: Work with management to have equipment checked or help employees document equipment failures and report them to the appropriate department.

More intrusive intervention: Take a position with management that the performance problem is in part an equipment or environment problem. Ask for a pilot study of a newer piece of equipment or of ways to improve the current work environment.

Example 6

Deficiency: The person does not have the skill. The skill has not been demonstrated in the past.

Often supervisors will respond affirmatively to this issue. 'Of course they can do it...' but the follow-up question of demonstration often makes it apparent that the manager has not actually witnessed the target behavior in their capacity as supervisor.

Less intrusive intervention: Institute the standard company training if this has not already been done. Ask if there is any competency requirement for exiting training. Often there is not; employees are simply asked to shadow another employee for a few hours or to view a video tape.

More intrusive intervention: Help the company determine some performance criteria for each behavior. Ask the question, 'How would I know if they had this skill?' When the on-the-job criterion is established make sure this is matched by similar criteria during training. Make sure that training is not considered completed until performance on the job, at criterion, is demonstrated. For more details about this sort of performance-based training, see Brethower and Smalley (1998).

Example 7

Deficiency: The task is not designed to be carried out in an efficient fashion. It could be streamlined or eliminated.

Many behavior analysts do not question the task that has been referred and may attempt to improve performance without considering other relevant variables. By taking in the larger picture of the context it may become apparent that other options are available.

Less intrusive intervention: Rather than trying to improve the performance, do a task analysis to see if there is an easier way to perform the task. Can some steps be eliminated? Can the task be facilitated with some device or piece of equipment or a job aid? Furthermore, (taking in an even larger picture) is the task affected by the performance of others in other tasks, departments, functions, or organizations? This latter point quickly leads us to some more advanced approaches to systems analysis and is beyond the scope of this chapter. However, we should say that to be an effective PM practitioner, one needs to be knowledgeable in behavioral systems analysis as well as applied behavior analysis. For more detail on systems analysis, see the systems chapters in this volume and Rummler and Brache (1995).

More intrusive intervention: Consider reengineering the task. That is, starting from scratch to determine how this function needs to be covered and how it should interact with other tasks and functions.

Example 8

Deficiency: There is response cost or some other punisher associated with performing the task.

This topic forces the Performance Management trainee to consider unintended but important consequences of the task under consideration. It is often the case that employees are reluctant to engage in a certain task because of the effort, discomfort or pain involved.

Less intrusive intervention: Try to eliminate any obvious effort, response cost, pain or discomfort associated with the task. In some cases this might involve training (e.g., in proper lifting to avoid back pain or injury). Some tasks might be made easier with the use of simple job aids, gloves, ear protection, and other forms of personal protective equipment.

More intrusive intervention: Consider the redesign of the job to eliminate the response cost or effort. Determine if more frequent breaks, job rotation, or redistribution of tasks would make the job easier to perform (consult an ergonomist for scientific analyses of these issues). Also, consider reassignment of the person to another task or outsourcing the job to temporary employees (although the latter may not always solve the problem).

Example 9

Deficiency: The behavior does not produce an observable effect.

As described above, this topic helps the practitioner to search for the natural consequences of the task at hand. Employees often more reliably complete tasks with natural reinforcers. If the task does not have an observable effect, potential interventions are listed below.

Less intrusive intervention: Determine what effect should be seen if the job is performed properly. Add mechanisms to highlight or bring these outcomes to the attention of the performer. In one example, field workers were handling toxic chemicals without wearing proper gloves, ostensibly because the chemicals appeared clear like water and had no immediate odor. An appropriate intervention in this case was to add coloring to the chemicals that created a stain when it touched the skin or clothing. This way, there was an observable effect of not using the appropriate gloves.

More intrusive intervention: Consider redesigning the task so that the natural consequences of excellent performance are obvious to the person. This might involve changing the flow of work or allowing the person to see data on their performance that would ordinarily not be part of the work setting.

Example 10

Deficiency: The person does not receive feedback from peers, customers, or supervisors for their performance.

This topic primarily addresses issues of social feedback for proper performance of a task.

Less intrusive intervention: Prompt peers and supervisors to provide feedback to each other on their performance. This will probably involve some training and setting up of special procedures, e.g. feedback cards, methods of showing appreciation and support. Brown and Sulzer-Azaroff (1994) devised a creative approach for soliciting and using social feedback at a bank. Tellers gave customers colored chips and asked them to drop the chips in a box indicating their level of satisfaction. This gave the tellers immediate social feedback on the outcomes of their service.

More intrusive intervention: More elaborate feedback systems might have to be set up that involves more complete training of supervisors, putting them on a feedback contract system where they are required to observe employees on a set schedule and provide positive feedback of an obvious nature. Behavior-based safety initiatives often use this approach or something similar. Many or most employees and supervisors are trained to observe safety behavior using a checklist, give each other feedback on the behaviors and summarize the data into percent safe scores that are then graphed and posted publicly.

Example 11

Deficiency: There is no intrinsic or tangible extrinsic reinforcement for the behavior.

This topic is also designed to help the student focus on issues pertaining to natural consequences of certain target behaviors as well as those related to how people are paid for the work they do. Some jobs can be made more intrinsically (naturally) rewarding by allowing employees to have some flexibility in how they complete the task or input into how it is done. A job that does not involve much customer contact might be redesigned to allow this to happen. As students, or even first-line supervisors for that matter, it is quite difficult to have any input on how people are paid. However, we have been involved in making suggestions about adding bonus system, on a trial basis, to determine if that might make a difference.

Less intrusive intervention: Through interviews ask employees how a job might be changed to make it more interesting or rewarding to them. Attempt to implement any reasonable suggestions.

More intrusive intervention: Work with management to implement improved pay systems that might provide for differential pay for extra effort or high performance. Arrange for bonuses if certain performance standards are met. One of the criteria we recommend to students in this case is to pay only for performance that results in some verifiable revenue for the organization. Otherwise such systems are far too complex for the novice to organize. For more advanced approaches to paying for performance, see Abernathy (1996).

Example 12

Deficiency: A competing behavior is being reinforced.

This topic directs students and supervisors to consider the possibility that the target behavior is not being completed because some other behavior is displacing it by being on a richer reinforcement schedule.

Less intrusive intervention: Working with management try to reduce the reinforcement available for the second task or to increase the reinforcement for the desired task. This might involve looking at both intrinsic and extrinsic reinforcers currently available for that task.

More intrusive intervention: Consider some programmatic change in the way that employees are paid for their jobs. Consider developing a Premack contingency in which the target task has to be completed before some higher rate task in which the employee is engaging. Consider a Performance Matrix (Daniels, 1989) as a method of changing the balance of extrinsic reinforcers available for multiple competing tasks.

Maintenance Plans. As an additional part of Step 6, a maintenance plan must be developed, and this tends to determine which interventions are most likely to succeed in the organization. For example, most assessments find that feedback and reinforcement are lacking for the desired performance. However, these are not always warranted, especially when simpler interventions (e.g., prompts or task redesign) are also warranted, because many organizations are not capable of (and some are not interested in) reliably administering and maintaining a feedback and reinforcement package. For this reason, we sometimes recommend that inexperienced practitioners find a suitable but yet simple intervention in place of more complex (yet potentially highly effective) interventions. However, this does seem to reduce the probability of success in some cases. This seems to occur most frequently in cases where both prompts and consequences are lacking, and the behavior is a difficult one to change. For example, we have seen many projects focusing suggestive selling in restaurants, and these often require consequences. Waitstaff tend to find it aversive to make suggestions, and therefore, task clarification or prompting often do not change behavior. These examples notwithstanding, we have found that students who design the intervention with maintenance in mind are more likely to see their interventions maintained. Therefore, we encourage and support planning for maintenance, even when it determines the focus and topography of the intervention.

Step 7: Perform a systems check. Organizations are complex systems. That is, when one dimension or variable is changed, many others may be affected. For more detail on viewing organizations as complex systems, see the organizational systems section of this volume. Throughout this chapter, we speak of Performance Management at the level of the individual, as this is the level at which applied behavior analysis principles function. However, the PM practitioner must recognize that when behavior and results change, this often significantly affects larger organizational outcomes (and such is among the goals of PM). This means that after planning the intervention, and before implementing it, we must verify that the intervention will have no adverse impact on the existing systems.

An impact analysis must be conducted through a focused meeting with the organizational contact person. During this meeting, the student and contact person should review the goals and objectives of the PM project. They may discuss questions such as, "If the target behaviors change significantly, what else might be impacted?" There are countless stories of organizations that significantly improved production output, only to have the result of increased inventory because sales did not achieve a corresponding increase. If the practitioner does not recognize this relationship between parts of the organization (and make the contact person aware of it as well), instead of reinforcement for the improvements, the contact person may be punished by the backlash from the other affected managers and departments.

This step is designed as a precaution against the possibility that an intervention might work in unintended ways to the disadvantage of other employees or management. Here, students must be able to predict certain outcomes of a successful PM intervention. If the goal is to increase suggestive selling or up-selling, and if the program were successful, would the kitchen be able to keep up with the increased demand? If the goal is to improve the interactions with customers could this possibly slow down the service overall? If improved housekeeping in a hotel were the goal, and maid supervisors had to do more frequent checking and provide more immediate feedback would you possibly put some of the housekeepers out of work? That is, with more efficiency, would the hotel need fewer cleaning personnel? Does such a system require more supervisors or supervisors of a different caliber who are able to be systematic enough to give consistent feedback? As behavior analysts we tend to think in terms of only positive outcomes for our interventions but looking at these 'best case' and 'worst case' scenarios might help us be more thoughtful in the design of our programs.

In one system installed recently in a restaurant, greater value was placed on getting wait staff to suggestively sell appetizers and desserts and a more accurate monitoring system was put in place as well. One outcome was that the new system allowed management to unobtrusively detect cheating on the part of employees and one person was fired as a result. In another case, transporters in a hospital were given more precise prompts for their performance as well as graphic and positive supervisor feedback. One possible outcome of faster transports was a greater increase in accidents or in other forms of poor customer service, e.g., being abrupt with patients, bumping into walls, furniture or other people in the halls. To counter this possibility, a customer service quality check system had to be implemented and extra prompts about safe transport being the primary goal was stressed.

Systems checks should be done both upstream and downstream. That is, we need to ask, if this project is successful, will the people upstream (completing tasks that come before the target task in the process stream) be able to cope with improved performance? Will they be able to provide the parts or service now required of an improved performance downstream from them? This, of course, requires us to ask how the performance of our target employees relates to others upstream. In addition, of course, we need to determine if there could be any downside to improved performance for those downstream. If we motivate sales people to sell more cars is the service department equipped to handle more service requests? Do they have the parts on hand? Do they have enough mechanics?

Step 8: Implement the plan. The actual implementation of PM programs is dealt with very sparsely in published studies we have discovered. Whereas the goal of the method section is to provide enough information for replication by competent researchers it is often not sufficient for implementation by students wishing to replicate a specific intervention. Several factors come into play when implementing a PM plan including: preparation, timing, training, monitoring, and troubleshooting.

In the preparation phase students will have to prepare the contact person in their business by presenting the results of their diagnostic analysis and their recommendations for possible interventions. We have learned that they should have at least two plans ready in case management rejects the first. The first plan is based on a 'best case' scenario in which management agrees to cooperate fully and the implementation needs of students can be met. Students are urged not to make great demands on the business but that they can make reasonable requests. They might want to post feedback on employee performance and they will need a commonly viewed place to locate the posters. They may need to have the supervisor view the graphs and give verbal feedback at a meeting each day or once a week. Many of these decisions cannot be made based on the research since certain variables have not been well examined yet, so common-sense extrapolations from basic principles and from whatever data do exist must be made. We don't know the optimal size of posters, colors to be used or ideal locations, based on research, for example, so we recommend fairly large sized posters [e.g., 20in x 30in] in fairly bright attractive colors located near a time clock or in a break room. Students are told to prepare all such materials including data sheets, coupons, file folders marked for each person, and all other materials necessary for the intervention to be implemented.

The timing of an intervention is complicated by the students' schedules, that of their contact person, and perhaps other variables within the company. On more than one occasion we were ready to rollout an intervention only to be superseded by a new company contest or short-term sales incentive system. This issue is also rarely discussed in published studies so again we are making extrapolations. We typically, if at all possible, like to begin interventions early in the week so that the students can do troubleshooting if necessary. In some cases, existing and standard company meeting times dictates the timing. In restaurants it is common to have meetings mid-week, for example. Meetings are critical for the types of interventions we are working with since in the vast majority of cases employees will need to be informed and perhaps receive training as part of the intervention.

Our recommendation is that the meetings and any training be run by the supervisor, both for the purposes of removing the students from association with the intervention (in hopes that it will be taken more seriously by employees) and to establish some 'buy-in' from the supervisor. This, of course, requires that the supervisor or manager be trained in how to conduct the in-service. The timing is critical here as well. If a program is to be kicked off on a Monday afternoon, the supervisor or manager should be trained that morning so that it is fresh in their mind. Training the person several days earlier has proven to be a disaster. The supervisor/ trainer may need some special materials and these need to be prepared with multiple copies made, and pilot tested for readability and simplicity, again by the students as part of their responsibility.

Monitoring the intervention to make sure that it was implemented properly is important to the success of the project. Unless their presence will somehow bias data collection, we stress that students should be present (but not participate) when the training (or intervention introduction) is conducted and that they should certainly be there almost every day thereafter to make sure the intervention is carried out properly. Our experience has been that 'Murphy's Law' absolutely prevails when it comes to these operations. Managers cooperative and ready to assist simply forget to call a meeting or call it and don't show up; materials laid out carefully with multiple copies suddenly disappear at the last minute; feedback sheets carefully prepared and posters neatly arranged are ripped down by someone unaware of their importance. It is difficult to prepare students for all of these eventualities but giving examples and reminding them to go over every detail a second and third time looking for possible problems seems to help.

Troubleshooting is one of the most difficult tasks for students, again since this is such a new enterprise for them. They will need to know what to do if their contact person quits or is fired and how to deal with employees who drop out of a study. Conditions need to be run 'to stability' and they will need some advice on how to handle very unstable data. Other common problems include contact persons who apparently become disinterested in the project or are otherwise distracted by other tasks at hand. If students or other PM trainees find that an intervention is not working for some reason they will need some help in reconfiguring their project to better address the intervention targets. This might involve doing another analysis of the target behavior, coming up with another way to provide feedback or installing a new incentive system.

Step 9: Continue monitoring data. This step can be described fairly simply since it involves the continued collection and display of data. We require students to collect their data at a minimum of twice per week and to bring it to class, newly graphed, with them every day that the class meets. Trainees in business settings will need to collect their data every day and show it to a training consultant once a week. Students and trainees are prone to panicking when an intervention does not have an immediate effect so they must be given support during rough periods. They must also understand that this is a most critical part of the study and that they cannot simply relax and let things slide. If at all possible we will want students to carry out a multiple baseline or perhaps reversal design to demonstrate experimental control and continuing to review the data to know when to make intervention changes is a must.

Step 10: Evaluate the impact. Evaluation of a study is important in that the student or trainee finally may come into contact with a more substantial reinforcer than simply looking at data points on a graph. Whole books can be written on evaluation but for our purposes we will lay out a few areas that seem important for students and trainees in Performance Management.

Behavior change as observed in daily or weekly data is the most obvious measurement dimension to consider. For social validity purposes we may also look at the size of the effect, whether it is found to be believable by employees and management, and whether it has some other implications that can be measured in more substantial terms. Although we discuss, with students, methods for measuring the financial impact of interventions, such as PVC analysis (Gilbert, 1978), we will only generally consider some successful outcomes of interventions here.

In a recent project involving getting patients and employees in a state hospital in for flu shots during the fall-winter flu season it was shown that with some extra prompting, changing of schedules, and a small incentive it was possible to get nearly 100% of patients inoculated and almost 50% of staff to get their shots. This was double the numbers for the previous three years of baseline. An accounting at the end, of savings to the hospital in terms of days of work lost, tests that did not have to be run and other medical interventions that did not have to be implemented, showed that the intervention saved over $100,000 in one year.

A student-run project on suggestive selling in one restaurant of a national chain showed that were the project to be run for one year, an increase in sales of over $7,000 could be expected; were the procedure to be adopted and successfully run by the entire chain of over nearly 1,000 restaurants the gross would exceed $6 million per year! A recent project in a shipping company was considered so successful that it was adopted by management and implemented in two additional locations. These and other forms of outcomes buttress the behavioral data which most of us find so interesting.

Concluding Remarks

The analysis or deconstruction of the process of Performance Management prepares the way for the development of more effective training materials and the design of better hands-on experiences for students. It also suggests areas where additional research and reporting needs to be done. For example, reporting assessment techniques in the research literature would greatly assist us in teaching it to students. Examples of systems analysis are very sparse in the behavioral literature; these too would greatly assist our training efforts.

We see training students to conduct PM projects as a cumulative effort, much like that of teaching other subject matter. That is, as we help lead new groups of students through the PM process each year, there are many lessons learned and we try to incorporate these into the curriculum as they come about. We try to communicate these to others through writing, and through presenting and sharing our experiences at conferences. It is important that this effort continue to grow – perhaps through the development of similar program replications across the country or perhaps through the development of new and improved PM training programs – so that we can continue to disseminate behavior analysis through the organizations in our nation.

References

Abernathy, W. B. (1996). *The sin of wages: Where the conventional pay system has led us and how to find a way out.* Memphis, TN: PerfSys Press.

Ackley, G. B. E., & Bailey, J. S. (1995). Teaching performance management using behavior analysis. *The Behavior Analyst, 18*(1), 73-81.

Austin, J. (2000). Performance analysis and performance diagnostics. In J. Austin & J. E. Carr (Eds.), *Handbook of applied behavior analysis,* (pp. 321-349). Reno, NV: Context Press.

Austin, J., Carr, J. E., & Agnew, J. L. (1999). The need for assessment of maintaining variables in OBM. *Journal of Organizational Behavior Management, 19*(2), 59-87.

Bailey, J. S., Riordan, M., Coleman, R. S., Hutchison, J. M., & Oswald, A., (1998, May). *Against all odds: Systematic performance management in state mental health.* Panel discussion at the Association for Behavior Analysis, International, Orlando, FL.

Brethower, D. M., & Smalley, K. (1998). *Performance-based instruction: Linking training to business results.* San Francisco: Jossey-Bass/Pfeiffer.

Brown, C. S., & Sulzer-Azaroff, B. (1994). An assessment of the relationship between customer satisfaction and service friendliness. *Journal of Organizational Behavior Management, 14*(2), 55-75.

Carr, J. E., & Burkholder, E. O. (1998). Creating single-subject design graphs with Microsoft Excel. *Journal of Applied Behavior Analysis, 31*(2), 245-251.

Daniels, A. C. (1989). *Performance management.* Tucker, GA: Performance Management Publications.

Eikenhout, N., & Austin, J. (2000). *Using goals, feedback, reinforcement, and the performance matrix to improve customer service in a large department store.* Unpublished manuscript.

Gilbert, T. F. (1978). *Human competence.* Amherst, MA: HRD Press.

Gilbert, T. F. (1982). A question of performance: The PROBE model. *Training & Development Journal, 36*(9), 20-30.

Kaplan, R. S., & Norton, D. P. (1996, Nov-Dec). Knowing the score. *Financial Executive, 12*(6), 30(4).

Luthans, F. (1982). Improving performance: A behavioral problem-solving approach. In L. W. Frederiksen (Ed.), Handbook of organizational behavior management, (pp. 249-279). New York: Wiley and Sons.

Mager, R. F., & Pipe, P. (1970). *Analyzing performance problems.* Belmont, CA: Fearon Publishers.

Mace, F. C. (1994). The significance and future of functional analysis methodologies. *Journal of Applied Behavior Analysis, 27,* 385-392.

New tool: "Reinforcement" for good work. (1971, December 18) *Business Week.*

Parsonson, B., & Baer, D. (1978). The analysis and presentation of graphic data. In T. R. Kratochwill (Ed.), *Single subject research: Strategies for evaluating change,* (pp. 101-165). New York: Academic Press.

Presbie, R. J., & Brown, P. L. (1985). *Behavior modification.* Washington, DC: National Education Association.

Rummler, G. A., & Brache, A. P. (1995). *Improving performance: How to manage the white space on the organizational chart* (2nd ed.). San Francisco, CA: Jossey-Bass.

Skinner, B. F. (1938). *The behavior of organisms.* Appleton-Century-Crofts.

Skinner, B. F. (1953). *Science and human behavior.* New York: Macmillan Company.

Author Notes

Dr. Jon Bailey can be reached at Florida State University, Department of Psychology, Tallahassee, FL 32306 or by e-mail at *bailey@psy.fsu.edu.*

Dr. John Austin can be reached at Western Michigan University, Department of Psychology, Kalamazoo, MI 49008 or by e-mail at *john.austin@wmich.edu.*

Discussion of Bailey and Austin

Opportunities and the Need for Deconstruction

Jacqueline E. Collins
University of Nevada

In "Deconstructing Performance Management Processes", Bailey and Austin provide a brief history of the background of Performance Management (PM) as being grounded in operant conditioning. This is followed by a break down of the skills required to conduct PM into 10 basic steps for purposes of training PM at the undergraduate level. This training process leads to a number of issues for discussion.

One issue for discussion is the value such a training procedure contributes to basic behavior analytic skills at the organizational level. There are many opportunities to obtain practical behavior analytic training at the level of the individual for undergraduates and graduates. This is not necessarily the case at the organizational level. Bailey and Austin argue that most organizational training occurs for consultants or researchers through journal or book publications. Providing this breaks down of PM skills at the undergraduate level might not only provide experience and opportunity for undergraduates, but may lead to further practical, organizational courses available at the graduate and professional levels.

Another area for discussion is the contribution the procedure can give to training research. It might be helpful to conduct follow up research regarding the activities of students after they have taken a desconstructing course. This could provide the field with information about the types of graduate programs or jobs attained by such students. Other research could look into the competitiveness of these students as consultants, researchers, or graduate students.

The specification of the skills needed in these 10 steps provides a methodology for training procedures that might be compared to the current journal and book format of training currently available. The authors state that it is "abundantly clear" that, over the course of a 10 year history, the training seems incomplete when certain steps are left out. On the surface it seems apparent that all steps are mandatory for the appropriate skills to be trained. However, by systematically breaking up the steps to see which ones might need more time to train accurately could lead to more efficient training procedures. Further, by testing the various types of antecedents (e.g. rules) and consequences (e.g. feedback) provided to students, the most effective training techniques of this procedure could be determined. Further research questions might compare this training to other areas of organizational research such as I/O or MBA programs.

Research questions could also be developed in undergraduate and graduate training. The field of behavior analysis has a unique opportunity through courses, practica, and administrative positions to conduct training research given the practical nature of the field. By promoting research and data collection in these types of activities, it would serve to promote this practical nature. Data collection should be a central part of all training not only to contribute to research, but to ensure the quality of the training that is taking place in the field.

A third area for discussion regards the prerequisites that may be necessary to take such a course to attain optimal levels of skill attainment. For example, some level of behavior analytic background should be required due to the techniques expected through these 10 steps of PM. Given the basis of PM in operant conditioning, a basic knowledge of the tenets surrounding operant conditioning would serve to make the training more efficient. The fact that behavior is measured in this process further emphasizes some prerequisites in behavior analysis. Students should also have some level of skill in the data collection processes utilized by behavior analysts. These include graphing skills that are necessary to represent the data collected. Bailey and Austin point out that graphing becomes a behavior analytic skill in PM because the graphs are done according to guidelines put forth by the *Journal of Applied Behavior Analysis*. If some level of prior behavior analytic knowledge is not a requirement, those teaching the course should include some training on behavior analytic techniques. This would help students better understand the implementation of the operant aspects of PM.

There are several areas where further data presentation would be necessary to emphasize the effectiveness of desconstructing PM. Much of this could be handled through research opportunities mentioned above such as looking at prerequisites with which students come to the course, and the acquisition of PM skills. It might also be interesting to see some data- based examples of various PM projects that have been conducted through this course. Such information might give some indication of the types of situations appropriate for this type of training. For example, it may be the case that certain organizational problems do not lend themselves to the most effective training either because they are too complex or simple for training purposes. Training at the undergraduate level might utilize more simple PM problems, but knowing where to draw the line in simplicity or complexity could be helpful to other schools trying to replicate the training.

In summary, deconstructing PM processes seems to be a unique and necessary training procedure. The practical areas of organizational behavior management could be greatly influenced by such a procedure. There are also a variety of basic research opportunities provided through this process. Pursuing such research areas could be instrumental to the growth of the field of PM and organizational behavior management.

Managing a Person as a System

Dale M. Brethower
Western Michigan University

Introduction

A person, a shoe store, a major corporation, or a university is a system. Each must be managed as a system if it is to be managed well. If I want to manage myself well, I must manage myself as a system because I am a system (see Ford, 1987). But what is a system? What is a "store" or "self" or "corporation" or "university?" The latter question is rhetorical but the answer is important. Neither a self nor a corporation is an entity. Try pointing at a university or a self and you will always miss the mark. Stafford Beer (Beer, 1961) made a similar point many years ago in a brilliant paper entitled "Below the twilight arch: A mythology of systems." A system such as a corporation is, by definition, a set of elements and relationships. The elements may be few in number but the relationships are too complex to understand or define precisely, Beer argued. Consequently, all that we have to work with are our conceptions, our myths about the system. Worse, any conception we have will be wrong, a misconception, according to Beer.

Why will any conception be a misconception? Because we are not omniscient. Everything, all the parts and all the relationships that comprise a university or self are much too complex to capture by pointing a finger or even by writing a book in several volumes. How then are we to manage a self or a university or a corporation? Behaviorists have an answer: We can't manage entities but we can manage behavior; we manage large organizations by managing specific behaviors of specific individuals. Cognitivists have a different answer: We can't manage entities but we can create mental models (Beer's myths) and manage in accord with our mental models. Both answers have something to recommend them but neither is adequate by itself. The weakness in the behavioral answer is that it doesn't answer a very important question: Which of the millions of behaviors are worth managing? The weakness of the cognitive answer is quite similar. It doesn't answer the question: Which of the millions of possible mental models is the one to use?

Behavioral systems analysis provides answers to both questions. Which behaviors? Those that contribute to worthy performance. Which models? Those that view the performer as a system. Behavioral systems analysis takes both answers and blends them together in useful and powerful ways.

Flawed Management Myths

The behavioral systems view, myth or not, is that we don't manage a "self" or an "organization"; we manage performance. We can manage almost any performance we pinpoint. But how does the top management group manage all the performances of an organization? How do managers manage all the performances of all the people in an organization? One performance at a time? No. Not only would that be too costly, it is also a logical impossibility, as the following logical exercise illustrates.

A Dangerous Myth: The Organization Chart

Imagine the traditional (and fatally flawed) myth of an organizational hierarchy. At the lowest level of the hierarchy is a worker. Who manages the worker? A supervisor? Perhaps, but who manages the supervisor? A low level manager, e.g., a department manager? Perhaps, but who manages a department manager? A middle level manager, e.g., a function manager? Perhaps, but who manages the middle level manager? A senior manager? Perhaps, but who manages the senior manager? The top manager or top management team? Perhaps, but who manages the top managers? A Board of Directors? Perhaps, but who manages the Board? Perhaps the customers manage the Board? Who manages the customers? The marketing department? They'd like to perhaps, but they aren't up to the task. Maybe the stockholders or stakeholders or government or somebody manages the Board or the Chief Operating Officer. But who manages the stakeholders or government? The question of "who" leads to an infinite regression: It doesn't end but keeps on going and going all the way to absurdity.

Where does that leave us? Perhaps we should just say "Ah, well, enough philosophizing. Let's get down to the practical stuff!" On the other hand, the philosophizing is enormously practical because it shows that there is no solution to the management problem of who manages whom. The management hierarchy, so treasured in organization charts and in colleges of management and in practice throughout the western world is a myth that misleads.

Rummler (see Rummler & Brache, 1988, 1995) has pointed out that the organization chart tells us about reporting relationships, not how the work gets done. In fact, the hierarchical organization chart is an impediment to getting the work done. Why? Because, among other things, people higher on the chart are tasked with managing people lower on the chart, with appraising their performance. In addition, wage and salary administration, the keepers of the financial reward structure, place financial rewards according to hierarchical placement, not according to the value and cost of work performed. Thus, the hierarchical organization chart impedes work and misaligns rewards. It is no surprise to the people in an organization that the organizational structure impedes work; that's one reason organizations reorganize so frequently. It is no surprise to the people in an organization that rewards are misaligned. But it might be a surprise to learn that the cause of the misalignment is not organizational politics—though surely politics is a factor—but a misalignment between organizational structure and organizational functioning. Organizational structures shown in organizational charts are about reporting relationships, not about how the work gets done.

The "who manages" question is a dead-end question. It has no meaningful and useful answer. A related question "Who do you report to?" has a meaningful but dangerous answer. Most people in an organization can answer by naming a specific person. Organization charts are drawn up to answer it. When organizations reorganize, one thing that is sure to change is the organization chart. "Who do you report to?" is answerable but a question that leads organizations astray. "Who do you report to?" supports the notion that an organization is "really" a social system that operates on the basis of political power or position power or command structure or something of the sort. Organizations, in fact, operate that way, because of the organization chart. Organizations also operate as systems and get things accomplished in spite of the organization chart.

A Flawed Myth: The Social System

Viewed as a social system, an organization is about the hierarchy described in the organization chart and the goal is to achieve vertical harmony, pleasing those higher on the pyramid and controlling those lower on the pyramid. Advancing means moving up the pyramid and getting a salary increase. The name of the organizational success game is climbing the pyramid. The organizational success game is largely driven by internal variables we might call "organizational politics." Once a manager successfully climbs the pyramid, however, the game changes and success is achieved and measured by external variables related to providing products or services in the marketplace.

The pyramid model is inherently limited, partly by organizational politics and partly because it is a centralized processing model in which major decisions are made near the top and people lower on the pyramid are not empowered to make consequential decisions. Such models assure that most people are only dimly aware of the big picture and the few that know the big picture are only dimly aware of the details of doing the work. Consequently, most decisions are made in the absence of important information. Centralized processing models are probably inherently less powerful than distributed processing models in which consequential decisions about the work are made close to the work. If persons are viewed as self-managing systems and managed as systems, it would be possible for an organization to function as a distributed processing model and, hence, to be managed as a system. An organization is a social system, to be sure, populated and operated by humans. But an organization is also a technical system, a system set up to perform work.

Better Management Myths

From the perspective of a technical system, "What do you report?' is a much better question than "To whom do you report?" There is a useful and informative answer. Furthermore, the same answer works for everyone. "What do you report?" Oversimplifying only slightly, the answer is "I report three things: Results, accomplishments, and progress."

Results, accomplishments, and progress: Each is important. Progress is important on a day to day and minute by minute basis. It is important to know whether we are progressing toward goals or progressing in directions unplanned. If a customer calls about an order, the customer wants the order fulfilled but second best is knowing progress toward order fulfillment. If a creditor calls about an unpaid bill, the creditor wants payment-in-full but second best is knowing progress toward payment. If an OSHA representative calls about safety violations, rest assured that OSHA wants progress reports toward improved safety. If a company calls a supplier about a quality problem, the company wants good quality products and a progress report on how quality problems are being prevented. "What do you report?" "Results (which are summaries of the cost and quality of accomplishments), accomplishments (which are stepping stones toward results), and progress (toward results and accomplishments)!"

The answer, "Results, accomplishments and progress!" makes sense. People are hired to accomplish something, today and every day. Each person, we hope, has accomplished some things recently and is making progress toward other accomplishments. If not, perhaps that person is the boss's nephew and the only accomplishment desired is keeping nephew out of the house and off the streets. Such exceptions are vexing to others in the organization and serve as non-examples that support the rule: People are at work to accomplish something. Reporting results, accomplishments, and progress is quite the sensible thing.

On the other hand, the three questions "What (results) do you report?" "What have you accomplished?" "What progress are you making?" are questions that people can't answer very well if they aren't managing as a system. For example, professors can answer the "What results do you report?" question with a little thought: "Grades, publications, and travel expenses." "What do you accomplish?" is a much more difficult question for a professor. Production workers can usually report time worked; commission sales people can report sales completed; managers can report being busy; the person-in-charge can report summary financial measures. But good things can happen when people have better measures of accomplishment and progress.

Who should have good measures of results, accomplishments, and progress? Arguably, everyone in an organization. A personal example will illustrate what that means. Several years ago I performed as the head of a university reading clinic. When I took on that role it seemed to me to be a very complex and demanding one. I asked my predecessor and mentor what I was responsible for. He replied, "Everything! If anything goes wrong, that's your responsibility. You should have prevented it; you must correct it as best you can; you should also make sure it doesn't happen again!" I agreed with the philosophy but as the person-in-charge-of-everything, I needed something more operational. My job was to manage the clinic and everything and everyone in it including myself. I thought, correctly, that it was an overwhelming task, not possible to perform.

I have talked to senior managers and business owners who agree with the philosophy of accepting responsibility and seek operational procedures for implementing it. There are hundreds of books offering advice and telling stories about how to do it but the books offer too much help. One bit of advice conflicts with other bits of advice, pulling the manager in multiple directions at once. The collection of books do not offer a coherent approach that is grounded in both theory and practice and supported by research.

This chapter provides such an approach, but with the academician's usual caveat: "More research is needed." However, the research cannot move forward expeditiously, I believe, unless there is a framework for it, an approach that is consistent with theory, research, and validated practice to date. The approach, I believe, is to set up organizations to enable people to function as self-managing systems and, thereby, enable organizations to be managed as systems.

Managing as a System

There are three elements to the approach, each of which I believe is essential. The first is the definition of performance. The second is a definition of the elements of a self-managing system. The third is a procedure for combining the elements and definition into a practical and readily implemented approach.

The Definition of Performance

The definition of performance is arbitrary but quite important. One well-known definition was articulated in Gilbert (1996): Behavior plus accomplishment. Behavior that doesn't accomplish anything is the enemy of performance. Behavior that doesn't accomplish anything is, however, very common. Perhaps one third to one half of all the behavior people engage in in organizations is behavior that doesn't accomplish anything other than, perhaps, filling in the time or yielding immediate reinforcers. What is the actual time on task in a classroom? Some studies show that it is very low, typically below 20%. What is the actual time on task in the workplace? Perhaps a bit higher than in classrooms but some studies show that it is typically below 50%. Behavior that accomplishes something but slowly is another enemy of performance. Behavior that accomplishes things, most of which are low in quality, is another enemy of performance. If performance is "good" the behavior is effective and efficient and the accomplishment is valuable.

The Elements of a Self-managing System

There are 7 elements of a self-managing system as I define the term: 1) A goal or purpose or mission or raison d'etre, 2) inputs, 3) a processing system, 4) processing system feedback, 5) outputs, 6) a receiving system, and 7) receiving system feedback. An example of a reading clinic (shown in Figure 1) will illustrate.

1) The mission of the reading clinic was to improve the reading performance of students. 2) The inputs were resources to run the clinic and the clients to be served by the clinic. 3) All the things we did to run the clinic and serve the clients comprised the processing system. 4) Processing system feedback included measures of service quality and economic efficiency. 5) Outputs were persons with improved reading performance. 6) The environments supplying resources and receiving the students comprised the receiving system. 7) Receiving system feedback included measures of how students fared after being served, referrals, and comments on our budgets and annual reports.

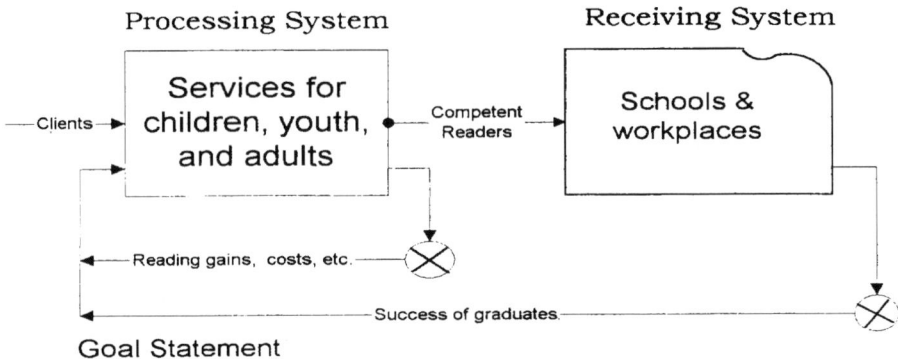

Goal Statement

The Reading Improvement Service enables readers to satisfy
standards for reading achievement and to attain academic or
workplace goals

Figure 1. Reading Improvement Service.

These seven elements comprise an adaptive system; remove or muddy one of
the elements and the system will function less well. For example, if the members of
a top management team worry more about climbing the next steps up the pyramid
than they do about serving customers, the organization will suffer. If there is a major
change in the inputs, clients or resources, the organization will be impacted. If there
are major changes in processes, e.g., because a key person leaves or because a new
technology is used, the organization will be impacted. If workers worry more about
office politics than work performance, the organization will be impacted.

Combining the Elements to Support Performance

Knowing the parts of an adaptive system, shown in Figure 1, allows us to answer
a very important question: "What support does a person require in order to perform
competently?" The answer is that a person requires 7 categories of support. The 7
categories correspond to the 7 elements of an adaptive system or what I have come
to call a total performance system. Examples showing what is necessary to support
the performance of two different knowledge workers will illustrate. Table 1 shows a
manager as a system, a knowledge worker; Table 2 shows a student as system, also
a knowledge worker (see Heiman & Slomianko, 1998). The wording of the examples
is deliberately parallel to show that in spite of different contexts, the performance
support is very similar.

Please note, also, that the adaptive system model, applied here at the task level,
is also applicable at the function level, as shown in Figure 1. Table 3, below, shows
a person as an adaptive system, demonstrating that the adaptive system can be used
at the task, person, and function level. It can also be used at the organization level
(see Brethower, 1970, 1982, 1995).

Performance Support	Performer
Goals—Knowledge of what results are to be achieved. Knowledge of why achieving the results is beneficial to the performer and to the organization.	If a manager knows that the goal of reading a consultant's report is to acquire answers to questions she and other managers have about the consultant's recommendations and knows why answering those question is important to her and to others, she is more likely to read it well than if she is clueless about such goals.
Outputs—Knowledge of what specific products are to be produced. Knowledge of the time, quality, and cost standards for the products.	If a manager knows that, after reading a report she should be able to answer specific questions, she will know what "reading the report" means and be much more likely to extract the correct information as she reads.
Processes—Specific ways of producing the outputs.	If a manager knows that answers to questions can be extracted one at a time and, at the same time, integrated & organized, she has a way to acquire the information that works much more effectively than if she tries to read the whole report and then think about answering the questions.
Inputs—Time, tools, materials, etc. Too little time, poor tools, or poor materials increases effort and decreases quality.	If a manager allocates the wrong amount of time, doesn't have a notebook or a calculator or whatever other tools are needed to do the task or has a poorly written report with too few examples and illustrations, her performance will suffer .
Process Feedback— Feedback from the work process that indicates whether or not the work is going smoothly.	If a manager can detect when she has lapsed into passive reading she can take corrective action. Similarly, if she can discriminate lapses due to faulty technique from lapses due to inadequacies in the report, she will do a better job of taking corrective action, perhaps by getting supplementary information by asking questions of the consultant or her peers or another consultant .
Receiving System— Knowledge of requirements and standards of people who receive the work output. Coaching or guidance from others.	If a manager knows the business standards required for excellent performance (or satisfactory or marginal performance), she has a better chance of setting her personal standards and adjusting her work habits so that she meets the requirements and standards. Similarly, access to coaching from mentors can be helpful.
Receiving System Feedback—Information about quality of the products, according to customer standards.	Managers who receive frequent external feedback on their performance are more able to perform well than managers who do not. This is true for managers who receive feedback in the form of frequent meetings with a mentor and for managers who seek and obtain feedback in other ways.

Table 1. A Manager as a System: A Knowledge Worker.

Performance Support	Performer
Goals—Knowledge of what results are to be achieved. Knowledge of why achieving the results is beneficial to the performer and to the organization.	If a college student knows that the goal of reading a chapter in a textbook is to acquire answers to personal or instructor questions and knows why answering questions and earning high marks is important to the student and others, he is more likely to read well than if he is clueless about such goals.
Outputs—Knowledge of what specific products are to be produced. Knowledge of the time, quality, and cost standards for the products.	If a student knows that, after reading a chapter he should be able to answer specific questions, he will know what "reading the assignment means" and be much more likely to extract the correct information as he reads.
Processes—Specific ways of producing the outputs.	If a student knows that answers to questions can be extracted one at a time and, at the same time, integrated & organized, he has a way to acquire the information that works much more effectively than if he tries to read the whole chapter and then think about answering the questions.
Inputs—Time, tools, materials, etc. Too little time, poor tools, or poor materials increases effort and decreases quality.	If a student allocates the wrong amount of time, doesn't have a notebook or a calculator or whatever other tools are needed to do the task, or has a textbook with too few good examples and illustrations, his performance will suffer.
Process Feedback—Feedback from the work process that indicates whether or not the work is going smoothly.	If a student can detect when he has lapsed into passive reading he can take corrective action. Similarly, if he can discriminate lapses due to faulty technique from lapses due to inadequacies in the text, he will do a better job of taking corrective action, perhaps getting supplementary information by asking questions of the instructor or other students or another text.
Receiving System—Knowledge of requirements and standards of people who receive the work output. Coaching or guidance from others.	If a student knows the academic standards required for excellent performance (or B or C performance), he has a better chance of setting his personal standards and adjusting his work habits so that he meets the requirements and standards. Similarly, access to coaching from instructors can be helpful.
Receiving System Feedback—Information about quality of the products, according to customer standards.	Students receiving frequent external feedback on their performance perform better than students who do not. This is true for students who receive the feedback in the form of frequent quizzes and for students who seek and obtain feedback in other ways.

Table 2. A Student as a System: A Knowledge Worker.

Regardless of the nature of the work, excellent performance is more difficult if there are deficiencies in any one of the seven areas. If there are deficiencies a number of categories, excellent performance becomes impossible. People who are highly motivated, well-educated, and well-trained can compensate for performance support deficiencies to some extent. For example, learners with poor instruction and managers with poor management can still succeed but only by expending extra energy. Over time, the energy demands can lead to poor performance, poor health, and other bad results.

The Managing-a-Person-as-System Myth

Let us be clear about one point. The only person a manager can manage as a system is the manager. But a manager, following the guidelines below, can manage information in a way that enables others to manage their own performance. The procedure, though difficult to achieve, is easy to describe. It begins by describing the system, in terms of the 7 elements of a performance system. Defining the system is not an easy task. To illustrate how to do it, I will use the job of the Chief of the Reading Improvement Service at the University of Michigan as it was when I had that job. Figure 1 above shows the context for that job, the system known as the Reading Improvement Service. Table 3 shows the 7 elements of the Reading Service as a System and of the Chief as a System.

System Component	The Reading Service as a System	The Chief of the Reading Service as a System
Goal	Provide services to clients that enable them to perform competently as readers.	Assure that Service goals are met.
Inputs	Staff, money, knowledge, supplies, clients, unsolved problems	Same as for Service
Processes	Reading instruction, research, staff management, administration, etc.	Same as for Service; Staff meetings; Coaching
Outputs	Clients with improved reading performance; staff with improved professional competence; publications	Progress reports, plans, budgets, strategic and operational goals, feedback systems, etc.
Internal Feedback	Reading gains, indicators of staff competence, etc.	Same as for Service, i.e., the data shown in the reports
Receiving System	Students and instructors in university classes; university administrators, etc.	Same as for Service; staff members, clients Chief serves, etc.
External Feedback	Continued success of students; requests for publications, etc.	Same as for Service; current and continued success of staff, clients.

Table 3. Two Systems: The Reading Service and the Chief.

Connecting Person to Organization

Table 3 documents the close relationship between the overall agency and the Chief of the agency. That is as it should be: Every performer within a system should be closely connected to the system. It should be possible to connect each performance of each person to the performance of the system as a whole. There are fewer connections between the part-time receptionist's performance and the Service than there are between the Chief's performance and the Service but that doesn't change the fact that it is the connection between the person's performance and the organization's performance that creates the value of the person's performance.

One analysis problem for many staff members would be to find the connections. The analysis problem for the Chief is to find differentiations, the key points of difference between organizational performance (for which the Chief is held responsible) and the Chief's performance, which is the only performance the Chief can actually manage. That, by the way, is reason the Chief's job is difficult, the Chief is accountable for a very large number of things the Chief can't control. That is the systems reason why a CEO might get ulcers or become a control freak.

Nevertheless, one advantage of the Chief's job is that the Chief has a clearer view of the organization than do many of the people who work within the organization. That vantage point explains why one of the tasks of leadership is to clarify and communicate a total vision for the organization (see Tosti & Jackson, 1999). The total vision is one point of connection between everyone in the organization and the organization. (Incidentally, one of the challenges for organizational design and strategy implementation is to assure that everyone in the organization can connect her or his performance to the work of the organization.)

One of the responsibilities of the Chief of the Reading Service should be to manage it as a system. I didn't know that when I was Chief, which is just as well because I didn't know how to do it. How can a leader be responsible for everything, be responsible for managing an organization as a system, when the leader can accomplishes only a small part of the work personally? In other words, while the systems model for the organization and for the leader are quite similar, how can they be differentiated so that the leader knows what the leader must accomplish to manage the organization as a system, i.e., assure that system goals are achieved?

Table 3 provides the beginnings of an answer. Notice that the major point of differentiation is in the Output row. The System Outputs all go to the Receiving System; they are truly outputs. However, many of the leader's outputs stay within the system. Publications generated personally by the leader are Outputs of the leader and the system. Internal reports and feedback systems are outputs of the leader but remain in the system. The value of such internal outputs, by the leader and by other personnel, is the support they provide to the primary or system outputs.

Notice that part of the Receiving System for the leader is outside, just as it is for the system as a whole but part of the Receiving System for the leader is inside, i.e., the "insiders" receive outputs of the leader. That is true of all Reading Service staff; some outputs are received by insiders and others are received by outsiders. (In large organizations many people generate outputs that are not received by outsiders, which creates special organizational design and management problems since these people do not have a "window" to the outside and must get Receiving System Feedback second hand.)

Monitoring Accomplishment

One of the major accomplishments of the leader is an Annual Report, a report that describes how well the system as a whole is functioning. The President of the United States does an annual State of the Union address; leaders of public corporations publish annual reports; the Chief of the Reading Clinic generated an annual report. (The Annual Report, is not, however, a major accomplishment of the organization —a point of differentiation between the leader and the organization. It is necessary but it is not a revenue generating output.)

An annual report, like other outputs, has quality requirements and standards. The financial data in annual reports is constrained by accounting standards but much of the other content can be relatively unconstrained self-promotion. Indeed, annual reports are often political or marketing pieces rather than balanced accounts of accomplishments. That was true in the case of the Annual Report for the Reading Service. It served as a tool for recognizing staff accomplishments but it was intended both as budget justification and as a marketing/political document designed to show the service in a favorable light when compared to competitors, both inside the university (e.g., the Psychological Clinic that "competed" for budget dollars) and outside (e.g., commercial reading courses). A leader that does not manage a system so that it can be described by a strong annual report is failing as a leader, whether or not the weakness in the annual report is due to external factors or internal mismanagement.

According to the model presented in Table 3, the Reading Service leader also has other key outputs: budgets, strategic goals, and feedback systems. This is, I believe, often an area of deficiency in the thinking of leaders. For example, some owners of small businesses are so busy "making it happen" themselves that they do not provide the infrastructure (goals, strategies, budgets, processes, and feedback systems) that are necessary to guide the efforts of others to "make it happen." Chief Operating Officers of larger organizations also know that they have a short window of time in which to "make it happen" and push for short term results rather than working strategically. They are much better, for example, at using budgets as planning and control devices for achieving quarterly objectives than they are at using budgets as the basis for feedback systems to support strategic objectives.

Suppose that, as Chief Operating Officer, I were to take seriously the notion that one of my most important responsibilities is to establish feedback systems. One of my first priorities is to establish feedback systems for the organization as a whole. But I also must assure that feedback systems are in place for each part of the Service and for each performer. And I must assure that all the feedback systems interlock, i.e., that they guide the several performances in the same direction.

Processing System   Receiving System

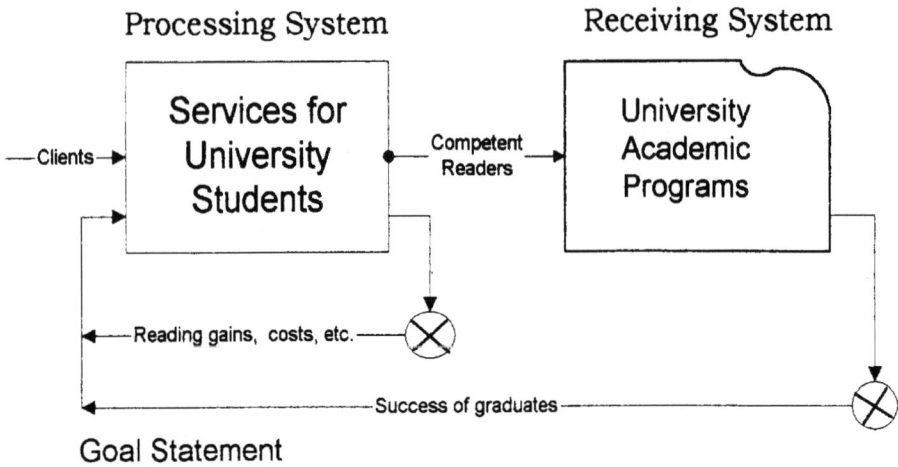

Goal Statement

The College Service enables college students to read & learn
effectively, thereby achieving more academically.

Figure 2. College Division.

The two feedback loops in Figure 1 show the major measures and indicators for
the system as a whole. Figure 2 shows one division of the Reading Service, the
division that provided services to college students. Notice that the feedback loops
for the division are essentially similar to the feedback loops for the Service as a whole.
The only difference is that the feedback loops for the division focus only on serving
one of the several client populations served by the Reading Service. Figure 3 shows
an instructor as a system. Notice that the feedback loops are somewhat different than
the feedback loops for the division. Notice also the differences in the Processing and
Receiving Systems.

All the systems look alike, in terms of the way they are depicted in Figures 1, 2,
and 3. That is because the Total Performance System diagram upon which they are
based is a way of depicting an adaptive system. An adaptive system is one that
performs intelligently over time. It can perform intelligently in the short run by
making adjustments based upon the internal feedback loop that monitors current
performance (Plan vs. Actual for the Instructor; Reading Gains for the Service). The
internal feedback loop symbolizes guidance, that is, adjusting performance as
required to achieve current objectives. But to perform intelligently over time, a
system must adapt, that is, change goals and objectives. Simply changing ways of
attaining goals and objectives, though necessary in the short run, is not enough in
the long run. The external feedback loop symbolizes feedback from the world at large
that allows the system to adapt to changing conditions by modifying goals and
strategies (Successes of learners; Successes of graduates). "Working smart" to attain

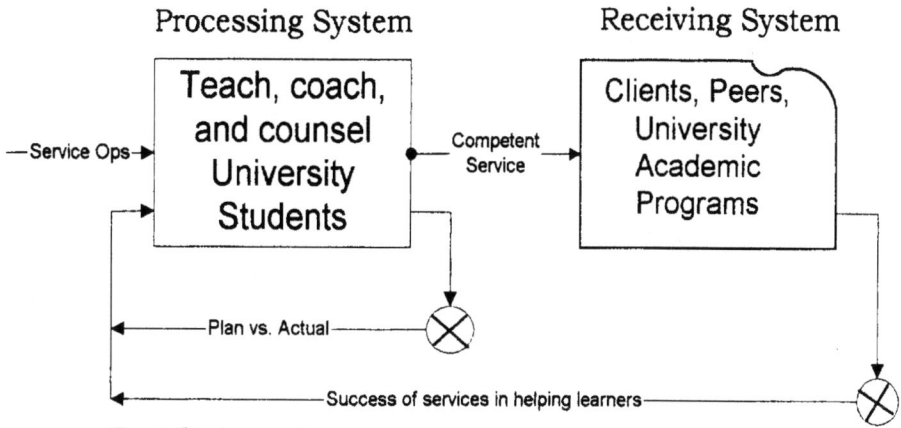

Goal Statement
The Instructor provides effective services that enable college
students to read & learn effectively, thereby achieving more
academically.

Figure 3. Instructor in the College Division.

current goals and "working smart" to adapt to changes in the external environment are both required for intelligent performance.

My thinking, as Chief, was that each staff member had to perform well and intelligently now and in the future. But each of us could be performing well from a subsystem perspective and we could be working at cross-purposes (as often happens in traditional organizational hierarchies). The goals shown in each diagram must align with the goals shown in all the diagrams and the goals must be adjusted as conditions change. The feedback loops make those adjustments possible. Thus, one reason the diagrams look alike is that they are all based upon an adaptive systems model. Another reason that I make the diagrams look alike is that the parts have to communicate well with one another if the whole is to function well. If the model describing each subsystem were different, it would be extremely difficult to even talk about our work. Langdon (1995) makes this point in his book, *The New Language of Work*. According to Langdon's observations, one reason people have so much trouble communicating with one another in organizations is that they have no common language. Different terminology is used in finance than in design than in human resources than in manufacturing than in marketing. That is as it should be in one sense; each area has specific and unique work to do and the language of each area should be tailored to that area. On the other hand, for the work of any area to be optimally valuable, it must coordinate with the work of the other areas. There is no common language for doing that. Langdon proposes a language of work to aid communication about work and also to aid in sharing "best management practices" between areas and coordinating work among areas.

In general, if each performer is to manage as a system, the performance supports must be there, i.e., the elements of a performance system must be in place. The goals and measures must be developed and continuously monitored. But for the goals and measures to be meaningful, each performer must have a performance logic, a way to connect daily performance to current goals and to strategic goals. Thus, it is not enough to know what the goals are and whether or not a performer is achieving the goals, the performer must also know how to "keep up the good work" when that is called for and "shape up" when that is called for. Continuous improvement requires both.

A Performance Logic

A performance logic consists of knowing what is to be accomplished, how it is to be accomplished, and how to maintain or modify performance as needed. A performance logic includes knowing the measures for monitoring and reporting accomplishment. A performance logic for the Chief is shown in Table 4.

The table shows a performance logic for three aspects of the Chief's role, labeled Things, People, and Data. For each aspect, major accomplishments or outputs are

Performance Logic

Outputs	Goals	Performance Strategies	Resource Management	Performance Measures
Things				
Classes taught (student achievement facilitated)	Double reading scores Completion by 80% + of students All students apply to academic work; GPA productivity increases for all	Model each process & product Coach each student individually each class: Praise progress, suggest improvements	Standardized tests for Pre- and Post-testing; Practice tests for each class Real texts Minimal special tools	Basic objectives achieved each class Measures taken for all goals Follow-up records of grades
People				
Staff developed External Relationships developed	All staff gaining Deans, etc. support budget Referrals continue	Assign duties @ .5 appt.; Group problem solving mode Keep in touch	No "people development" or "marketing" budget	Progress relevant to development goals for staff Budget changes, referral flow
Data				
Annual Report Research Reports Evaluation Reports	Retain budget & support of Chief, Bur Psych Services 2 publications or professional presentations per staff per yr. Reports show economic value greater than cost from University & stakeholder perspectives	Establish Feedback systems for staff and clients, incorporating feedback into service processes Model self-management & request regular progress reports from each staff member.	Minimal clerical support and minimal budget. Use establishing the feedback systems to enable thesis & dissertation research by staff	Data on all clients and classes, broken out for all stakeholder groups. Count how many staff are self-managing how many aspects of their performance.

Table 4. Chief, Reading Improvement Service.

shown, then the goals relevant to the output, then performance strategies used to generate the output, a note about relevant tools and resources, and, finally, the measures used to track the accomplishment. The top part, labeled Things, shows the lead worker role of the chief, modeling the process of providing services to clients, using specific performance strategies, and guiding the work by performance data. The middle part, labeled People, shows the staff development and external relationship roles. The bottom part, labeled Data, shows what the Chief reports; in addition, it shows that establishing feedback systems is a major performance strategy. Establishing feedback systems for each performer is a performance strategy used by the Chief to get everything else to work.

In another setting, let us say a larger organization or any organization in which the principal manager is not a lead worker, establishing feedback systems could be shown as a major output. For example, for the Reading Service, I could replace the Things accomplishment above with "establishing feedback systems" as shown in Table 5.

Notice that this part of the executive's job supports all other aspects of the executive's performance. According to this model the executive's job is to self-manage using performance measures very closely aligned with the organizational performance measures. As Chief, I measured me against learning gains of clients (my personal clients and those of the Service), publications (mine and the staff's), and development of staff as measured by the gains of their clients, their publications, and their progress through degree programs. In addition, but less formally, I measured me by the extent to which I could provide an environment containing feedback systems that enable staff and clients to function as self-managing systems. I could manage one person, me, as a system, and then establish the feedback systems necessary to enable staff members to manage themselves as systems. Unless staff had

Performance Logic For Feedback Systems

Outputs	Goals	Performance Strategies	Resource Management	Performance Measures
Things				
Feedback systems established for major processes and for all performers	Every process owner and every performer should have the feedback needed to perform intelligently	Model self-management. Request "How's it going?" reports regularly from each process owner. Encourage each process owner to request reports from others.	Allocate dollar and human resources to establishing and continuously improving feedback systems	Count how many processes are monitored by effective feedback systems vs. how many are not. Count number of performers who are and are not self-managing.

Table 5. Any Senior Executive or Manager.

the goals, feedback, and tools necessary to function intelligently, they could not self-manage well and I could not successfully manage the Reading Service as a system.

Summary

The alternative to managing organizations and persons as systems is to continue to function as we do now. In the typical organization, organizational hierarchies create an artificial game in which climbing the pyramid is the most obvious measure of success. The artificial hierarchies assure that self-serving performance is rewarded at the expense of customer serving performance. Pyramid climbing is a zero-sum rather than value adding game. Intelligent performance must assure that value is added. Intelligent performance assures win/win/win relationships among individuals, organizations, and customers. Such relationships are too complex to be driven by a central authority in a rapidly changing world. It is necessary to set up organizations so that intelligent performance can be distributed throughout the organization. This is a new challenge for managers and executives, but the concept of managing persons (and organizations) as adaptive systems provides clear guidance in meeting the challenge, as does the work of Tosti and Jackson (1999).

Individual performance is the resultant of interactions between a person and an environment. And the performances of many people are required for a large organization to function well. In the work environment, a person should report results, accomplishments, and progress so that others can coordinate their work. The ability to report significant results, worthy accomplishments, and realistic progress is enhance by managing persons as systems. If a person is to manage his work performance as a system, he must do 3 things:

1.   Specify his performance, identifying what he reports, how he performs, and how he measures or monitors his performance. A performance logic table such as those shown is Table 4 and Table 5 is one way to do that.
2.   Identify the elements of a performance system. A system description such as those shown in Table 1 and Table 2 and a total performance system diagram such as those shown in Figure 2 and Figure 3 help to do that.
3.   Find ways to align the self-as-system models with organization-as-system models such as those shown in Figure 1 and Table 3.

Similarly, organizational performance is the resultant of interactions between an organization and an environment. When the individual performer is an organizational leader, she must manage herself and the organization as systems. To do so, she must specify her performance (e.g., as shown in Table 4 and Table 5), identify the elements of the performance system that describes the total organization, and find ways to align self-as-system with organization-as-system. The leader can lead by example, operating as a self-managing system, while establishing the infrastructure that enables others to manage self-as-system and support managing the organization as a system.

References

Beer, S. (1961). Below the Twilight Arch-A Mythology of Systems. *Systems: Research aid design*. John Wiley & Sons.

Brethower, D. M. (1970). *The classroom as a self-modifying system*. Unpublished doctoral dissertation, University of Michigan.

Brethower, D. M. (1982). The total performance system. In R. M. O'Brien, A. M. Dickinson, & M. P. Rosow (Eds.), *Industrial Behavior Modification: A management handbook* (pp. 350-69). New York: Pergamon Press.

Brethower, D. M. (1995). Specifying a human performance technology knowledgebase. *Performance Improvement Quarterly, 8*(2), 17-39.

Ford, D. H. (1987). *Humans as self-constructing living systems: A developmental perspective on behavior and personality*. Hillsdale, NJ: Earlbaum.

Gilbert, T. (1996). *Human competence: Engineering worthy performance*. Washington, D.C.: The International Society for Performance Improvement.

Heiman, M., & Slomianko, J. (1998). *Learning to learn: Thinking skills for the 21st century* (7th ed.). Cambridge, MA: Learning-To-Learn.

Langdon, D. (1995). *The new language of work*. Amherst, MA: HRD Press.

Rummler, G. A., & Brache, A. P. (1995). *Improving Performance: How to manage the white space on the organization chart* (2nd ed.). San Francisco: Jossey-Bass.

Rummler, G. A., & Brache, A. P. (1988). The systems view of human performance. *Training, 25,* 45-53.

Tosti, D., & Jackson, S. (1999). Influencing others to act. In H. Stolovitch & E. Keeps (Eds.), *The Handbook of human performance technology* (2nd ed., pp. 759-775). San Francisco: Jossey-Bass.

Discussion of Brethower

Dilemma in Organizational Behavior Management

Patrick M. Ghezzi
University of Nevada

Behavior science, like every other science, breeds specialization. This is seen at numerous levels that range from the conceptual, experimental, and applied analysis of behavior to specializations that are nested within specializations. For instance, in the applied domain there are specializations in education, gerontology, clinical, and developmental disabilities. Still narrower specializations include autism in developmental disabilities and behavioral medicine in the clinical specialization, to name just a few.

Organizational behavior management, or OBM, is another specialization in applied behavior analysis (Hall, 1980; Mawhinney, 1984). Its subjects range from business and industry executives to rank and file factory workers, and its locales range from corporate board rooms to assembly lines. These characteristics are unimportant to identifying OBM as a specialization in applied behavior analysis, however. What is important is the degree to which the principles, concepts, and methods of behavior science are consistently and thoroughly applied to understand, predict, and control the behavior of an individual in a socially important and scientifically convincing manner (Baer, Wolf, & Risley, 1968, 1987). Casting OBM in this way as a specialization within applied behavior analysis establishes the basis for these comments on Professor Brethower's paper, "Managing a person as a system."

One impression given by Brethower's analysis is that it is unclear how it relates to applied behavior analysis. We read, for example, that a person is best conceived as a system interacting in and with organizational systems, and that in order to improve the interactions between the systems we must alter the performance of the person-system in relation to the organization-system. Ideally, the person-system must become a self-managed system in the sense of being capable of continuously adapting or adjusting itself to feedback provided by the organization-system. How this is achieved is outlined in various tables and flow charts showing how the systems work together to ensure personal and organizational success.

But again, Brethower does not tell us how his analysis relates to the principles and concepts of behavior science. Furthermore, he does not provide any hard evidence that shows us what his analysis can do to ameliorate a specific problem. In the end, then, we are left with an analysis that has the look of something other than applied behavior analysis.

If this impression is anywhere near the mark, then Brethower is caught in the same dilemma that others who work in OBM are caught: Whether or not to maintain an identity with applied behavior analysis.

In order to maintain an identity with applied behavior analysis, Brethower would have to translate his analysis into behavioral language, and he would have to demonstrate how his analysis performs under the scrutiny of persons in both the working world of business and industry and the scientific world of applied behavior analysis.

It is doubtful that Brethower's analysis would survive the scrutiny of workers in both worlds. On the one hand, Brethower knows far better than most how difficult it is to speak the technical language of applied behavior analysis consistently to an audience of executives whose concerns always center on "managing the behavior" of a large group of people. The difficulty here is that only individuals behave, and any analysis that proceeds as if a group behaves is not within the accepted cannon of behavior science. Thus, to stand firm with respect to the cannon would preserve an identity with the science, but at the expense of losing executives in a sea of technical terms and arcane concepts that do not pertain to their everyday concerns. On the other hand, moving outside the accepted canon, for example, by likening the behavior of the individual to the collective activity of many individuals, may keep the executives interested, but at the expense of losing an identity with behavior science.

There is no way to resolve this dilemma. Subtle changes in terms, for example, from controlling behavior to "managing performance" or from delivering reinforcement to "providing feedback" is no resolution, and in fact only serves as a reminder that OBM is moving toward creating an identity that differs from applied behavior analysis. Brethower, a long-time behavior analyst and leader in OBM, admits as much by suggesting that his analysis may be used to create "a language of work to aid communication about work." Evidently, he believes that the language of behavior analysis does not serve that purpose. Instead, Brethower has chosen to move outside the accepted cannon of behavior science to develop an analysis that he believes is better suited to the working world of business and industry.

It would be a mistake to misinterpret these comments by jumping to the conclusion that Brethower's analysis, or OBM more generally, has little or nothing in common with applied behavior analysis, and that consequently there would be no point in maintaining anything other than an historical relationship. To the contrary, much is to be gained by continuing the relationship, but in a way that takes advantage of the inherently interdisciplinary character of OBM.

What comes to mind as an example of interdisciplinary study is behavioral economics, which combines microeconomic concepts, principles, and measures with concepts, principles, and methods developed by behavior analysts. The synthesis of behavior analysis and economics has stimulated a great deal of conceptual and experimental analysis, and has also been applied to understanding and treating substance abuse, gambling, and obesity at both the individual and community level (see Bickel & Vuchinich, 2000).

One obvious advantage of introducing behavioral economics to OBM is that it gives behavior analysts a way to communicate with executives in business and industry in their native language. Obvious, too, is that workers in OBM can proceed to develop their agendas with relative ease by taking advantage of the conceptual, experimental, and applied foundation that has already been established for behavioral economics. On this course, OBM can set itself apart from other specializations within applied behavior analysis, but not so far apart from them to be isolated from, or ignored by, the behavioral community.

References

Baer, D. M., Wolf, M. M., & Risley, T. R. (1968). Some current dimensions of applied behavior analysis. *Journal of Applied Behavior Analysis, 1*, 91-97.

Baer, D. M., Wolf, M. M., & Risley, T. R. (1987). Some still-current dimensions of applied behavior analysis. *Journal of Applied Behavior Analysis, 20*, 313-327.

Bickel, R. E., & Vuchinich, R. E. (2000). *Reframing health behavior change with behavioral economics*. Hillsdale, NJ: Lawrence Erlbaum Associates.

Hall, B. (1980). Editorial. *Journal of Organizational Behavior Management, 2*, 145-150.

Mawhinney, T. C. (1984). Philosophical and ethical aspects of organizational behavior management: Some evaluative feedback. *Journal of Organizational Behavior Management, 6*, 5-31.

Notes

Thanks to Ken MacAleese for his assistance in gathering materials relevant to this commentary.

3. First line supervision and management (M1 and M2 in the diagram) is monitoring operational outputs such as "units shipped" and "sales made". In addition to formal measures on the computer printout, they are relying heavily on ad hoc data such as manual "hourly counts" and personal observations from making joint-calls with sales reps. They know what desired performance (operational) is, how well they are performing, and generally, what operational "knobs" to turn to affect operational performance.

4. Middle management (M3, 4, and 5 in the diagram) is monitoring a combination of financial and operational meters on their respective "dashboards" (more financial near the top and more operational near the bottom). Generally,
   a) they don't know the link between the financial measures and the operational measures. As a result, they are unclear what operational knobs to *have* turned. (They turn very few knobs themselves.)
   b) the operational measures aren't as plentiful as the financial measures.
   c) they end up trying to manage operations with financial measures.
   d) they are expected by top management to deliver the *financial* results through *operations*, even though nobody has figured out the clear link between the two. By and large, each manager is left to their own devices to figure out the relationship between the two.
   e) they are removed several levels from the knobs that need to be turned. As a result, they are in the uncomfortable position of being accountable for performance reflected in the financial measures, but not able to turn the operational knobs that impact those measures.

Because there is no clear link between the financial measures and the operational measures (no clear link between the "top of the house" and the "bottom of the house") there is also the issue of the time lapse between the top level of meters and the turning of the key knobs at the low end of the hierarchy. Specifically, top management is looking primarily at financial measures, which are clearly "lagging" indicators of performance. They are history. Managing with these measures is like driving through the rear-view mirror.

What is required is a way to tie meters to relevant knobs and thereby link the various management levels. And I think I have uncovered a way to do just that-to wire the organization together. That is what I would like to present today.

But first, permit me a quick review of the key conceptual (but practical) building blocks that have gotten me to this point.

1. *The notion of the organization as an adaptive system.* Figure 1 is a current manifestation of the General Systems Model that Dale Brethower drew for me in 1965. Key principles related to this view of the world are:

Performance Logic: The Organization Performance Rosetta Stone

Geary A. Rummler
Performance Design Lab

One of the great challenges in organization effectiveness is to link the "top" of the organization (as represented by financial measures) to the "bottom" of the organization (represented by operational measures) and to have them both going in the same direction at the same time. Using Figure 1 as a reference, the challenge looks like this to me:

1. Earnings are derived from the sale of products/services that are produced through complex organization processes such as strategy formulation and planning, product development, marketing, sales, order fulfillment, installation, billing, service, etc.

2. Management monitors both the earnings and product/service outputs and ideally makes decisions about direction, priorities, and resource allocation that will optimize both outputs. However, key to doing this is:

   a) understanding exactly how operations (i.e. processes) impact earnings and the link between the two.

   b) knowing what measures (represented by the "meters" in the diagram) need to be monitored, by whom, to detect deviations from desired operational performance.

   c) knowing what operational "knobs" (shown as residing within the processes in the diagram) need to be turned, by whom and when, in order to get the meters back within desired limits.

However, the reality is the following:

1. The link between meters and knobs is complex and seldom understood by management. For the meter measuring "market share", there is no one knob management can turn to alter that meter reading. Instead, perhaps six other subordinate meters need to be consulted and 12 knobs turned to begin to impact that one measure. Management seldom understands the complex operating "system" that produces earnings.

2. Top Management (M6 in the diagram) is interested in the earnings output almost exclusively and is looking at an instrument panel made up primarily of financial measures. They know what desired performance (financial) is and how well the organization is performing in that regard. They tend not to know what operational "knobs" need to be turned to affect financial performance, other than cutting costs.

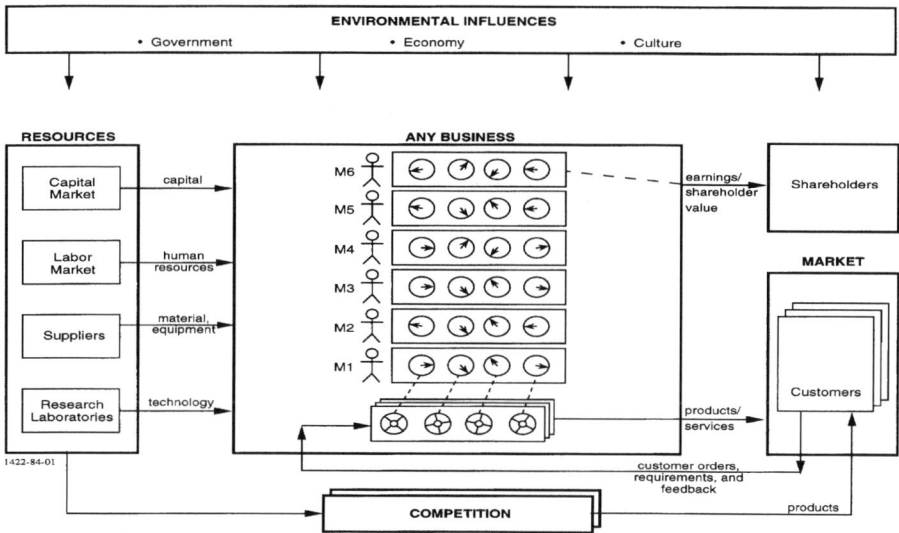

Figure 1. Performance measurement vacuum.

a) An organization is a system, taking in various inputs and producing valued products and services for its customers (and in the private sector, providing an economic return for its stockholders.)

b) An organization system exists in a larger system, a "super-system" consisting of
   - it's markets
   - it's competition
   - the resources it needs to produce the necessary outputs (capital, technology, human resources, and material)
   - it's general geo-political environment consisting of the economy, legislation, and prevailing cultural mores.

c) An organization is an adaptive system, adapting to changes in its supersystem and internal workings. The fundamental truth is that this entity must "adapt or die".

2. *The notion that there are Three Levels of Performance* that we need to focus on in an organization; The Organization, Process, and Job/Performer Levels. (See Figure 2) This "Three Level view" is an elaboration of a notion that Dale and I had in 1965 and which formed the underpinnings of a workshop we started at the University of Michigan that year called The Training Systems Workshop. The key to organization effectiveness is the alignment of these three critical *interdependent* levels. The overall performance of an organization (how well it meets

the expectations of its customers) is the result of goals, structure, and management actions at all three levels. If a customer receives a shipment of faulty widgets, for example, the cause may lie in any or all of the three levels. The *performer* may have assembled the widgets incorrectly and/or let faulty widgets be shipped. The *processes* that influence widget quality (including design, procurement, production, and distribution) may be at fault. The *organization*-represented by top managers who determine the role of widgets in the organization's strategy, provide the budget for staff and equipment, and establish the goals and measures-may also have caused the problem.

Assembly *performers* can be trained in statistical process control techniques, can be grouped into self-managed work teams, and can be empowered to stop the line if they encounter defects. However, those actions will have little effect if the design *process* has produced a widget that is difficult to assemble correctly, or if the purchasing process can't acquire enough sub-assemblies, or if out-of-sync sales and forecasting processes lead to product changeovers that require the assembler to follow a different procedure each day. The desire of the assembler to produce a high quality widget will be further compromised if, in this *organization*, the primary measure and basis of reward is "the number of units shipped", regardless of quality.

3.   *The notion of the Performance Management System.* Consistent, high-performance is a function of the three components illustrated in Figure 3.

   a)   *Performance Planned*-goals are established, plans are set and imple-mented (made operational) and communicated to the "per-former".

   b)   *Performance Executed*-the "performer" delivers the performance set forth in the goals and plans.

   c)   *Performance Managed*-actual performance is monitored against the goals and plans and as a result, there may be a "change" signal sent to the "performer" to change their execution in some way and/or there may be a "change" signal sent to the Performance Planned component to either change the goals or the plans to accomplish the goals.

   d)   *Performance Planned* (again)-changes goals and/or plans based on feedback from Performance Managed and data on "external" events. The three components shown in Figure 3 make up the Performance System.

The *Performance Planned and Performance Managed* components constitute the "brains" or "central cortex" of the Performance System and are referred to as the Performance Measurement and Management System. The Performance Measure-ment and Management System (PMMS) is what makes it possible for the

Performance System to *adapt* to external changes and react to execution failures. It is the mechanism whereby the Performance System is an *adaptive* (or learning) system.

The Performance Measurement and Management System exists at all three levels of performance:

    a)   Job/Individual Level (See Figure 4) - a job requires:
        - goals and plans for achieving the goals
        - performance as planned
        - review of performance and corrective action if necessary to improve performance

    b)   Process Level (See Figure 5) - a work process such as "new product development" needs a Process Performance Measurement and Management System for that process that will:
        - develop the goals and plans for that process
        - review the performance of the process and determine what must be done to improve the performance of the process
        - review the performance results and the external world to see if the process goals and/or plans must be modified.

    c)   Organization Level (See Figure 6) - the organization is an adaptive system made up of a myriad of processes, all of which must adapt to the changing external world and actual performance results. The Organization Performance Measurement and Management System is the mechanism or "central cortex" that makes it possible for the organization system to adapt.

    4.   *The understanding that the Three Levels of Performance, Organization, Process, and Job/Performer are linked* through the Performance Measurement and Management Systems at each Level, as shown in Figure 7. As you can see, every manager has a unique PMMS or is part of a PMMS. They have specific goals and areas for which they plan and meters which they must monitor, and consequently, actions to take in the event of deviations from performance goals. The organization is a hierarchy of PMMS's.

The CEO's *planning* concerns are corporate strategy and earnings, EVA, and market share goals. They are overseeing the development of corporate plans and budgets for achieving these goals. The CEO's *managing* concerns including the monitoring of earnings, EVA, and market share performance, asking questions about significant negative deviations, and directing appropriate corrective action. These actions may be immediate, such as instructing a reduction in expenses, or delayed, such as preparing to modify corporate strategy at the next quarterly strategy review meeting.

The Sales Manager's *planning* concerns are establishing sales objectives, account plans, and sales territories for their sales district and the 12 sales reps they manage. The Sales Manager's *managing* concerns include monitoring sales, proposal

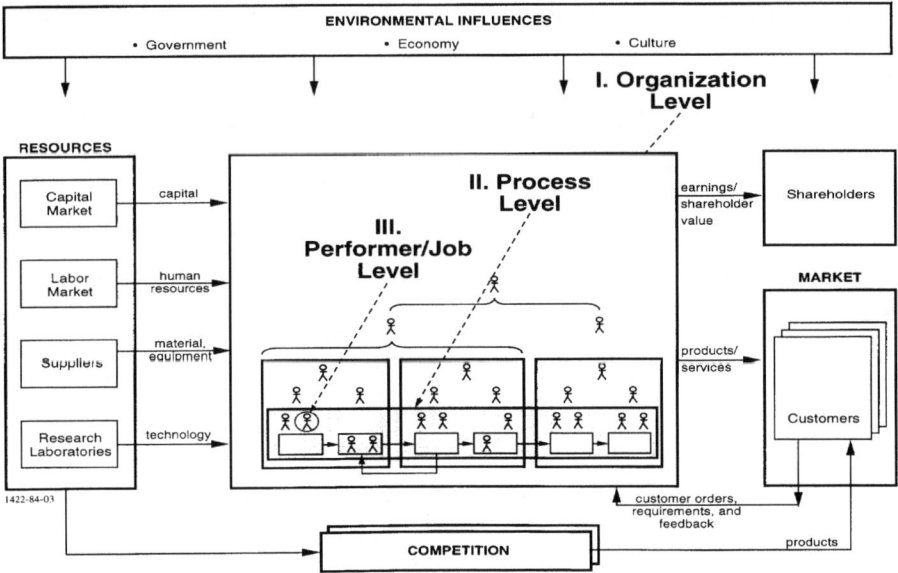

Figure 2. Organization as an adaptive system and 3 levels of performance.

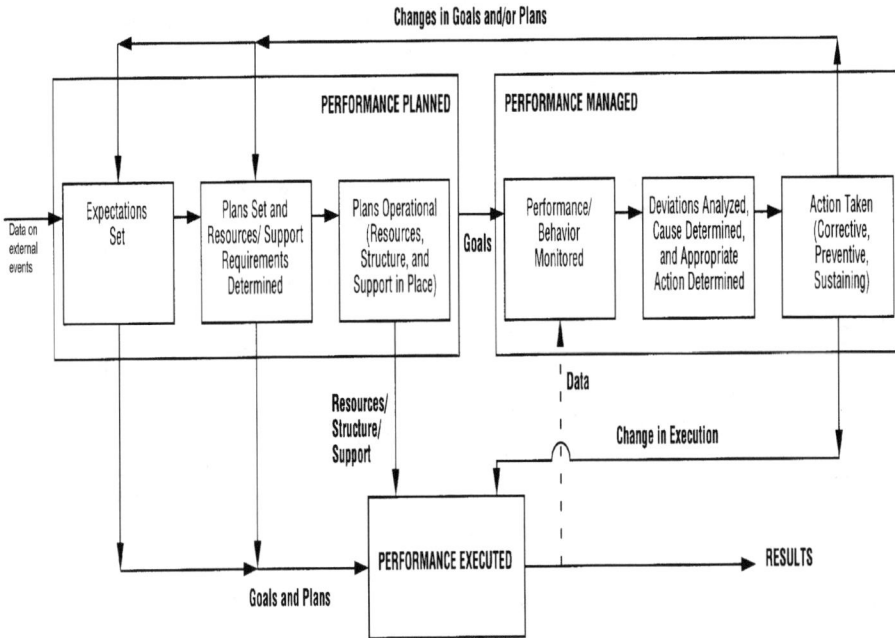

Figure 3. Any performance system.

JOB PERFORMANCE PLANNED

EXPECTATIONS SET
- Relevant Process and Function Strategy and Goals Received
- Job Mission Determined and Communicated
- Job Accomplishments and Specifications Determined and Communicated
- Job Outputs and Specifications Determined and Communicated
- Job Tasks and Specifications Determined and Communicated

PLANS SET
- Plans Developed
- Budgets Developed

PLANS OPERATIONAL
- Job Designed
- Performers Available (Capable and Prepared)
- Performance Support Systems in Place (Consequences, Tools, Feedback)
- Job Input Requirements Met
- Performance Maintenance Systems in Place (Benefits, Safety, Compensation)
- PMMS in Place
- Decision Rules in Place
- Policies and Procedures in Place
- Resources Available

JOB PERFORMANCE MANAGED

PERFORMANCE MONITORED
- "Performance Managed" Roles Determined and Understood
- Performance Data Available (Measurement System)
- Performance Data Communicated/ Distributed
- Data Monitored

PERFORMANCE DEVIATION ANALYZED
- Cause Determined
- Appropriate Action Determined

ACTION TAKEN
- Corrective
- Preventive
- Sustaining

JOB
INPUTS → JOB → OUTPUTS → **JOB PERFORMANCE**
JOB PERFORMANCE EXECUTED

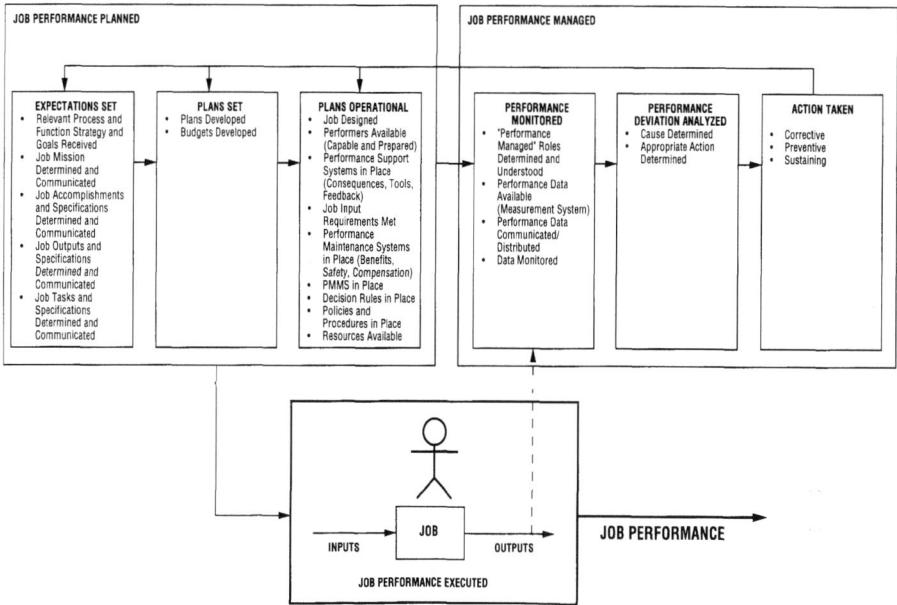

Figure 4. Job performance measurementand management system.

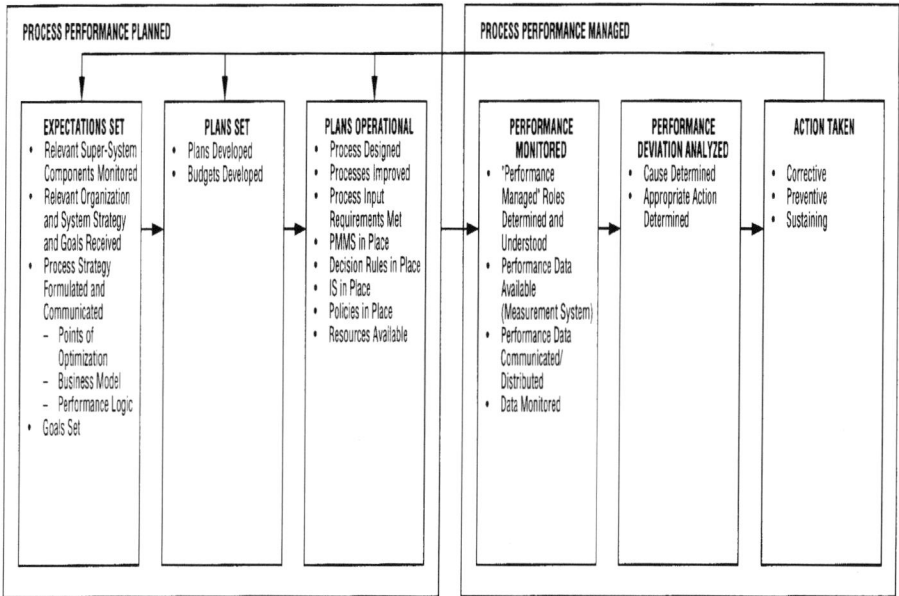

PROCESS PERFORMANCE PLANNED

EXPECTATIONS SET
- Relevant Super-System Components Monitored
- Relevant Organization and System Strategy and Goals Received
- Process Strategy Formulated and Communicated
  - Points of Optimization
  - Business Model
  - Performance Logic
- Goals Set

PLANS SET
- Plans Developed
- Budgets Developed

PLANS OPERATIONAL
- Process Designed
- Processes Improved
- Process Input Requirements Met
- PMMS in Place
- Decision Rules in Place
- IS in Place
- Policies in Place
- Resources Available

PROCESS PERFORMANCE MANAGED

PERFORMANCE MONITORED
- "Performance Managed" Roles Determined and Understood
- Performance Data Available (Measurement System)
- Performance Data Communicated/ Distributed
- Data Monitored

PERFORMANCE DEVIATION ANALYZED
- Cause Determined
- Appropriate Action Determined

ACTION TAKEN
- Corrective
- Preventive
- Sustaining

Figure 5. Process performance measurement and management system.

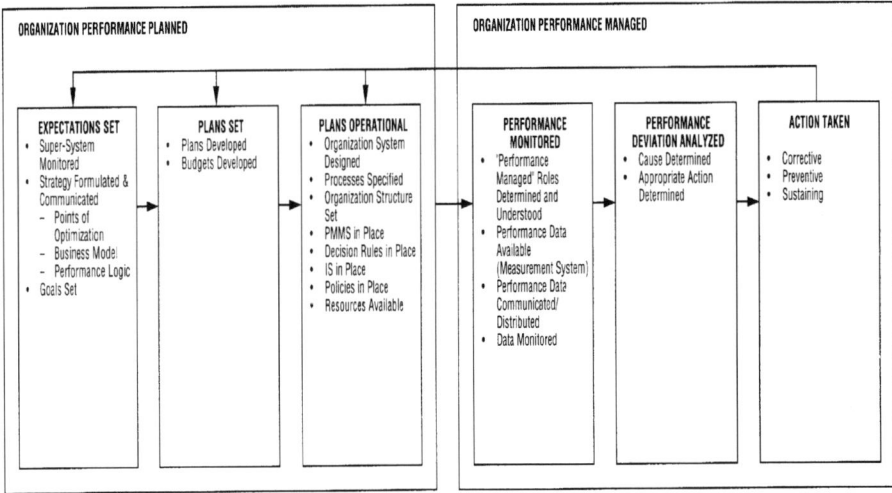

Figure 6. Organization performance measurement and management syste.

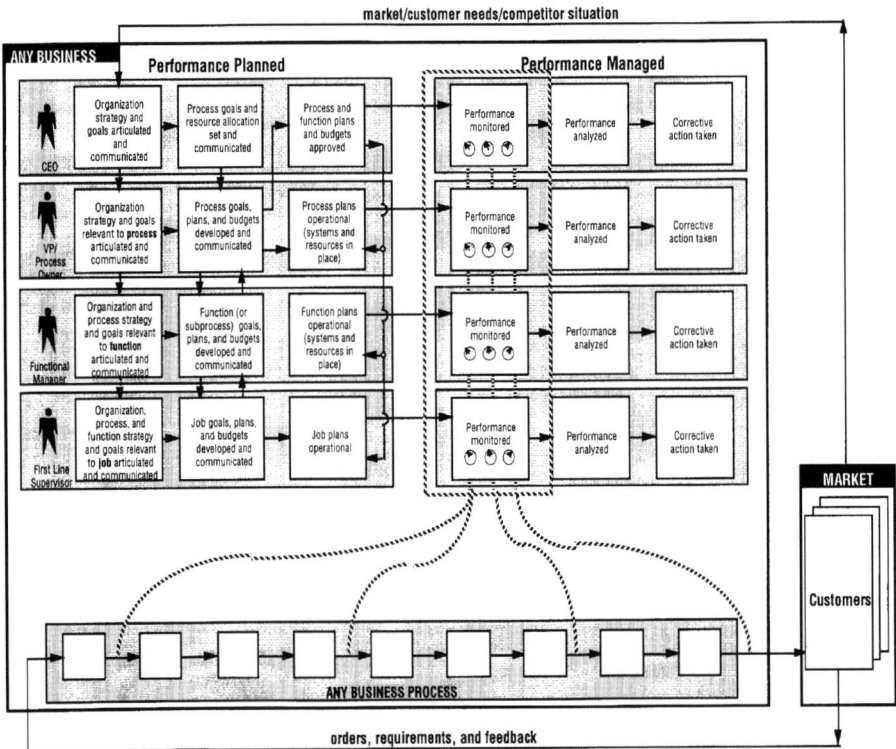

Figure 7. Performance measurement and management system and the organiztional hierarchy.

submission rate, call rate, expenses, etc., for their district as a whole and for the individual sales reps. They must analyze any significant negative deviations from desired performance, and take appropriate corrective action.

An Approach to Meeting the Challenge-The Performance Logic

And now we come to the missing piece of the puzzle. In figures 2-7, we have made the case for linking the Three Levels of Performance in order to get consistent, high-performance in an organization. We further believe that the Organization, Process, and Job/Performer Levels are in fact, linked by an underlying *logic* or what we are calling a Performance Logic. A *Performance Logic* (PL) is a network of variables or factors that affect a given output ("Output 'X' is a function of these variables...."). Figure 8 contains an example of a Performance Logic for a portion of the public workshop business for a training company. This diagram is called a Performance Logic Map (PLM) and shows the relationship between the variables as they affect the output "profit".

Not all variables in the Performance Logic are "born equal". Some are more critical to the desired output than others. We call these variables "*Leverage Points*" - those variables in the PL which will have the greatest impact on the desired output and should therefore be measured, monitored, and managed. A variable may become a Leverage Point as a function of some event, such as the Arab oil embargo in 1973. Overnight, the relatively benign variable of "cost" became the dominant variable in the global petroleum industry. This is an example of a Leverage Point for an entire industry, a variable that all companies in the industry must work with or around. However, any given company in an industry may select particular Leverage Points that they will emphasize in order to give them a competitive edge.

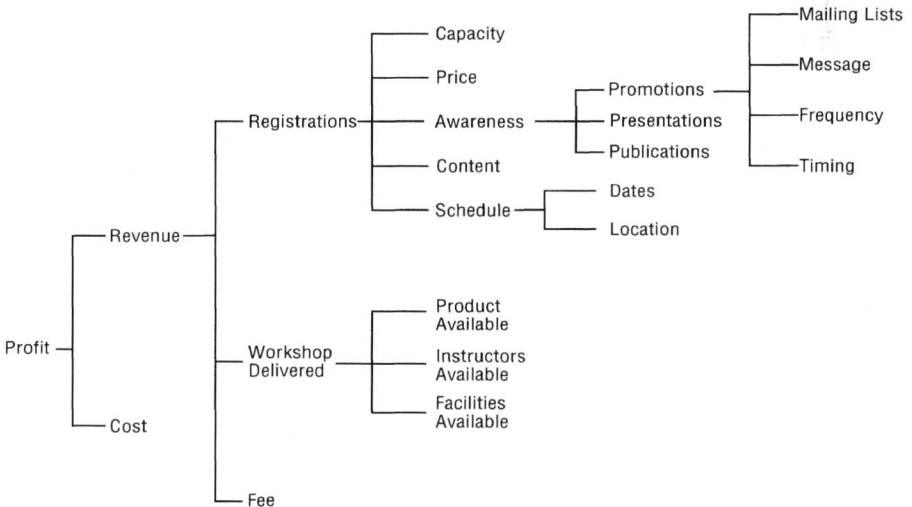

Figure 8. Partial performance logic for workshop business.

A current example is how Walmart has revolutionized the retail industry by concentrating on the variables of "inventory cost" and "out-of-stocks", making them competitive Leverage Points. Referring to Figure 8, we can assume that the variables affecting revenues in the "public workshop industry" are virtually the same for all companies in that industry. However, Company A may have some extraordinary ability to develop new workshops and may choose to make "Product Available" a Leverage Point and competitive advantage. Company B may be leveraging an advantage they have in marketing (i.e. , "Awareness") and Company C an advantage they have in "Price". Thus there is usually a basic Performance Logic for an industry, but different Leverage Points for companies in that industry, depending on their individual strategies and economic or organizational strengths and weaknesses.

Performance Logics are seldom articulated and therefore seldom understood. Yet they often represent the *hidden* key to success. Our contention and assumption is that there is such a Performance Logic for most of what we do in organizations and that it is identifiable and documentable. The identification and documentation of this Performance Logic is what has been missing in the management of organizations. Failure to identify and document this Logic is a major contributor to why financial measures and operational measures have never been linked.

Once such a Logic is exposed and documented for an organization, it is possible to:

1. Determine the Leverage Points.
2. See what must be managed.
    a) what performance variables to monitor, which in turn identifies what performance must be measured.
    b) what variables or "paths" to pursue in trying to understand the cause of poor performance. (Troubleshooting poor performance.)
    c) what action to take (or knobs to turn) to improve performance.
3. See what must be planned for and what the relationship of performance goals for the variables needs to be.
4. Overlay performance data on the logic and determine which variables or paths
    a) fail most frequently
    b) have most impact on performance
    c) are "leading indicators" of future performance.

This analysis reveals which variables need to be most closely monitored and controlled and suggests key measures.

Understanding the Performance Logic of an organization is akin to having a Rosetta stone that breaks the "code" of organization performance. Once the variables and their relationship is known, it is clear what is required for success. Although the Performance Logic links the Organization, Process, and Job/Performer levels of performance in an organization, there are also distinct Organization Level Performance Logics, Process Level Performance Logics, and Job/Performer Level Performance Logics for a single organization.

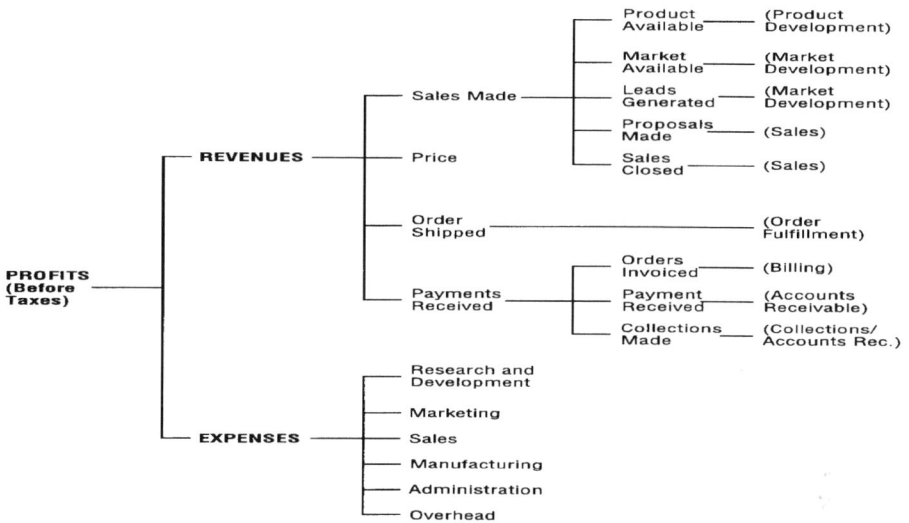

Figure 9. Organizational level performance logic map (and related processes) Eagle Inc.

The *Organization Performance Logic* shows the relationship between the organization's ultimate outputs (e.g., EVA, profits) and operations (specifically processes). This logic remains unarticulated in most businesses and is the reason why the relationship between various financial meters and operational "knobs" remains a mystery. Figure 9 shows a partial Organization Performance Logic for a business, linking the enterprise output of profits to the various processes (shown in parentheses) that impact the variables that determine profits. Now we have a "map" linking the "meter" on profits to the processes containing the "knobs" that affect profits.

The *Process Performance Logic* is implicit in the input-output relationship of a work process flow. However, in most cases it is beneficial to make the Process Logic explicit with a Process Performance Logic Map. Figure 10 contains a partial Process Performance Logic for the "Customer Order Process" identified in Figure 9. Through process improvement work, many businesses have begun to understand process level performance logic. However, it has done little good because the processes were not linked to "top level" business measures because the Organization Performance Logic was never made explicit, and therefore understood by management.

The *Job/Performance Logic* is implicit in the accomplishment/sub-accomplishment based Job Models (Rummler, 1979) developed by Praxis Corporation and practiced by The Rummler-Brache Group and others. There is a logic in the accomplishment/sub-accomplishment format of the Job Model. In addition, we have frequently developed job flow charts and job "decision-trees", which imply a job performance logic.

Order Shipped & Invoice Sent

Order Submitted — Credit Pre-Approved — Carrier Approved / Credit Data Complete — Data Requested / Personnel Trained

Credit Checked — Current Credit Data — Data Requested

Order Entered — Order Data Complete — Order Heard / Order Recorded — Personnel Trained / System Operation

Order Data Correct — Order Heard / Order Recorded — Personnel Trained / System Operation

Order Scheduled — Inventory Checked — Inventory Data Correct

Material Ordered — Approved Suppliers Available — Approval Procedure / Supplier Perf. / Specifications Known

Production Scheduled — Print Capacity — Equipment / Personnel

Assembly Capacity — Equipment / Personnel

Invoice Prepared — Order Stopped / Order Data Complete — Credit Disapproved.

Order Produced — Material Printed — Raw Material Available — Supplier Performance / Inventory Located / Equipment Operational / Personnel Available / Specifications

Order Assembled — Raw Material Available — Supplier Performance / Inventory Located / Equipment Operational / Personnel Available / Specifications

Order Shipped — Order Picked — Inventory Available — Forecast / Production Rate

Order Packaged — Packing Mail Available / Packing Instructions / Ship to Info / Personnel Available

Invoice Inserted — Invoice Available

Order Loaded and Dispatched — Carrier Available / Loaders Available / Equip. Available

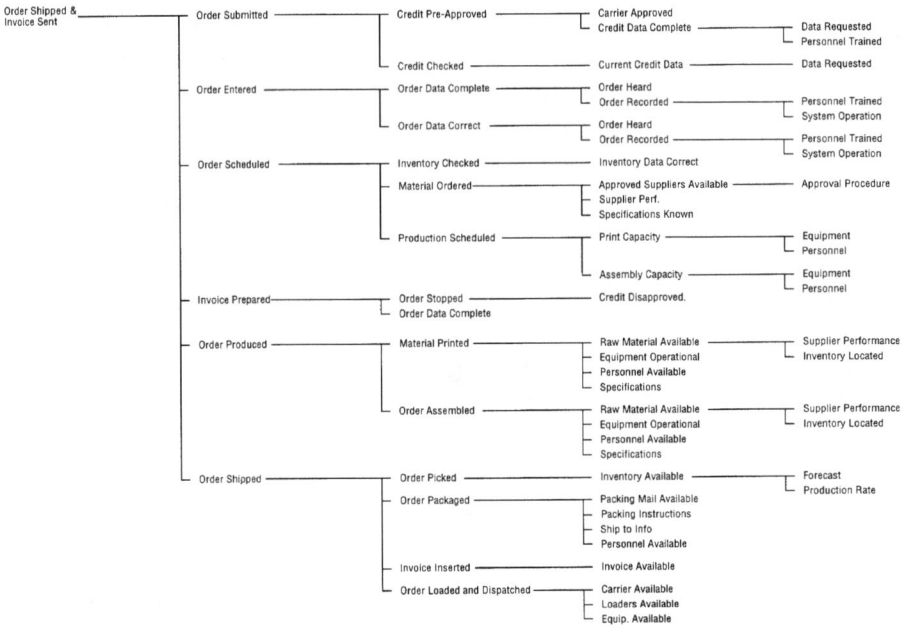

Figure 10. Customer order process performance logic.

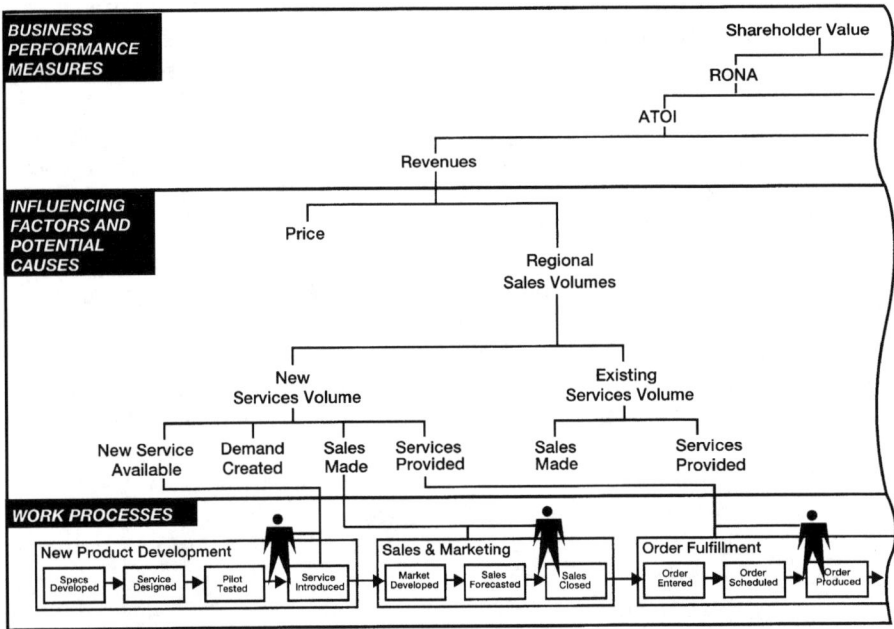

BUSINESS PERFORMANCE MEASURES

Shareholder Value — RONA — ATOI — Revenues

INFLUENCING FACTORS AND POTENTIAL CAUSES

Price — Regional Sales Volumes

New Services Volume — New Service Available / Demand Created / Sales Made / Services Provided

Existing Services Volume — Sales Made / Services Provided

WORK PROCESSES

New Product Development: Specs Developed → Service Designed → Pilot Tested → Service Introduced

Sales & Marketing: Market Developed → Sales Forecasted → Sales Closed

Order Fulfillment: Order Entered → Order Scheduled → Order Produced

Figure 11. Performance logic.

Figure 11 shows another view and example of a Performance Logic Map, linking the organization output of Shareholder Value to the processes (and variables therein) that affect/impact it.

There are a number of applications of the Performance Logic. However, the one I would like to discuss in some detail is its application to the design of a measurement and management system. Other applications will be discussed briefly, later.

An Example

Referring to Figure 7 again, the question is "how do we determine what should be measured in an organization and who should be looking at what measures and taking what action?" The situation we found at the client I am about to describe was not a-typical from my experience:

- The executive committee wanted a "balanced scorecard" because it was the thing to do.
- The controller was commissioned by the CFO to determine what the measures (financial and non-financial) needed to be.
- The Executive VP of Operations was commissioned by the CEO to come up with an operational set of measures because he was tired of getting numbers that didn't tally across the organization.
- The same Executive VP of Operations had been trying unsuccessfully for nine months to get all function heads to submit their top 10 KPI's (Key Performance Indicators).
- The Information Technology group had formed a committee of 30 people to decide the priorities for automating various performance measures.
- The newly formed Process Management department was telling any manager who would listen that they needed to begin managing by Statistical Process Control Charts.

Our entry into this situation was a request by the Executive VP of Operations to develop a measurement system to meet the CEO's requirements. The company had three lines of business, A, B, and C. We started our work with Division A because our early interviews told us the division General Manager shared our "systems view" of the world. Once we had built a prototype measurement system for that division, we did the same for the other two divisions, and then built a measurement "cap" linking the divisions to Corporate. The sequence of events within Division A was as follows:

1. Based on interviews with managers, and some experience with this industry, two Rummler-Brache Group (RBG) consultants developed a "straw" Performance Logic Map for the division. There was an Organization Level PLM for Division A (See Figure 12) and Process Level PLM's for several significant processes that supported all three divisions.
2. The "straw" PLM was reviewed by the Division A management team and finalized. The team was asked to then identify the high-leverage

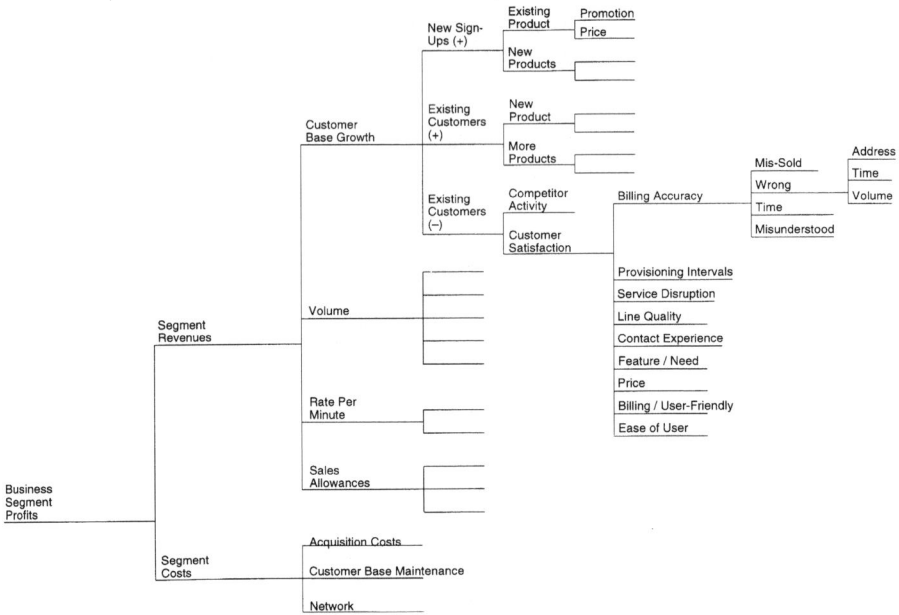

Figure 12. Performance logic.

variables (i.e., Leverage Points) in the PLM. Next, they were asked what measures they thought would be appropriate for these high-leverage variables.

3. The two consultants finished populating the Organization Level PLM and the Process PLMs with measures, based on their growing understanding of the business. (See Figure 13.)

4. The consultants met again with the management team and finalized the Organization Level measures. During this meeting the consultants also worked with the management team to decide who in the organization should be monitoring what measures, with what frequency, and taking what kind of action. This is a very important event. The management team is determining who is responsible for what performance at every level in the organization, and specifying the measures they should be monitoring and acting upon to get the desired performance. The division management is no longer leaving performance to chance (See Figure 14). Subsequent meetings were held with the various process management teams to finalize the process PLMs and measures.

5. Each measure on the Measurement Hierarchy (Figure 13) was color coded to reflect whether that measure currently did not exist, existed and was automated, existed but needed to be automated, and existed

New Sign-Ups (+)
Number

Existing Product
New Products

Promotion
Price

Customer Base Growth
Customer Count

Existing Customers (+)
Number

New Product
More Products

Mis-Sold
Wrong
Time
Misunderstood

Address
Time
Volume

Existing Customers (−)
Number

Competitor Activity
Customer Satisfaction
Satisfaction Index

Billing Accuracy

Provisioning Intervals
Service Disruption
Line Quality
Contact Experience
Feature / Need
Price
Billing / User-Friendly
Ease of User

Segment Revenues
Segment Gross Revenues

Volume
Average $/ Customer

Rate Per Minute
Average $/ Minute

Sales Allowances
Total $

Business Segment Profits
Segment Gross Margins

Segment Costs

Acquisition Costs
Customer Base Maintenance
Network

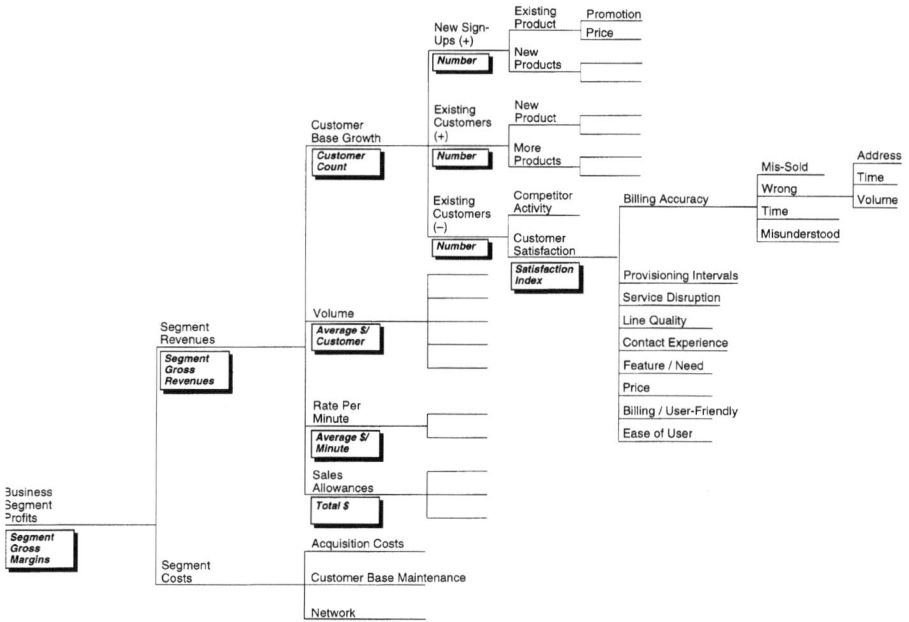

Figure 13. Performance logic and measures hierarchy.

PERFORMANCE LOGIC & MEASURES	MEASURES SUMMARY	POSITION AND PROCESS						
		GM	MKTING	SALES		PROVIS.	BILLING	NPD
	Segment Gross Revenues							
Customer Base Growth / Customer Count	Segment Gross Margins							
	Segment Revenue by ...							
	Customer Count by ...							
Segment Revenues / Segment Gross Revenues / Volume / Average $/ Customer	Disconnects by ...							
	Customer Sat. Index							
Rate Per Minute / Average $/ Minute	Provision Ct. by ...							
Sales Allowances / Total $	Provision On-time to Provise							
Business Segment Profits / Segment Gross Margins	Ct. to Problem Resolution ...							
Segment Costs	Abandonment Rate ...							
	Trouble Reported ...							

Figure 14. Measurement system.

but did not need to be automated. Then the management team established the automation priorities for the Division.

6.   Automation commenced, using an intranet/Web Page format.

7.   A Management System was designed to support the Measurement System. This consisted of communicating what managers would be reviewing what measures with what frequency and taking what types of action. These roles and responsibilities were formalized through a series of regularly scheduled meetings of key managers.

The same pattern was followed in the remaining two divisions, starting with the validation of the PLM's. There were relatively small, but significant differences in the PLM's for each business. Once the PLM's were validated and the Points of Leverage agreed-upon, development of the measurement hierarchy was relatively straight-forward.

Features of a Performance Logic-Based Measurement System

Once we understand the underlying Performance Logic of a business, we can begin to put the Performance Measurement and Management System (as represented in Figures 4, 5, and 6) in place. The relationship of the PMMS to the Performance Logic is the same as the relationship between the banks of complex meters/gauges that are monitored in a chemical processing plant and the underlying process and logic diagrams the engineers have developed and used to build the plant and the processes. The same as the relationship between the displays and dials in an aircraft cockpit and the underlying system logic which reflects the relationship between the variables of engine power, wing flaps, and tail flaps.

The *performance logic* is what is *behind* the meters of the instrument panels (as represented by the "measures tower" in Figure 7). It is what tells us:

- what performance is required at all levels of the logic

- what performance to monitor

- what performance to measure

- what questions to ask about performance deviations

- what actions to take to modify performance

What we have done too long in too many organizations is debate and negotiate what meters go in the instrument panel without an inkling of the underlying performance logic. We have meters stuck in instrument panels, but they frequently aren't connected to one another-or to knobs that can change anything.

Features of a measurement system based on a Performance Logic include:

1.   The measures are driven by business results.

2.   There is a comprehensive set of measures reflecting all the critical organization outputs, thus providing a "balanced scorecard".

3. There is a measures *hierarchy*, not a just a list of measures with no sense of their relationship. It is readily understood how one measure impacts another.

4. The measures are integrated. That is, all the measures that might appear on an executive "balanced scorecard" (profit, market share, customer satisfaction) can all be linked to a set of common processes through the Performance Logic. Thus it is possible to see the relationship between all the measures on the executive dashboard. (This is a unique feature which is not found in the standard approach to developing "balanced scorecards".)

5. The measures hierarchy is superimposed on the PLM so managers know what the underlying logic of the business is at all times. Thus all managers will be following the same "troubleshooting" routine or template to determine the cause of a performance deviation.

6. The business has ALL the measures necessary to manage the business at all levels, not the just the "critical few". (What would be the "critical few" measures you would like the cockpit crew on your next flight to be limited to?) Obviously, no one manager is monitoring more than a handful of measures at one time. But when faced with a performance deviation, they can "drill-down" through the measures hierarchy to determine root-cause or identify who to turn to for root-cause and corrective action.

The results of this approach to performance measurement include having:

1. Linked the "top" and the "bottom" of the organization.

2. Linked "meters" and "knobs".

3. Linked financial and operational measures.

4. Integrated all the Enterprise Measures (that might make-up the "Balanced Scorecard") at the process level.

5. Made it possible to systematically "troubleshoot" poor performance.

6. Made it possible for performers at every level see how they impact Enterprise Performance.

7. Built in the ability to respond quickly to changes in customer requirements and market conditions.

8. Made it possible to begin managing by "logic" versus "myth".

Applications of the Performance Logic

The design of a measurement and management system is one application of the Performance Logic. Other potential applications include:

1. Competitive Analysis

Once management understands the Performance Logic for their industry, they can use this framework to deduce the strategy of competitors. What are their leverage points? What "levers" are they currently pushing? How do we counter that thrust?

2. Stock/Financial Analysis

Once a stock analyst develops a Performance Logic for an industry, they can describe major companies in that industry by the leverage points they have and the "levers" they are pushing. They can make buy/sell recommendations based on their opinion of whether companies are attending to the right variables and whether they will be able to execute.

3. Mergers and Acquisitions

Prior to a merger or acquisition, a management should compare the respective Performance Logics of the two businesses and determine the compatibility of their respective leverage points. Will the two Performance Logics remain separate and compliment one another or is the intent to convert one company's PL to the other's. If the latter is the plan, what is the impact on the processes of the company that is expected to change? What is involved (time and money) in changing those processes?

4. Business Analysis

A Performance Logic should be developed for every business as a Rosetta stone for understanding the fundamentals of the business. From that basic blue print, it is possible to see both problems and opportunities. In a recent case, when we attempted to build a PL for an organization, we quickly learned that three different PL's where required because the company was in fact in three different businesses. However, the company was trying to be in three businesses as once by following one not well articulated "logic", resulting in decisions that always seriously sub-optimized performance in two of the markets/businesses.

5. Performance Analysis/Training Analysis

When a training function has a Performance Logic for each business units they serve, they can:

    a)   identify areas where training will impact critical organization outputs and see where to look to evaluate the effectiveness of the training.

b) deflect requests for training that will not contribute to organization performance.

6. Strategy Formulation

Understanding the Performance Logic of an industry is invaluable in identifying the Leverage Points that will give a company a competitive edge. The Logic will also identify those processes critical to successfully establishing and maintaining that competitive edge.

7. Planning and Modeling

The Performance Logic and related Leverage Points point out what variables need to be planned for, and managed, to achieve the desired organization output. The relationship between these key variables can be modeled if appropriate.

8. Goal Setting

Once the Performance Logic has been articulated and the Leverage Points identified, there is a framework for determining appropriate performance goals for each variable/factor that impacts the desired organization output. Goal setting is no longer a matter of negotiation between positions and levels of management-it is driven by needs of the business and guided by the Performance Logic.

9. Education and Communication Tool

We have seen the Performance Logic of organizations used to:
  a) Help a management team gain insight into the complexity of their business.
  b) Help a management team gain understanding of the current reality of their business.
  c) Develop a shared understanding of a business and a shared vision of what it might become and what will be required to do so.

10. Supporting becoming a "Learning Organization" as defined by Peter Senge (1990).

The Performance Logic Map is a powerful tool for:

a) gaining insight into the nature of complexity in organizations.

b) seeing where "high leverage" lies.

c) understanding "current reality" and restructuring the view of reality.

d) developing shared visions.

e) articulating and communicating mental models.

f) aligning "espoused theory" with "theory in use".

g) designing "scenario analysis" exercises.

Implications and Conclusion

The notion of an organization Performance Logic has substantial implications for:

1. *The business press and journalism.* Recently I read an article about the management style of a seemingly successful executive of an organization that owned over 50 franchises of a particular fast-food restaurant chain. The article described his hard-nosed and controlling approach to management and how well it worked. But how much more valuable and interesting this article would have been if it had started with a discussion of the Performance Logic of this industry, the Points of Leverage this particular franchisee was exploiting, and how and why this executive's management style worked in *this particular situation.* And perhaps then the article could have drawn some conclusions and helped the reader understand why this "50's" approach to management was appropriate and effective in this situation, but would not be so in other situations, both in and out of the fast-food restaurant industry. Why couldn't/shouldn't every story written in the popular business press include a "grounding" in the Performance Logic of that industry and company, and go on to describe how the content of this particular story impacted the PL variables and desired organization outputs. If a business story cannot relate to the Performance Logic of the subject company, why is it being written anyhow?

2. *Understanding and managing the growing complexity of today's businesses.* In the past, when a business organization got too large and/or complex to manage, the solution was to break it into smaller, "more manageable" components such as groups, sectors, divisions, strategic business units, regions, districts, and in some cases, separate businesses. The response was basically to segment the business in some fashion and delegate responsibility for results downward-sort of a "divide and conquer" response. Sometimes this segmentation made sense. Often it did not in terms of optimizing the business. As today's business has gotten more global and interdependent and the lines between suppliers, customers, and competitors is getting very fuzzy, it is harder to ignore the fundamental fact that our business organizations are *systems* and they cannot be arbitrarily whacked into segments small enough so that some executive can get their "head around" it. It is time to face the fact that "it's a system, stupid!" A classic example of the "divide and conquer" approach to complexity was the way many of the major petroleum companies divided their Value Chain of exploration, production, refinement, distribution, and retail sales into separate companies.

Today, however, it is necessary to manage all these components of the value chain as a system-as a single entity-in order to optimize the return from a barrel of crude. A daunting task, but necessary and possible with the appropriate "systems view" and today's information technology. In order to manage the complexity of today's businesses, it is necessary to:

    a)   understand the total business system, including the *performance logic* of the industry and company.

    b)   select the Points of Leverage that will provide the necessary competitive edge.

    c)   establish the Performance Measurement and Management System required to manage the "organization as a system". Then you can begin to manage the organization as the complex system that it is.

3. *Managing.* To a large extent, a great deal of management these days could be characterized as "management by myth" - each individual executive/ manager is operating on the insight they have figured out for their corner of the business. Every district sales manager has their unique insights into what must be managed for success, learned through years of experience. Same for every department head on every shift in manufacturing, to say nothing of every plant or facility manager. And likewise, for everyone in procurement, from individual buyer to vice president. Each has developed or inherited a "myth" for what is important to manage, and each is very reluctant to share their myth, as it is their "black magic" or individual "competitive edge", so to speak. (You can see why trying to develop a rational measurement system in such an environment is an impossible task.) And of course, Management by Myth in turn contributes to the perception that a business is overwhelmingly complex. Application of the notion of Performance Logic can lead to Management by Logic, rather than Myth. With the PL, it is possible to:

    a)   identify and articulate the variables, and their relationship, that impact the necessary organization outputs. This Logic can be driven down from organization outputs such as profit to every corner (i.e., shift, district, product, etc.) of the business.

    b)   get agreement from all members of management as to the variables, their relationship, and Points of Leverage. Individual "myths" are dragged out of the dark and tested against the bright light of the developing Performance Logic of the business. Based on the collective experience of managers, agreement is reached on the best action to take in the event of deviations from desired performance.

    c)   communicate to all managers, regardless of level, what variables they need to watch and what action they are to take in the case of deviations from target.

    d)   develop a measurement system that will provide the information necessary to manage the agreed upon Points of Leverage at every level in the organization.

When managing by Logic, we will no longer tell managers "as long as you get the results, we don't care what goes on in your operation". Managers will be expected to identify, articulate and communicate the performance logics they are following. These logics will be "public" and will undergo close scrutiny by senior management. Measures will be continuously reviewed by all levels of management to assure that they reflect the latest Points of Leverage. In one organization where we introduced this form of management, an old line executive commented that we had "taken the virility out of management". Perhaps, but we also doubled profits and reduced expensive turnover by 90% in the first six months.

Based on our experience with the Performance Logic, the only conclusion I can reach is that the Performance Logic is the key to unlocking the secrets to organization effectiveness and success. And I challenge you to give it a try.

References

Rummler, G. A. (November, 1979). *Job Performance Standards and Measures*. A Series of Research Presentations and Discussions from the ASTD Second Annual Invitational Research Seminar, Savannah, Georgia.

Senge, P. M. (1990). The leader's new work: Building learning organizations. *Sloan Management Review*, *32*(1), 1-23.

Discussion of Rummler

Organizational Change and Its Relation to Cultural Change

Ramona Houmanfar
University of Nevada

The behavioral sciences have offered many approaches to the prediction and management of behavior in organizational settings. The impact of behavioral sciences has been mainly demonstrated by their ability to specify techniques and procedures that result in clear and well-documented improvements in performance. These techniques and procedures have enabled organizational analysts and managers to better observe and articulate the role of organizational systems in relation to human performance. The establishment and maintenance of a coherent approach for the analysis of human performance within organizational systems that adheres to fundamental behavior analytic concepts and principles is a challenging task, however. Many scholars and professionals in the field of organizational behavior management have identified this challenge and have made it a subject of many commentaries and discussions in academic and professional settings (e.g., national conferences). In that regard, Rummler's *Performance Logic: The Organizational DNA* is one of a few models that provide a clear basis for understanding human performance within a context of organization systems.

Rummler's Performance Logic establishes the connection between human performance and organization systems by emphasizing and demonstrating the interrelation of performance accomplishments at different levels of the organization. Through establishing this connection, Rummler adds the process level of the organization between the levels of individual performance and the organization systems effect. Accordingly, his model starts at the organization level, with the goal of identifying processes with performance payoffs. At the process level, process improvement steps and jobs with performance payoffs are identified. Finally, job improvement actions are specified at the job performer level. Overall, Rummler's model allows for congruence across three levels —organization, process, job performer— and assures the participation of all employees at all organizational levels in the facilitation of the accomplishment goals of the organization (Dean, 1997).

Rummler's approach toward performance improvement suggests the interrelationship among the accomplishments of top management, middle management and the front line workers. Often, this element of performance analysis is lost or not made explicit and results in speculations regarding the adherence of such an analysis to behavior analytic principles that require the focus on individual performance in relation to others and/or environment.

In general, Rummler's Performance Logic provides a technical approach to organizational change that takes into account the arrangement of social, financial, and technical resources for the production of desired outcome in the context of environmental threats and opportunities. This arrangement implies a large scaled organizational change that influences the organization's culture. However, the interaction between the large scaled change and the culture of the organization and its impact on organizational outcome are not clearly articulated in Rummler's Performance Logic. Before further elaboration on this issue, let us identify and clarify the role of culture in the context of organizational change.

Culture and Organizational Change

From a behavior analytic standpoint, culture in a given organization can be defined as a group of individuals who share similar responses to environmental/organizational stimuli (e.g., rules, policies, mission, vision, other organizational members, etc.). The dominant patterns of behaviors of organizational members resulting from the development of this sort of cultural group are perhaps the most challenging components of any organizational system since they are somewhat informal, contextual, implicit and are strengthened and transmitted interindividually as well as intraindividually. Therefore, the challenge in designing interventions lies in making explicit and available what is usually implicit.

Different factors may influence the degree of consistency among organizational members' behaviors with regard to the organizational stimuli. One factor is the size of organizational environment. The larger the size of the organization, the more susceptible it will become to cultural incongruent. In addition, stability of cultural conduct is said to depend upon the characteristics of the stimulus objects (e.g., logos, plaque, title, etc.) associated with it, such that the more indefinite and pervasive the stimulus object, the more stable the cultural behavior (e.g., ideals, beliefs, etc.) (Kantor, 1982).

One other important factor that may participate in the occurrence of cultural incongruent is cultural diversity. Cultural diversity may occur along such dimensions as ethnic background, education, professional identification, sex and age (Tichy, 1983). Organizational change is also a major factor in the establishment of cultural incongruent.

Types of issues such as size, cultural diversity and organizational change that are inherent parts of any organizational change suggest the importance of organizational alignment in the implementation of such a change (Dean, 1997). One organizational model that deals with these sorts of issues is "Organizational Alignment" model (Dean, 1997). Organizational Alignment model focuses on the interrelationship between strategic and cultural paths to the organizational results and defines these paths and their interdependence. According to this model, the cultural content changes like the technical changes should be examined in relationship to each component of organizational model including the mission strategy, the tasks, the prescribed networks, people, processes and emergent networks. The underlying element in this process is the communication system by which the top management articulates the organizational change. This includes a clear description of what the top management is doing, why are they doing it and how does the change affect the organization's accomplishments and goals. In addition, the top management's support for change should be demonstrated by their actions in an on ongoing manner that will serve as evidence of long-term commitment to the change. Another important component of a desirable cultural change is the clarification of how the new principles/values and practices apply to everyone, from the front line to the boardroom. The clarification of individual's roles in relation to the organizational change can be tied with the ongoing measurement of progress toward the desired outcomes. Further, languages and symbols may influence the maintenance of organizational members' attention and commitment to the ongoing change. Changes in languages and symbols may help organizational members understand the effects of the organizational change on current and desired practices. (Dean, 1997).

In summary, the implementation of Organizational Alignment model provides opportunities for the establishment of a high management credibility, a balance between high productivity and commitment to organizational member, open communication, ownership of strategy, increased innovation, strong productivity and nondiscriminatory ethic. It is the implementation of this sort of model that may insure the achievement and maintenance of change from technological as well as cultural standpoints in any type of organization (public or private). In other words, organizational alignment model allows for the establishment and maintenance of organizational members' shared responses to organizational stimuli that are subject to change in a majority of organizational interventions.

In short, Organizational Alignment perspective allows for further elaboration on Rummler's Performance Logic model in the area of cultural change. One may suggest that an elaboration on cultural change would be a redundant task when dealing with system models such as Performance Logic since such a change is apparent and inherent within the implementation of this type of model. However, the world is full of theories and models about the ways by which groups and individuals should interact, work and live together. The question is how many of these theories and models are successfully implemented and therefore "bough in to" and practiced by individuals and groups? As record shows, Rummler has achieved and maintained the success of his model through its many successful implementations. This type of success however makes one wonder even more about how the issue of "resistance to change" as it pertains to cultural change has been dealt with by successful organizational consultants such as Rummler? In other words, how is organizational alignment achieved through the implementation of Performance Logic? How the effect and/or influence of Performance Logic model on organizational culture is measured or systematically manipulated?

Conclusion

The challenge in designing organizational interventions lies in making explicit and available what is usually implicit (i.e., cultural practices). From a technological standpoint, Rummler's Performance Logic provides a comprehensive approach toward the implementation of a productive system of management. The implementation of this model suggests the establishment of a democratic vs. autocratic or horizontal vs. vertical system of performance management. However, the precise specification and demonstration of the means by which such changes influence the culture and the dominant patterns of organizational members' behaviors is a challenge that is worth the direct attention of behavior analysts- engineers of human behavior- in the field of Organizational Behavior Management.

References

Dean, P. J., & Ripley, D. E. (Eds.). (1997). *Performance improvement pathfinders: Models for organizational learning.* Washington, DC: The International Society for Performance Improvement.

Dean, P. J., & Ripley, D. E. (Eds.). (1997). *Performance improvement interventions: Culture & systems change.* Washington, DC: The International Society for Performance Improvement.

Kantor, J. R. (1982). *Cultural psychology.* Chicago, IL: Principia Press.

Tichy, N. M. (1983). *Managing strategic change: Technical, political, and cultural dynamics.* New York, NY: John Wiley & Sons, Inc.

Organization-Environment Systems as OBM Intervention Context: Minding Your Metacontingencies

Thomas C. Mawhinney
University of Detroit Mercy

Introduction

Most if not all of the participants in The Nevada Conference on Organizational Change are members of a human culture called Organizational Behavior Management (OBM) by people outside the culture and by many of its participants. As the culture's name implies, people involved in changing organizations in the OBM tradition are concerned with the effective management of behavior in organizations. However, they are not often interested in the management of behavior simply to show that it can be managed. More often than not they are interested in devising ways of managing behavior so it more reliably contributes to effective organizational performance and improved quality of working life among members of organization(s) in which performance is improved (Daniels, 1977). Effective organizational performance arises from accurately describing and then creating and managing the relations among system components that result in the organization being "competitive, adaptive (reactively and proactively), and focused on continuous performance improvement" (Rummler & Brache, 1995). Effective organizational performance, of course, arises from correctly defining, measuring, and rewarding performances of organizational members as individuals and/or as groups (Abernathy, 1996; Komaki & Reynard, in press). The policies, programs, and tools they adopt with respect to the management of human motivation and skills required to improve organizational performances are dominated by positive as opposed to aversive methods of behavior change management and control (Abernathy, 1996; Brethower, 1982; Daniels, 1977, 1989, 1994; Mawhinney, 1984). They know what constitutes coercion (Sidman, 1989) and exploitation (Baum, 1994, 1995). More importantly, from a normative vantage point, they prefer to avoid creating cultures in which aversive and coercive behavior change and control policies and programs constitute the typical modus operandi (Abernathy, 1996; Daniels, 1994).

In this chapter the following ideas are presented and developed: 1) the OBM culture is not a monolith, 2) it is comprised of two easily discriminated subcultures, 3) both recognize the need to conduct organizational analyses to simplify problem spaces before developing solutions, 4) both work from the assumption that selection by consequences explains evolution of behavior repertoires, 5) selection by consequences operates on variation within populations across time and on operant behavior within individuals resulting in stimulus control of behavior, 6) verbal behavior is operant behavior that comes under stimulus control of its environment and is observed in verbal rule-governed behavior and problem solving behavior, 7) organizational cultures can be described by classes of verbal behavior called emic and/or etic, 8) behavior in and performance of organizational cultures is described by their respective metacontingencies that interact within an organizational ecology, 9) selection by consequences operates on the variation among organizations that compete within a common organizational ecology, and 10) organizational leadership involves the management of organizational metacontingencies.

Two Subcultures of OBM

Within the OBM culture one can identify two traditions or subcultures. Systematic research would likely reveal additional subcultures. I focus on these because of their readily identifiable practices that distinguish between them while recognizing that the work of some OBM researchers reflects elements of both subcultures (e.g., LaFleur & Hyten (1995) and Redmon & Mason (in press)). Each approaches the design and evaluation of OBM interventions from somewhat different yet compatible vantage points. One I shall term the *natural sciences* vantage point and the other the *engineering and systems sciences* vantage point. The term science appears in the name I have applied to each culture. And the ways in which members of these subcultures approach the causal analyses of individual, group, and organizational behavior and performance can be called scientific (cf., Skinner (1953) and Gilbert (1992)).

The natural sciences vantage point includes a concern for developing and using terms and concepts from the evolving science of behavior called behavior analysis (see Baum, 1994). In addition to improving organizations, members of this subculture seek to foster use of behavior analytic terms and concepts in descriptions of organizational phenomena. They usually pay some attention to validating generality of behavioral principles in field settings using ABA reversal and multiple baseline intervention designs (Komaki & Goltz, in press; Parsonson & Baer, 1978; Sidman, 1960) to establish reliability of OBM intervention effects in work organizations. The engineering and systems science vantage point, on the other hand, reflects less concern for extending the use of terms, concepts, and research methods of behavior analysis within their field interventions. Members of this subculture appear more concerned with how behavior principles fit into the design and optimization of larger performance systems. They often focus on entire organizational systems or organizational cultures as the context in which behavior principles are *presumed* to operate within and in conjunction with organizational system processes (Rummler & Brache, 1995).

Tom Gilbert (1978) provided insights into the pivotal practice that distinguishes these two subcultures from one another. He devoted virtually all of one chapter entitled "The behavior engineering model" to explicating what he considered differences between what I have called the natural science conception of behavior and performance as *valued accomplishments* that depend on other factors in complex organizations *in addition to behavior per se*. In Gilbert's (1992) words, *"Behavior, you*

take with you; accomplishments, you leave behind" [emphasis in the original text] (p. xv).
He also noted that philosophers of science had once evaluated scientific contributions "using a three-edged ruler: *parsimony, elegance,* and *utility*" [emphasis in the
original text] (Gilbert, 1992, p. xv). More import to my current contention, that the
natural sciences and engineering and systems science approaches to OBM are
compatible, is Gilbert's (1992) comparison of Skinner's system for describing the
development of behavior-environment relations with development of Newtonian
physics:

> If we look at the development of Newtonian physics, we see how closely
> it adhered to these characteristics [parsimony, elegance, and utility]. The
> same is true of Skinner's rules of reinforcement: they explain development
> of behavior patterns with great parsimony, elegance, and utility. (p. xv)

The two subcultures overlap with one another and are, for the most part,
compatible. Links between the two cultures are the works of B. F. Skinner (1953),
Dale Brethower (1972; 1982), Tom Gilbert (1978), and more recently, Rummler and
Brache (1995). (Work by Rummler and Brache (1992) appears to be indirectly
connected to Skinner's work via connections between their conceptual framework
and Brethower's.)

Simplicity and Brethower's Bridge

The work of Dale Brethower (1972, 1982) may represent some of the earliest and
most direct recognition of linkages between the complexity of human behavior and
management of complex behavior systems in organizations so as to achieve desired
consequences from their environments. One of his more important insights can
appear paradoxical. He contends that complexity of individual and group operant
behavior and organization-environment relationships can and must be reduced to
an underlying simplicity before it can be effectively managed.

The bridge between simplicity of behavior explained in terms of contingencies
of reinforcement (Skinner, 1953; 1969) and the complexity of behavior in organizational systems appears in Brethower's (1972; 1982) conception of a *Total Performance System* (TPS). A central point of Dale's approach to analysis of behavior in
organizational systems and the management of a system's performance is that
complexity of behavior and performance systems must be reduced to a level that
brings understanding and solutions within the kin of human information processing
capabilities (Brethower, 1982). For this reason Dale's model aims to simplify the
complex before attempting to manage it. This feature of the TPS model and
approach to management permitted me to effectively introduce the idea of behavior
systems and organizational systems management to hundreds of business students;
and they gave it a good reception.

Dale's (Brethower, 1982) generic TPS model (see Figure 1) can be applied to
identify contingencies among goal directed actions within a processing system (in
conjunction with inputs to it), outputs resulting from those actions and the
environmental consequences of those outputs. Outputs of a system can be evaluated
relative to the system's internal output goals and standards via the processing system

feedback loop. Usually, however, ultimate effectiveness of a processing system depends on effects its outputs have on its receiving system. And, assessment of these effects relative to effects sought by managers of a processing system, e.g., in formal for-profit organizations, depends on delayed feedback from the receiving system via the receiving system feedback loop. The processing system can be defined as a person, a group of persons, a department in a complex organization, or a goods producing or service delivery organization. The objective of this sort of simplification of complex processing system-receiving system interactions is to reveal when, why, and how activities of the processing system must be changed to adapt its goals, objectives, and outputs to requirements of its receiving system. Survival of the processing system usually pivots on its satisfying requirements of its receiving system, e.g., customers and clients. The TPS is essentially an outline or guide to effective performance system analysis and performance system engineering and management when the objective is to adapt the processing system to its receiving system. This basic model can be elaborated to comprehend the complexity of modern corporate structures as Rummler and Brache (1995) have demonstrated. And, I shall deal with additional complications when I eventually develop the organizational metacontingency concept. In terms of the simple TPS in Figure 1, a metacontingency is the "if ... then" relationship between all behavior within the processing system and all consequences of it measured by the receiving system's response to processing system outputs which feeds back to the processing system via the receiving system feedback loop.

Total Performance System Model Including Elements of a Simple Metacontingency

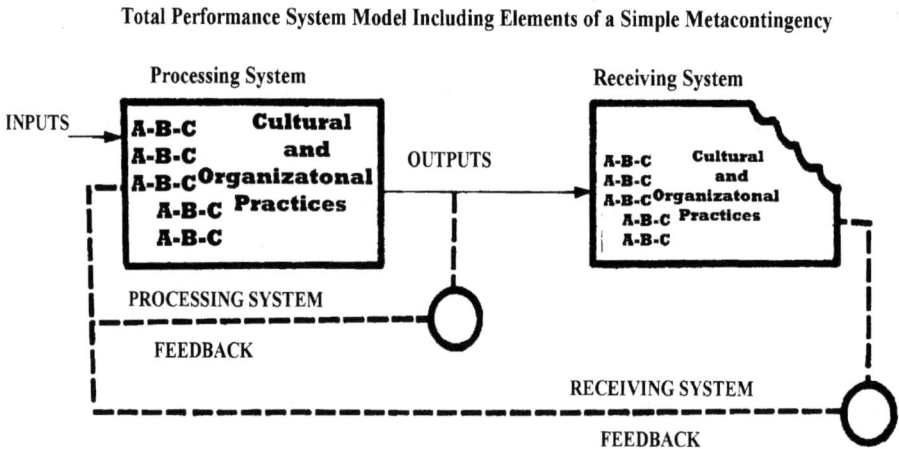

Figure 1. An adaptation of Brethower's (1972) Total Performance System model showing basic elements of a metacontingency between practices controlled by behavioral contingencies (A-B-Cs) within a processing system (human culture) and consequences of them arising from behavioral contingencies (A-B-Cs) of a receiving system in response to the processing system's outputs.

I have placed A-B-Cs within the processing system and the receiving system components of the generic organizational TPS depicted in Figure 1. Some of them are labeled cultural practices and some are labeled organizational practices. Their presence in the figure is intended to emphasize the fact that in the absence of human behavior as defined by the natural sciences OBM subculture *there would be no point in talking about systems processes and their performance* upon which the engineering and system sciences subculture focuses its attention. What should be clear is that what people do within a processing system or organizational culture has delayed environmental consequences that are complicated by their interactions with what other people do, e.g., consumers of their goods or services delivered as outputs. Effects of competitors will be observed in receiving system feedback, but with some delay and need for interpretation of feedback. For example, receiving system feedback can change because of a change in processing system outputs or a change in the way the receiving system responds to those outputs because of a change in the outputs (competing products or services) of another processing system, i.e., a competitor. Whether individuals and groups within a processing system can directly respond to them or not, there exist contingent relationships between the behavior and practices of all members of a focal processing system and aggregate behavior of their customers or clients. These contingent relations are what is called an organization's metacontingency and, as noted above, Figure 1 represents a bare bones model of a metacontingency. This and related concepts will be fleshed out in more detail later.

I shall not develop a detailed integration of the natural science and engineering and systems science vantage points in OBM. Suffice it to say I think the connection between the two ways of talking about complex organizational phenomena will become apparent as I develop several themes in the remainder of this chapter.

Selection by Consequences as a Causal Mode: A Unifying Concept

I believe both subcultures, implicitly if not explicitly, agree that selection by consequences is the fundamental causal mode responsible for evolution of individual behavior repertoires and organizational cultures. Rummler and Brache (1995) express de facto agreement with this proposition when they assert that organizations "adapt or die." Organizations that are better managed have a better chance of survival than poorly managed organizations. And management groups that foster and engage in "deadly" practices will contribute to the death of their organizations as well as the eventual extinction of their "deadly" management practices, at least in the organizations that perish because of them (Mawhinney, 1992a).

It is now accepted as fact that species and living entities (e.g., human cultures and formal organizations) that have not adapted to environmental requirements for their continued life have perished from the community of living things on earth. Every *living entity*, including human cultures called formal organizations, at any given time, is a product of the causal mode of selection by consequences extant that point in time (Lovelock, 1988). Having survived up to some moment in time, however, does not insure survival beyond that point in time.

In "Selection by Consequences" (1981) Skinner pointed out the fundamental difference between laws of physics stated in ahistoric equations of classical mechanics and the causal mode of selection by consequences that takes history into account when explaining current events. Selection by consequences is well accepted as an explanation of the origin of species by natural selection. Although less well accepted as an explanation of human action, it is also evident in the origins of operant behavior repertoires. These human repertoires include *language* defined in terms of verbal behavior of a verbal community (Skinner, 1957). And verbal behavior, according to Skinner, is much involved in the creation of human cultures and practices that occur within them (Skinner, 1981). Skinner's more controversial position holds that human cultural practices and whole human cultures are the product of the casual mode of selection by consequences. Before turning to an analysis of organizational culture defined by dominant cultural practices comprising an organization and the organization-environment system they create, I want to present several literally graphic examples of this causal process in action.

Examples of the Process of Selection by Consequences as a Causal Mode

A hypothetical example of the way in which natural selection produces an anatomical trait such as long necks among members of a giraffe population reveals the dynamic character of natural selection. The minimum requirements for natural selection by consequences to operate on something like length of giraffe necks in a population of giraffes through some number of successive generations are the following (Baum, 1994):

1. Whatever environmental condition makes longer necks contribute a better survival and reproduction rate among giraffes with longer necks must remain in place long enough to have an impact on successive generations of giraffe.

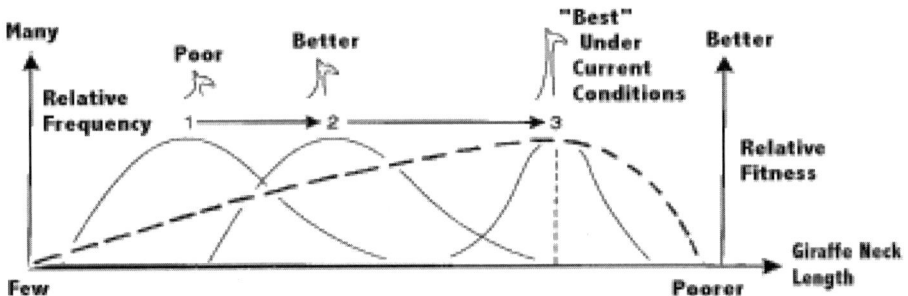

Figure 2. Dynamics of an anatomical trait (giraffe neck length) change during evolution explained by the causal mode of selection by consequences as adapted from Baum (1994).

2. The variation in neck length must reflect at least some influence of genetic variation.
3. There must be competition such that longer necks make for an advantage in reproduction among giraffe that inherit genes for longer necks.

Figure 2 is a graphic depiction of the hypothetical evolution of increased frequency of longer neck length among successive generations of giraffe as a function neck length contribution to fitness within a given environmental niche. The long dashed curve depicts relative fitness of short and successively longer neck lengths given whatever environmental conditions make longer neck length advantageous. As successive generations of giraffe with longer necks are more productive of offspring carrying the genetic material responsible for longer necks, the frequency of giraffe with longer necks increases; note the succession of bell-shaped curves, 1, 2, and 3, under three different neck lengths pictured. The increase in neck lengths terminates at some point when it begins to be dysfunctional and the distribution of neck lengths narrows around a relatively optimal length.

To explain the length of necks among giraffe one does not appeal to local events and the mechanics of neck lengths. And, changing neck lengths cannot be observed at a moment in time since natural selection is *a process that unfolds through time and across generations*. In addition, the explanation of neck length *does not reside in the present*. It resides in the history of the species interactions with environmental conditions that selected for this trait. And, for that reason, neck length could become *maladaptive* or *dysfunction* if environmental conditions for which it best fitted the species for survival *changed* in a way that nullified this erstwhile anatomical advantage. Later I note how highly adaptive organizational practices during one era of an organization's life can, in similar fashion, become deadly following a shift in what its environment defines as adaptive practices.

Anyone who has shaped the topography of an operant behavior under highly controlled laboratory conditions will recognize the parallel, but not an isomorphism, between the hypothetical example above and empirical evidence of effective operant behavior shaping. (For an excellent graphic depiction of shaping in the pigeon see Eckerman, Hienz, Stern, and Kowlowitz (1980) Figures 2 and 3 (pp. 303-304)). For an example of a complex human team behavior shaping experiment see Burnstein and Wolff (1964).)

Selection by consequences as a causal mode can be directly observed in operant conditioning processes. It is observed when behavior changes in conformity with the law of effect (Baum, 1973). The law of effect selects for increased frequency of effective behavior topographies and other targeted dimensions of behavior. *Effectiveness* is defined in terms of contact with reinforcement and escape from or avoidance of punishment. By the same token, it selects against ineffective behavior by extinguishing it from the individual's operant repertoire in a given environmental context. As in natural selection, there must be environmental conditions that remain in effect long enough for effective and ineffective dimensions of behavior to be respectively selected for (reinforced) and against (extinguished). This role is filled by three-term (A-B-C) environmental contingencies (Poling & Braatz, in press) that

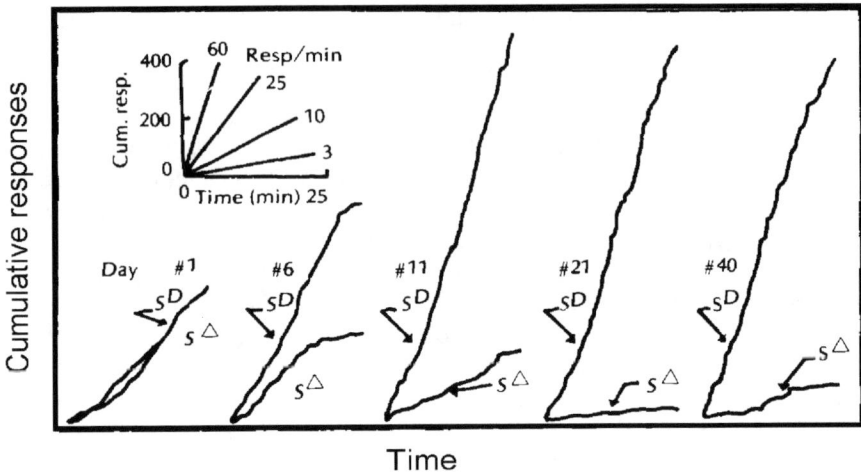

Figure 3. Selected daily cumulative records from daily sessions of one rat exposed to forty days of discrimination training (Herrick, Myers, & Korotkin, 1959).

arrange for differential reinforcement and extinction to select for and against variations in dimensions of the individual's behavioral outputs.

Just as natural selection cannot be observed at a moment in time, selection by consequences as observed in the operation of the law of effect on dimensions of behavior cannot be observed at a moment in time. When selection by consequences is *operating* on behavior some dimension of the behavior will be changing (e.g., topography, rate, or both) due to reinforcing consequences arising from the behavior's interactions with environmental contingencies (A-B-Cs). This will be most evident when environmental contingencies change such that some behavior or dimension(s) of a behavior undergoes extinction while another behavior or another dimension of a behavior is subjected to reinforcement.

Figure 3 reveals evolution of operant behavior discrimination in the rat as a function of reinforcement in the presence of an S^D and extinction in the presence of an S^Δ when the two conditions were randomly alternated through time (Herrick, Myers, & Korotkin, 1959). (I have used data from the rat because the data from human subjects is not often presented in graphics that so clearly reveal the evolutionary nature of the behavioral process. For reliable evidence of discrimination learning among normal adult humans see Terrace (1974).) At first, the cumulative frequencies of the operant in the presence of the S^D and the S^Δ overlap. As the behavior interacts with the two contingencies, the slopes (rates of responding) in the presence of the S^D and the S^Δ diverge. What is observed is evolution of discriminated operant behavior or different dimensions of behavior (rate in this case) in the presence of different *environmental contexts* where *environmental context* refers to three-term contingencies.

People, however, are often observed in environmental contexts that are stable with respect to reinforcement contingencies. How does one *see* selection by consequences when the individual's environment is not changing and the individual's behavioral repertoire within that environment has already been selected by the causal mode of selection by consequences? The simple answer is that one cannot see it in action under these conditions. But the products of this causal mode can be observed in stimulus control of a behavior that arises from an observed history of reinforcement.

Stimulus control is a change in behavior that occurs when the context of the behavior changes. Put another way, *stimulus refers to a change in context* and *control* refers *to a correlated change in behavior* (Baum, 1994). Stimulus control arises from a history of discrimination learning that brings different behavior under the control of different contexts or different S^Ds. Nevertheless, both people and other animals experience stimulus control of their behavior in the presence of contexts with which they have no specific experience and therefore, no specific reinforcement history. This occurs because invariably some element of their reinforcement history will include experience with contexts that resemble the current context of behavior. Therefore, some sort of behavior occurs even in what are relatively novel situations for the individual. For example, some of the effect of reinforcement in the presence of an S^D usually spreads out or *generalizes* to environmental stimuli ranging above and below the S^D on some stimulus dimension such as sound amplitude, tone, intensity of light, or facial features. The degree to which these other values of environmental stimuli have been selected to control behavior by virtue of their proximity to the S^D can be estimated. Guttman (1956) reinforced pigeon pecks in the presence of a 550

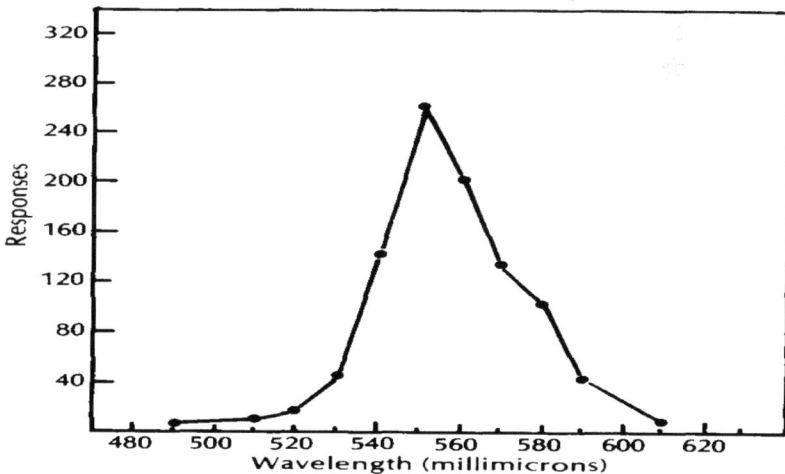

Figure 4. Responses emitted in the presence of different wavelengths randomly illuminating the pecking key one key at a time from beginning to end of extinction of all responding (Guttman, 1956).

millimicron wavelength of light. Then he subjected all behavior emitted by them to extinction. During extinction of all behavior, however, he randomly presented the wavelength used in training (S^D = 550 millimicron) and wavelengths above and below it (i.e., a range of S- s above and below the S^D value). A picture of the subject's "subjective" response to or "perception" of the similarity among antecedent stimuli was then plotted as total number of responses made in the presence of each stimulus value during "total" extinction of responding to antecedent stimulus presentations. Figure 4 is a plot of the resulting behavior frequencies for one such post discrimination training test. The curve in Figure 4 is called a *generalization gradient* and the phenomenon depicted is called *stimulus control* and *generalization*. This generalization gradient provides a picture of stimulus control arising from the causal mode of selection by consequences that selected for the highest rates of responding in the presence of the S^D. To explain this instance of stimulus control, one does not appeal to the *force of the stimulus*, as it were, *knocking* the responses *out of the subject* like a billiard ball's equal and opposite reaction to being struck by a cue ball. Rather, one appeals to a variable that is *not directly observed in the current setting*. That variable is a particular *history of reinforcement* that produces the most reliable stimulus control by the S^D. That same history in conjunction with the biological makeup of the species (a result of natural selection) accounts for the fact that the individual also responds to these other wavelengths. Note, however, that less and less reliable stimulus control is exerted by stimulus values farther and farther from the S^D in each direction. In principle at least, the history of reinforcement that contributed to stimulus control by the S^D and the resulting generalization gradient can be captured and recorded under controlled laboratory conditions such as those recorded and depicted in Figure 3, given data in Figure 3 was a record collected for the pigeon and wavelengths of light rather than the rat and its discriminative stimulus.

Virtually all of us have experienced generalization of stimulus control. It is evident when we call out the name of a person "we know" only to learn that the person to whom we have directed the exclamation is not the person with whom we have a history but a "look alike."

Verbal Behavior, Rules, Rule-governed Behavior, and Problem Solving

Verbal behavior of a speaker can exert stimulus control over the behavior of a listener and vice versa, *if they belong to the same verbal community* (Skinner, 1957). If they belong to the same verbal community their reinforcement histories with respect to this behavior are similar. Verbal behavior can also function as a reinforcer, e.g., approval, praise, or threat. Just as the a 550 millimicron wavelength of light functioned as a S^D due to the pigeon's history of differential reinforcement in its presence the verbal behavior of a speaker often functions as a S^D and exerts stimulus control of the behavior of a listener. Except for covert verbal behavior, verbal behavior emitted by a speaker typically depends on presence of a listener in addition to other dimensions of the speaker's physical environment. When a parent says

"Dinner is served, come and get it," *hungry* (a long time since last eating) children move quickly to the dinner table; during the school day ringing of the school's "lunch bell" has a similar effect on their behavior, but they move quickly to the school's cafeteria. The 550 millimicron wavelength of light, the parent's verbal behavior, and the school lunch bell are all examples of what Skinner (1969) called *contingency specifying stimuli* (or CSS). They point to "if ... then" relations among three-term A-B-C (and more complex) environmental contingencies. Although the specific histories that account for the behavior of the pigeon and children as well as topography and other dimensions of the S^Ds differ among these examples, they all exemplify stimulus control of behavior arising from the casual mode of selection by consequences. The pigeon will not come to the dinner table when "called" by the parent and a 550 millimicron wavelength of light won't bring the children to the dinner table. These examples all share a very important feature. They point to particular reinforcement histories that transformed each class of CSS from a neutral event into one that functioned as an S^D because the CSS effectively predicted when the class of behavior it eventually evoked was reliably followed by a class of events called reinforcers. But, as indicated below, some CSS not only exert stimulus control of a behavior, they "create" or establish consequences as reinforcers associated with the behavior. This possibility has important implications for the management of behavior, particularly in organizational cultures.

Rule-Governed Behavior, Proximate and Ultimate Contingencies

According to Baum (1994) "Skinner (1953, 1969) defined a rule as a verbal discriminative stimulus that points to a contingency" (p. 132). Therefore, in Baum's scheme, *rule-governed behavior* is behavior controlled by verbal discriminative stimuli. As such the rule points to some reinforcement likely to follow the behavior specified and evoked by the speaker's rule statement or CSS. Baum (1994) also contends that "Rule-governed behavior always involves two contingencies: a long-term, *ultimate* contingency – the reason for the rule in the first place – and a short-term, *proximate* contingency of reinforcement for following the rule" (p. 136). In keeping with the natural sciences orientation of behavior analysis, Baum characterizes the long-term or ultimate contingency as one that when followed contributes to the health and reproduction of people who follow the rule. Thus in the example depicted in Figure 5 the speaker's behavior (Bv) is a CSS in the form of a Mand (Skinner, 1957), "Wear shoes," the listener's compliance is the behavior of putting on shoes, which the speaker immediately reinforces with verbal approval or some other sign of affection (S^R). (For alternative terms and concepts used in accounts of verbal behavior and its effects see Cerutti (1989) and Hayes, Zettle, and Rosenfarb (1989).) The connection between putting on shoes and health and eventual opportunity to reproduce is by no means evident to the child being taught to follow the rule. Eventually, however, the mere presence of rough ground out of doors or cold weather may suffice to evoke the practice of putting on shoes. Control of the

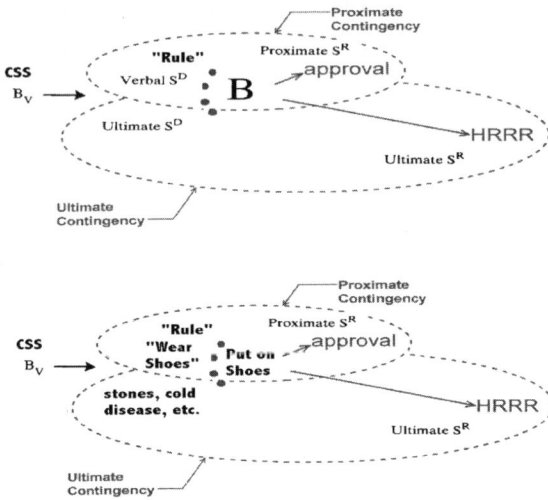

HRRR= Health, Resources, Relationships, & Reproduction

Figure 5. An adaptation of Baum's (1994, 1995) depiction of the two contingencies (proximate and ultimate) responsible for rule learning and rule following behavior. The generic model appears above and a specific example below. The ultimate contingency justifies the proximate rule and can eventually control the behavior in the absence of the rule.

shoe wearing practice, or rule following, is eventually shifted to environmental conditions that justified creation of the rule in the first place.

The parallel in organizational life is found in behavior of formally appointed leaders, unit heads, and managers in whom control over reinforcers in the work place is vested (Mawhinney, in press). They may state many rules of conduct across an array of conditions that they presume will evoke follower behavior in support of organizational goals and objectives. These rules and tactics for insuring organizational members will follow them are supposed to be derived from an analysis of behavior required to support effective organizational performance so that compliance with them contributes to effective organizational performance (Gilbert, 1978). Effective organizational performance arising from member performances should, if properly related to one another, create an ultimate contingency that through time results in organizational performance, survival and job security among organizational members (Brethower, 1982; Deming, 1982; Mawhinney, 1992, 1992a, 1992b; Rummler & Brache, 1995).

What Baum (1994, 1995) calls a proximate contingency is what Malott (1992) calls a *direct acting contingency* or what has traditionally been called a three-term contingency of reinforcement (i.e., $S^D : B \rightarrow S^R$). And, what Baum calls an ultimate contingency is what Malott (1992) calls an *indirect acting contingency*. Both agree that rules stated at the level of indirect acting contingencies are less likely to be effective rules, i.e., less likely to evoke and control behavior. This is because the typical ultimate contingency refers to reinforcers that are delayed or improbable or involves consequences too small to be discriminated even though they reliably accrue to a large amount through time.

Rules Functionally Defined

Rules can, however, be defined functionally. This approach obviates the necessity of drawing a distinction between proximate and ultimate contingencies and effective and ineffective rules. Put most simply, rules can be defined as CSS that have effects on behavior evident in changed behavior after as compared to before contact with the CSS. Why they have any effect, however, still requires some consideration. This approach involves recognizing that contingency specifying stimuli in general and verbal CSS in particular can produce effects that resemble what Michael (1982) has termed establishing operations or EOs. The EO is an event or procedure that alters the functional relations among initially neutral antecedents of behavior transforming them into antecedents that exert stimulus control of behavior (whether they technically qualify as S^Ds or not) or consequences that function as reinforcers (S^Rs) or into both. This idea has been extended to remote stimuli that can exist as environmental contingencies that Baum (1994, 1995) calls ultimate and Malott (1992) calls indirect acting contingencies. And, Agnew (1998) has interpreted a traditional cognitive explanation of goal settings effects (Locke, 1980). These terms and concepts permit OBM theorists and researchers to explain goal setting phenomena using terms and concepts that conform to standards of explanation in the natural as compared to the social sciences (Baum, 1994). For example, consider the following CSS uttered by a speaker: "Anyone who makes quota tomorrow will be awarded $100." This cannot function as a rule of the sort defined by Baum (1994) because the statement cannot immediately function as a S^D that evokes making quota that is immediately followed by receipt of $100. Even if this does accurately describe an ultimate contingency, according to Malott (1992) the reinforcer is too long delayed to function as a reinforcer and probability of attaining the "reinforcer" is not certain. In addition, an event that has not occurred cannot control current behavior unless one is willing to accept a teleological explanation of the intervening behavior. However, the CSS might simply change the functional relationship of all environmental stimuli within contingencies the listener encounters between the time the CSS was stated and the time the listener finishes work the following day, whether the quota is achieved and $100 received or not. For example, a person to whom the CSS was addressed might self-state and follow a rule of setting the alarm clock so as to be awakened earlier than usual the next morning. The person might also depart for work earlier than usual. The person might also spend more time upon arriving early to work arranging work-related tools and materials in ways known to support more efficient performance of the work.

Agnew and Redmon (1992) have suggested that members of the OBM community adopt a definition of "rules" stated and advocated by Schlinger and Blakely (1987) (Blakely & Schlinger, 1987; Schlinger & Blakely, 1994); it comprehends this sort of behavioral phenomenon. *Rules are function-altering contingency specifying stimuli* (Agnew & Redmon, 1992). Whether they qualify as S^Ds when stated or not, therefore, rules as defined by Schlinger and Blakely are *by definition effective* since they must be CSS that evoke behavior change to qualify as rules. If the CSS alters the function of some stimuli from neutral to the status of S^Ds, even with some delay after the CSS has occurred, they result in stimulus control on the occasion of a behavior that would not have occurred absent contact with the CSS. If they alter the function of a behavior's consequences from neutral to the status of reinforcer/punisher with resulting reinforcement/punishment of the behavior, they account for this change in behavior rate that would not have occurred absent the occurrence of the CSS.

Problem solving behavior is essentially a chain of behavior that culminates in the behavior of the problem solver coming under the stimulus control of a CSS that is a solution to the problem (Skinner, 1969). For example, there were two important consequences of Henry Ford's creation of the assembly line. One was a dramatic reduction in time required to assemble a car and the other was an almost equally dramatic rise in worker turnover as skilled crafts workers fled from the routine assembly line work (Halberstam, 1986). Without a sufficient supply of workers demand for cars could not be satisfied no matter how fast an individual worker could assemble them. At some point a verbal CSS occurred regarding the possible effects of increased pay on the supply of workers and the five dollar day pay plan was introduced; it did solve the problem (Halberstam, 1986).

Whether rules as defined above are effective from the vantage point of the speaker *and* contribute to organizational performance is another matter altogether. Other elements of the context in which CSS of a speaker aimed at evoking member rule following behavior that supports ultimate organizational missions, goals, and objectives are likely to determine whether rule statements have desired and planned effects on the behavior of listeners to whom they are directed. One thing seems clear, however. Organizational members can respond to CSS by coming under the control of rules as defined by Agnew and Redmon (1992) while the rules statements they evoke among individuals, e.g., self-stated rules, can vary across individuals as a function of their unique histories of reinforcement.

For example, Fellows and Mawhinney (1997) described an organizational setting in which all telemarketers working in a subunit of a larger telemarketing organization were assigned to a telemarketing pilot study commissioned by a potential client. Their instructions involved verbal CSS describing proximate contingencies in the form of individual daily quotas of phone surveys each was to complete. The justification for this proximate contingency (CSS) was stated in a CSS regarding the ultimate contingency between all telemarketers in the study (N = 7 per day and per evening shift) achieving quota every day for eight five day work weeks and the telemarketer group winning the contract and keeping their jobs. They were also informed (CSS) that failing to achieve quotas and not winning the contract would result in management disbanding the subunit and terminating their employment. During the first three weeks of the pilot study total daily calls completed by both shifts fell appreciably short of the required goal. At the same time, some telemarketers were achieving quota several days of each week while number of calls completed by two telemarketers who worked in adjacent booths exhibited a decidedly downward trend. There was no doubt at that point that absent dramatically improved telemarketer performance during the remaining five weeks the contract was sure to be lost and the work unit disbanded. Management had first to bring its behavior under control of CSS defining a solution. I assisted in this successful problem solving process. A lottery based incentive system was introduced with verbal CSS describing it. Only then did performance improve enough to win the contract.

Managers CSS descriptions of ultimate contingencies in ways *they think* will evoke desired behavior often fail to be confirmed by desired follower behavior changes. More often than not this occurs because managers do not have a good technical understanding of the behavior's controlling variables. This is not to say managers never "get it right." It is only to say that at least sometimes they "get it wrong." And, much of what constitutes the repertoire of managerial thinking (as verbal behavior) arises from their memberships in a national culture, a professional culture, and a specific organizational culture. But, what is meant by the term culture appears to be culturally determined as well.

Emic and Etic Descriptions of Organizational Culture-Organizational Environment Relations

The behavior analytic vantage point on human cultural evolution (Glenn, 1988, 1991; Lamal, 1991) involves interpretation and elaboration of the natural science paradigm cultural anthropologist Marvin Harris (1979) calls cultural materialism. From the vantage point of *cultural materialism,* the behavioral practices and technologies upon which production of life supporting resources and reproduction of one generation after another depend are ultimately selected for and against on the basis of their contributions to these accomplishments. Thus, practices and technologies change in predictable ways with changes in the culture's social and environmental ecology. If fishing techniques are dominant practices resulting in a food supply and the fish population is depleted, another food source and practices required to exploit it must take the place of the fishing-based culture. When a culture's ecology changes in this way the culture will perish unless it discovers practices and technologies required to feed its members and reproduce another generation under the new conditions, i.e., it must engage in problem solving behavior.

Harris (1979) draws on the work of Pike (1967) to identify and distinguish between descriptions of the origins and justification of cultural practices that define human cultures. A culture's practices can be described, understood, and explained from the vantage point of its members or the terms, concepts, methods and analytic procedures of a natural science can be used to describe and explain origins and maintenance of a culture's practices from the vantage point of natural scientists. The former is called an *emic* and the latter an *etic* account. The test of whether an emic account is adequate is whether a native of the culture would understand it. In the words of Harris (1979):

> The test of the adequacy of etic accounts is simply their ability to generate scientifically productive theories about the causes of sociocultural differences and similarities. Rather than employ concepts that are necessarily real, meaningful, and appropriate from the native point of view, the observer is free to use alien categories and rules derived from the data language of science. Frequently, etic operations involve the measurement and juxtaposition of activities and events that native informants may find inappropriate or meaningless. (p. 32)

Currently popular accounts of behavior in organizations and characterizations of what constitutes an organization's culture, while often called scientific, more closely resemble what Harris would call emic than etic accounts of cultural phenomena. The characterization of formal organizational culture developed below, like the account of human rule making and following above, is decidedly and intentionally etic in its approach to the subject matter.

Etic Description of Organizational Culture

An organization's culture is defined in terms of the dominant practices of its members, an explanation of the origins and maintenance of these practices (Redmon & Mason, in press) and connections among these practices and their environmental consequences for the culture as a whole. Cultural practices are learned behavior repertoires that are transmitted from one generation of the culture's membership to another and between cultural groups without benefit of genetics (Harris, 1979). Transmission of culture involves social operant behavior reinforcement processes including modeling and imitative behavior in conjunction with shaping via differential reinforcement among members of the cultural unit (Glenn, 1988; 1991). (These modes of transmission also fall into the category of experiences that have function altering effects on elements of environmental contingencies and thereby change behavior repertoires (Schlinger & Blakely, 1994).) In conformity with the way Harris (1979) accounts for evolution of cultural practices, Redmon and Mason (in press) note that these practices are characterized in terms of their effects on the environment "(e.g., production, reproduction): practices which are effective in gaining resources or offsetting threats are repeated, whereas those which are ineffective in producing survival-related outcomes occur less often and, eventually disappear." In complex modern organizational cultures, however, practices that were once functional can be maintained by powerful behavior level reinforcement contingencies that survive in the culture long after a change in the organization's environment has transformed them from functional to potentially deadly practices (Mawhinney, 1992a).

One of the most important functions of organizational leadership is analysis of relations between practices in the organization and their survival related environmental consequences. If the organization's leadership does not recognize environmental changes that transmute practices from functional to deadly and act quickly and effectively enough to extinguish (replace) them, they will "eventually disappear." But, the reason for disappearance of these offensive practices will have been death of the organizational culture within which they once resided (Mawhinney, 1992a). According to Redmon and Mason (in press), "a model of cultural change should include methods of observing and describing what is done and techniques for identifying variables which influence what is done." This orientation reflects a concern for identifying and extinguishing *dysfunctional practices* that may occur in an organization and fostering adoption and maintenance of more *functional practices* with functional and dysfunctional being defined with respect to practices that make for a more *adaptive organization* (Rummler & Brache, 1995).

However, the model that management develops in the form of verbal CSS describing how their organization is related to its environment has much to do with where and how management looks for clues regarding environmental changes that might call for changes in their cultural practices. Management has historically been trained to think of themselves as commanders of the fate of their organizations who can set up and achieve a wide array of objectives. While management thinking and action remains critical to organizational performance, it is now recognized that forces larger than any given management group play an important role in an organizational culture's evolution and survival. This is revealed in the natural science based description of selection by consequences operating at the level of a population of organizational types that share and compete within an organizational ecology (Hannan & Freeman, 1989; Mawhinney, 1992a). The concept that connects the vantage points of cultural materialism and organizational ecology is "metacontingencies."

Etic Description of Organizational-Environment Systems: Metacontingencies

Organizational metacontingencies are contingent relations between dominant practices in an organization and outcomes of those practices (Glenn, 1991; Mawhinney, 1992a; Redmon & Mason, in press). For example, the outcome of the management practice of simply providing a verbal CSS to telemarketers concerning the ultimate contingency between making quota, winning the contract, and survival of the telemarketer group described above was ineffective and would have proven deadly to that group if it had not been supplemented with another practice. When that practice was supplemented with a lottery-based incentive for making quota the group's outputs changed in that performance rates improved dramatically among telemarketers. As a consequence of improved performance the contract was won and the telemarketer group not only survived, it prospered (Fellows & Mawhinney, 1997). Given the simplicity of this organizational unit and its receiving system (a client that would award a multi-million dollar contract contingent on effective

performance during the eight week pilot study) it can be depicted as a variation of
Figure 1. This would involve identifying the quota system as a dominant organizational practice within the processing system during baseline or prior to any
performance improvement intervention. To this processing system one would add
the practice of providing a one week lottery-based incentive system. To evaluate a
change in the metacontingency from the vantage point of Figure 1, one would have
to examine processing system outputs relative to the output goal specified by its
receiving system; the telemarketers' client in this instance. This would involve
evaluation of receiving system feedback as its own outputs relative to the receiving
system's goal. Processing system feedback can be more or less useful depending on
how it is treated for purposes of evaluating performance. The data plotted in Figure
6 permit the observer to see, week-by-week, any differences between cumulative
number of calls completed by all telemarketers for seven weeks of the pilot study and
the receiving system's cumulative call completion requirements upon which winning the contract (solid line) depended. When the receiving system's requirements
(the solid goal line) are plotted and processing system outputs are plotted relative to
those requirements, the relative performance of the processing system is graphically
depicted through time, thus it provides a picture of a rudimentary metacontingency
through time. If one knew the exact decision rule the client would apply when
awarding the contract and also had data on performance of other processing systems
competing for the contract a more complicated version of the metacontingency
could be depicted, i.e., how "our" telemarketers are stacking up against the
competition from day-to-day. For all we know, function altering effects of CSS in the
form of metacontingency feedback of this sort might have "motivated" effective
telemarketer performance in the absence of either quotas or a lottery-based incentive. What is clear, however, is that the incentive system was added to the quota

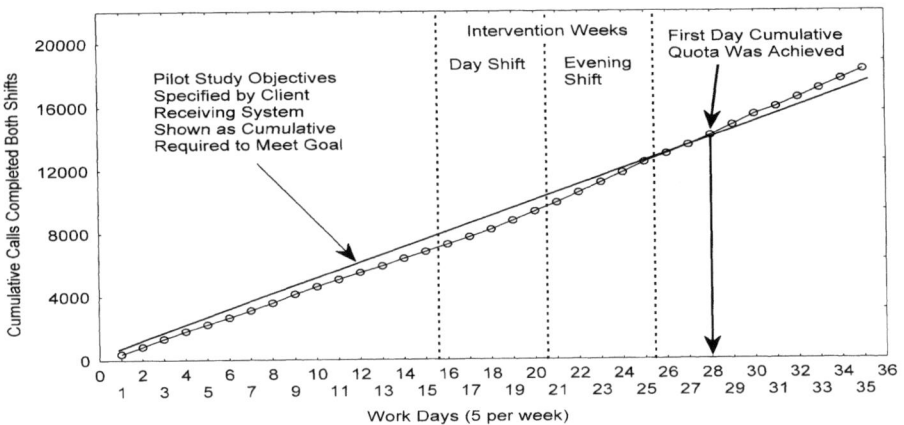

*Figure 6. Cumulative calls completed (open circles) compared to pilot study goal/objective
(solid line) for seven weeks of an eight week pilot study (Fellows & Mawhinney, 1997).*

system for each shift of telemarketers for one week in multiple baseline fashion. And, even with addition of the lottery, the "survival" requirement (cumulative calls above the goal or solid line) was not reached until three days after the second leg of the intervention with the evening shift.

Functional Definition of Organizational Metacontingency

Few organizational cultures are simple enough that their survival can be accounted for by a single dominant practice briefly added to other practices with consequences of the added practice as clearly evident as those plotted in Figure 6. Yet, each complex organizational culture, at least in principle, can be described in terms of its *unique* organizational "metacontingency." Redmon and Mason (in press) have succinctly characterized the complex generic *metacontingency* concept as follows:

> A metacontingency describes how classes of practices common to a group are related to molar consequences and refers to collective practices which determine the survival of a group as a whole. Metacontingencies operate concurrently with local contingencies which affect the practices of individuals or subgroups and may be compatible with or in conflict with local contingencies. In the case of a metacontingency, if the practices of large numbers of members of a culture lead to adaptation to the environment and survival, then the practices which succeeded are likely to be passed on to other members and be perpetuated.

Each complex formal organizational culture is defined by a complex metacontingency the outcomes of which are only partially under the direct control of the culture's leadership. This is because the more complex the culture the more

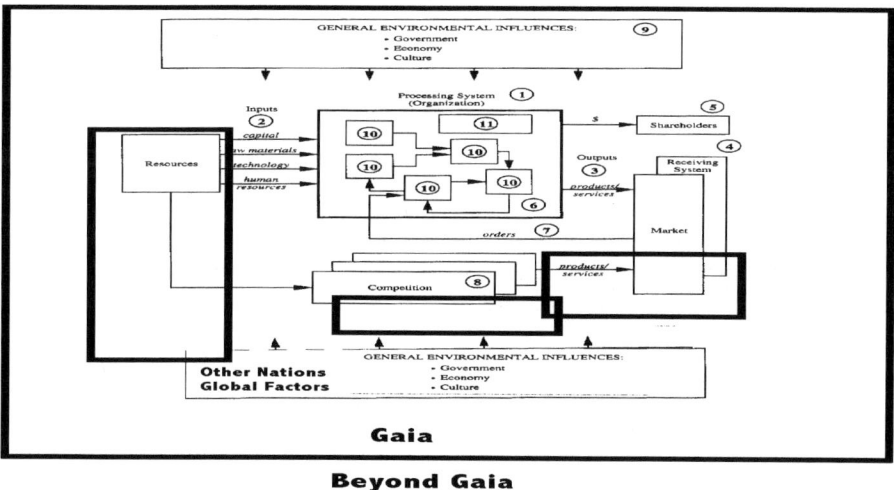

Figure 7.

the effects of its outputs on customers or clients as feedback from them (e.g., satisfaction, rate of consumption, and prices paid) depend on the actions of other organizational cultural units in its environment. In addition, these competing organizational cultures have effects on the supply and costs of human, financial, and raw materials inputs of the culture. This complexity becomes evident when Dale's (1972; 1982) simple generic TPS is sufficiently elaborated to reflect virtually all the other organizational cultural units (in addition to individual customers or clients) the activities of which interact with those of the focal culture's practices in determining its performance. I have added global elements to the Rummler and Brache (1995) elaboration of the TPS so that it reflects complexities arising from global competition (see Figure 7).

Organizational Ecology and Selection by Consequences

Figure 7 depicts a focal organizational culture in relation to its environment using a *block diagram*. What this sort of model does not include is a specific account of the dynamic relationships among all the organizational cultural entities comprising an organizational population and its environment. An account of these dynamic relations is provided by the academic theorists and researchers who work within the discipline called *organizational ecology* (Hannan & Freeman, 1989). Researchers in this tradition of organizational behavior and theory have developed methods of describing and predicting how the casual mode of selection by consequences operates *across metacontingencies of organizational cultures* that compete within an organizational ecology. This vantage point resembles the vantage point of selection for long necks among giraffe, but it is not isomorphic. The grist for the selection mill in this case is variation *among* organizational cultures that comprise an organizational population within a given ecology. This would include the focal organization in Figure 7 and all its competitors. Their metacontingencies are interrelated by virtue of the fact that they compete for common resources on the input side and common consumers or clients on the output side. Rather than being fixed, as in the case of the giraffe's environment, the selecting environment in the case of organizational cultures is typically dynamic. The bases of competition tend to change as organizational cultures discover and invent new ways of attracting customers to their outputs at the expense of other cultures. But, if those other cultures "catch on" quickly enough and change effectively they remain in the competitive "game" of life in their ecology. Staying in this game or surviving depends on changing in ways and at rates dictated by their evolving environment or better, being a leader of effective (e.g., best practices) change in that environment. Cultures that don't evolve practices or imitate leaders or change as their environments change, *perish*, sooner or later. That is, *their metacontingency ceases to exist*. I have described the connection between this paradigm and OBM in some detail elsewhere (Mawhinney, 1992a). Here I shall only sketch out the important lessons that can be drawn from the research results of organizational ecologists. These lessons should be of interest to OBM people whose theoretical and research efforts are aimed at learning how complex organizational cultures can be developed to perform better with performance including a capacity for relatively nimble adaptation to changing environmental conditions (cf. Rummler & Brache, 1995).

Selection by Consequences Across Organizational Metacontingencies: The Auto Industry

When Hannan and Freeman (1989) looked for evidence of highly adaptive, nimble, and long lived organizational cultures they did not find as many as they had anticipated. This led them to consider the possibility that selection by consequences did not operate solely on variation in innovative cultural and technological practices within organizations selecting for practices that were more adaptive and against those less adaptive. They began contemplating the possibility that selection by consequences might sculpt improved cultural and technological practices among members of an organizational population from variation that occurs among organizations populating a given organizational ecology or industry group.

The focal organization in Figure 7, its competitors, suppliers, and so on constitute one way of envisioning an organizational ecology. Hannan and Freeman (1989) looked for evidence that the activity among organizational cultures populating an organizational ecology through a sufficiently long time would reveal effects of the causal mode of selection by consequences operating across variations in their practices, technologies and other features of organizational cultures. From this vantage point, I have contended that selection by consequences will cull from a given organizational population or members of a common niche or ecology, those that engage too long in deadly practices. This will leave the population or ecology with survivors that, at the moment at least, have not engaged in deadly practices too long.

From their empirical work, Hannan and Freeman (1989) learned that rates of births, deaths and survival within an industry were predicable using methods analogous to those used to analyze biological populations that compete for niches within a common domain of natural resources. According to this view, practices and technologies of an organizational culture might be effective for relatively long time intervals making it unlikely they can be changed quickly if something changed the culture's environment in ways that changed existing practices from functional to deadly. Organizations that perish because they cannot change quickly enough when their practices turn deadly take those deadly practices with them, as it were, to their grave. And, members of surviving organizations in the same population, one would think, would avoid those practices while seeking to imitate the practices of surviving industry leaders. But, the leader's practices might be functional only until the next environmental shock might call them into question or some other organization might ascend to industry leadership. Ford's failure to quickly follow GM's lead with respect to the practices of offering consumers paint color options and sleek body styles cost him 50% of his market share (Halberstam, 1986), the Big Three all suffered when Japanese producers successfully entered their markets and they changed too slowly, and GM's market share has been in something of a decline ever since (Mawhinney, 1992a).

If this is a realistic scenario, it suggests why it is so important to design or engineer into formal organizational cultures practices that will contribute to their maintaining some degree of flexibility and some level of nimbleness that will permit them to adapt when adaptation is called for. To a certain extent, however, adaptation is an ongoing process. One of the variables that Hannan and Freeman (1989) identified that distinguished between survivors and casualties during the evolution of an industry was rate of technological innovation. Members of an industry or competitive organizational ecology that fell off the pace of industry leaders were more likely to perish than those that remained close to the leader's pace. Older cultures were found to be more vulnerable to death given a major shift in the organizational ecology *if new organizations were still being created with some frequency.* This occurred because the new organizational cultures were founded on practices among mangers and workers fitted specifically to the most advanced production or service technologies used by the newly created cultures. Older cultures required to adopt these new technologies were also required to extinguish old practices and introduce and reinforce adoption of new ones. It should come as no surprise that the longer organizations survive the more difficult it is to change practices that have a long history of success and acceptance. Unless those practices support (reinforce) being constantly flexible and judiciously innovative per se they can become deadly when the environment shifts. Organizational ecologies that have a long evolutionary history during which the causal mode of selection by consequences has been operating should show some signs of this process. And, the domestic auto industry does.

It is worth noting that the vantage points reflected in the work of Hannan and Freeman (1989) are etic and not emic. Thus, there is no reason to expect that current industry leaders will accept or believe their account of the evolution of their particular industry. By the same token, there is no reason to believe that leaders and

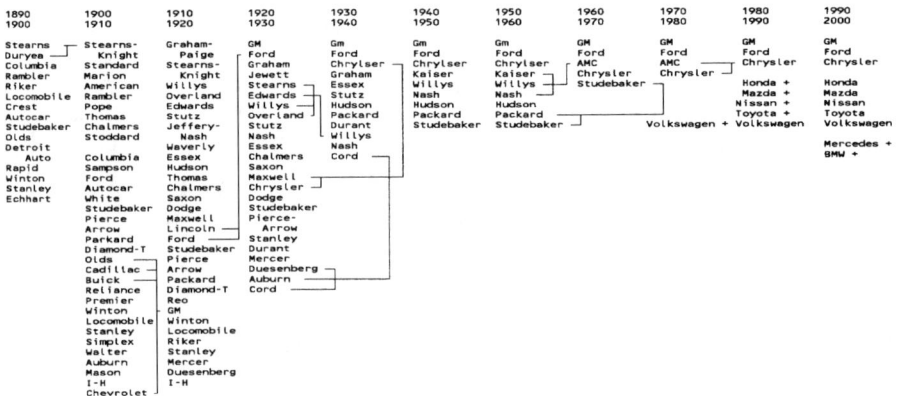

1890 1900	1900 1910	1910 1920	1920 1930	1930 1940	1940 1950	1950 1960	1960 1970	1970 1980	1980 1990	1990 2000
Stearns	Stearns-Knight	Graham-Paige	GM	Gm	Ford	Gm	GM	GM	GM	GM
Duryea	Standard	Stearns-Knight	Ford	Ford	Chrylser	Ford	Ford	Ford	Ford	Ford
Columbia	American	Willys	Graham	Chrylser	Graham	Chrylser	Chrysler	AMC	Chrysler	Chrysler
Rambler	Rambler	Overland	Jewett	Graham	Essex	Kaiser	AMC	Chrysler		
Riker	Pope	Edwards	Stearns	Essex	Stutz	Kaiser	Chrysler		Honda +	Honda
Locomobile	Thomas	Stutz	Edwards	Stutz	Hudson	Willys	Studebaker		Mazda +	Mazda
Crest	Chalmers	Jeffery-	Willys	Hudson	Packard	Willys			Nissan +	Nissan
Autocar	Stoddard	Nash	Overland	Packard		Nash			Toyota +	Toyota
Studebaker		Waverly	Stutz	Durant		Hudson			Volkswagen +	Volkswagen
Olds	Columbia	Essex	Nash	Willys		Packard				
Detroit Auto	Sampson	Hudson	Essex	Nash		Studebaker		Volkswagen +		Mercedes +
Rapid	Ford	Thomas	Chalmers	Cord						BMW +
Winton	Autocar	Chalmers	Saxon							
Stanley	White	Saxon	Maxwell							
Echhart	Studebaker	Dodge	Chrysler							
	Pierce	Studebaker	Saxon							
	Arrow	Ford	Dodge							
	Parkard	Lincoln	Studebaker							
	Diamond-T	Pierce	Pierce-							
	Olds	Arrow	Arrow							
	Cadillac	Packard	Stanley							
	Buick	Diamond-T	Durant							
	Reliance	Reo	Mercer							
	Premier	GM	Duesenberg							
	Winton	Winton	Auburn							
	Locomobile	Locomobile	Cord							
	Stanley	Riker								
	Simplex	Stanley								
	Walter	Mercer								
	Auburn	Duesenberg								
	Mason	I-H								
	I-H									
	Chevrolet									

Figure 8.   Evolution of the U.S. auto industry through ten plus decades: 1890–present. Plus signs indicate foreign producer's initiating production in the U.S. (Adams , 1986).

managers of auto companies and their unions will find the data I present on evolution of the U.S. auto industry evidence of selection by consequences. However, this chapter is not directed at these audiences. It is directed at behavior scientists with histories of reinforcement that make it more likely they will see the "wisdom" of this casual account of industrial development.

Figure 8 is a record of the U.S. auto manufacturing companies founded, disbanded, and merged or acquired per decade from 1890 almost up to 2000. The lines connecting names of several organizations indicate mergers and the right most name is the name of the company following the merger or acquisition. It should be noted that in the decade 1970-1980 Volkswagen began production of its vehicles in the U.S. as did Honda, Mazda, Nissan, and Toyota in the decade 1980-1990. During the current decade Mercedes and BMW also built plants and began production in the U.S. These events should make it clear that evolution of an industry's organizational ecology does not move to some optimal condition and settle there in quiet repose. They also call into question the notion organizations can or should seek some sort of equilibrium with their environments. Unless, that is, the equilibrium condition is stated in dynamic terms such as growing at a rate that matches evolution of markets, changing at rates that keep it up to date relative to technologies, products, and practices required by competitive market conditions.

The auto industry data reveal the fact that selection by consequences is an amoral and "heartless" process that simply selects against survival of any organizational culture that fails to do what is required to survive given the type and pace of

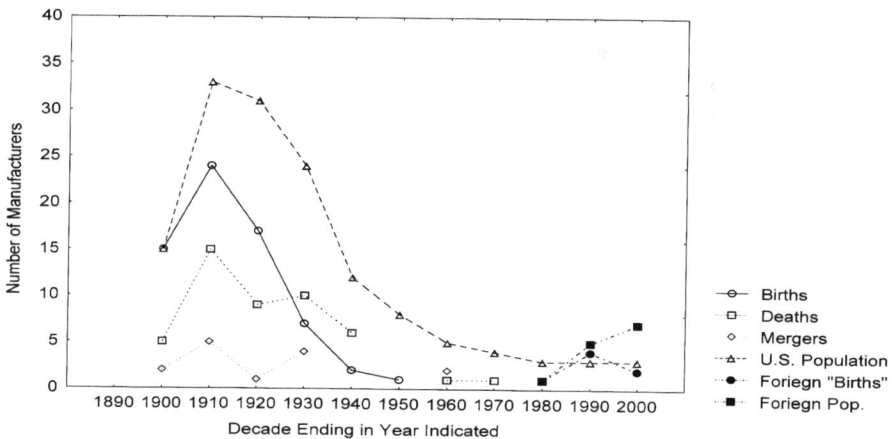

Figure 9. *Evolution of the U.S. auto industry through ten decades: 1890-1990. Line graphs link producer births, births, mergers across and U.S. population size (number of producers), "births" of foreign production operations in the U.S., and population size (number of producers) of foreign cultures in the U.S. over ten-plus (up to 1998) decades. Data are plotted for status of the industry during the last year of each decade, except for the 1990-2000 decade. These data plots extent those reported by Mawhinney (1992a).*

change in its environment. The pace of change may be steady, rapid or slow, it may cycle from slow to rapid and back to slow, or the pace may be relatively constant for long periods of time but punctuated from time to time by dramatic spikes in demand for rapid change. Absent government intervention there is no telling what might have happened to the U.S. auto industry following the oil crises and Japanese entry into its markets. The picture of the auto industry's evolution without respect to company names but in "cold hard" numbers appears in Figure 9 as a plot per decade of the number of companies founded (births), disbanded (deaths), and merged. (Number of foreign owned manufacturers recently establishing production operations in the U.S. appear separately in Figure 9. The recent merger between Daimler-Benz and Chrysler is not reflected in Figure 9.)

Who's the Boss? Nature!

The forgoing analyses of the roles played by the causal mode of selection by consequences at the level of individual, group, and organizational cultural behavior should put teeth into the assertion by Rummler and Brache (1995) that organizations must "adapt or die." The consequences of failing to adapt and do so at a rate demanded by an evolving environment can be quick and deadly. The telemarketer group would have been disbanded had they not successfully completed the pilot project within eight weeks. And that success would not have occurred if management had continued to rely on effects of CSS regarding daily achievement of individual quotas (proximate contingencies) and potential job loss in the absence of quota achievements (ultimate contingency) to create rule-governed behavior in compliance with the quota system. Or, it can appear to occur in slow motion. Although it occurred in the field, the telemarketer study represented a type of micro culture with near laboratory conditions for examining the concept of organizational metacontingency and effects of a change in practice on survival of the cultural unit. The GM culture, on the other hand, continues to be threatened with loss of domestic market share. In addition, the current evidence of rule-governed behavior among UAW members and GM management suggests that this culture is not yet in complete agreement concerning which practices will accommodate goals and objectives of union and management subcultures and their continuing need to compete in an environment that continues to evolve, nevertheless.

As individuals we may appreciate the idea that it is difficult to see ourselves as others see us. But, if we adopt etic as opposed to emic methods of describing what we do and the conditions under which we do it, we are likely to get an unvarnished picture of our various "habits" including our particular peccadilloes. The advantage of creating and using etic terms and concepts to define organizational culture is that these terms and concepts refer to events that are located in dimensions of time and space. They can, therefore, be measured using the same metrics from one organization to another just as individual's we can compare dimensions of our behavior to that of others if we use etic descriptions (e.g., behavior rates) rather than impressions of it. And, that is why I have attempted here to demonstrate the general applicability of the causal mode of selection by consequences as an etic account of human and organizational behavior. It explains phenomena as apparently diverse as the origins of stimulus control of a pigeon's and a person's behavior and stimulus control of a person's behavior by spoken words and phrases of another person. Perhaps the most striking application of this causal mode is in the explanation of changing dominant practices within organizational cultures arising from the extinction of organizational metacontingencies that include, regardless of their origins, deadly practices. The vantage point on organization-environment systems that is created by looking at those systems using the terms and concepts developed in this chapter (e.g., rule-governed behavior, cultural/organizational practices, and metacontingencies) prepares one to understand the other portion of the chapter title; minding your metacontingencies.

Minding Metacontingencies

Minding one's metacontingencies requires that one be able to describe the dominant practices of one's organizational culture that play a critical role in its survival at the moment. In addition, attention must also be focused on the dynamics of the environment with particular attention devoted to occasions when the environment shifts; all the better if those practices include organization-environmental analyses that permit environmental shifts to be predicted. When a shift is detected, an audit of practices will be essential. The vantage point developed here suggests this because it indicates that such shifts can have the effect of transforming once highly functional practices into deadly practices. It also suggests that rule-governed behavior is related to the consequences of following rules. Thus, if the designer of a culture seeks to keep rules of conduct its members follow aligned with those required by the organization, consequences likely to function as reinforcers need to be correlated with desired behaviors and accomplishments (Austin, Kessler, Riccobono, & Bailey, 1996; Clayton, Mawhinney, Luke, & Cook 1997; Langeland, Johnson, & Mawhinney, 1998). And one *system* or array of practices that conforms with the values of the OBM culture and achieves these results is what Abernathy (1996) calls *positive leadership* in conjunction with a performance measurement *system* that permits establishment of a correlation between measured performance and earned income. Another system that suggests how to remove barriers between behavior of individuals or groups and their ability to contribute to organizational flexibility and efficiency of operations is the Rummler and Brache (1995) approach to identifying, making palpable, and filling in the white space of organizational authority structures.

Both subcultures of OBM are concerned with establishing positive leadership in complex organizations while assisting upper level leaders fulfill their responsibility of fitting their organizations as human cultures and processing systems for survival in the larger systems that are their competitive environments (Brethower, 1982; Rummler & Brache, 1995). Knowledge provided by both subcultures can and should be used by those responsible for minding the metacontingencies of complex organizational cultures. However, in some cases it will be our responsibility to do analyses from the vantage point of natural scientists using etic terms and concepts while presenting what we learn from those analyses to organizational leaders using emic terms and concepts (Agnew, 1998). There remains an interesting alternative to this approach. Might it be possible to educate prospective organizational culture leaders in the use of etic terms, concepts and methods? If so, natural scientists would be able to speak with them more directly. In the mean time, the OBM culture will probably have to speak two languages. We might call one call emic OBM and the other etic OBM. Regardless what language we speak, our task remains the same, improving organizational metacontingencies (performance) (Rummler & Brache, 1995) and quality of life in organizational cultures (Daniels, 1977).

References

Abernathy, W. B. (1996). *The sin of wages.* Memphis, TN: PerfSys Press.

Agnew, J. L. (1998). The establishing operation in organizational behavior management. *Journal of Organizational Behavior Management, 18*(1), 7-19.

Agnew, J. L., & Redmon, W. K. (1992). Contingency specifying stimuli: The role of "rules" in organizational behavior management. *Journal of Organizational Behavior Management, 12*(2), 67-75.

Austin, J., Kessler, M. L., Riccobono, J. E., & Bailey, J. S. (1996). Using feedback and reinforcement to improve the performance and safety of a roofing crew. *Journal of Organizational Behavior Management, 16*(2), 49-75.

Baum, W. M. (1973). The correlation-based law of effect. *Journal of the Experimental Analysis of Behavior, 20,* 137-153.

Baum, W. M. (1994). *Understanding behaviorism: Science, behavior, and culture.* New York: HarperCollins.

Baum, W. M. (1995). Rules, culture, and fitness. *The Behavior Analyst, 19,* 1-21.

Blakely, E., & Schlinger, H. (1987). Rules: Function-altering contingency-specifying stimuli. *The Behavior Analyst, 10,* 183-187

Brethower, D. M. (1972). *Behavioral analysis in business and industry.* Kalamazoo, MI: Behaviordelia.

Brethower, D. M. (1982). The total performance system. In R. O'Brien, A. Dickinson, & M. Rosow (Eds.), *Industrial Behavior Modification* (pp. 250-369). New York: Pergamon.

Burnstein, D. D., & Wolff, P. C. (1964). Shaping of three-man teams on a multiple DRL-DRH schedule using collective reinforcement. *Journal of the Experimental Analysis of Behavior, 7,* 191-197.

Cerutti, D. T. (1989). Discrimination theory of rule-governed behavior. *Journal of the Experimental Analysis of Behavior, 51,* 259-276.

Clayton, M. C., Mawhinney, T. C., Luke, D. E., & Cook, H. G. (1997). Improving the management of overtime costs through decentralized controls: Managing an organizational metacontingency. *Journal of Organizational Behavior Management, 17*(2), 77-98.

Daniels, A. C. (1977). Editorial. *Journal of Organizational Behavior Management, 1*(1), v-vii.

Daniels, A. C. (1989). *Performance management: Improving productivity through positive reinforcement.* Tucker, GA: Performance Management Publications.

Daniels, A. C. (1994). *Bringing out the best in people.* New York: McGraw-Hill.

Deming, W. E. (1982). *Quality productivity and competitiveness or out of the crisis.* Cambridge, MA: MIT Center for Advanced Engineering Study.

Eckerman, D. A., Hienz, R. D., Stern, S., & Kowlowitz, V. (1980). Shaping the location of pigeon's peck: Effects of rate and size of shaping steps. *Journal of the Experimental Analysis of Behavior, 33,* 299-310.

Fellows, C., & Mawhinney, T. C. (1997). Improving telemarketers' performance in the short-run using operant concepts. *Journal of Business and Psychology, 11,* 411-424.

Gilbert, T. F. (1978). *Human competence: Engineering worthy performance.* New York: McGraw-Hill.

Gilbert, T. F. (1992). Foreword. In H. D. Stolovitch & E. J. Keeps (Eds.), *Handbook of human performance technology* (pp. xiii-xviii). San Francisco: Jossey-Bass Publishers.

Glenn, S. S. (1988). Contingencies and metacontingencies: Toward a synthesis of behavior analysis and cultural materialism. *The Behavior Analyst, 11,* 161-179.

Glenn, S. S. (1991). Contingencies and metacontingencies: Relations among behavioral, cultural, and biological evolution. In P. A. Lamal (Ed.), *Behavioral analysis of societies and cultural practices* (pp. 39-73). Washington, D.C.: Hemisphere.

Guttman, N. (1956). The pigeon and the spectrum and other complexities. *Journal of Experimental Psychology, 2,* 449-460.

Halberstam, D. (1986). *The reckoning.* New York: Avon Books.

Hannan, M. T., & Freeman, J. (1989). *Organizational ecology.* Cambridge, MA: Harvard University Press.

Harris, M. (1979). *Cultural materialism: The struggle for a science of culture.* New York: Random House.

Hayes, S. C., Zettle, R. D., & Rosenfarb, I. (1989). Rule-following. In S. Hayes (Ed.), *Rule-governed behavior: Cognition, contingencies, and instructional control* (pp. 191-220). New York: Plenum.

Herrick, R. M., Myers, J. L., & Korotkin, A. L. (1959). Changes in S^D and S^Δ rates during the development of an operant discrimination. *Journal of Comparative and Physiological Psychology, 52,* 359-363.

Komaki, J. L., & Goltz, S. (In press). Within-group research designs: Going beyond program evaluation questions. In C. M. Johnson, W. K. Redmon, & T. C. Mawhinney (Eds.), *Organizational performance: Behavior analysis and management.* New York: Haworth Press.

Komaki, J. L., & Reynard, M. L. (In press). Developing performance appraisals: Criteria for what and how performance is measured. In C. M. Johnson, W. K. Redmon, & T. C. Mawhinney (Eds.), *Organizational performance: Behavior analysis and management*. New York: Haworth Press.

LaFleur, T., & Hyten, C. (1995). Improving the quality of hotel banquet staff performance. *Journal of Organizational Behavior Management, 15*(½), 69-93.

Lamal, P. A. (Ed.). (1991). *Behavioral analysis of societies and cultural practices*. Washington, D.C.: Hemisphere.

Langeland, K. L., Johnson, C. M., & Mawhinney, T. C. (1998). Improving staff performance in a community mental health setting: Job analysis, training, goal setting, goal setting, feedback, and years of data. *Journal of Organizational Behavior Management, 18*(1), 21-43.

Lovelock, J. (1988). *The ages of Gaia: A biography of our living earth*. New York: W. W. Norton.

Malott, R. W. (1992). A theory of rule-governed behavior and organizational behavior management. *Journal of Organizational Behavior Management, 12*(2), 45-65.

Mawhinney, T. C. (In press). Leadership: Behavior, context and consequences. In Johnson, C. M., Redmon, W. K., & Mawhinney, T. C. (Eds.), *Handbook of organizational performance: Behavior analysis and management*. New York: Haworth Press.

Mawhinney, T. C. (1984). Philosophical and ethical aspect of Organizational Behavior Management: Some evaluative feedback. *Journal of Organizational Behavior Management, 6*(1), 5-31.

Mawhinney, T. C. (1992). *Organizational culture, rule-governed behavior and organizational behavior management: Theoretical foundations and implications for research and Practice*. New York: The Haworth Press.

Mawhinney, T. C. (1992a). Evolution of organizational cultures as selection by consequences: The Gaia hypothesis, metacontingencies, and organizational ecology. *Journal of Organizational Behavior Management, 12*(2), 1-26.

Mawhinney, T. C. (1992b). Total quality management and organizational behavior management: An integration for continual improvement. *Journal of Applied Behavior Analysis, 25,* 225-243.

Michael, J. (1982). Distinguishing between discriminative and motivational functions of stimuli. *Journal of the Experimental Analysis of Behavior, 37,* 149-155.

Parsonson, B., & Baer, D. (1978). *The analysis and presentation of graphic data*. In T. R. Kratochwill (Ed.), *Single subject research: Strategies for evaluating change* (pp. 101-165). New York: Academic Press.

Pike, K. L. (1967). *Language in relation to a unified theory of the structure of human behavior*. The Hague: Mouton.

Poling, A., & Braatz, D. (In press) Principles of learning: Respondent and operant conditioning and human behavior. In C. M. Johnson, W. K. Redmon, & T. C.

Mawhinney (Eds.), *Handbook of organizational performance: Behavior analysis and management*. New York: Haworth Press.

Redmon, W. K., & Mason, M. A. (In press). Organizational culture and behavioral systems analysis. In Johnson, C. M., Redmon, W. K., & Mawhinney, T. C. (Eds.), *Handbook of organizational performance: Behavior analysis and management*. New York: Haworth Press.

Rummler, G. A., & Brache, A. P. (1995). *Improving performance: How to manage the white space on the organizational chart* (2nd ed.). San Francisco: Jossey-Bass.

Schlinger, H., & Blakely, E. (1987). Function-altering effects of contingency-specifying stimuli. *The Behavior Analyst, 10,* 41-45.

Schlinger, H. A., Jr., & Blakely, E. A. (1994). A descriptive taxonomy of environmental operations and its implications for behavior analysis. *The Behavior Analyst, 17,* 43-57.

Sidman, M. (1960). *Tactics of scientific research*. New York: The Free Press.

Sidman, M. (1989). *Coercion and its fallout*. Boston: Authors Cooperative.

Skinner, B. F. (1953). *Science and human behavior*. New York: Macmillan.

Skinner, B. F. (1957). *Verbal Behavior*. New York: Appleton-Century-Crofts.

Skinner, B. F. (1969). *Contingencies of reinforcement*. New York: Appleton-Century-Crofts.

Skinner, B. F. (1981). Selection by consequences. *Science, 213,* 31 July, 501-504.

Terrace, H. S. (1974). On the nature of non responding in discrimination learning with and without errors. *Journal of the Experimental Analysis of Behavior, 22,* 151-159.

Discussion of Mawhinney

Evolutionary Epistemology

William O'Donohue and Adrian H. Bowers
University of Nevada

Selection by consequences is an appropriate causal model for the analysis of the practices in Organizational Behavioral Management (OBM). One caveat that we hold about the applicability of an evolutionary model to OBM is the tacit rate of change that many take evolution to imply. Usually evolution is discussed as occurring over thousands of years. The rate of change that is seen in the evolution of companies should not be likened to the extinction of the dinosaurs. The life cycle of the common fruit fly (i.e., a number of hours) is often closer to the scale of the rate of change in business. Changes in business are clearly based on selection; but selection at a frantic pace—a high speed time lapsed film of biological evolution.

We like Professor Mawhinney's use of evolutionary metaphor so much that in our commentary we would like to set it in its larger context. We want to suggest that all knowledge–including the knowledge involved in running a business is a product of blind variation and selective retention. This general model of knowledge is known as evolutionary epistemology and is based on the work of the social psychologist, Donald Campbell; the philosopher of science, Karl Popper; the analytic philosopher W.V.O. Quine; and finally, the learning researcher B. F. Skinner (see O'Donohue & Henderson, 1999).

Humans are products of evolution (in fact descendants of the first organic replicating molecule). Our abilities to know and learn are also product of variation and selective retention. Popper (1979, p. 261) gives a nice general characterization of evolutionary epistemology: "The theory of knowledge which I wish to propose is a largely Darwinian theory of the growth of knowledge. From the amoeba to Einstein, the growth of knowledge is always the same: we try to solve our problems, and to obtain, by a process of elimination, something approaching adequacy in our tentative solutions".

This knowledge occurs in two major ways. First, organisms are literally embodiments of knowledge. As Bartley (1987) states, "evolution is a process in which information regarding the environment is literally incorporated, incarnated, in surviving organisms through the process of adaption" (p. 23). Second, science and any criticism process can select and eliminate proposed solutions. Popper (1974, p vi) illustrates how theories can be allowed to die in our stead:

> The way in which knowledge progresses, and especially our scientific knowledge, is by unjustified (and unjustifiable anticipations, by guesses, by tentative solutions to our problems, by conjectures. These conjectures are

controlled by criticism; that is, by attempted refutations, which include severely critical tests. They may survive these tests; but they can never be positively justified; they can neither be established as certainly true nor as 'probable (in the sense of probability calculus). Criticism of our conjectures is of decisive importance: by bringing out our mistakes it makes us understand the difficulties of the problem which we are trying to solve. This is how we become better acquainted with our problems, and able to propose more mature solutions: the very refutation of a theory–that is, of any serious tentative solution to our problem–is always a step forward that takes our nearer to the truth. And this is how we can learn from our mistakes."

Thus the traditional philosophical issue of epistemology becomes naturalized. Human knowledge is regarded as a natural phenomenon that can best be studied according to the same methods that other natural phenomena are studied. In this case however, the psychological learning laboratory become particularly important (Quine, 1969; Skinner, 1984). This turns traditional justificationist epistemology on its head. Radnitzky (1988, p. 288) nicely illustrates the contrast between justificational and critical, selectionist accounts:

The justificationist asks: When is it rational to accept a particular theory (or belief); and he suggests an answer on the lines; When it has been verified or probabilified to a sufficient degree. In the critical context the key question is; when is it *rational* fallibly to prefer a particular position (statement, view, standard, etc.) over its rival(s)? The answer suggested is along the lines: It is rational fallibly to prefer a position over its rivals if and only if it has so far withstood criticism–the criticism relevant for the sort of position at stake–better than did its rivals."

In this model of knowing those wanting a business or part of an organization to prosper would attempt to maximize nonlethal criticism of their tentative solutions to their problems. It is important to note that the evolutionary metaphor can be applied at various levels of analysis–to the entire organization–to parts of the organization and even to super-organizational domains such as the horse buggy industry. Good quality assurance procedures generally conform to this model. These attempt to supply information regarding deviations from standards or goals. This can falsify any (potentially lethal or injurious) complacency on the part of the business or organization. It can do this by showing that problem solutions are inadequate or that problems that have not been on the radar screen should be.

Thus, organizational analysts and business professionals can do well be using the evolutionary analysis. The metaphor can guide them to the importance of: 1) understanding all their problems and their problem formulations (ignorance of a problem or a poor problem statement can lead to further problems). An important aspect of these problem statements is an evaluation of the competition in the niche. It is fortuitous that evolutionary theorists and business analysts both use "competition" as a key term. 2) creatively proposing tentative solutions that are not judged on their "justification" but rather are efficiently criticized. Campbell's classic "Reforms as Experiments" provides an useful model for this process. 3) Recycling this process. Thus, we join Professor Mawhinney in looking forward to the day when business and organization analysis is not simply based on gurus or the fad of the day, but rather is based on an analysis of the selective forces operating on tentative solutions.

References

Bartley, W. W. (1987). Philosophy of biology versus philosophy of physics. In G. Radnitzky & W. W. Bartley (Eds.), *Evolutionary epistemology, rationality, and the sociology of knowledge* (pp. 121-138). La Salle, IL: Open Court.

O'Donohue, W., & Henderson, D. (1999). Evolution and psychotherapy: The promise of evolutionary epistemology. *American Psychologist*, under editorial review.

Popper, K. R. (1979). *Objective knowledge: An evolutionary approach*. Oxford: Clarendon Press.

Popper, K. R. (1974). *Conjectures and refutations: The growth of scientific knowledge*. London: Routledge & Kegan Paul.

Quine, W.V.O. (1969). Epistemology naturalized. In Quine, W.V.O. *Ontological relativity and other essays*. New York: Columbia University Press.

Radnitzky, G. (1988). In defense of self-applicable critical rationalism. In G. Radnitzky & W. W. Bartley (Eds.), *Evolutionary epistemology, rationality, and the sociology of knowledge* (pp. 279-312). La Salle, IL: Open Court.

Skinner, B. F. (1984). Selection by consequences. *Brain and Behavioral Sciences, 7*, 477-510.

Beyond the Flaw of Averages: Managing Organizational Performance and Financial Risk

Dwight Harshbarger and Anthony Broskowski
Pareto Solutions

An organization is an interesting and sometimes puzzling place. What you see is not what you always get. What you get may not be what you thought you saw. An organization is physically bounded in time and place, and contains people, technology and many kinds of resources, all aimed at achieving a mission or purpose. It has a virtual reality that transcends its physical presence, not just electronically, but in the lives of its participants. It has many layers and divisions, each of them at times simultaneously presenting different faces internally to members, and externally to the outside world of vendors, customers and stakeholders. It contains something called a culture, patterns of rewards and punishments that alternatively shape and maintain normative and deviant behavior in everyday organizational life. It is a place where human performance yields innovation, and sometimes stagnation, in products and services. It consumes often-substantial resources, requiring a continuing stream of revenue in order to stay alive and healthy. Financing must be secured and, at least in the private sector, once financial resources are secured they are immediately put at risk – for there are no guarantees that products and services will be sold for more than their costs, or sold at all.

An organization is a place where human behavior becomes organizational performance; a place where the bottom line of financial performance shapes future possibilities; a place where people manage the behavior of themselves, each other and their technologies while simultaneously managing resources and financial risk. As they do this, they implicitly or explicitly deal with three simply stated but far-reaching questions (Sulzer-Azaroff and Harshbarger, 1995).

1. What is a good job?
2. How do I – how do we - know if we're doing a good job?
3. What happens when I –when we- do a good job?

In answering these questions, *managers must deal with two fundamental challenges: Can we effectively manage human performance while simultaneously managing financial risk?* In this paper we will look at some factors that play important roles in effectively meeting these challenges. We also hope to question conventional wisdom, and perhaps you, with some approaches to these challenges that diverge from the well-traveled roads of past practices.

Pareto Solutions

Over the past two years we have been building computer based statistical models of organizational performance, revenues and costs, and using them to simulate performance and financial risk. We began our work based on some conceptual and statistical models Broskowski (1991, 1993, 1995, 1997; Broskowski and Marks, 1992) developed while working for major health care and managed care organizations. Our company, originally called Managed Care Solutions, was later named Pareto Solutions to honor the work of the Italian economist and sociologist, Vilfedo Pareto (1848-1923). He is perhaps best remembered for the mathematical distribution bearing his name, one expressing the importance of the significant few and the relative unimportance of the insignificant many, commonly known as "the 80-20 rule".

Our firm's work began as an effort to help public not-for-profit mental health or behavioral health organizations bear financial risk as they enter the world of managed behavioral health care. For many years these organizations have operated as corporate entities, but only on the edges of the private sector. With a continuing base of relatively secure federal, state, county and local tax-based revenues, these organizations, principally community mental health or behavioral health centers, have operated with relative financial security and relatively low financial risk. With the advent of managed care, and approval by the federal government in state after state to place Medicaid services under managed care, behavioral health organizations have found themselves entering the private sector; a world of financial risk, profit and loss. A few have prospered, and a few have gone into Chapter 11. Virtually all of them are re-examining ways of structuring and delivering behavioral health services, and searching for cost-effective ways to meet client needs. Together we are all learning the complex ways that clinical practices are inextricably joined with the economics of those practices under managed care (Broskowski and Harshbarger, in press; Harshbarger, 1997).

We have recently begun to extend our work into other areas. We have built statistical models of pathways of cancer treatment as well as models of special educational services in school systems. We are currently working with a major corporation to develop and apply a computer-based statistical model of safety cost, performance and financial risk to its workplaces, and project future financial risk for the corporation.

In this paper we will focus on two topical areas, behavioral health services and safety performance, and use them to illustrate our concepts and methods in managing human performance and financial risk.

Understanding Risk

Risk is a frequently misunderstood and oversimplified concept. In the history of the Western World, until the Reformation and Renaissance we put our faith in God or Gods, and assumed that the future, with all its unknowns, was under these sources of external control. In pre-Reformation Western society, there were no institutions, other than perhaps the church, to help us anticipate and prepare for the risk inherent in future events. Risk and a calculus of future probabilities were beyond our control.

Prior to the 17th century, the discipline of mathematics, with its power to calculate and quantify risk, did not exist. Bernstein (1996) persuasively makes the point in his book, *Against the Gods: The Remarkable Story of Risk*, that we can separate modern from pre-modern Western societies on the basis of how risk is managed. Our modern society, Bernstein suggests, may be better dated from the advent of mathematics and probability formulas than from any other single societal factor. What separates us from our ancestors is the combination of our development of statistical probabilities of outcomes and the ensuing exercise of our systematically behaving in ways to influence those outcomes.

To many people, risk simply means a threat to the expected. We're planning a picnic and it may rain. Others equate risk with costs. High cost means high risk. For example, expensive patient care means high risk patients. We view risk as having three independent dimensions.

1. Uncertainty about an outcome – will gain or loss occur?
2. The size of the outcome – how much will be gained or lost?
3. Choices and decisions – what can we do to influence, even control, outcomes?

Bernstein notes that the origin of the word *risk* lies in its Latin root, *risicare*, meaning *to choose*. What choices can we make to manage factors bearing on risk? Risk is about uncertainty and probabilities – how much will be gained or lost? What are the probabilities associated with different levels of gain or loss? It is about variation. It is about choice –What can we do about it? It is about the interplay between variation in outcomes, and choices in the management of decisions and performance leading to those outcomes.

Risk Sharing and Risk Bearing

In managed behavioral health care. Under managed behavioral health care, an organization is contractually responsible for the provision, usually through subcontracts to a panel of providers, of all the behavioral health services needed by a defined population of members. Financially this organization bears risk for the provision of behavioral health services to the population of eligible potential users of services. This is done through payment of a fee for each member enrolled as a "covered life", and is usually referred to as a "per member per month" (PMPM) rate of payment. An employer, for example an auto manufacturer, might enter into a contractual relationship with a managed care organization (MCO) for the MCO to bear responsibility and financial risk for the provision of health or behavioral health services to all employees and their families. To do this, the MCO is paid a monthly fee for all services, however large or small. This fee is described as a capitated rate, i.e., it is a per eligible person rate of payment for covered employees and their families, whether or not they use any behavioral health services.

The following formula contains the chief factors affecting the total cost of services under a PMPM risk-sharing arrangement:

Total $ Cost = 1 x 2 x 3 (below)
  1. Number of Covered Lives x Number of Users/1000
  2. Service Units per User (number and types of units per user)
  3. Price per Unit (by type of unit)

Total Cost = ((100,000 lives) x (100 users per 1000 lives)) x (10 units per person)
  x ($100 per unit)

Total Cost = (10,000) x (10) x ($100) = $10,000,000

Per Member Per Month (PMPM) Rate = Total Cost / Covered Lives / 12

PMPM = ($10,000,000) / (100,000) / (12) = $8.33

In managed behavioral health care services, financial risk can be defined as *the probability that a defined array of services to a defined population of potential users over a defined time period will be delivered for a given cost, or more than that cost.*

The PMPM rate of payment fixes incoming revenue. This is not the fee for service world. Providers do not earn more by doing more. Providers must deliver effective, high quality services within available revenues. In the above example, $8.33 PMPM is the fixed revenue. In a commercially insured population it may be in the $2 - $4 range. In a Medicaid population the PMPM may be $35 - $40, or higher. What are the chances that the costs will exceed the revenue, and by how much? The financial risk in this arrangement is that the treatment cost will exceed revenue. Or, 1) What is the probability that the costs will exceed a threshold cost? and 2) Should this happen, how much greater might these costs be?

In safety performance. In an annual business plan, all planned costs, projections of what we estimate costs will be, must be specified prior to approval of the plan. Near the end of a plan revenues are compared to costs, and expected profitability is calculated. One of these costs is the cost of unsafe performance, all the costs resulting from incidents producing workplace injuries and illnesses. These costs go well beyond workplace injuries and illnesses, including, for example, service or production losses, equipment and property losses, employee replacement and retraining costs, alternative or temporary work assignment programs, etc. An employer bears risk for all these costs. An employer who purchases workers' compensation insurance, property damage insurance, etc., bears indirect risk for some of these costs through insurance coverage and premiums, and bears full risk for others, such as the hiring and training of replacement staff, alternative work programs for injured employees, etc. We will assume, just to keep things simple, that our employer is a large self-insured corporation bearing full risk for the cost of unsafe performance.

The following formula contains the factors affecting the total cost of unsafe performance, and the associated financial risk:

Total $ Cost = 1 x 2 x 3 (below)

1. Number of Incidents (by type of incident)
    a. Indemnity (lost time incidents)
    b. Medical costs only (no lost time)

2. Cost Units per Incident (number and types of cost units)
    a. Indemnity and Associated Cost Units (for lost time incidents; not a complete list)
        · Wage-Salary (days or months)
        · Med-rehab (frequency and/or duration treatment units)
        · Lost services or production (number service or production units)
        · Temporary Alternative Duty (number TAD days)
        · Staff replacement (number replaced)
    b. Med Only (non-lost time incidents) and Associated Costs
        · All the above, except Salary

3. Cost per Unit (by type of unit)
    a. Indemnity and Associated Costs
        · Wage-Salary cost per day
        · Med-rehab cost per unit of treatment
        · TAD cost per day
        · Staff replacement cost per replacement
    b. Med Only and Associated Costs
        · Same logic as above

In an annual profit plan projections are made about the number of incidents, types of incidents, the expense units associated with them, and the cost per expense unit. From these calculations, a number is developed and entered in a business plan for the cost of unsafe performance.

For example, there may be 100 lost time workplace incidents, lasting on average 10 days at a cost of $120 per day, totaling $120,000. In addition, each incident resulted in 2 hours of lost production @ $2,000 per hour (100 x 2 x $2,000 = $400,000). Beyond this there were such costs as: Placing some injured employees into Temporary Alternative Duty (50 employees x 4 days x $50 per day = $10,000) for a period of recovery while working; a need to replace some employees who were away from work for longer periods of time in order to recover (50 employees x 10 days x $140 per day = ($70,000), as well as other costs not included here.

Financial risk can be defined as *the probability that the number incidents and their associated costs for a defined population of employees over a defined time period will be at or above a given estimated cost.*

The profit plan, once completed, puts in place fixed estimates of safety costs. What are the chances that costs will exceed these estimates? By how much? How many incidents will there be? What is the cost per incident for wages, medical treatment, lost production, etc.? The financial risk in this arrangement is that the cost of unsafe performance will exceed your estimates, and impact your revenue stream and profitability. What is the probability that these costs will exceed a threshold cost. If this should this happen, how much greater might these costs be?

The grocery industry is a very low margin business. For example, a multi-billion dollar wholesale food products company employing thousands of people may hope to achieve 1.5% net profit at year end. Since this is a percent of a substantial revenue base, the potential profit number is relatively large. At the same time, with only a 1.5% margin, it is a very vulnerable number. If cost controls slip, for example through an increase in unsafe performance and its human and financial costs, profit margins can be significantly reduced. Managing human performance in order to manage financial risk around safe performance becomes very important to the economic health of the company.

Factors Creating Uncertainty in Risk

In managed behavioral health care.

1.   Risk in estimating users of services

1a. Underlying needs: Potential users of services

The number of potential users of health care is, of course, a function of the underlying level of need for services within the eligible population. Level of need is equated with what epidemiologists call the "prevalence" of the disease, which in this case are alcohol, drug, and mental health (ADM) disorders. Unfortunately, there is little reliable information on the prevalence of ADM within the general population and even less on the prevalence among Medicaid-eligible persons. A report by Cille and Manderscheid (1992) indicated that among the entire U.S. population with Supplemental Security Income (SSI) or Supplemental Security Disability Income (SSDI)–subcategories of Medicaid eligibility for those with diagnosed disabilities– an estimated 23.9 percent of SSDI, and 27.4 percent of all disabled persons had a "mental disorder." That rate is equivalent to about 5.24 percent of the general U.S. population.

1b. Risk for actual users of services

The number of persons "in need" who will actually use services must also be estimated. Many providers confuse prevalence or "need" with the probability of actual utilization or "demand." For example, it is not uncommon to find that in a given year as few as 65 percent to 68 percent of the estimated number of seriously mentally ill (SMI) persons will, in fact, receive treatment.

Barbara Burns (1997) reported that 45 percent of SED-diagnosed children with "public insurance" (primarily Medicaid) self-reported using some mental health services during a two-year period, while only 37 percent of SED children with private insurance did so. The percent of publicly insured children with any mental health diagnosis using any mental health services was 25 percent, while for children with any mental health diagnosis with private insurance, the rate of use of any service was only 21 percent. Thus, holding severity constant, there does appear to be a higher probability of use among publicly insured children. Interestingly, Burns also found that among children with *no* diagnosable condition, 12 percent of those with public insurance received services compared with only 7 percent of those with private insurance.

There is even less information on the number of Medicaid-eligible adults who access mental health and substance abuse treatment services. In a review of the early years of the MH/SA "carve-out" in Massachusetts, Callahan et al., reported that there were 222.6 unduplicated users per 1,000 eligible Medicaid members (i.e., a 22.26 percent penetration rate). This seems to be much larger than the usual rate of access. The present authors have observed from other databases that the rate of access to behavioral services among Medicaid-eligible persons (all ages and SSI and AFDC combined) is closer to 10 percent.

Inappropriate over-utilization can also affect estimates that are based on historical databases of care users. Many of those served in the fee-for service environment were, in fact, below a threshold of what medical necessity criteria would consider "in need" of care. Table 1 summarizes data from a national epidemiological survey that examined the annual prevalence of mental health and addictive disorders and the prevalence of treatment for these disorders (Bourdon et al., 1994).

The broader the scope of services, the more difficult it becomes to estimate the probabilities of the many different service utilization patterns or combinations. For example, one of the distinctive features of the Medicaid population is its pattern of service utilization. For many reasons related to poverty, life stresses, unreliable transportation, discriminatory access, discontinuity in eligibility, and so forth, Medicaid-eligible person are more likely to use emergency-based services over

Patterns of Needs and Treatment

Receive Treatment?

		Yes	*No*	*Total*
Need Treatment?	*Yes*	**8.1%**	20.0% *in need but unserved*	28.1%
	No	6.6% *unnecessarily served*	**65.3%**	71.9%
		====	====	====
		14.7%	85.3%	100.0%

Table 1.

appointment-based services, and to use brief acute hospitalizations often followed by little or no follow-up care. Outpatient care will be characterized by many persons dropping out of treatment after one to three visits.

2.   Risk for utilization

This risk includes two distinct kinds of uncertainties: How many eligible persons will use care (i.e., how many "eligibles" will become "patients"), and how much care each patient will use. The question of how much care is also a question about the pattern of care –whether it will be episodic, chronic, non-compliant, emergency-based or scheduled and predictable.

Estimates are typically based on averages and historical trends. For example, last year a service provider had 1000 clients enter the organization for services, and 10 service units were consumed per client. Will 1000 clients enter next year? Will they consume an average of 10 units apiece?

3.   Risk for cost or price

Even though there is more certainty about what a unit of service will cost, there are unknowns that make life difficult for providers bearing financial risk. It is often easier for providers to estimate cost or price than it is to estimate utilization, since providers usually have better records about, and more control over, costs. But, the addition of new staff, the signing of new bargaining unit contracts, the construction of a new facility and many other potential developments can lead to higher unit costs. Note, however, that cost and price are not always the same thing. The provider's cost describes actual cost (e.g., salary + phone + rent). The provider's charge (price) is likely to exceed the provider's cost.

In behavioral health care, combining estimates of the three factors. A "most likely" estimate of the total cost of providing services is based on the estimated average values for each of the three factors (users, units per user, and cost per unit). Actuaries under contract to the payer usually carry out this step. In practice, the actuaries may simply divide the historical total costs by the historical member months to calculate a per member per month (PMPM) premium. They may not break out the relative contribution of each of the three distinct factors.

Recalling that risk involves possible variation from averages, the "risk" is that in practice the actual number of users/1000, units per user, and cost per unit will exceed the estimated average number. In other words, the risk inherent in assuming total liability for the total cost is the possible upside variation in any one or more of these three factors. And, since these three factors are multiplied by one another to arrive at a PMPM rate, the cumulative risk is greater than the possible variation in any single factor.

Reliable information on each of these three variables may or may not be readily available to a provider who is considering the assumption of full risk through a PMPM contract. For example, the provider usually knows, on average, how many clients entered each of the several different programs that the provider directly operates. But the provider may *not* know the size of the population from which these users emerged, and thus cannot estimate the *true rate* of users/1000 eligible lives, which is needed to estimate potential users within the new population. If the provider's past clients had commercial insurance their rate of demand and utilization patterns will not generalize to the Medicaid population. The provider may also not know if its past patients received additional services elsewhere, or if additional users of care never visited the provider's organization but did use services from other organizations. If the provider is assuming liability for all services on a PMPM basis, then it is critical that the provider estimate the total probability of *any* eligible lives entering into care *anywhere* over a given time period.

It is also extremely difficult to get reliable estimates of the *variation around averages* for the number of users, the units per user, and the cost per unit. Finally, once the provider has possible values for each of these three factors and is aware that each value can vary, it is difficult to know what combination of these values is the correct one to use in calculations leading to a contractual PMPM rate, and the assumption of financial risk.

In safety performance. Among safety professionals, the word incident is replacing the word accident, even though the dictionary definitions of these words are quite similar. *Incident: an event that disrupts normal procedure or causes a crisis. Accident: something occurring unexpectedly or unintentionally; fortune or chance.* It is the latter part of the definition of accident, fortune or chance, that creates the problem. An accident, it is often said, is a chance event. Who can control chance? The Gods? It is this sense of fatalism and lack of control accompanying the word "accident" that is leading to its being shelved by safety and risk professionals and many line managers. An incident is an event in the workplace, one that is potentially under the control of managers and workers.

1.   Risk in estimating incidents

1a. Underlying conditions

There are many factors that shape the relative safety of industries and workplaces. For example, goods-producing companies have higher incidence rates for injuries and illnesses per 100 workers than service-producing companies. Among goods-producing companies, manufacturing had the highest incidence in 1995 at 11.6 per 100 workers, followed by construction at 10.6 per 100 workers. In the service sector, transportation and public utilities were highest at 9.1 per 100, followed by retail and wholesale trade 7.5 per 100 (Bureau of Labor Statistics, 1997). While these statistics vary moderately from year to year, their relative consistency across the many sectors of industry in the United States speaks to the continuing presence of underlying conditions that reliably characterize the on-going hazards in the work demands of different industry sectors.

Industry patterns of change create new challenges for managers and employees who are working to build safe workplaces. New technologies, materials, substances and working conditions create new hazards and challenges. Economic cycles lead to rising and falling production and service demands. How certain are we that incidence rates for last year will characterize incidence rates for next year?

1b. Workplace injury and illness incidents

Within an industry or within a given organization, how can we assess the risk we are facing for incidents and their costs? We know our past. How confident are we that the past we know will reflect the future we don't know?

For example, assume you head a company operating nursing and personal care homes. Your past performance in safety has paralleled that of the industry. It is one of relatively high rates of incidents and risk. Industry-wide in 1995 nearly 1.5 million people were employed in this industry, over 85% of them women. The injury rate that year was 595 per 10,000 workers, or 5.95 per 100, yielding an estimated 82,000 injuries and illnesses. Injuries typically occurred to nursing aides, orderlies and attendants, and were injuries principally associated with overexertion, primarily while lifting and maneuvering patients and residents. Most injuries involved sprain or strain, often to the back. About 75% of injured workers returned to work within 4 days, and about 25% were absent from work for 11 or more days because of their injuries (Bureau of Labor Statistics, 1997).

If you wanted to estimate your rate of incidents and potential financial risk for next year's business plan, you might use the above statistics to guide your analysis. Would you do this?

Or, would you ask in what ways will next year's safety performance be similar to or different from last year? How specific might you be in detailing and quantifying expected changes? Simply using last year's rates assumes nothing will change. Changing the rates assumes you know something about probable change.

What if, for example, you planning to fund and implement a behavioral safety program to reduce injuries? Alavosius and Sulzer-Azaroff (1990) have demonstrated how a behavioral safety program can build correct performance in the lifting and moving of nursing home patients. From baseline data of 50-60 percent of procedures correctly performed, they were able, through training and feedback, in as few as 2 and as many as 25 days, to increase the percent of correct procedures to 93-99%.

2.   Risk for Units of Cost

If an injury producing incident occurs, it will be more or less expensive depending on its severity. Severity has two dimensions. First, the extent and duration of the injuries to the person or persons affected by the incident. Second, the scope of impact of the incident. For example, John might improperly operate a machine, causing an injury to his arm. Or, he might operate a machine improperly resulting in a fire injuring others, causing damage to the physical plant and stopping production for 2 hours.

Lost time injuries, by definition, are injuries so severe that the injured employee must leave the workplace for one or more days. Again, we calculate the average length of time per lost time injury, and then make assumptions about lost time, knowing only the rate of injuries. But Harshbarger and Rose (1990) have demonstrated how the frequency and costs of workplace injuries in an athletic footwear distribution center can be substantially reduced through a combination of behavioral worksite programs and a carefully planned return to work program. For an overview of behavioral approaches to improving safe performance at work, see Geller (1997).

In addition to the variation of units per incident, there is the problem of the inclusion of units. Very often organizations carefully monitor their costs of wages and medical-rehabilitation due to workplace injuries and illnesses, but for those same incidents fail to include the cost of lost services and production, the use of emergency equipment, equipment damage, the recruiting-hiring-training of replacement workers, etc. The under inclusion of units leads to a significant underestimation of the true cost of workplace injuries and illnesses (see Leigh et al., 1997, for a thoughtful review of this problem in national safety data).

3.   Cost per unit

Of the three variables, cost per unit is likely to vary least, though it will vary. New contracts and higher wages, more expensive and now damaged equipment or technology, increases in the cost of recruiting-hiring-training, are only a few of the changing, usually rising, cost per unit factors that are common in creating variation in cost per unit.

In safety performance, combining estimates of the three factors. The logic and mathematics of combined estimates follows the same path as that discussed earlier in combining estimates of the three factors in estimating behavioral health care costs. "Most likely" estimates of total cost are based on the estimated average values for each of the three factors (incidents, units per incident and cost per unit). Actuaries usually project trend lines based on historical incidence rates and costs, then calculate an insurance premium.

Remember, risk involves variation from averages. The *real risk* is that in practice the actual number of incidents/1000, units per incident, and cost per unit will exceed the estimate based on averages. As in health care, the risk inherent in assuming total liability for the total cost of unsafe performance is the possible upside variation in any one or more of these three factors. And, since these three factors are multiplied by one another, the cumulative risk is greater than the possible variation in any single factor.

It is difficult to get reliable estimates of the *variation around averages* for the number of incidents, units per incident, and the cost per unit. Most data systems do not commonly monitor measures of variation in performance and cost. Though, on the positive side, most data systems have the capacity to do this, if asked and perhaps prodded a bit. Finally, once the possible values for each of the three factors are known, it is difficult to know what combination of these values is the correct one to use in calculations leading to projections of safety performance and the assumption of financial risk.

Risk and "The Flaw of Averages"

When most people are told of an average value, (e.g., the average number of outpatient visits per closed outpatient episode, the average annual number of workplace injuries in a facility), they generally do *not* consider the impact of variation around that average value. If they do consider possible variation, they generally assume a bell-shaped, symmetrical distribution of variation around the average value, called a "normal" distribution. The problem is that most distributions of health care services and safety performance and costs *are not normally distributed.* Rather, there are "skewed" distributions, in which the average value typically is greater than the "modal" value (i.e., the most likely value) because there are a small number of very high values that "drag up" the average. In other words, there are small probabilities of very large values and very large probabilities of moderate or small values.

In addition, the reliability of the average variability that can be expected is a function of the total number of lives under risk. With very large populations and very large numbers of episodes, incidents and service units, some skewed distributions will begin to approach "normality" in shape.

Because variation is not likely to be symmetrical, one should not look only at average values for these three variables. Paramount in estimating possible risk and reward is also understanding and measuring the possible variation above or below the average that can occur in both cost and utilization.

A full exposition of the various types of theoretical statistical distributions that can occur is not possible here. Some of these distributions can be extremely skewed, (i.e., Pareto distributions) and others less skewed or nearly normal (i.e., Poisson distributions). Examine the distributions in Figures 1 – 4. Two of them are non-normal and skewed. The two normal distributions vary widely in their variation. Note that they all have the same mean, $110.

Variation in the Medicaid population and behavioral health care. To measure variation, one needs to understand the underlying factors that are "driving" it. Many sources of variation can be managed or controlled in order to reduce the upside variation. For example, formal algorithms for triage to service programs and formalized treatment protocols can reduce variation attributable to the day-to-day decisions made by clinicians. Other factors that affect variation cannot be easily managed and changed in the short run, such as poverty or the prevalence of disease in a particular population.

It is safe to assume that average utilization estimates based on commercially insured lives cannot be readily generalized to the Medicaid population. Not only will the average measures be different, it is likely that Medicaid populations will reflect a greater variability around these averages. In other words, even if the averages are comparable, the "shapes" of the distributions will vary, with Medicaid distributions having more upside deviation or "skew."

Another important source of variation in utilization and cost are the payer's requirements for unique or specialized services for individual users. The more

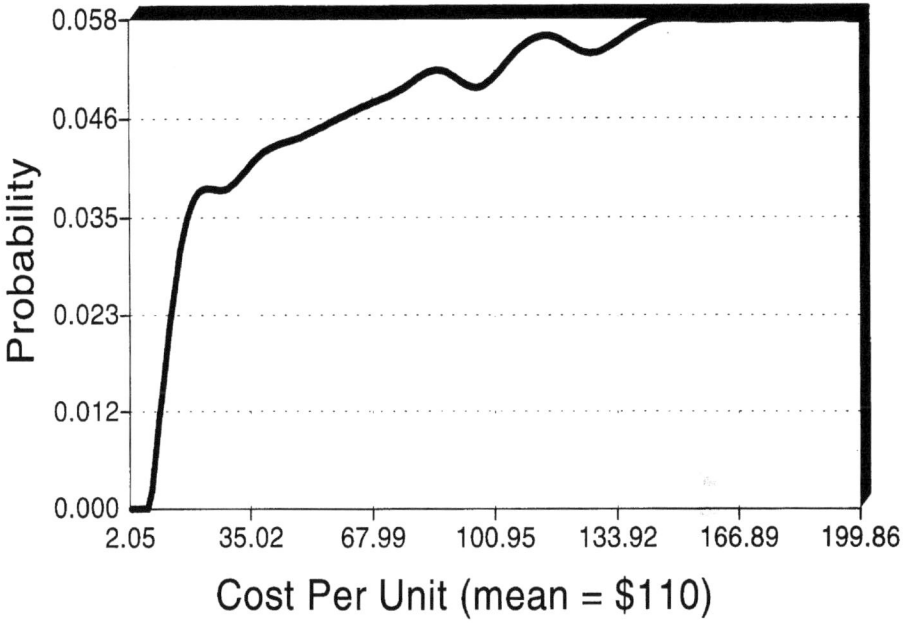

Figure 1. Distribution of Unit Costs.

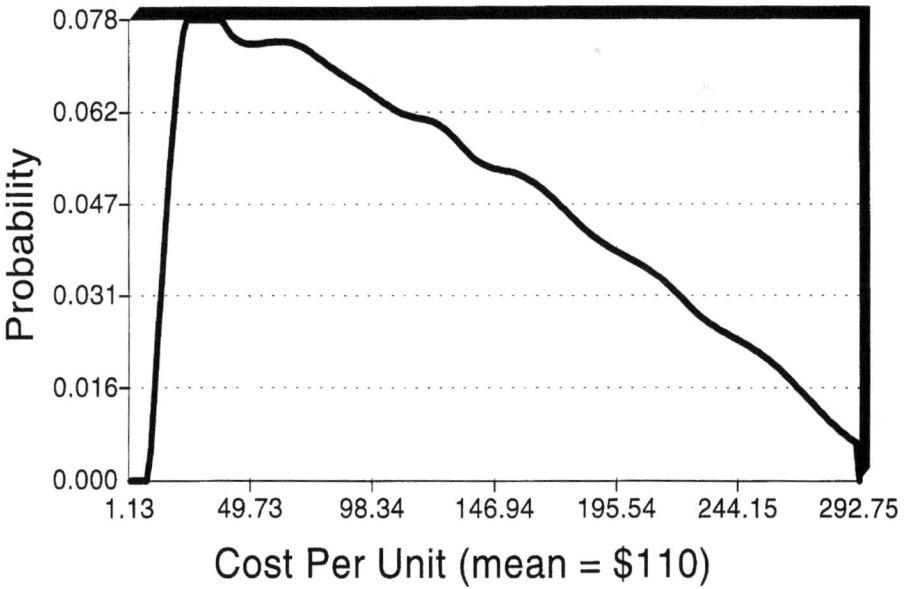

Figure 2. Distribution of Costs

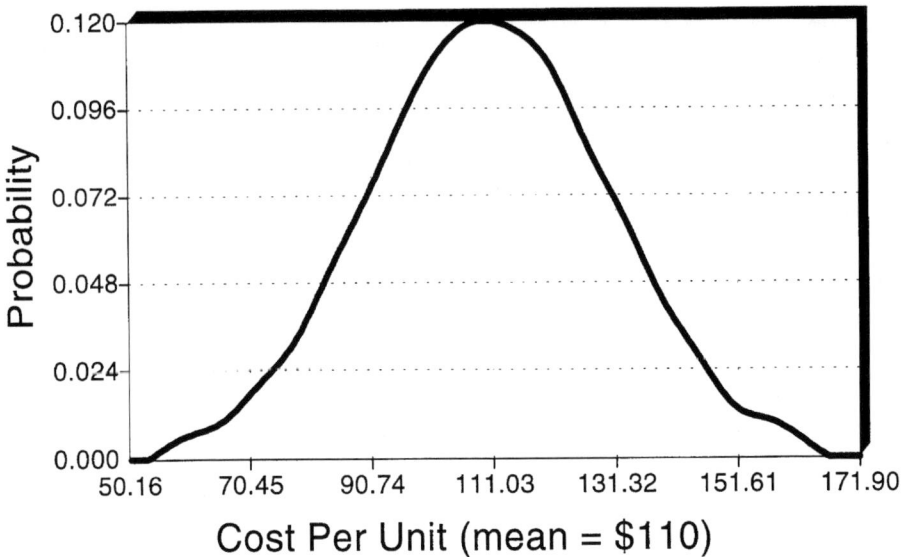

Figure 3. Distribution of Unit Costs.

customized features that are required and provided, the higher the cost of the overall system. For example, if direct service providers must be multilingual or if they must support multiple access points in a neighborhood, then costs will be greater. In accepting risks, providers should be alert to contract requirements of the payer that can introduce increased variation in the estimated utilization or unit-cost factors.

Variation in eligibility status over time is also greater in the Medicaid population. This variation can translate into higher acute-care cost because of lower investment in continuity of care and long-term solutions. If Medicaid eligibility and enrollment with a provider is a monthly, on-again, off-again phenomenon, or if the provider has a short-term contract (i.e., one year) to assume risks for a population with unstable eligibility, then providers are less likely to be motivated to invest in long-term preventative strategies that require long-term reciprocal commitments of patient and provider.

Variation in safety performance and costs. The number or rates of injury or illness incidents in a company or major location within a company, or an employee group are commonly known. Variation in those rates by workgroup or subsets within locations are not usually known, though they sometimes can be retrieved from organizational data bases. Variation across major locations is likely to be expressed only as averages or rates with no description of variation.

In safety performance, similar to health care, units and costs due to injuries and illnesses are typically expressed as averages. Note Figures 1 – 4 and the problems this presents. As mentioned earlier, analysts typically assume "normal" distributions around these averages, usually tight distributions with short tails on either side of the average. However, in most areas of safety performance the distributions are highly skewed. There are many small, low cost incidents that in aggregate are expensive. Their mode, however is quite low. The mean is "dragged up" by a smaller number of expensive incidents, then treated as if it represented the mean of a normal distribution.

"The Actuarial Fallacy"

Actuaries have valuable skills and provide often important services. Their methodology assumes that the future is best predicted by trends based on past performance. Is our future reflected by our past?

When behavioral health providers move from the world of fee-for-service to the world of risk-bearing under managed care, are they moving into a world of new performance contingencies, or a world much like the one they have known? We suggest that under managed care the contingencies shaping organizational performance are radically altered, and service patterns and their costs are also often dramatically changed. The fee-for-service past does not dictate the optimal operating procedures for the risk-bearing environment of next year.

In safety performance, behavioral safety programs have consistently demonstrated the power to sharply improve safe performance and significantly reduce the numbers and rates of workplace injuries and illnesses. This occurs though a strengthened use of systematic feedback and coaching in the workplace to achieve the criteria for safe performance. Not surprisingly incidents and costs decrease. In one company, performance was so poor that *no* insurer would accept risk. Based on actuarial projections, the company was placed in the "assigned risk pool" for the

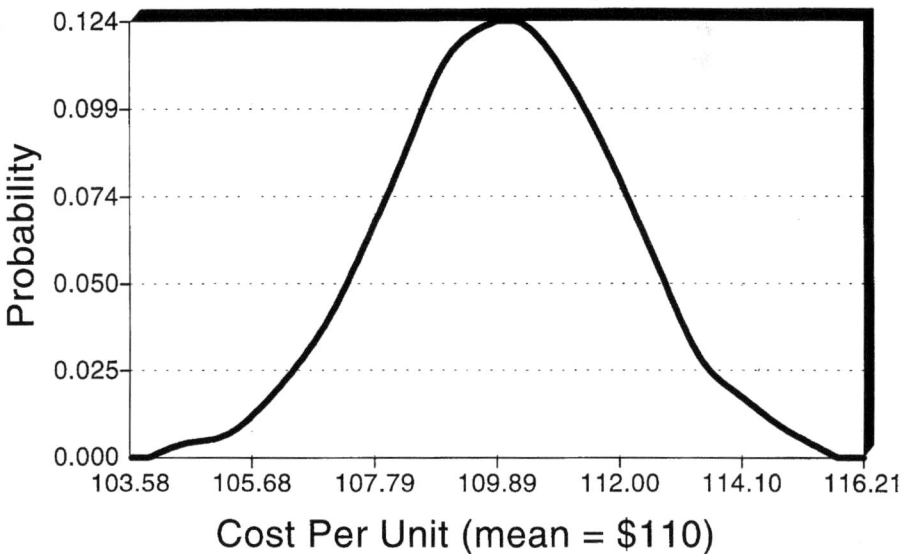

Figure 4. Distribution of Unit Costs.

state. One year later, following the implementation of behavioral safety and return to work programs, incidents and costs had been cut in half, and continued to decline over the next two years (Harshbarger & Rose, 1991).

"The Actuarial Fallacy" is this:

> We can not assume that the future is a linear function of past performance. Accurate actuarial predictions of future performance are possible under two principal conditions. First, when the aggregate sample size and data base of experience across multiple worksites is so large that organizational differences are statistically "washed out"; the law of large numbers applies. Second, when it can be said with confidence that for the period of future time in question there will be no significant changes in the operating environment. When we do such things as implement new programs and technologies, expand or shrink a business, hire and lay off employees, we violate the second assumption. It happens all the time and is the rule, not the exception. At the operating level for most companies, and for virtually all workplaces, the future is only occasionally a linear trend from the past.

Actuarial versus Prospective Modeling of Performance and Risk

The "actuarial fallacy" not withstanding, we still face the challenge of predicting and managing organizational performance and financial risk. The question is how do we approach this challenge?

In behavioral health care the principal paradigm used to establish a PMPM premium for bearing risk is one growing out of traditional actuarial methods. PMPM premiums are based on the use of historically-based averages trended forward, perhaps with some "adjustments" made to account for elements in the system that were not present during the historical time period, (e.g., additional services being covered, new and more expensive drugs, the application of utilization management). Similar methodologies are used in actuarially projecting safety performance and its financial risk.

As discussed earlier, behavioral health care providers are unlikely to be able to use an actuarial approach because adequate, detailed historical data is usually unavailable. In addition, in both behavioral health care and safety performance the historical data is unlikely to reflect the conditions under which future operations, programs and service programs will occur, including the presence of risk-sharing incentives around performance.

In the absence of needed historical data, we propose an alternative strategy called *prospective modeling*. It is one we have used extensively in our work with clients. Table 2 summarizes the major difference between the traditional actuarial and prospective modeling methods.

Most organizations perform their calculations by using averages, as shown in Tables 3 and 4, allowing for a little "slippage" or change in the averages—a type of best-case/worst-case scenario planning. This is generally a hit-or-miss approach, reflecting the subjective risk biases of the person making the estimates.

Differences Between Actuarial and Prospective Estimates and Modeling

Actuarial	Prospective
Assumes the future will be like the past	Assumes the future can be dramatically different than the past
Easy to "lock in" past performance and service patterns	Can forecast multiple and varied performance and service scenarios
Assumes historical data is complete with respect to future plans	Allows systematic planning when historical data is missing or incomplete
Cannot directly account for programs and services not covered or not available in the past	Allows one to estimate the costs of treatment based on protocols and treatment guidelines; new methods, programs to build safe performance
Creates a "Black Box" with little or poor understanding of how much each variable contributes to the final estimation of the cost	Allows one to estimate the costs of contributions of: Rates of Users-Incidents/1000, Episodes-Units per User or Incident, and Cost per Unit
Uses average values calculated from aggregated data. Encourages further use of "average patients and "average incidents" which in reality rarely exist	Uses distributions of raw data that can reflect the reality of: Variation in clinical practice in response to individual patient differences; management decisions and programs altering safety performance and costs

Table 2.

Example in behavioral health care. Assume you are heading a service providing organization and have been told that the PMPM rate the payer will pay for mental health and substance abuse services for a Medicaid eligible population is $30. Assume further that this is a blended rate, (i.e., the rate is the result of blending a $100 PMPM for every SSI-eligible person and a $5 PMPM for every AFDC-eligible person). Assume that this blended rate is the same for all age groups. Your challenge is to use *estimates* of potential users, units and cost per unit to calculate what you think it would cost to serve a blended population of Medicaid-eligible persons. Your worksheet might look like the worksheet in Table 3.

Calculation of PMPM Based on Averages

Population = 50,000

Service	Users Per 1000	Units Per User	Cost Per Unit	Total Cost
Emergency Care	40	3	$250	$1,500,000
Inpatient Care	15	21	$600	$9,450,000
Partial Hospital	35	12	$125	$2,625,000
Outpatient Care	100	8	$ 85	$3,400,000
				Total $16,975,000

$16,975,000 / 50,000 = $339.50 Capitated cost per member per year

$339.50 / 12 months = **$28.29 PMPM**

Table 3.

Looking at the initial assumptions, averages for Users, Units and Cost, it appears that the offered $30 PMPM will be adequate since you project your costs at $28.29. The offered rate of $30 is 5.7% higher than $28.29, a reasonable profit. Right? Pause a moment and reflect on your answer. Although the average values may accurately describe the past, do they describe the future? Were there normal or skewed distributions around these averages?

What if, following your negotiation of the contract, several things happen:

- Welfare reform reduces the number of AFDC-eligible persons but not the SSI-eligible, so the actual number of SSI as a percentage of Total Eligibles goes from 20 percent to 25 percent.
- The relatively greater number of SSI members leads to increased use (more users) of emergency care coupled with more frequent uses within the year (4 times vs. 3).
- There are more re-admissions to the hospital so the effective admission rate is 22/1000 lives and not 15/1000.
- You were able to reduce the average length of stay from 21 days to 14 days but the SSI users tended to use more partial hospital care and have more sessions.
- Due to the population's greater difficulty in maintaining levels of compliance with scheduled appointments, your staff's productivity level was reduced and your effective cost per unit of counseling went up to $95 per hour.

If these events were to come to pass, then your actual cost would be $33.14 PMPM compared with your anticipated cost of $28.29. This difference occurred because inputs varied from the expected averages.

How can you possibly accommodate or anticipate all of the potential combinations of increases or decreases in access rates, service units, and unit costs across all the programs your organization operates? In the above example, there were three variables for each of four programs, or 12 total variables. If each variable's value is independent of every other variable's value, and each variable could take on as few as five possible values (a very conservative assumption), there are 5x5x5x5x5x5x5x5x5x5x5x5 = 244,140,625 combinations of values or possible PMPM calculations! Granted, some of these possible PMPM combinations will be identical because increases in one variable can be offset by decreases in another, but one is still left with a huge number of possible combinations.

Example: In safety performance. Assume that you are a regional manager responsible for the operation of four large distribution centers in a market leading home products company. Your company is in a highly competitive market, and is pressing you to control costs. In examining safety performance and cost, you are hopeful that last year's safety performance and costs will hold for the coming year. Your performance and cost assumptions for lost time injuries and illnesses are outlined in Table 4.

As you complete your business plan for the coming year, you outline the changes you anticipate in your operations.

- Sales volume is expected to grow by 20%, principally though expanded units sold. New sales and marketing programs seem to be working effectively. However, competitive market pressures will continue to push price per unit downwards, intensifying the need to achieve cost controls.
- To handle the increase in unit volume, you plan on expanding the workforce in each Center, adding a total of 400 Order Selectors, 200 Forklift Operators and 200 Loaders.
- Unemployment is low throughout the region. Skilled or experienced people are hard to find.

Distrib. Centers	Employees	Incidents	Per Incident	Total Cost
Center 1	1,000	89	$2,196	$195,444
Center 2	2,000	75	$1,827	$137,025
Center 3	1,500	103	$2,359	$242,977
Center 4	500	68	$1,905	$129,540
			Total	$704,986

Table 4. Calculation of Safety Indemnity Cost, Based on Averages.

- Safety performance among Forklift Operators deteriorated last year. Further, it typically is at its worst among new drivers in their first year.
- Back injuries among Order Selectors and Loaders have increased in frequency and severity over the past two years. Injuries are highest and most costly among 1) new employees and 2) employees with more than 6 years of service. You have plenty of the latter, and plan on hiring more of the former.

The safety performance and cost data in Table 4 deal only with indemnity costs (wages plus medical treatment), i.e., the costs incurred by workplace injuries and illnesses with lost time. There are also medical treatment costs for incidents with no lost time. Further, the additional costs incurred as a result of injury incidents need to be calculated and included, for example property damage from forklift incidents, the hiring and training of employees to replace those who must leave work, the cost of incident investigations, temporary duty programs, etc.

Among lost time injuries and illnesses, the modal cost per claim in Center 1 was $500, even though the average cost per claim was $2,196. Similar patterns, some a little better, some a little worse, held in the other Centers. There were lots of small, relatively low cost incidents, and a few very expensive incidents in each Center. Do calculations based on an average cost per claim reflect this reality? If the true underlying performance is reflected in Figure 5, would you use the mean of the distribution to estimate next year's indemnity costs due to lost time injuries?

Welcome to Monte Carlo

To handle a large number of possible variables and combinations of Users-Incidents, Units and Cost, we recommend the development and use of a formal mathematical model of performance that incorporates at least the three critical

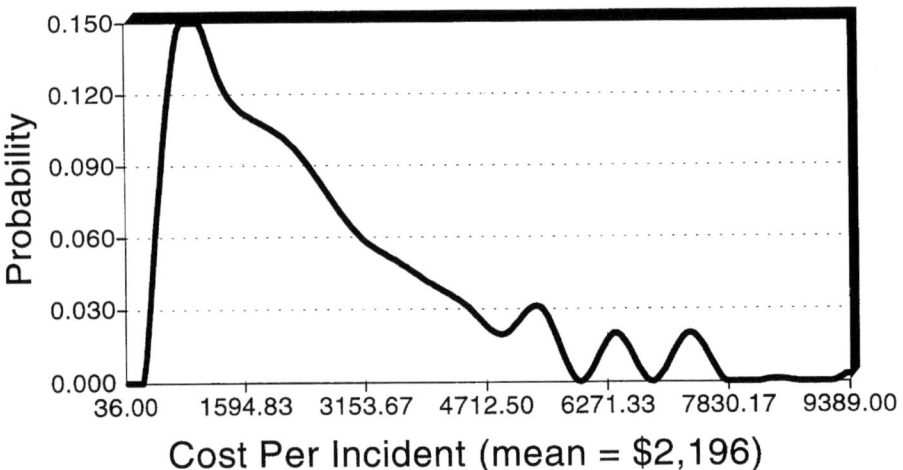

Figure 5. Distribution of Cost Per incident.

variables of users or incidents, units and cost per unit. (It may also be necessary to incorporate additional variables that can affect the values of the "big three"; in behavioral health care , using such variables as readmission rates, staff productivity, patterns of assignment of patients across multiple programs, and ratios of fixed-to-variable costs; in safety performance, the different types of costs created by an injury incident, such as employee replacement, temporary duty, etc.) When these variables are expressed in terms of their potential for variation or as variable distributions, they can be mathematically joined using "Monte Carlo" simulation methods (Rubinstein, 1981) to reflect the overall financial risk for the organization. This risk is expressed as *the probability of a given PMPM cost, or the probability of the cost of workplace injury and illness incidents.*

For any given variable, such as length of stay in treatment, or length of time away from work, one could enter estimates of the likely minimum value, maximum value, average value, and modal value (the length of stay for most admissions, or length of time away from work for lost time incidents). You can then "simulate" the expected range of possible costs and examine a frequency distribution of all possibilities. You can determine the probability of any given PMPM rate coinciding with the specific rate the payer wants to pay; or, the probability that your injury costs will be at or above your threshold value in your business plan. If there is a high likelihood of loss (i.e., cost exceeds revenue in more than 50 percent of the simulations), you can reexamine your projections and perhaps use your simulation data to renegotiate rates or revise your business plan.

There is commercially available software such as Crystal Ball or @Risk, that can be used to create spreadsheets in which all the possible variable inputs (e.g., average units per user or incident, average cost per unit) are linked to calculations of all the desired outputs (e.g., cost per member per month; total cost of workplace injuries and illnesses). The software allows the modeler to replace the input values in spreadsheets, averages, with statistical distributions. The analyst can then run simulations of alternative scenarios. On each trial of the simulation, the software replaces these variable input values with possible alternative values that might be expected to arise, in proportion to their relative probability of occurrence. All the "downstream" calculations (for example, PMPM or total injury costs) that depend on these variable inputs will also change each time the inputs change. If the analyst were to run 100 iterations, 100 possible "results" would be generated. Using the computer, the iterations can be run quickly, and the relative probability of alternative output values can be plotted (see below).

With this approach you can free yourself from the flaw of historical averages and replace your historically based averages with estimated distributions of future possibilities. The distributions can be based on what you think your organization can possibly accomplish through good clinical and workplace performance and management. These estimates can include statistical parameters of variation.

A good prospective model will likely contain the following attributes or structural features.

In behavioral health care.

- Stratification of population cohorts by attributes that are correlated with their probability of becoming users (i.e., SSI versus AFDC; adults versus children, etc.).
- Stratification of users or patients by cohorts that reflect their potential for differential use of programs and differential service use patterns (i.e., seriously mentally ill versus substance abusers versus dually diagnosed versus developmentally disabled).
- For each population cohort, the estimated prevalence of each patient cohort.
- For each patient cohort, the estimated rates of demand for services (i.e., the treated prevalence rate).
- Organizational service capacity, including assumptions about available service time and staff productivity relative to payroll hours, full salary and fringe benefit costs.
- Triage, or projected assignment of clients in each cohort to available clinical programs.
- Fixed and variable costs for each direct service program, as well as organizational overhead costs properly allocated to each direct service program.
- Projected distributions of service utilization within each program for each cohort.
- Based on the variable inputs, formulas to calculate for each cohort within each program and for all programs combined:

  Costs per unit of service
  Episode costs (cost per person for an episode of care within a program)
  Case costs (cost per person across multiple programs)
  PMPM costs

In safety performance.

- Stratification of a population of employee cohorts by attributes that are correlated with their probability of experiencing workplace injuries and illnesses, such as occupational groups and/or workplace locations.
- Stratification of injury and illness incidents to reflect their potential for differential use of programs and differential service patterns (lost time injuries and medical only non-lost time injuries and the direct and indirect costs associated with each form of incident).
- For each incident, the estimate of associated cost units and the cost per unit, including salary-wage costs, medical-rehabilitation costs, the cost of lost productivity or services, employee replacement costs, property damage, etc.

- Projected distributions of incidents, units and costs for each cohort.
- Based on the variable inputs, formulas to calculate for each cohort within each cost element, and for all cost elements combined:

Cost for each type of cost element
Cost per unit within the different types of cost elements
Total cost for each cohort group and/or each location
Business performance ratios
    Cost as a % of sales
    Cost as a % of payroll
    Cost per employee hour worked
Total costs

An example, Monte Carlo and PMPM pricing. Using Monte Carlo simulation, a continuum of probabilities can be generated reflecting a continuum of possible PMPM costs or per-case costs based on the information entered into a model. We ran such a simulation on the model presented in the top half of Table 3, *replacing each average input value entered there with a probability distribution of the range of possible values based on the degree of variation we would expect in those average values.* After running 1,000 simulation trials, we had 1,000 possible PMPM values. These values were then plotted as frequency distributions and cumulative curves.

The frequency distribution of PMPM possibilities arising from the simulation of the model from Table 3 is presented in Figures 6 and 7. Figure 6 is a histogram in which the exact probability of each possible PMPM cost is reflected by the height of each bar over each specific PMPM value. Note the approximate point representing the average expected PMPM cost value of $30. Also note the probability of PMPM costs higher than $30.

Figure 7 presents the same information recast as a cumulative frequency curve. Here, the vertical Y-axis is the *cumulative* probability of a given PMPM value *or less* – that is, the probability that the cost will be the indicated PMPM value along the X-axis or some amount lower than this value. From this curve you can also determine the probability that the PMPM cost will be greater than a given PMPM value. In this case, the probability of a PMPM greater than $30 is equal to 100 percent minus the probability it will be equal to $30 or less than $30.

If you were negotiating a PMPM price, it is likely that you would want to be somewhere in the probability range of .60 to .80 that a given PMPM, or a lower amount, would be likely to occur. Using Figure 7, a PMPM of $31 to $38 would put you in this probability range. It is well beyond the $30 offered, and certainly beyond the $28.29 of our original calculation based on averages.

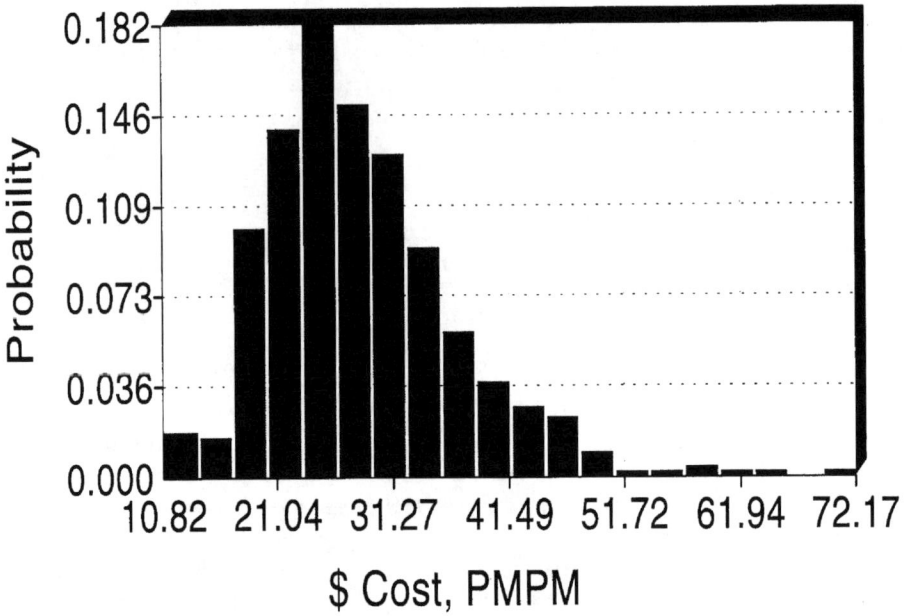

Figure 6. Distribution of Per Member Per Month Cost

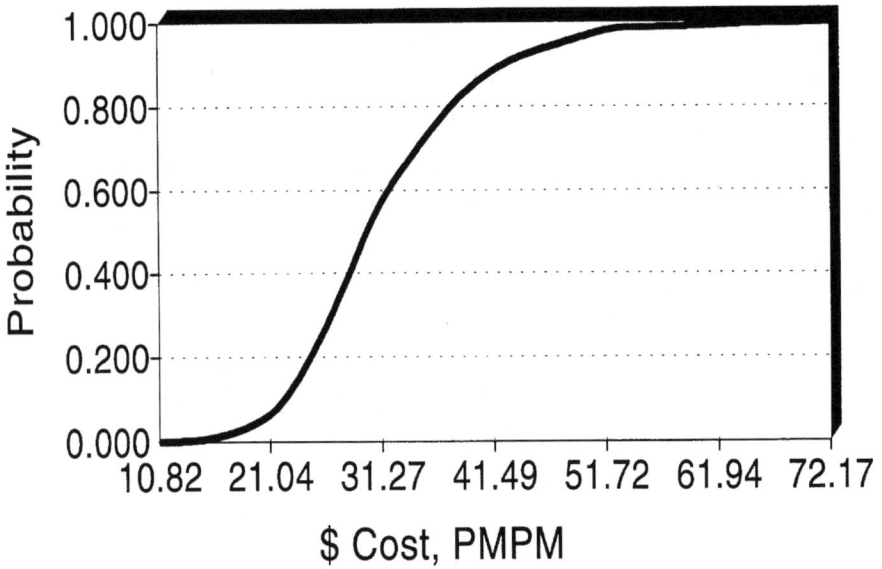

Figure 7. Distribution of Per Member Per Month Cost.

The Y-axis in our graphs gives the likelihood that the PMPM cost will be "$X.xx or less than $X.xx". This "equal to $X or less than $X" measurement reflects the reality that risk-taking is all about an organization's comfort level in not exceeding a given cost level. Using a cumulative probability curve, a probability value can be attached to any given level of PMPM or less. This feature allows managers using Monte Carlo simulation models to make informed judgments about the level of risk they are willing to accept. The range of probable PMPM costs also supports the consideration of various mechanisms to "buffer" the risks. (e.g., withhold pools for catastrophic care, risk corridors). Similar graphs can be generated for any other output (case rates, total cost, units per 1,000, etc.).

Would you be willing to bear financial risk under these conditions:
1.   A probability of .50 or less of just breaking even?
2.   A non-normal distribution that could produce some very high costs?

It's not likely. You would probably want to be funded with a PMPM rate that is high enough to yield a probability of .60 to .80 that your costs will be at or below this level. However, if you are operating in a competitive environment, and other behavioral health care providers are bidding and competing with your organization for the same managed care contract, are you likely to be successful with a conservative but higher PMPM bid of, say, $40? If not, are there steps you might take to alter and reduce your cost structure? You can do this using prospective modeling by changing your operating assumptions and modeling different configurations of organizational performance. You then can enter these new values into the prospective model, and can run a new simulation of 1000 iterations and examine probable outcomes.

Beyond estimating cumulative downside risk, a formal simulation model allows behavioral health care providers to perform a detailed service and financial analysis of programs by cohort groups. Such a model can also be designed to track the flow of patients entering the system of care, and the probabilities of their movement from one program to another. This type of model allows the planner to test the cost-effectiveness of strategies to change the flow. For example, would a Centralized Case Management and Triage program improve the flow of patients into the most cost-effective pathways, reducing the overall PMPM? Finally, such a model can be used to evaluate program performance, examine the variability in per-patient costs, and support continuous quality improvement activities designed to reduce controllable variations.

In safety performance, these models allow organizations to project the distributions of the costs of injuries and illnesses for employee groups by location and/or type of job being performed. The calculation of business performance ratios help executives see the full impact of safety performance costs on the financial health of the business. More accurate forecasting becomes possible. What are the costs of unsafe performance likely to be next year? What are the relative contributions of the different cost elements, such as lost days, medical and rehabilitative costs, return to work programs, temporary duty programs, the hiring and training of replacement employees, lost productivity, etc.? Prospective modeling can give statistically based answers to these questions.

Having built this kind of safety performance and financial risk model, it is then possible to enter into "what if" scenarios. What if, for example, we invested $150,000 in worksite behavioral safety programs in our distribution centers? What if we invested $50,000 in more carefully managing return to work programs? What if we placed $2,000,000 into ergonomic changes our conveyers and loading equipment? Could we expect performance changes? If so, what would be their magnitude? What would the impact be on the distribution and probabilities of cost elements and total injury costs? These and many other questions can be specifically and quantitatively answered across various cost elements and for the total organization using the statistical distributions contained in performance models.

Concluding Comments

Quantifiable, mathematically based prospective models of organizational performance and cost can help providers make sound programmatic and business decisions by incorporating risk and variation into decision making. Prospective models are among the best tools available for estimating risk of behavioral health care and safety performance costs. Even when reasonably good historical data on past performance can be obtained, if we face a future operating environment that is likely to depart from the past, new tools for guiding future performance and risk management will be needed. Statistical models that simulate performance and project costs can be valuable tools for planning and managing organizational performance.

The performance of organizations, reflecting aggregate behaviors and costs within work units, is best characterized using distributions, not point averages. Integrating these distributions into prospective models of organizational performance further strengthens this method of forecasting costs. The effective management of human behavior to produce valuable outcomes under conditions of risk-bearing will be enhanced by models of performance incorporating statistical distributions of performance and costs.

Once in place, the quantitative dimensions of models of organizational performance and cost can be used to specify the criteria for the evaluation of the performance of work teams, departments and other organizational units. These dimensions become the criteria for evaluating the quality of performance and the quality of its management. They form the foundation for answering fundamental questions about the quality of performance:

1. What is a good job?
2. How do we know if we're doing a good job?
3. What happens when we do a good job?

If you quantify your answers to these questions using point averages, means, you are likely to be wrong. Just how wrong, and the human and financial consequences of your errors, will depend on the nature and shape of the ι distributions that you have neglected. As a manager and decision ma of your answers to the "good work questions" and your decisions b answers will be improved by using statistical distributions and prospective models of organizational performance and financial risk.

References

Alavosius, M. P., & Sulzer-Azaroff, B. (1990). Acquisition and maintenance of health-care routines as a function of feedback density. *Journal of Applied Behavior Analysis, 23,* 151-162.

Bernstein, P. (1996). *Against the Gods: The Remarkable Story of Risk.* New York: John Wiley & Sons.

Bourdon, K. A., Rae, D .S., Narrow, W. E., Manderscheid, R. W., & Regier, D. A. (1994). National prevalence and treatment of mental and addictive disorders. In R. W. Manderscheid & M. A. Sonnenschein (Eds.), *Mental health, United States* (pp. 22-51). DHHS Publication No. (SMA) 94-3000. Washington, DC: U.S. Government Printing Office. Washington D.C.

Broskowski, A. (1991). Current mental health care environments: Why managed care is necessary. *Professional Psychology: Research and Practice; Special Issue, 22,* 1-9.

Broskowski, A., & Marks, E. (1992). Managed mental health care. In S. Cooper & T. Lentner (Eds.), *Innovations in Community Mental Health.* Sarasota, FL Professional Resource Exchange.

Broskowski, A. (1993). Mental health financing. In F. McGuirk & A. Sanchez (Eds.), *Managed care and finance reform.* Boulder, CO: Western Interstate Commission for Higher Education.

Broskowski, A. (1995). Financing case management services within the insured sector. In B. Friesen & J. Poertner (Eds.), *Building on Family Strengths: Case Management for Children with Emotional, Behavioral, or Mental Disorders.* Baltimore, MD: Paul Brookes Publishing Co.

Broskowski, A. (1997). The role of risk-sharing arrangements. In L. Scallet, C. Brach, & E. Steel (Eds.), *Managed Care: Challenges for Children and Family Services.* Baltimore, MD: Annie E. Casey Foundation.

Broskowski, A., & Harshbarger, D. (1998). Predicting costs when working with the Medicaid population. In K. Coughlin (Ed.), *1999 Medicaid managed behavioral care sourcebook: Strategies and opportunities for providers and purchasers* (pp. 215-224). New York: Faulkner and Gray, Inc.

Bureau of Labor Statistics (1). *Workplace Injuries and Illnesses in 1995.* Website release, March 12, 1997.

Bureau of Labor Statistics (2). *Lost-worktime Injuries: Characteristics and Resulting Time Away from Work, 1995.* Website release, June 12, 1997.

Burns, B. J., et al. (1997). Insurance coverage and mental health service use by adolescents with serious emotional disturbance. *Journal of Child and Family Studies, 6*(1), 89-111.

Callahan, J., et.al. (1995). MH/SA Treatment in Managed Care: The Massachusetts Experience. *Health Affairs, 14.*

Friedman, R., Katz-Leavy, J., Manderscheid, R., & Sondheim, D. (1996). Prevalence of serious emotional disturbance in children and adolescents. In R.W. Manderscheid & M. A. Sonnenschein (Eds.), *Mental health, United States* (pp. 77-91). DHHS Publication No. (SMA) 96-3098, Washington, DC: U.S. Government Printing Office.

Geller, E. S. (1997) Key processes for continuous safety improvement: Behavior-based recognition and celebration. *Professional Safety*, October.

Harshbarger, D., & Rose, T. (1991). New possibilities in safety performance and the control of workers' compensation costs. *Journal of Occupational Rehabilitation, 1*(2), 133-143.

Harshbarger, D. (1997). Taming Killer Variance: Modeling and managing financial risk and clinical services in managed behavioral health care. In M. A. Freeman (Ed.), *The Breakthrough Innovation Sourcebook and Mutual Consultation Guide* (pp. 198-200). Tiburon, California: CentraLink Publications.

Kochnar, S., & Scott, C. (1995). *Social Security Bulletin, 58*(1).

Leigh, J. P., Markowite, S. B., Fahs, M., Shin, C., & Landrigan, P. J. (1997). Occupational injury and illness in the United States: Estimates of costs, morbidity, and mortality. *Archives of Internal Medicine, 157*, 1557-1568.

Rubinstein, R. Y. (1981). *Simulation and the Monte Carlo method.* New York: John Wiley & Sons.

Sulzer-Azaroff, B., & Harshbarger, D. (1995). Putting fear to flight. *Quality Progress*, December, 61-65.

Discussion of Harshbarger

From Benevolent Gods to Mathematical Prediction: Placing a Value on the Vagaries of the Future

Michael C. Clayton
Jacksonville State University

While quite technical in spots, the preceding paper "Beyond the Flaw of Averages: Managing Organizational Performance and Financial Risk" offers a solid methodology that is refreshingly broad in applicability. For over two decades, the field of financial engineering has been developing and applying the same principles to everything from the stock market to the weather. As it turns out, the uncertainties of a market crash or the next hurricane can be priced, divided into marketable chunks, and sold to someone who is willing to bear the risk; in exchange for a fee or a future stream of revenue. The technology allows one to completely manage the risks of an entire organization.

Before preceding, it is important to understand that there is no "hocus pocus" involved, reliable mathematical models are being utilized, to great effect. In fact, the 1998 Nobel Prize for economics went to Myron Scholes and Robert Merton, two of the creators of the options-pricing model that has helped to fuel the explosion of activity in the derivatives markets.

Financial engineering attempts to put a price on uncertainty (Stix, 1998). In the stock markets it can be thought of as *purchasing volatility*. Financial risk in the preceding paper can be thought of as the probability that the number of misfortunes and associated costs for a defined population of employees over a given time period will be at or above a given estimated cost. Essentially, money is being made on the basis of being able to predict any variation (however slight) about a mean.

The "Flaw of Averages" in the paper's title refers to the assumption of a linear progression of yesterday, through today, and into tomorrow. It reflects a common human tendency to predict that tomorrow will be very similar to today, maybe a little better or maybe a little worse. Most of the time, this prediction holds true. When someone is told of an average value they generally do not consider the impact of variation around that average value. The standard deviation about a mean can be more telling than the mean itself. Even when the standard deviation is considered, one normally assumes a bell-shaped, symmetrical distribution of variation about the mean, the so-called "normal" distribution.

The problem with his assumption is that, in the "real" world, distributions are rarely normally distributed. With regard to health care services, safety performance, and agency costs, the distribution is, in fact, skewed. It is important to realize that a small number of very high values can "drag up" the average value. That is, there are small probabilities of very large values and very large probabilities of moderate or small values.

The "Managing risk" portion of the title posits that if we can make an educated guess or somewhat accurate prediction into the immediate future we will be better off than the other guy. Traditionally, risk simply meant a threat to the expected. Whereas, more accurately, risk is about uncertainty or probabilities; how much will be gained or lost? What are the probabilities associated with different levels of gain or loss? Simply, risk is about variation. Bernstein (1996) suggests that we can separate modern from pre-modern Western societies on the basis of how risk is managed. Previously, organizations put their faith in God or Gods and assumed that the future, with all of its unknowns, was under existential sources of control.

Managing risk becomes increasingly important as public not-for-profit behavioral health services enter the world of managed behavioral health care. Historically, these public organizations operated with relative financial security and relatively low financial risk. With the advent of managed care, behavioral health organizations have found themselves entering the private sector; a world of financial risk, profits and losses.

While the prospective modeling techniques being discussed in the previous paper allow one to manage risk more effectively, models are not without risks all their own. Needless to say, any model is only as good as the data that it operates upon. Thus, mathematical models can be quite brittle. The bankruptcy of Orange County, California presents a startling example of how complacency when utilizing modeling techniques can lead to unexpected results. The members of the school boards simply accepted the projections spun forth by the mathematicians without taking into account the existence of a 5% chance of a billion-dollar-plus loss. The result was a rare, but extreme, loss of $1,700,000,000. Modeling techniques sometimes fail to capture the magnitude of rare and unlikely events. This, of course, is the nature of managing risk. Managing risk implies that you will manage your risks while your competitors will not.

Finally, when balancing profit and loss to achieve the most beneficial outcome, it is increasingly easy to lose track of quality of care issues. The ideal situation would be one in which health care services could be provided to all that need them. This would be done without over-budgeting, creating surplus, or under-budgeting, and then being unable to provide quality care to everyone.

The difference between a successful organization and an unsuccessful one comes down to the ability to predict, with some accuracy, variation about means. How much service will be enough without going over on either end of the spectrum? A surprising implication of this is the case in which financial managers plan for a certain, definable future. If a behavioral safety program changes the dynamics of safety costs dramatically, i.e., decreasing plant accidents by 50%, then the projected health care costs will miss the mark. In fact, the successful safety intervention will end up *costing* the organization more than it saved as a result of misjudged risk.

The societies of antiquity placed everything in the hands of Gods. If crops were abundant, then gratitude was owed to the Gods. If the baby died soon after birth, then a more pious life-style was indicated. The sources of control were existential and beyond our ability to comprehend the whys of our existence. Today's organizations are attempting to place a value upon the vagaries of the future. In this future, it may be possible to imagine a security for every condition in the world; and any risk, from bankruptcy to a rained-out picnic, could be shifted to someone else. I will leave it to the reader to ponder exactly how far civilization has come with regard to managing the risks associated with our delicate existence.

References

Bernstein, P. L. (1996). *Against the gods: The remarkable story of risk.* New York, NY: John Wiley & Sons, Inc.

Stix, G. (1998). A calculus of risk. *Scientific American, 278*(5), 92-97.

Outside the Box: The Analysis of Consumer Behavior

Donald A. Hantula and Diane F. DiClemente
Temple University
Amy K. Rajala
Liberty Mutual Group

....don't be caught consuming less than your share.
(Aldous Huxley, *Brave New World*)

Ours is a culture of consumption. In post-industrial society, consumption, not production is the primary economic activity. Indeed, many readers of this chapter, their family and their friends will probably never produce tangible, fungible goods during decades of work. Yet, each day, these same individuals will consume dozens of goods and services in their personal and professional lives. Even when tangible goods are consumed, it is often within the context of simultaneously consuming particular services, such as in the case of a McDonald's hamburger or a Gateway computer (Schneider & Bowen, 1995). This transition from manufacturing to malling has not gone unnoticed; it was anticipated, discussed, and appraised by a spectrum of social commentators as varied as Baudrillard (1970/1997), Borsodi (1929), Gailbrath (1958), and Huxley (1932). While it may seem self-evident that anyone interested in organizations would be expert in matters of consumer behavior, ironically, the study of consumption has a long past but a short and sparse history both within Industrial/Organizational Psychology (see, Foxall, 1997; Van De Water, 1997) and within Organizational Behavior Analysis (see Buckley, 1982).

From a first glance at the academic literatures in management and marketing, it would seem that studying, understanding, and managing the behavior of customers is intrinsically different from studying, understanding, and managing the behavior of employees. But the organisms, methods, and theories are the same in each case. That "management" and "marketing" has become so divided as to be viewed as wholly separate entities or boxes on the organizational chart, and separate departments or boxes within colleges and schools of business is more a case of evolved administrative overspecialization than it is of actual epistemic difference. The only real dissimilarity may be the placement of boxes. Just as "employee" was a deliberately manufactured social construct of the industrial age, "....the same knowledge used to produce the producers of products became the same knowledge used to produce the needs of the consumer." (Jacques, 1996, p. 153). Thus, the locus and context for employee behavior and consumer behavior are the same; each are engaging in behavior highly subject to the immediate and distal influences of the organization or its products. As such, the behavior of consumers is an entirely appropriate matter for study in Organizational Behavior Analysis.

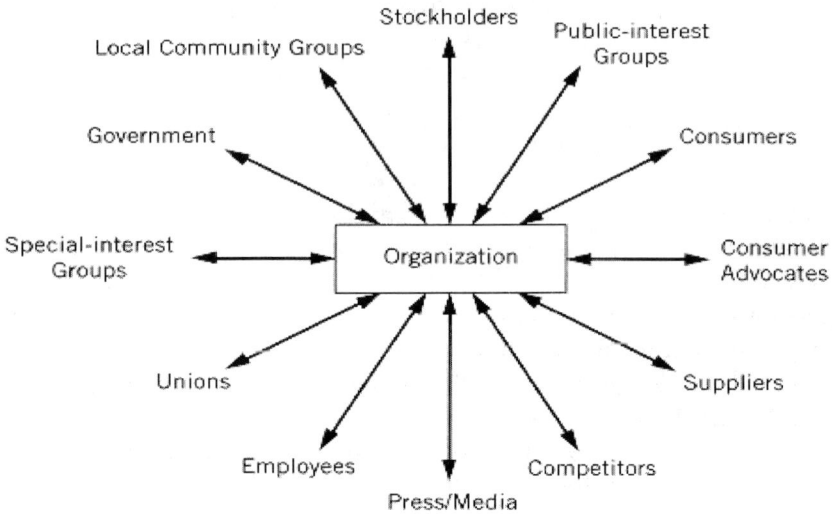

Figure 1. The organizational box, as depicted in the stakeholder model of the organization (from J. L. Bowditch and A. M. Buono, 1997 A Primer on Organizational Behavior (4th ed.). NY: Wiley. Used by permission).

Accordingly, in this chapter we step outside the traditional organizational box to present an emergent behavioral analysis of consumption. After a brief historical review to establish some context, the contemporary status of consumer research from a behavioral perspective is assessed. Three current and complementary research streams are identified and discussed. Intellectual trends in consumer behavior research, especially the rise of classical conditioning in advertising and postmodern influences in consumer inquiry are presented as possible establishing operations for further behavior analytic work in consumption. Finally, a modern research agenda in the analysis of consumer behavior is proposed.

Inside the Box: Managing Organizations

Curiously, organizations are often depicted as boxlike fortresses, with thick, solid walls and a clear demarcation between those individuals who are inside the organization and those who are outside the organization. For example, Figure 1 shows a common illustration of the organization in its environment, as presented in a leading graduate management/organizational behavior text (Bowditch & Buono, 1997). The people inside the box are referred to as "employees." "Management" is the discipline concerned with their behavior, and the umbrella of "human resources" comprises the various organizational functions relating to employees[1].

Intra-organizational behaviors. The behavior of employees acting within the organization are termed **intra-organizational behaviors**. Since the advent of the

Organizational Behavior Management (OBM) movement, a substantial literature documenting many successes in modifying intra-organizational behaviors has developed (see Frederiksen, 1982; O'Brien, Dickinson, & Rosow, 1982; Stajkovic & Luthans, 1997). Illustrative applications of operant-based procedures for changing employee behavior include those which: increase productivity (e.g., Anderson, Crowell, Hantula, & Siroky, 1988; Johnson, Welsh, Miller, & Altus, 1991; Welsh, Luthans, & Sommer, 1993; Wikoff, Anderson, & Crowell, 1982), improve safety (e.g., Alavosius & Sulzer-Azaroff, 1990; Babcock, Sulzer-Azaroff, & Sanderson, 1992; Fox, Hopkins, & Anger, 1987; Hopkins, Conard, Dangel, Fitch, Smith, & Anger, 1986; Komaki, Barwick, & Scott, 1978; Rhoten, 1980), increase attendance/decrease absenteeism (e.g., Gaetani, Johnson, & Austin, 1983; Kopelman & Schneller, 1981; Silva, Duncan, & Doudna, 1981), reduce waste (e.g., Eldridge, Lemasters, & Szypot, 1978; Runnion, Watson, & McWhorter, 1978), and win hockey games (Anderson, Crowell, Doman, & Howard, 1988).

Boundary behaviors. However, an organization does not survive by intra-organizational behaviors alone. As an integral part of their duties, many employees interface between the organization and members of its environment. The behaviors of employees who interface with extra-organizational actors while acting within the organization are termed *boundary behaviors*. Just as is the case in modifying intra-organizational behaviors, a large literature describing successful OBM interventions with boundary behaviors exists. Illustrative applications of OBM to boundary behaviors include work with airline reservation agents (Feeney, Staelin, O'Brien, & Dickinson, 1982), waitpersons (George & Hopkins, 1989; Ralis & O'Brien, 1986), real estate sales people (Anderson, Crowell, Sucec, Gilligan, & Witkoff, 1982), department store clerks (Brown, Malott, Dillon, & Keeps, 1980; Luthans, Paul, & Baker, 1981), bank tellers (Crowell, Anderson, Abel, & Sergio, 1988), and fast food franchise employees (Komaki, Blood, & Holder, 1980; Komaki, Waddell, & Pearce, 1977; Martinko, White, & Hassell, 1987; Welsh, Bernstein, & Luthans, 1992).

Extra-organizational behaviors. In a functional management-centric view, the behaviors of extra-organizational actors are important only to the extent to which they impact directly on boundary behaviors or intra-organizational behaviors. And, not surprisingly, in the OBM literature, scant attention (relative to other emphases) has been paid to modifying the behavior of extra-organizational actors. Granted, the behavior of many extra-organizational actors such as government agency employees, union officials, and other stakeholders may be entirely outside of the organization's sphere of influence. Thus, we have a conceptualization of organization in which behaviors are defined by their locus with respect to the organization's formal boundaries. Just like "management" in general, OBM is in the box.

The Organic Organization

McDonald's has more employees than U.S. Steel.
Golden arches, not blast furnaces, symbolize the American economy.
(George F. Will)

The four-walled depiction of the organization-cum-fortress is a holdover from medieval times and the industrial age. So long as goods are produced within the organizational walls and made available to consumers through extra-organizational distribution channels, this conceptual division may be adaptive. However, that economy disappeared decades ago. It would have made little sense to analyze or run a factory as if it were a farm; and it makes little sense now to analyze or run a service business as if it were a factory. Just as "employee" was manufactured as a part of the industrial revolution (Jacques, 1996), "consumer" is created as part of the post-industrial revolution. But unlike an employee, a consumer is not confined by the box walls.

Consumers are intimately involved in the "production" of services (Albrecht & Zemke, 1985; Schneider & Bowen, 1995). And, because services are not fungible, they cannot be created in the absence of the consumer and stored for future use. Thus, in order for an organization to survive, consumers must be able to easily pass in and out of it as they need. This suggests a different metaphor for organization, one not based on construction and machinery, but rather on biology. Perhaps a more suitable view is one of organization-as-cell. A cell is distinct from its environment, and contains intracellular (or intra-organizational) functions, but the cell wall is a *permeable* boundary that allows certain entities to pass in and out of the cell. Further, a cell is dynamic, adaptive, and responsive to its environment; attributes which presumably characterize thriving organizations in the fluid economy.

Metaphors control the way we think (Skinner, 1957). The metaphor of an organic organization with a permeable cell wall should occasion significant reconsideration of the definition of extra-organizational behaviors on the part of consumers. Spatial and temporal constraints implied by the organizational box dissipate with the metaphor of organism-organization. As consumers move in and out of the organization spatially as in a storefront, they may also engage the organization in more temporally distant manners, such as through mail, telephone contact or through the Internet, as occurs with such retailers as Land's End, CD Now, or Amazon Books. Further, when repeated movement in and out of an organization is the primary mode of interface, the consumer is no longer a single individual acting with respect to the organization at a single point in time (such as when purchasing a good or service once), but instead engages in a temporally extended relationship with the organization.

In modern commerce, consumers become human resources, leaders, and consultants to successful organizations (Schneider & Bowen, 1995). Indeed, when a consumer places an order for a particular good or service to be completed to their specifications (e.g., a Wendy's spicy chicken sandwich without mayonnaise or a Dell computer with two floppy disk drives), the consumer becomes, albeit briefly, a manager. It is at this point that the consumer is directing the work of the organization's employees and is engaging in intra-organizational behavior. Johnson (1985) provides an example of how a consumer used prompts and reinforcement to modify newspaper distribution to coin operated boxes.

Because organizations exist to direct and control the behavior of their members (Scott, 1987), a question arises; to what extent should the consumer's behavior be controlled by the organization? Broad management prerogatives regarding the control of employee behavior are culturally accepted and codified legally. However, organizational control of consumer behavior is controversial (Markin & Narayana, 1975). It may be argued that because employees are "part" of the organization, their behavior is rightfully subject to strong organizational control. Yet this argument is an endorsement of the fortress-organization and ignores the realities of the modern marketplace. Employees are not captives of the organization; they can choose to enter or leave an organization's employment, just as a consumer can choose to enter or leave. When consumers interface with most modern organizations, they become part of that organization, and are therefore subject to greater control by the organization. Indeed, the purpose of advertising, promotions, merchandise display, and store layout design is to control consumer behavior, although this may not be always explicitly acknowledged by practitioners of these professions. Perhaps the real point of contention is not the extent to which organizational control of consumer behavior is permitted, but rather the extent to which organizational control of consumer behavior is frankly recognized, and the degree to which haphazard, unacknowledged control is preferred to deliberate, acknowledged control (Skinner, 1971).

The Analysis of Consumer Behavior in 30 Year Cycles

Although behavioral applications in management are well established, behavioral work in consumption preceded the OBM movement by decades. Interest in the behavioral analysis of consumption has waxed and waned in 30 year cycles and its history reads much like a history of behavior analysis. Initial work was done by Watson (emphasizing classical conditioning), later work was accomplished by of one of Skinner's students (emphasizing reinforcement schedules), followed by more recent explorations that expanded the analysis to include verbal behavior and adaptive/evolutionary perspectives.

Cycle 1: J. B. Watson in the 1930's

In 1920 John B. Watson joined the J. Walter Thompson advertising agency. The national advertising industry in the 1920's grew as a response to the outgrowth of a system of industrial production that was becoming increasingly geared toward distributing goods on a national scale. Because of the tremendous growth of products and services, advertisers looked to psychology to facilitate the distribution and marketing process, and Watson was a well-known psychologist of his day.

In a presentation to a graduating class of R. H. Macy Co. executives, Watson (1922, p. 3) stated, "The consumer is to the manufacturer, the department stores and the advertising agencies, what the green frog is to the physiologist." Watson's analogy of the customer and the green frog illustrates how the marketplace was seen as a laboratory for the advertising industry and how the consumer was akin to the experimental subject whose behavior was subject to deliberate control by the advertiser. As a former laboratory scientist, it is not surprising that Watson emphasized the need to establish consumer reactions under laboratory conditions, using sample populations of consumers as subjects, so that advertisers could refine their techniques scientifically. The goal of advertising was not limited to providing information about given products or services, but it was about creating a society of consumers and controlling their consumption behavior.

Because mass production rendered many competing products indistinguishable in quality and function, Watson was convinced that marketing goods depended not upon an appeal to reason but upon emotional conditioning and stimulation of desire. Watson believed control of consumption could be achieved by the use of behavioral techniques to condition emotional responses, as evidenced in a statement to his advertising colleagues, "To get hold of your consumer, or better, to make your consumer react, it is only necessary to confront him with either fundamental or conditioned emotional stimuli." To assure the appropriate reaction from consumer, Watson instructed advertisers to "tell him something that will tie up with fear, something that will stir up a mild rage, that will call out an affectionate or love response, or strike at a deep psychological or habit need." These "secret and hidden springs of action" were the "powerful genii of psychology," (Watson, cited in Buckley, 1982, p. 212).

In an analysis of Watson's advertisements developed for Pond's facial cream, Coon (1994) identified three common features; evoking emotion rather than cognition, providing specific instructions for using the product, and employing direct testimonials. Testimonials had long been used by manufacturers of patent medicines and were generally held in low esteem by most advertisers. However, under Watson's direction the Thompson agency revived testimonial advertising which sparked a re-evaluation of testimonials by the industry. Some of Watson's direct testimonials linked the product with an appeal to authority or a desire for emulation. But it was through indirect testimonials that employed symbols to stimulate responses of fear, rage, and love that Watson felt that brand appeal depended on factors other than usefulness or product reliability.

Although Watson's academic credentials lent a certain legitimacy to the burgeoning advertising industry, it is not clear how much his brand of behaviorism influenced advertising. Certainly the appeals to emotion through "classical conditioning," and providing specific behavioral guidelines for using a product may have been occasioned by his previous behavioral research, it appears that he actually improved upon existing advertising techniques rather than developing anything new (Coon, 1994). Recounting a 1955 interview with Watson, Burnham (1994, p. 68) writes: "I asked him how his training in psychology affected his work in the advertising agencies. He said psychology was irrelevant and had no effect on his work."

Cycle 2: O. R. Lindsley in the 1960's

In contrast to Watson's emphasis on Pavlovian conditioning, Ogden Lindsley introduced operant conditioning and direct recording of ongoing consumer behavior using conjugate reinforcement schedules as the basic analytic tool. Under a conjugate reinforcement schedule, a subject will directly and immediately control the intensity of a continuously available reinforcing stimulus, such as a television show. In a typical study of this type, subjects sat in a room with a television receiver or projection device. The subject could use a hand or foot switch to produce a slight increase in the brightness of an image. High rates of responding kept the picture brightly illuminated, and moderate responses kept the picture at dimmer levels, and no response kept the picture dark. The cumulative records furnished a direct measure of the consumer's moment to moment interest in the advertisement, program or text (Lindsley, 1962). By using the conjugate schedules to study television viewing, Lindsley proposed that researchers should examine specific aspects of television viewing such as selecting an appropriate program for a given commercial, examining interprogram comparisons, selecting an appropriate selection of media, describing the specific consumer targets, and choosing the proper technical procedures.

This conjugate reinforcement trend continued in the 1960's when several advertising researchers used a device called CONPAAD, (Conjugately Programmed Analysis of Advertising) to measure advertising effectiveness. CONPAAD was used to study attention to story board and finished versions of advertisements (Nathan & Wallace, 1965), the effects of satiation on advertising (Grass & Wallace, 1969), magazine article interest (Wolf, Newman, & Winters, 1969), and readership of magazine articles (Winters & Wallace, 1970). Although popular and pragmatic, the CONPAAD technology fell into disuse due to the rise of eyetracking technology (e.g., Russo, 1978), and Lindsley's pursuit of other research projects (O. R. Lindsley, personal communication, May 24, 1998).

Cycle 3: BPM and Behavioral Ecology

As the OBM movement came of age in the 1980s, some researchers began turning their attention to more theoretical studies in analog settings of such organizationally important topics as leadership (Rao & Mawhinney, 1991), intrinsic motivation (Mawhinney, Dickinson, & Taylor, 1989), and financial decision making (DeNicolis-Bragger, Bragger, Hantula, & Kirnan, 1998; Goltz, 1992, 1993, in press; Hantula & Crowell, 1994a, b; Hantula & DeNicolis-Bragger, 1999). This expansion of the field may be attributed to a number of coinciding factors including the proliferation of powerful low-cost microcomputers and advances in programming languages which allowed many of these studies to be conducted (DiFonzo, Hantula, & Bordia, 1998), a maturing of the field (Hantula, in press), an infusion of new researchers seeking their own niches, and the behavioral momentum of over 20 years of collective reinforcement from many successful applied studies.

Concurrent with this expansion into more theoretical research was the advent of two independently developed behavior analytic research programs in consumption, the Behavioral Perspectives Model (Foxall, 1990) and the Behavioral Ecology of Consumption (Rajala & Hantula, in press). Although the occasional conceptual article appeared either calling for a behavioral analysis of consumption, or introducing consumer researchers to the basic tenets of behavior analysis (e.g., Foxall, 1986a, b, 1987; Geller, 1989; Kunkel & Berry, 1968; McSweeney & Bierley, 1984; Nord & Peter, 1981; Peter & Nord, 1982; Rothschild & Gaidis, 1981), these two research programs represent the first thematic behavioral approaches to the study of consumption.

The Analysis of Consumer Behavior: Current Status

Although it may appear that there are as many conceptual articles on the behavioral analysis of consumption as there are empirical studies, there exists a growing literature documenting behavior analytic studies of consumers which have clearly followed several distinct trends. Beginning in the early 1960's television viewing was the first clearly defined trend in consumer literature (e.g., Grass & Wallace, 1969; Lindsley, 1962; Nathan & Wallace, 1965). Studies in the environmental realm were the next boom in behavior analytic consumer research beginning in the early 1970's, ranging from conserving electricity (e.g., Winett, 1977) to conserving paper to increasing bus ridership (Deslausiers & Everett, 1977; Everett, Hayward, & Meyers, 1974). These types of studies continue to appear in the more recent literature (e.g., Austin, Hatfield, Grindle, & Bailey, 1993). The next wave in consumer research focused on Pavlovian conditioning in the early 1980's. Gorn's (1982) classical conditioning study clearly sparked a debate over the effectiveness of classical conditioning in advertising and marketing arenas that has lasted until today (e.g., Janiszewski & Warlop, 1993; Tom, 1995). The health conscious 1980's sparked an interest in healthy food choice studies (e.g., Wagner & Winett, 1988). Now the trend is shifting towards more theoretically oriented explorations of consumption.

The Applied Analysis of Consumer Behavior

Applied Behavior Analysis is focused on applying the principles and procedures of the basic science of behavior analysis to improve socially important behaviors. Research in Applied Behavior Analysis spans a wide range of endeavors from habilitation work with individuals with developmental disabilities (e.g., Matson, 1989) to the behavior of consumers. Most of the Applied Behavior Analysis studies of extra-organizational behaviors have focused either on managing behaviors *other* than purchasing behaviors such as, resource conservation (Foxx & Hake, 1977; Geller, Chaffee, & Ingram, 1975; Seaver & Patterson, 1976; Winett, 1977; Winett, Hatcher, Fort, Leckliter, Love, Riley, & Fishback, 1982; Winett, Kaiser, & Haberkorn, 1977; Winett, Leckliter, Chin, Stahl, & Love, 1985; Winkler & Winett, 1982; Witmer & Geller, 1976), environmental preservation (Austin, et al., 1993; Burgess, Clark, & Hendee, 1971; Clark, Burgess, & Hendee, 1972; Geller, Farris, & Post, 1973; Kohlenberg & Phillips, 1973; Powers, Osborne, & Anderson, 1973), customer safety belt usage (Cope, Moy, & Grossnickle, 1988; Hagenzieker, 1991; Malenfant & Van Houten, 1988; Rudd & Geller, 1985; Sowers-Hoag, Thyer, & Bailey, 1987; Williams, Thyer, Bailey, & Harrison, 1989), and other prevention behaviors (Cope & Allred, 1991; Cope, Allred, & Morsell, 1991; Honnen & Kleinke, 1990; Jason, Neal, & Marinakis, 1985; Lombard, Neubauer, Canfield, & Winett, 1991; Ragnarsson &

Bjorgvinsson, 1991; Stock & Milan, 1993; Van Houten, Rolider, Nau, Friedman, Becker, Chalodovsky, & Scherer, 1985), or have "accidentally" discovered interesting modifiers of consumer behavior such as prompting or pricing strategies through research of a different focus (Martinko, 1987).

However, some research on modifying purchasing behaviors in retail environments has been conducted. Studies of techniques to increase consumption include McNally and Abernathy (1989) who used reinforcement schedules to increase Automatic Teller Machine (ATM) use, and McCall and Belmont (1996) who studied the influence of credit card insignia on tipping as an instance of stimulus equivalence. Studies focused on changing consumption centered largely on modifying food choices of customers towards healthier foods (Mayer, Heins, Vogel, Morrison, Lankester, & Jacobs, 1986; Wagner & Winett, 1988; Winett, Kramer, Walker, Malone, & Lane, 1988; Winett, Moore, Wagner, Hite, Leahy, Neubauer, Walberg, Walker, Lombard, Geller, & Mundy, 1991) or less expensive foods (Greene, Rouse, Green, & Clay, 1984), and training children in appropriate shopping deportment in a grocery store (Barnard, Christophersen, & Wolf, 1977). Studies of decreasing consumption include those of the effect of response cost procedures on local directory-assistance calls (McSweeny, 1978), the impact of law enforcement practices on sales of cigarettes to minors (Jason, Billows, Wyatt-Schnopp, & King, 1996), and techniques for reducing shoplifting (Carter & Holmberg, 1992; Carter, Holmstrom, Simpanen, & Melin, 1988; Carter, Kindstedt, & Melin, 1995; Gaetani & Johnson, 1983; McNees, Egli, Marshall, Schenlle, & Risley, 1976) which is, after all, a method of consumption. One study (Carter, et al., 1995) found, interestingly, that labeling items as "on sale" increased the probability of their being stolen, perhaps acting as an establishing operation for consumption.

What is noteworthy in the above literature is the distinction made between managing the elimination of behavior (e.g. littering, consumption, wasting, illegally parking in handicapped spaces, shoplifting, unsafe driving practices) or "deconsumption" in marketing terms, and managing the acquisition of behavior (e.g. recycling, purchasing). It appears that the majority of the work to date has been concentrated on "social marketing" issues (Geller, 1989; Kotler & Zaltman, 1971), rather than on consumption issues as generally understood within marketing. While most of the research cited above prescribes guidelines for reducing certain consumer behaviors, there is a conspicuous absence of literature on managing consumer behavior from an operant perspective, especially with respect to acquisition of purchasing behaviors. These studies simply demonstrate that applied behavior analysis can be used to modify consumer behavior. Yet, there is not a coherent body of research which is theoretically and practically relevant to marketers, consumer behavior managers, and researchers as the more general body of OBM work is to those who study and practice management.

The Behavioral Perspective Model (BPM)

Foxall (1990, 1994a) delineates the Behavioral Perspective Model (BPM) of purchase and consumption which contextualizes the various prepurchase, purchase, and postpurchase responses by situating them at the interaction of consumer and behavioral setting. In the BPM the concept of the consumer situation, consisting of the interaction of the consumer and the behavior setting in which the consumer acts, is paramount. The consumer's genetic, state variables, and the consumer's learning history are abstracted in the BPM (Foxall, 1994a). The other component of the consumer situation is the behavior setting. It consists of the physical and social discriminative stimuli and the verbal rules (plys, derived from mands; tracks, derived from tacts; and augmentals) that specify the contingencies of reinforcement among setting variables, behaviors, and their consequences (Skinner, 1969). These physical, social, and verbal discriminative stimuli combine to determine the relative openness of the consumer setting in which purchase and/or consumption occur.

The consumer behavior setting. The consumer behavior setting consists of the immediate contextual influences on a consumer's behavior: physical surroundings, social surroundings, and the verbal community. These discriminative stimuli signal the types of consequences likely to follow from a particular behavior. Consumer behavior settings can be described on a continuum from relatively open to relatively closed. Open settings constitute low control over reinforcement delivery and are typical of most marketplace situations. In closed settings, however, reinforcement delivery can be controlled to a greater extent. The relatively open setting in which the consumer browses within an exclusive department store, making decisions among a vast array of consumer innovations and luxuries can be contrasted with the relatively closed setting in which authorities exact taxations which must be paid if the consumer is to retain his or her rights of citizenship (Foxall, 1994a). In the relatively closed setting, the physical, social, and regulatory environments are arranged almost entirely by persons other than the consumer. Such settings encourage conformity to the behavioral repertoire they sustain and they achieve this by making reinforcement contingent on such conformity, which usually consists of the performance of one or two very carefully specified operant responses while punishment is contingent on deviation from the specified response (Foxall, 1994a). Finally, the behavior setting in the BPM refers not directly and simply to the immediate environment but to the source and nature of control it exerts, including the possibility of self-control in which the consumer is in a position to arrange the contingencies to which s/he is subject.

The nature of reinforcement in BPM. The contingent consequences signaled by the discriminative stimuli that compose the behavior setting are conceptualized in the BPM as hedonic reinforcers, informational reinforcers, and aversive stimuli. Hedonic reinforcement is that which is associated with feelings of fun, amusement, arousal, sensory stimulation, enjoyment, or pleasure and strengthens subsequent responses of purchase and consumption (Foxall, 1992a). Informational, or non-hedonic, reinforcers operate by providing feedback on the correctness or appropriateness of a consumer's performance not only in terms of economic rationality, but in terms of the wider socio-economic ramifications such as status, prestige, and social acceptance that accrue to the individual as a result of following prescribed behavior patterns (Foxall, 1992a). Finally, aversive consequences, the unpleasant outcomes of buying and using goods and services, have both hedonic and informational components (e.g., the loss of money to purchase the good or service, the trouble of obtaining/using it).

Classes of consumer behavior. Purchase and consumption behaviors can be classified according to the pattern of hedonic and informational reinforcement on which they are maintained. Four general classes of behavior can be distinguished: Maintenance, Accumulation, Pleasure, and Accomplishment (Foxall, 1993a, b). Given the situational context in which the consumer behaviors that produce them occur, most acts of prepurchase, purchase, and consumption can be fairly unambiguously assigned to one of these classes of consequence. Maintenance refers to a pattern of consequences incorporating low levels of both hedonic and informational reinforcement. Accumulation is consumer behavior maintained principally by informational reinforcers and only secondarily by hedonic reinforcers. Pleasure consists of consumer behavior which is maintained mostly by hedonic reinforcers and secondarily by informational reinforcement. Finally, Accomplishment is behavior maintained by high levels of both hedonic and informational reinforcement.

The BPM offers a theoretically coherent and far-reaching behavioral analysis of consumption including the possibility of a hierarchy of consumer behaviors over the consumer life cycle using household saving and financial asset management as a reference point (Ghez & Becker, 1975), as well as a depiction of consumer behavior over the product-market life cycle including of the adoption and diffusion of innovations among consumers (Foxall, 1994b). Although the BPM has been the subject of much theoretical development (Foxall 1990; 1992a, b, c; 1993a, b; 1994a, b; 1995a, b; 1997), empirical support for this account has not yet been published.

The Behavioral Ecology of Consumption

Humans, like all other animals, browse, purchase, and consume as part of a biobasic activity (Sherry, 1991). The Behavioral Ecology of Consumption (Rajala & Hantula, in press) applies methods and concepts from work in Optimal Foraging Theory (Stephens & Krebs, 1986) to human consumption. In the Behavioral Ecology of Consumption, shopping is analogous to foraging, and the mathematical models of foraging (e.g., Elsmore & McBride, 1994; Fantino, 1991; Fantino & Abarca, 1985; Stephens & Krebs, 1986) are used to predict consumer behavior and guide experimentation. Thus, the Behavioral Ecology of Consumption goes beyond descriptive anthropological work such as Winterhalder's (1981) study of food procuring strategies of the Cree, with a goal of predicting and modifying consumer behavior.

Foraging may be viewed as a natural analogue to time and response matching found in laboratory studies of choice (Abarca & Fantino, 1982). Behavioral ecologists have studied foraging patterns of organisms in the wild while operant psychologists have studied choice behavior in the laboratory. The question is whether the two disciplines' predictions about decision-making converge, and results from experiments suggest the affirmative (e.g., Abarca & Fantino, 1982; Baum, 1974a; Fantino, 1985; Fantino & Abarca, 1985). The following sections introduce concepts from behavioral ecology regarding foraging situations and attempts are made to relate them to concepts within consumer behavior.

Prey selection. Models of prey selection deal with what a forager should do when it successively encounters items of different types. On each encounter it must decide whether to accept the item at hand or continue searching (Shettleworth, 1988). The question to be answered is how prey should be selected to maximize the net rate of energy intake (or, in operant terms, reinforcement). Prey types could be construed as products or services for which a consumer is shopping (foraging). Operant studies have shown that prey selection depends on the time spent traveling to a patch (Abarca & Fantino, 1982; Fantino & Abarca, 1985; Werner, Mittelbach, & Hall, 1981). Specifically, the more time an organism spends traveling to a patch, the less selective it will be in deciding what to eat. Applying this to consumer behavior, the time it takes to travel to get to a store or the number of stores one must go to before one finds a particular item may be related to how selective the consumer is once s/he gets there. Travel time may also be a variable to describe or explain the apparent inconsistencies of consumer behavior.

Risk. Risk is another variable that may have some important ramifications for consumer behavior. In the foraging literature, it has been demonstrated that animals who have most often been risk averse, that is, not willing to forage in variable patches, will display risk prone behavior when they are food deprived or given food at a low rate. Animals who become risk prone will consume less than satisfactory prey and forage in highly variable environments. Open and closed economies affect the rate of reinforcement and should also be considered with reference to risk. The economy in which a consumer operates may directly indicate when the consumer will display "finicky" behavior and when the consumer will display behavior such that they will purchase/consume an item considered to be below the consumer's standards. However, other variables such as product (prey) selection and travel times are involved as well. Again, delay to reinforcement is the important factor under consideration here. Relative deprivation (supply/demand aspects) and the associated risk prone behavior may help explain the matching behavior (Baum, 1974b; Davison & McCarthy, 1988; DeVilliers, 1977; Herrnstein, 1961, 1970, 1974) found in animals and may also be an important consideration for the explanation of the matching (not maximizing) behavior found with humans (Herrnstein, 1990).

Time horizons. Few organisms forage continuously. Often, they are interrupted by the arrival of predators or rivals, or may need time to groom, drink, or rest. Thus, the time available for foraging, or the animal's time horizon, is limited. It has been shown that with given prey items and densities, predators are less selective when foraging in short bouts. Likewise, selectivity decreases toward the end of a foraging bout if the total foraging time is known by the animal (Shettleworth, 1988). For example, if a consumer is aware of the time a store closes, but still has several items left on a list of things to buy when a five-minute warning until closing comes over a speaker, the consumer may become less selective in the choices s/he makes and purchase less-than-satisfactory goods. Likewise, if the consumer is on a lunch break and has just a few minutes to run some film to a store to get it developed, s/he may go to a nearby store which charges more money rather than spend the time to go to a store down the block that is less expensive. Even though the quality of film developing is the same in both stores, the consumer is less selective (willing to pay more) when in a time crunch (foraging in short bouts). Therefore, as with risk sensitivity due to relative satiation/deprivation, time horizons may be an important variable in human purchasing and consumption.

Patch sampling. Another foraging problem is how a forager selects a patch. There may be two types of maximization that occur in animals. First, a forager might attempt to maximize its food intake by always foraging in the patch with the highest expected reward rate (momentary maximizing). Alternatively, the forager might attempt to maximize its intake over the total foraging time and sacrifice short-term gain in order to acquire more information about other patches. Studies of operant behavior suggest that animals nearly always choose the alternative that maximizes reinforcement momentarily (Staddon, 1983). If patches may be considered functionally equivalent to groups of stores (malls, supermarkets, outlets) or geographic locations (an area where one can shop for groceries, go to a drug store, and go to a laundromat), it may be assumed that a consumer would choose the patch that allows the most shopping/consumption to be accomplished in the least amount of time, or is closest to home (both are reinforcing). This could be thought of as momentary maximization. Likewise, the consumer may sacrifice short-term reinforcement for more information regarding other stores or locations where s/he may do business.

Patch departure. In order to leave a resource-depleted patch at the optimal time, a forager must in some way keep track of its rate of food intake in the current patch and compare this to the state of the rest of the environment. Operant research indicates that an organism should leave a patch when the amount of food in a patch equals the average amount of food in the environment (Shettleworth, 1988). Information about the environment includes travel times, rates of gain in other patches, and probabilities of encountering different patch types. This information about the environment may be related to reinforcement histories of consumers.

Research in the Behavioral Ecology of Consumption thus far has explored aspects of prey selection, patch sampling, and patch departure in the context of Internet shopping. Using a simulated Internet mall microworld (DiFonzo, Hantula, & Bordia, 1998), the quantitative predictions of the Delay Reduction Hypothesis (Fantino & Abarca, 1985) and of the Matching Law (Baum, 1974b; Davison & McCarthy, 1988; DeVilliers, 1977; Herrnstein, 1961, 1970, 1974) have been tested. In general, the data indicate that the human consumption conforms both qualitatively and quantitatively to the predictions of Optimal Foraging Theory and the Delay Reduction Hypothesis in studies of delay in online shopping (DiClemente & Hantula, 1998; Rajala & Hantula, in press). Further research has yielded data consistent with both qualitative and quantitative predictions of the Matching Law in a single alternative choice situation investigating preference for shipping costs/ delayed delivery (Hutcheson & Hantula, 1998), and in a multi-alternative choice situation (cf. Elsmore & McBride, 1994) investigating the effect of in-stock probability on consumer choice in an online mall (Hantula, Rajala, & Bryant, 1997).

This nascent research program has been more concerned with data collection and model testing than with theory building. All of the current studies have been conducted in a simulated Internet mall or Internet store, with subjects purchasing music CDs. The degree to which these results generalize to other goods, services, or shopping situations remains to be seen. However, in all cases the data are consistent with both human and non-human animal data gathered in functionally and conceptually similar settings.

A Strategic Moment for Conceptual Brand Switching

Consumer behavior is an active, growing field, but there is much dissension regarding its conceptual bases (Foxall, 1984, 1986b, 1997; Sherry, 1991) and dissatisfaction with the "cognitive consumer" model which has pervaded the literature since the publication of Howard and Sheth's (1969) influential *The Theory of Buyer Behavior*. Although it has sparked much research, Howard and Sheth's theory and the cognitive consumer paradigm has not led to the promised coherent depiction of consumption (Foxall, 1990). Instead, to the marketer following the cognitive consumer paradigm, consumers seem fickle, seemingly changing their tastes in products with every promotion that rolls around. Stigler and Becker (1977) concede:

> ...no significant behavior has been illuminated by assumptions of differences in tastes. Instead, they, along with assumptions of unstable tastes, have been a convenient crutch to lean on when the analysis has bogged down. They give the appearance of considered judgment, yet really have only been ad hoc arguments that disguise analytical failures. (p. 89)

In his 1977 presidential address to the Association for Consumer Research, Kassarjian called for a more parsimonious view of consumer behavior, pointing out that consumer behavior started out being able to be explained by drive, response, cue, and reinforcement, and proceeded to be made more complicated by theories such as cognitive dissonance, personality, perceived risk, and attribution theory. In addition to the problem of parsimony, Kassarjian also points out another questionable assumption that cognitive theories make: "For the countless thousands of insignificant decisions that are made by the consumer, to assume a thinking, reasoned, attitudinally influenced decision may well be a classic example of anthropomorphism" (1978, p. 13).

A Trial Purchase: The Growing Popularity of Classical Conditioning

Of growing interest in the consumer behavior literature is the analysis of certain advertising techniques as classical conditioning procedures (see Cohen & Areni, 1991; Shimp, 1991 for reviews). In 1984, McSweeney and Bierley published an influential introduction to classical conditioning in the consumer behavior literature. Classical conditioning has been included in consumer behavior textbooks (e.g., Wilkie, 1994) and classical conditioning experiments have appeared regularly in the consumer behavior literature. Pairing pleasant scenery, beautiful women, music, or colors, for example, (about which a consumer presumably already has a known attitude) with a product or service is an attempt to transfer the attitude toward the former to the latter and has been used extensively (e.g., Allen & Madden, 1995; Allen & Jaiszewski, 1989; Bierley, McSweeney, & Vannieuwkerk, 1985; Gorn, 1982; Janiszewski & Warlop, 1993; Kellaris & Cox, 1989; Kim, Allen, & Kardes, 1996; Kleine, Macklin, & Bruvold, 1986; Kroeber-Riel, 1984; Macklin, 1983; Milliman, 1982; Petty, Cacioppo, & Schumann, 1983; Shimp, Stuart, & Engle, 1991; Stuart, Shimp, & Engle, 1987; Tom, 1995). Attempts to use classical conditioning principles in advertising, however, have proceeded under the assumption that attitudes may be classically conditioned (Petty et al., 1983). Such conditioning of attitudes is termed the peripheral route to advertising, defined as attitude change brought about by the association of the attitude issue or object with positive or negative cues or by the person making a simple inference about the merits of the advocated position based on cues in the persuasion context.

The consumer's mood is another variable that has been manipulated in classical conditioning studies to investigate product evaluation and product choice (Groenland & Schoormans, 1994). Some authors have examined consumers' attitudes toward the advertisement itself to predict advertisement effectiveness and attitudes toward the brand (Edell & Burke, 1984; Gresham & Shimp, 1985) and others have used second-order negative conditioning procedures to study attitudes toward brands (Blair & Shimp, 1992).

This approach is not without its critics who point out that classical conditioning procedures have been developed mostly in carefully controlled laboratory studies with animal subjects and have not been tested on a wide scale with consumers in the marketplace (e.g., Foxall, 1987; Kahle, Beatty, & Kennedy, 1986). Furthermore, little research has been done to compare the conditioning of attitudes with the conditioning of visceral or overt voluntary behavior, and how the procedures for obtaining each may or may not differ. Despite this oversight, advertising and promotion strategies continue to be developed with the goal of changing or shaping consumers' attitudes toward products or services in hopes that these attitudes will drive or influence purchases.

However, the understanding of classical conditioning as represented in the consumer behavior literature is much less sophisticated than that in the basic behavior analytic literature. A more thorough behavior analytic perspective on classical conditioning in advertising may serve to disentangle some of the controversies in the marketing literature, as well as provide avenues for future research. It also remains unclear whether classical conditioning or Relational Frame Theory (Hayes, 1994) is the best account for the findings thus far. Indeed, a Relational Frame Theory account of advertising is a potentially profitable research stream.

A Change in Fashion: The Rise of Postmodern Consumer Inquiry

Some consumer theorists have argued that consumer research has become intellectually moribund, and have advocated postmodern and social constructionist alternatives to the current normal science straitjacket (e.g., Holbrook, 1995; Hirschman & Holbrook, 1992; Sherry, 1991). In particular, postmodern analyses have questioned the adequacy of statistically driven hypothetico-deductive research methods and experimental designs (e.g., Sherry, 1991), the validity of Cartesian dualism (Hirschman & Holbrook, 1992), and the dominance of the cognitive consumer paradigm (Foxall, 1990; Sherry, 1991).

All of these questions point to an amenable fit with current behavior analytic theory. Metatheoretically, postmodernism and behavior analysis are extremely compatible. The contextualist approach to theory embodied in behavior analysis (Morris, 1988) is entirely consistent with postmodern thought (Guerin, 1992). Indeed, Skinner's 1957 analysis of verbal behavior anticipated current postmodern analyses of language and text (compare for instance, Skinner's 1972 "on having a poem" with Foucault's 1970 "what is an author"). Postmodern management scholar Jacques (1996) readily acknowledges that Skinner (1953) is one of the few works in all of social science that treats the social control of behavior and socially constructed reality seriously.

While the metatheoretical convergence between behavior analysis and postmodernism is heartening, the most important aspect of the postmodern movement in consumer research is its outright rejection of a dominant paradigm in favor of multiple avenues of inquiry. Thus, the paradigmatic dominance alleged in psychology which has been increasingly cognitivist (Friman, Allen, Kerwin, & Larzlere, 1993) may not be as limiting to a behavioral analysis of consumption as the "cognitive revolution" in Psychology has been to behavior analysis. Indeed, Hirschman and Holbrook conclude their 1992 book *Postmodern Consumer Research* with a prayer that exhorts consumer researchers to "Remember..... that multiple viewpoints with different but equally valid claims to truth and beauty exist as alternative bases on which to conduct consumer research." and "... acknowledging the mutual coexistence of potentially contradictory research paradigms." (p. 226).

Toward a Behavioral Analysis of Consumption

Perhaps the third time is the charm. The dissatisfaction with the current cognitive consumer model, acceptance of classical conditioning research and rise of postmodern inquiry within the consumer behavior field may serve as potent establishing operations for a behavioral analysis of consumption. It is interesting to note that the beginnings of a behavioral analysis of consumption were Watson's attempts to generalize from classical conditioning to advertising, an approach that has resurged in modern consumer research. In over two decades of systematic research and application, the OBM movement has proven its mettle as a theoretically and practically important area of management, and is ready to break out of its box.

Concurrent schedules of reinforcement. The three current approaches to a behavioral analysis of consumption presented herein (Applied Analysis of Consumer Behavior, Behavioral Perspective Model, Behavioral Ecology of Consumption) are complementary and should not be viewed as mutually exclusive. In addition, the growing research in behavioral economics has significant implication for the analysis of consumer behavior. In the postmodern spirit of encouraging a chorus of other voices, all of these approaches should be encouraged and viewed as concurrent schedules with no COD penalty. In fact, it is an eloquent testimony to the theoretical richness of behavior analysis that distinctly different research streams in consumption could emerge.

The Applied Analysis of Consumer Behavior approach is high in social validity and follows from the body of work in OBM. Once the organizational box walls are flattened, consumer implications for many current OBM research programs will become clear. For example, expanding behavioral safety research to include managing the safety of consumers (i.e., reducing slip and fall accidents in stores, promoting safe use of products in the home), managing the "productivity" of consumers (i.e., interventions to help consumers use and enjoy their purchases more effectively, set up and modify home computers) making consumers more effective managers of employee behavior, and studying the effect of OBM interventions on consumer behavior (e.g., Brown & Sulzer-Azaroff, 1994 who replicated and assessed the customer impact of the Crowell et al., 1988 bank teller friendliness intervention) are rich areas for future research.

The BPM (Foxall, 1990) provides a framework for studying consumption as an explicitly social process in terms of Skinner's (1953, 1957) analyses of social control and verbal behavior. Further, the BPM offers much prescriptive advice for applications in managing consumption. Beyond the behavioral aspects of the BPM, its social constructionist-ish framework is in sync with current intellectual trends in the humanities and the interpretive movements in disciplines such as anthropology and sociology. Hence, the BPM can tie empirical, conceptual, and applied behvaioral work to the forefront of social science inquiry, serving as a reminder that present-day behavior analysis remains an intellectually vigorous enterprise.

The Behavioral Ecology of Consumption (Rajala & Hantula, in press) descends directly from current laboratory work in the experimental analysis of behavior and in evolutionary biology. By making explicit the ties between shopping and foraging, this approach is perhaps the first to bring evolutionary theory to bear on consumption in a systematic manner. In addition, because the experiments have been done in the context of Internet shopping, behavior analysis is brought into the burgeoning arena of cybershopping (Krantz, 1998; Poppe, 1998), as well as into current thinking in the natural sciences which emphasizes a Darwinian analysis of human behavior (e.g., Dawkins, 1990, 1996; Wilson, 1998). Lea (1981) questioned whether models of non-human animal foraging could be extended to humans, which this research answers in the affirmative. The mathematical models established in previous research with non-human animals serve as an invaluable guide for new experiments which further the shopping-as-foraging analogy. Thus, The Behavioral Ecology of Consumption appears to be a fruitful patch for much future research.

Commonalties between economic theory and behavior analytic theory have been noted by many authors (e.g., DeNicolis-Bragger, et al., 1998; Hursh, 1980; Kagel, Battalio, & Green, 1995). In particular, basic economic concepts such as supply and demand, demand elasticity, open/closed economies, and substitution/complementarity have been successfully operationalized and studied in the operant laboratory (Lea, 1981). Indeed, the demand curve in economics was shown to be analogous to response rate functions based on reinforcement rate by Lea (1978) who compared data sets from operant laboratory experiments to data sets from econometric studies. This research and theory in behavioral economics provides models for further behavioral studies of consumption, including the means for including substitutable and complementary goods, income, demand functions, and elasticity in current quantitative models of choice. Behavioral economics has recently been extended to analyzing drug use (Green & Kagel, 1996), which underscores the self-evident point that drug use is yet another class of consumption. This work could lead to an interesting synthesis of consumer behavior, behavior analysis, and behavioral pharmacology which may provide a much richer understanding of causes and cures of drug addiction.

Back to the Future to the End

It may be said that all studies of operant behavior are in fact studies of consumption. The key pecks which produce access to grain in an operant laboratory experiment may not be terribly dissimilar from the money used to purchase a loaf of bread. The bar presses which postpone aversive stimuli in an avoidance study may not be functionally dissimilar from the dollars spent on a safe apartment. A theoretically driven, operant analysis of consumer behavior may be close at hand. The spirit of Watson's initial work in classical conditioning and advertising is spurring new work by current consumer researchers, Skinner's analyses of social control and verbal behavior are embraced by postmodernists, and foraging concepts from Darwin's work are being applied to behavior on the Internet. The intellectual groundwork that is the history and present of behavior analysis provides a fertile field for cultivating a coherent understanding of consumption.

As consumers drift in and out of permeably walled organizations and engage in more spatially and temporally distal interfacing with organizations, the necessity of a contextualist approach to consumption which can abide temporally extended relationships, assumptions of arationality, and interdisciplinary thinking while at the same time providing actionable research and application becomes clearer. Just as one would not run a factory as if it were a farm or understand behavior as an epiphenomenon of consciousness, one should not try to comprehend consumer behavior as something simply manufactured by and for the producers of goods and services. Instead, consumption is worthy of study in its own right, independent of reference to production, industrial organization, and the walls it constructs. The

Behavioral Analysis of Consumption is presented herein as concurrent schedules, from which an individual researcher may choose freely. Perhaps if individual researchers in this burgeoning field match their efforts to the returns provided by each schedule, we will maximize.

References

Abarca, N., & Fantino, E. (1982). Choice and foraging. *Journal of the Experimental Analysis of Behavior, 38*, 117-123.

Alavosius, M. P., & Sulzer-Azaroff, B. (1990). Acquisition and maintenance of health-care routines as a function of feedback density. *Journal of Applied Behavior Analysis, 23*, 151-162.

Albrecht, K., & Zemke, R. (1985). *Service America! Doing business in the new economy.* Homewood, IL: Dow Jones-Irwin.

Allen, C. T., & Janiszewski, C. A. (1989). Assessing the role of contingency awareness in attitudinal conditioning with implications for advertising research. *Journal of Marketing Research, 26*, 30-43.

Allen, C. T., & Madden, T. J. (1985). A closer look at classical conditioning. *Journal of Consumer Research, 12*, 301-315.

Anderson, D. C., Crowell, C. R., Doman, M., & Howard, G. S. (1988). Performance posting, goal setting, and activity-contingent praise as applied to a hockey team. *Journal of Applied Psychology, 73*, 87-95.

Anderson, D. C., Crowell, C. R., Hantula, D. A., & Siroky, L. M. (1988). Task clarification and performance posting for improving cleaning in a student-managed university bar. *Journal of Organizational Behavior Management, 9*, 73-90.

Anderson, D. C., Crowell, C. R., Sucec, J., Gilligan, K. D., & Witkoff, M. (1982). Behavioral management of client contacts in a real estate brokerage: Getting agents to sell more. *Journal of Organizational Behavior Management, 4*, 67-95.

Austin, J., Hatfield, D. B., Grindle, A. C., & Bailey, J. S. (1993). Increasing recycling in office environments: The effects of specific, informative cues. *Journal of Applied Behavior Analysis, 26*, 247-253.

Babcock, R. A., Sulzer-Azaroff, B., & Sanderson, M. (1992). Increasing nurses' use of feedback to promote infection-control practices in a head-injury treatment center. *Journal of Applied Behavior Analysis, 25*, 621-627.

Barnard, J. D., Christophersen, E. R., & Wolf, M. M. (1977). Teaching children appropriate shopping behavior through parent training in the supermarket setting. *Journal of Applied Behavior Analysis, 10*, 49-59.

Baudrillard, J. (1970/1997). *The Consumer Society: Myths and Structures (Theory, Culture and Society).* Newbury Park, CA: Sage.

Baum, W. M. (1974a). Choice in free-ranging wild pigeons. *Science, 185*, 78-79.

Baum, W. M. (1974b). On two types of deviation from the matching law: bias and undermatching. *Journal of the Experimental Analysis of Behavior, 22*, 231-242.

Bierley, C., McSweeney, F. K., & Vannieuwkerk, R. (1985). Classical conditioning of preferences for stimuli. *Journal of Consumer Research, 12*, 316-323.

Blair, M. E., & Shimp, T. A. (1992). Consequences of an unpleasant experience with music: A second-order negative conditioning perspective. *Journal of Advertising, 21*, 35-43.

Borsodi, R. (1929). *This ugly civilization*. New York, NY: Simon & Schuster.

Bowditch, J. L., & Buono, A. F. (1997). *A primer on organizational behavior* (4th ed.). New York, NY: Wiley.

Brown, M. G., Mallot, R. W., Dillon, M. J., & Keeps, E. J. (1980). Improving customer service in a large department store through the use of training and feedback. *Journal of Organizational Behavior Management, 2*, 251-265.

Brown, C. S., & Sulzer-Azaroff, B. (1994). An assessment of the relationship between customer satisfaction and service friendliness. *Journal of Organizational Behavior Management, 14*, 55-75.

Buckley, K. W. (1982). The selling of a psychologist: John Broadus Watson and the application of behvaioral techniques to advertising. *Journal of the History of the Behvaioral Sciences, 18*, 207-221.

Burgess, R. L., Clark, R. N., & Hendee, J. C. (1971). An experimental analysis of anti-litter procedures. *Journal of Applied Behavior Analysis, 4*, 71-75.

Burnham, J. C. (1994). John B. Watson: Interviewee, professional figure, symbol. In J. T. Todd & E. K. Morris (Eds.), *Modern perspectives on John B. Watson and classical behaviorism* (pp. 65-73). Westport, CT: Greenwood Press.

Carter, N., & Holmberg, B. (1992). Theft reduction in a grocery store through product identification. *Journal of Organizational Behavior Management, 13*, 129-135.

Carter, N., Holmstrom, A., Simpanen, M., & Melin, L. (1988). Theft reduction in a grocery store through product identification and graphing of losses for employees. *Journal of Applied Behavior Analysis, 21*, 385-389.

Carter, N., Kindstedt, A., & Melin, L. (1995). Increased sales and thefts of candy as a function or sales promotion activities: Preliminary finding. *Journal of Behavior Analysis, 28*, 81-82.

Clark, R. N., Burgess, R. L., & Hendee, J. C. (1972). The development of anti-litter in a forest campground. *Journal of Applied Behavior Analysis, 5*, 1-5.

Cohen, J. B., & Areni, C. S. (1991). Affect and consumer behavior. In T. S. Robertson & H. H. Kassarjian (Eds.), *Handbook of consumer behavior* (pp. 188-240). Englewood Cliffs, NJ: Prentice-Hall.

Coon, D. J. (1994). "Not a creature of reason": The alleged impact of Watsonian behaviorism on advertising in the 1920s. In J. T. Todd & E. K. Morris (Eds.), *Modern perspectives on John B. Watson and classical behaviorism* (pp. 37-63). Westport, CT: Greenwood Press.

Cope, J. G., & Allred, L. J. (1991). Community intervention to deter illegal parking in spaces reserved for the physically disabled. *Journal of Applied Behavior Analysis, 24*, 687-693.

Cope, J. G., Allred, L. J., & Morsell, J. M. (1991). Signs as deterrents of illegal parking in spaces designated for individuals with physical disabilities. *Journal of Applied Behavior Analysis, 24*, 59-63.

Cope, J. G., Moy, S. S., & Grossnickle, W. F. (1988). The behavioral impact of an advertising campaign to promote safety belt use. *Journal of Applied Behavior Analysis, 21*, 277-280.

Crowell, C. R., Anderson, D. C., Abel, D. M., & Sergio, J. P. (1988). Task clarification, performance feedback, and social praise: Procedures for improving the customer service of bank tellers. *Journal of Applied Behavior Analysis, 21*, 65-71.

Davison, M., & McCarthy, D. (1988). *The matching law: A research review*. Hillsdale, NJ: Erlbaum.

Dawkins, R. (1990). *The extended phenotype : The long reach of the gene*. NY: Oxford University Press.

Dawkins, R. (1996). *River out of Eden : A Darwinian view of life* NY: Harper-Collins.

DeNicolis-Bragger, J., Bragger, D., Hantula, D. A., & Kirnan, J. (1998). Hysteresis and uncertainty: The effect of uncertainty on delays to exit decisions. *Organizational Behavior and Human Decision Processes, 74*, 229-253.

Deslauriers, B. C., & Everett, P. B. (1977). Effects of intermittent and continuous token reinforcement on bus ridership. *Journal of Applied Psychology, 4*, 369-375.

de Villiers, P. A. (1977). Choice in concurrent schedules and a quantitative formulation of the law of effect. In W. K. Honig & J. E. R. Staddon (Eds.), *Handbook of operant behavior* (pp. 233-287). Englewood Cliffs, NJ: Prentice-Hall.

DiClemente, D. F., & Hantula, D. A. (1998). *An examination of the Delay Reduction Hypothesis on cybershopping*. Paper presented at the 24th annual meeting of the Association for Behavior Analysis-International, Orlando, FL.

DiFonzo, N., Hantula, D. A., & Bordia, P. (1998). Microworlds for experimental research: Having your (control and collection) cake, and realism too. *Behavior Research, Methods, Instruments, & Computers, 30*, 278-286.

Edell, J. A., & Burke, M. C. (1984). The moderating effect of attitude toward an ad on ad effectiveness under different processing conditions. In T. C. Kinnear (Ed.), *Advances in consumer research, 11* (pp. 644-649). Provo, UT: Association for Consumer Research.

Eldridge, L., Lemasters, S., & Szypot, B. (1978). A performance feedback intervention to reduce waste: Performance data and participant responses. *Journal of Organizational Behavior Management, 1*, 258-266.

Elsmore, T. F., & McBride, S. A. (1994). An eight-alternative concurrent schedule: foraging in a radial maze. *Journal of the Experimental Analysis of Behavior, 61*, 331-348.

Everett, P. B., Hayward, S. C., & Meyers, A. W. (1974). The effects of a token reinforcement procedure on bus ridership. *Journal of Applied Behavior Analysis, 7*, 1-9.

Fantino, E. (1985). Behavior analysis and behavioral ecology: A synergistic coupling. *The Behavior Analyst, 8*, 151-157.

Fantino, E. (1991). Behavioral ecology. In I. H. Iversen & K. A. Lattal (Eds.), *Experimental analysis of behavior* (Part 2, pp. 117-153). Amsterdam: Elsevier.

Fantino, E., & Abarca, N. (1985). Choice, optimal foraging, and the delay-reduction hypothesis. *The Behavioral and Brain Sciences, 8*, 315-330.

Feeney, E., Staelin, J., O'Brien, R., & Dickinson, A. (1982). Increasing sales performance among airline personnel. In R. M. O'Brien, A. M. Dickinson, & M. P. Rosow (Eds.), *Handbook of industrial behavior modification* (pp. 141-158). New York, NY: Pergamon.

Foucault. M. (1970). *The order of things*. New York, NY: Pantheon.

Fox, D. K., Hopkins, B. L., & Anger, W. K. (1987). The long-term effects of a token economy on safety performance in open-pit mining. *Journal of Applied Behavior Analysis, 20*, 215-224.

Foxall, G. R. (1984). Evidence for attitudinal-behavioral consistency: Implications for consumer research paradigms. *Journal of Economic Psychology, 5*, 71-92.

Foxall, G. R. (1986a). The role of radical behaviorism in the explanation of consumer choice. *Advances in Consumer Research, 13*, 187-191.

Foxall, G. R. (1986b). Theoretical progress in consumer psychology: The contribution of a behavioral analysis of choice. *Journal of Economic Psychology, 7*, 293-314.

Foxall, G. R. (1987). Radical behaviorism and consumer research: Theoretical promise and empirical problems. *International Journal of Research in Marketing, 4*, 111-129.

Foxall, G. R. (1990). *Consumer psychology in behavioral perspective*. London: Routledge.

Foxall, G. R. (1992a). The behavioral perspective model of purchase and consumption: From consumer theory to marketing practice. *Journal of the Academy of Marketing Science, 20*, 189-198.

Foxall, G. R. (1992b). The consumer situation: An integrative model for research in marketing. *Journal of Marketing Management, 8*, 383-404.

Foxall, G. R. (1992c). The consumer situation: An intergrative model for research in marketing. *Journal of Marketing Management, 8*, 392-404.

Foxall, G. R. (1993a). Situated consumer behavior: A behavioral interpretation of purchase and consumption. *Research in Consumer Behavior, 6*, 113-152.

Foxall, G. R. (1993b). Consumer behaviour as an evolutionary process. *European Journal of Marketing, 27*(8), 46-57.

Foxall, G. R. (1994a). Behavior analysis and consumer psychology. *Journal of Economic Psychology, 15*, 5-91.

Foxall, G. R. (1994b). Consumer choice as an evolutionary process: An operant interpretation of adopter behavior. *Advances in Consumer Research, 21*, 312-317.

Foxall, G. R. (1995a). Environment-impacting consumer behavior: An operant analysis. *Advances in Consumer Research, 22*, 262-268.

Foxall, G. R. (1995b). Science and interpretation in consumer research: A radical behaviourist perspective. *European Journal of Marketing, 29*, 3-99.

Foxall, G. R. (1997). The explanation of consumer behaviour: From social cognition to environmental control. In C. L. Cooper & I. T. Robertson (Eds), *International Review of Industrial and Organizational Psychology*. West Sussex: John Wiley & Sons Ltd.

Foxx, R. M., & Hake, D. F. (1977). Gasoline conservation: A Procedure for measuring and reducing the driving of college students. *Journal of Applied Behavior Analysis, 10*, 61-74.

Frederiksen, L. W. (Ed.). (1982). *Handbook of organizational behavior management*. New York, NY: Wiley.

Friman, P. C., Allen, K. D., Kerwin, M. L. E., & Larzelere, R. (1993). Changes in modern psychology: A citation analysis of the Kuhnian displacement thesis. *American Psychologist, 48*, 658-664.

Gaetani, J. J., & Johnson, C. M. (1983). The effect of data plotting, praise, and state lottery tickets on decreasing cash shortages in a retail beverage chain. *Journal of Organizational Behavior Management, 5*, 5-15.

Gaetani, J. J., Johnson, C. M., & Austin, J. T. (1983). Self management by an owner of a small business: Reduction of tardiness. *Journal of Organizational Behavior Management, 5*, 31-39.

Gailbrath, J. K. (1958). *The affluent society*. New York, NY: Houghton-Mifflin.

Geller, E. S. (1989). Applied behavior analysis and social marketing: An integration for environmental preservation. *Journal of Social Issues, 45*, 17-36.

Geller, E. S., Chaffee, J. L., & Ingram, R. E. (1975). Prompting paper recycling on a university campus. *Journal of Environmental Systems, 5*, 39-57.

Geller, E. S., Farris, J. C., & Post, D. S. (1973). Promoting a consumer behavior for pollution control. *Journal of Applied Behavior Analysis, 6*, 367-76.

George, J. T., & Hopkins, B. L. (1989). Multiple effects of performance-contingent pay for waitpersons. *Journal of Applied Behavior Analysis, 22*, 131-141.

Ghez, G. R., & Becker, G. S. (1975). *The allocation of time and goods over the life cycle*. New York: National Bureau of Economic Research.

Goltz, S. M. (1992). A sequential learning analysis of decisions in organizations to escalate investments despite continuing costs or losses. *Journal of Applied Behavior Analysis, 25*, 561-574.

Goltz, S. M. (1993). Examining the joint roles of responsibility and reinforcement history in recommitment. *Decision Sciences, 24*, 977-994.

Goltz, S. M. (in press). Can't stop on a dime: The roles of matching and momentum in persistence of commitment. *Journal of Organizational Behavior Management*.

Gorn, G. J. (1982). The effects of music in advertising on choice behavior: A classical conditioning approach. *Journal of Marketing, 46*, 94-101.

Grass, R. C., & Wallace, W. H. (1969). Satiation effects of TV commercials. *Journal of Advertising Research, 9*, 3-8.

Green, L., & Kagel, J. H. (Eds.). (1996). *Advances in behavioral economics: Vol 3. Substance use and abuse*. Norwood, NJ: Ablex.

Green, C. W., Reid, D. H., Perkins, L. I., & Gardner, S. M. (1991). Increasing habilitative services for persons with profound handicaps: An application of structural analysis to staff management. *Journal of Applied Behavior Analysis, 24,* 459-471.

Greene, B. F., Rouse, M., Green, R. B., & Clay, C. (1984). Behavior analysis in consumer affairs: Retail and consumer response to publicizing food price information. *Journal of Applied Behavior Analysis, 17,* 3-21.

Gresham, L. G., & Shimp, T. A. (1985). Attitude toward the advertisement and brand attitude: A classical conditioning perspective. *Journal of Advertising, 14,* 10-17.

Groenland, E. A. G., & Schoormans, J. P. L. (1994). Comparing mood-induction and affective conditioning as mechanisms influencing product evaluation and product choice. *Psychology and Marketing, 11,* 183-197.

Guerin, B. (1992). Behavior Analysis and the social construction of knowledge. *American Psychologist, 47,* 1423-1433.

Hagenzieker, M. P. (1991). Enforcement or incentives? Prompting safety belt use among military personnel in the Netherlands. *Journal of Applied Behavior Analysis, 24,* 23-30.

Hantula, D. A. (1992). The basic importance of escalation. *Journal of Applied Behavior Analysis, 25,* 575-579.

Hantula, D. A. (in press). Schedules of reinforcement in organizational performance: Application, analysis, and synthesis. In: C. M. Johnson, T. C. Mawhinney, & W. Redmon (Eds.), *Handbook of organizational performance.*

Hantula, D. A., & Crowell, C. R. (1994a). Behavioral contrast in a two-option analogue task of financial decision making. *Journal of Applied Behavior Analysis, 27,* 607-617.

Hantula, D. A., & Crowell, C. R. (1994b). Intermittent reinforcement and escalation processes in sequential decision making: A replication and theoretical analysis. *Journal of Organizational Behavior Management, 14,* 7-36.

Hantula, D. A., & DeNicolis-Bragger, J. L. (1999). The effects of feedback equivocality on escalation of commitment: An empirical investigation of decision dilemma theory. *Journal of Applied Social Psychology, 29,* 424-444.

Hantula, D. A., Rajala, A. K., & Bryant, K. (1997). *Of mice and men (and women): Studying consumer choice in an online mall.* Paper presented at the FABA/OBM Winter meeting, Daytona Beach, FL.

Hayes, S. C. (1994). Relational Frame Theory: A functional approach to verbal events. In S. C. Hayes, L. J. Hayes, M. Sato, & K. Ono (Eds.), *Behavior analysis of language and cognition* (pp. 9-30). Reno, NV: Context Press.

Herrnstein, R. J. (1961). Relative and absolute strength of response as a function of frequency of reinforcement. *Journal of the Experimental Analysis of Behavior, 4,* 267-272.

Herrnstein, R. J. (1970). On the law of effect. *Journal of the Experimental Analysis of Behavior, 13,* 243-266.

Herrnstein, R. J. (1974). Formal properties of the matching law. *Journal of the Experimental Analysis of Behavior, 21,* 159-164.

Herrnstein, R. J. (1990). Rational choice theory: Necessary but not sufficient. *American Psychologist, 45*, 356-367.

Hirschman, E. C., & Holbrook, M. B. (1992). *Postmodern consumer research: The study of consumption as text.* Newbury Park, CA: Sage.

Honnen, T. J., & Kleinke, C. L. (1990). Prompting bar patrons with signs to take free condoms. *Journal of Applied Behavior Analysis, 23*, 215-217.

Hopkins, B. L., Conard, R. J., Dangel, R. F., Fitch, H. G., Smith, M. J., & Anger, W. K. (1986). Behavioral technology for reducing occupational exposures to styrene. *Journal of Applied Behavior Analysis, 19*, 3-11.

Howard, J. A., & Sheth, J. N. (1969). *The theory of buyer behavior.* New York, NY: Wiley.

Holbrook, M. M. (1995). *Consumer research: Introspective essays on the study of consumption.* Newbury Park, CA: Sage.

Hursh, S. R. (1980). Economic concepts for the analysis of behavior. *Journal of the Experimental Analysis of Behavior, 34*, 219-238.

Hutcheson, A. M., & Hantula, D. A. (1998). *Delay sensitivity to demand moderated by desire in on-line shopping behaviors.* Paper presented at the 24th annual meeting of the Association for Behavior Analysis-International, Orlando, FL.

Huxley, A. (1932). *Brave new world.* Garden City, NY: Doubleday, Doran, & Co.

Jacques, R. (1996). *Manufacturing the employee: Management knowledge from the 19th to 21st centuries.* Newbury Park, CA: Sage.

Janiszewski, C., & Warlop, L. (1993). The influence of classical conditioning procedures on subsequent attention to the conditioned brand. *Journal of Consumer Research, 20*, 171-189.

Jason, J., Billows, W., Wyatt-Schnopp, D., & King, C. (1996). Reducing the illegal sales of cigarette to minors: Analysis of alternative enforcement schedules. *Journal of Applied Behavior Analysis, 29*, 333-344.

Jason, L. A., Neal, A. M., & Marinakis, G. (1985). Altering contingencies to facilitate compliance with traffic light systems. *Journal of Applied Behavior Analysis, 18*, 95-100.

Johnson, C. M. (1985). Customer feedback to the main office: Selling newspapers plot, stock, and bare shelf. *Journal of Organizational Behavior Management, 7*, 37-49.

Johnson, S. P., Welsh, T. M., Miller, L. K., & Altus, D. E. (1991). Participatory management: Maintaining staff performance in a university housing cooperative. *Journal of Applied Behavior Analysis, 24*, 119-127.

Kagel, J. H., Battalio, R. C., & Green, L. (1995). *Economic choice theory.* New York, NY: Cambridge University Press.

Kahle, L. R., Beatty, S. E., & Kennedy, P. (1986). Comment on classically conditioning human consumers. *Advances in Consumer Research, 14*, 411-414.

Kassarjian, H. H. (1978). Presidential address, 1977: Anthropomorphism and parsimony. In H. K. Hunt (Ed.), *Advances in consumer research, 5.* Ann Arbor, MI: Association for Consumer Research.

Kellaris, J. J., & Cox, A. D. (1989). The effects of background music in advertising: A reassessment. *Journal of Consumer Research, 16,* 113-118.

Kim, J., Allen, C. T., & Kardes, F. R. (1996). An investigation of the mediational mechanisms underlying attitudinal conditioning. *Journal of Marketing Research, 33,* 318-328.

Kleine, R. E., Macklin, C. M., & Bruvold, N. T. (1986). Print ads and Pavlov: Are they compatible? In *Proceedings of the 1986 Conference of the American Academy of Advertising* (pp. 97-102). Provo, UT: Academy of Advertising.

Kohlenberg, R., & Phillips, T. (1973). Reinforcement and rate of litter depositing. *Journal of Applied Behavior Analysis, 6,* 391-396.

Komaki, J., Barwick, K. D., & Scott, L. R. (1978). A behavioral approach to occupational safety: Pinpointing and reinforcing safe performance in a food manufacturing plant. *Journal of Applied Psychology, 63,* 434-445.

Komaki, J., Blood, M. R., & Holder, D. (1980). Fostering friendliness in a fast food franchise. *Journal of Organizational Behavior Management, 2,* 151-163.

Komaki, J., Waddell, W., & Pearce, G. (1977). The applied behavior analysis approach and individual employees: Improving performance in two small businesses. *Organizational Behavior and Human Performance, 19,* 337-352.

Kopelman, R. E., & Schneller, G. O. (1981). A mixed-consequence system for reducing overtime and unscheduled absences. *Journal of Organizational Behavior Management, 3,* 17-28.

Kotler, P., & Zaltman, G. (1971). Social marketing: A planned approach to social change. *Journal of Marketing, 35,* 3-12.

Krantz, M. (1998, July 20). Click till you drop. *Time,* 34-39.

Kroeber-Riel, W. (1984). Emotional product differentiation by classical conditioning. In T. C. Kinnear (Ed.), *Advances in consumer research, 11* (pp. 538-543). Provo, UT: Association for Consumer Research.

Kunkel, J. H., & Berry, L. L. (1968). A behavioral conception of retail image. *Journal of Marketing, 32,* 45-52.

Lea, S. E. G. (1978). The psychology and economics of demand. *Psychological Bulletin, 85,* 441-466.

Lea, S. E. G. (1981). Animal experiments in economic psychology. *Journal of Economic Psychology, 1,* 245-271.

Lindsley, O. R. (1962). A behavioral measure of television viewing. *Journal of Advertising Research, 2,* 2-12.

Lombard, D., Neubauer, T. E., Canfield, D., & Winett, R. A. (1991). Behavioral community intervention to reduce the risk of skin cancer. *Journal of Applied Behavior Analysis, 24,* 677-686.

Luthans, F., Paul, R., & Baker, D. (1981). An experimental analysis of the impact of contingent reinforcement on salespersons' performance behavior. *Journal of Applied Psychology, 66,* 314-323.

Mace, F. C. (1994). Basic research needed for stimulating the development of behavioral technologies. *Journal of the Experimental Analysis of Behavior, 61,* 529-550.

Macklin, M. C. (1983). Classical conditioning effects in product/character pairings presented to children. *Advances in Consumer Research, 13,* 198-203.

Malenfant, J. E. L., & Van Houten, R. (1988). The effects of nighttime seat belt enforcement on seat belt use by tavern patrons: A preliminary analysis. *Journal of Applied Behavior Analysis, 21,* 271-276.

Markin, R. J., & Narayana, C. L. (1975). Behavior control: Are consumers beyond freedom and dignity? *Advances in Consumer Research, 3,* 222-228.

Martinko, M. J. (1987). An organizational behavior modification analysis of consumer behavior. *Journal of Organizational Behavior Management, 8,* 19-43.

Martinko, M. J., White, J. D., & Hassell, B. (1989). An operant analysis of prompting in a sales environment. *Journal of Organizational Behavior Management, 10,* 93-107.

Matson, J. L. (Ed.). (1989). *Handbook of behavior modification with the mentally retarded* (2nd ed.). New York, NY: Plenum Press.

Mawhinney, T. C., Dickinson, A. M., & Taylor, L. A., III (1989). The use of concurrent schedules to evaluate the effects of extrinsic reward on "intrinsic motivation." *Journal of Organizational Behavior Management, 10,* 109-129.

Mayer, J. A., Heins, J. M., Vogel, J. M., Morrison, D. C., Lankester, L. D., & Jacobs, A. L. (1986). Promoting low-fat entree choices in a public cafeteria. *Journal of Applied Behavior Analysis, 19,* 397-402.

McCall, M., & Belmont, H. J. (1996). Credit card insignia and restaurant tipping: evidence for an associative link. *Journal of Applied Psychology, 81,* 609-613.

McNally, K. A., & Abernathy, W. B. (1989). Effects of monetary incentives on customer behavior: Use of automatic teller machines (ATMs) by low frequency users. *Journal of Organizational Behavior Management, 10,* 79-91.

McNees, M. P., Egli, D. S., Marshall, R. S., Schenlle, J. F., & Risley, T. R. (1976). Shoplifting prevention: Providing information through signs. *Journal of Applied Behavior Analysis, 9,* 399-405.

McNees, M. P., Schnelle, J. F., Kirchner, R. E., & Thomas, M. M. (1980). An experimental analysis of a program to reduce retail theft. *American Journal of Community Psychology, 8,* 379-385.

McSweeny, A. J. (1978). Effects of response cost on the behavior of a million persons: Charging for directory assistance in Cincinnati. *Journal of Applied Behavior Analysis, 11,* 47-51.

McSweeney, F. K., & Bierley, C. (1984). Recent developments in classical conditioning. *Journal of Consumer Research, 11,* 619-631.

Milliman, R. E. (1982). Using background music to affect the behavior of supermarket shoppers. *Journal of Marketing, 46,* 86-91.

Morris, E. K. (1988). Contextualism: The world view of behavior analysis. *Journal of Experimental Child Psychology, 46,* 289-323.

Nathan, P. E., & Wallace, W. H. (1965). An operant behavioral measure of TV commercial effectiveness. *Journal of Advertising Research*, 13-20.

Nord, W. R., & Peter, J. P. (1981). A behavior modification perspective on marketing. *Journal of Marketing, 44*, 36-47.

O'Brien, R. M., Dickinson, A. M., & Rosow, M. P. (Eds.). (1982). *Handbook of industrial behavior modification.* New York, NY: Pergamon.

Peter, J. P., & Nord, W. R. (1982). A clarification and extension of operant conditioning principles in marketing. *Journal of Marketing, 46*, 102-107.

Petty, R. E., Cacioppo, J. T., & Schumann, D. (1983). Central and peripheral routes to advertising effectiveness: The moderating role of involvement. *Journal of Consumer Research, 10*, 135-146.

Poppe, D. (1998, June 7). Look for a boom in electronic commerce. *The Philadelphia Inquirer*, D3.

Powers, R. B., Osborne, J. G., & Anderson, E. G. (1973). Positive reinforcement of litter removal in the natural environment. *Journal of Applied Analysis, 6*, 579-586.

Rajala, A. K., & Hantula, D. A. (in press). Towards a Behavioral Ecology of Consumption: Delay-Reduction effects on foraging in a simulated Internet mall. *Managerial and Economic Decision.*

Rao, R., & Mawhinney, T. C. (1991). Superior-subordinate dyads: Dependence of leader effectiveness on mutual reinforcement contingencies. *Journal of the Experimental Analysis of Behavior, 56*, 105-118.

Ragnarsson, R. S., & Bjorgvinsson, T. (1991). Effects of public posting on driving speed in Icelandic traffic. *Journal of Applied Behavior Analysis, 24*, 53-58.

Ralis, M. T., & O'Brien, R. M. (1986). Prompts, goal setting, and feedback to increase suggestive selling. *Journal of Organizational Behavior Management, 8*, 5-18.

Rhoten, W. W. (1980). A procedure to improve compliance with coal mine safety regulations. *Journal of Organizational Behavior Management, 2*, 243-249.

Rothschild, M. L., & Gaidis, W. C. (1981). Behavioral learning theory: Its relevance to marketing and promotions. *Journal of Marketing, 45*, 70-78.

Rudd, J. R., & Geller, E. S. (1985). A university-based incentive program to increase safety belt use: Toward cost-effective institutionalization. *Journal of Applied Behavior Analysis, 18*, 215-226.

Runnion, A., Watson, J. O., & McWhorter, J. (1978). Energy savings in interstate transportation through feedback and reinforcement. *Journal of Organizational Behavior Management, 1*, 180-191.

Russo, J. E. (1978). Eye fixations can save the world: A critical evaluation between eye fixations and other information. *Advances in Consumer Research, 5*, 561-570.

Seaver, W. B., & Patterson, A. H. (1976). Decreasing fuel-oil consumption through feedback and social commendation. *Journal of Applied Behavior Analysis, 9*, 147-152.

Schneider, B., & Bowen, D. E. (1995). *Winning the service game.* Boston, MA: Harvard Business School Press.

Scott, W. R. (1987). *Organizations: Rational, natural and open systems* (2nd ed.). Engelwood Cliffs, NJ: Prentice-Hall.

Sherry, J. F., Jr. (1991). Postmodern alternatives: The interpretive turn in consumer research. In T. S. Robertson & H. H. Kassarjian (Eds.), *Handbook of consumer behavior* (pp. 548-591). Englewood Cliffs, NJ: Prentice-Hall.

Shettleworth, S. J. (1988). Foraging as operant behavior and operant behavior as foraging: What have we learned? In G. H. Bower (Ed.), *The psychology of learning and motivation, 22* (pp. 1-49). San Diego: Academic Press.

Shimp, T. A. (1991). Neo-Pavlovian conditioning and its implications for consumer research. In T. S. Robertson & H. H. Kassarjian (Eds.), *Handbook of consumer behavior* (pp. 162-187). Englewood Cliffs, NJ: Prentice-Hall.

Shimp, T. A., Stuart, E. W., & Engle, R. W. (1991). A program of classical conditioning experiments testing variations in the conditioned stimulus and context. *Journal of Consumer Research, 18*, 1-12.

Silva, D. B., Duncan, P. K., & Doudna, D. (1981). The effects of attendance-contingent feedback and praise on attendance and work efficiency. *Journal of Organizational Behavior Management, 3*, 59-69.

Skinner, B. F. (1953). *Science and human behavior.* New York, NY: Free Press.

Skinner, B. F. (1957). *Verbal behavior.* New York, NY: Appleton-Century-Crofts.

Skinner, B. F. (1969). *Contingencies of reinforcement: A theoretical analysis.* Englewood Cliffs, NJ: Prentice-Hall.

Skinner, B .F. (1971). *Beyond freedom and dignity.* New York, NY: Knopf.

Skinner, B. F. (1972). A lecture on "having" a poem. In: *Cumulative record: A selection of papers* (3rd. ed.) (pp. 345-355). New York, NY: Appleton-Century Crofts.

Skinner, B. F. (1984). Selection by consequences. *The Behavioral and Brain Sciences*,

Sowers-Hoag, K. M., Thyer, B. A., & Bailey, J. S. (1987). Promoting automobile safety belt use by young children. *Journal of Applied Behavior Analysis, 20*, 133-138.

Staddon, J. E. R. (1983). *Adaptive behavior and learning.* Cambridge: Cambridge University Press.

Stajkovic, A. D., & Luthans, F. (1997). A meta-analysis of the effects of organizational behavior modification on task performance, 1975-1995. *Academy of Management Journal, 40*, 1122-1149.

Stephens, D. W., & Krebs, J. R. (1986). *Foraging theory.* Princeton, NJ: Princeton University Press.

Stigler, G. J., & Becker, G. S. (1977). De gustibus non est disputandum. *The American Economic Review, 67*, 76-90.

Stock, L. Z., & Milan, M. A. (1993). Improving dietary practices of elderly individuals: The power of prompting, feedback, and social reinforcement. *Journal of Applied Behavior Analysis, 26*, 379-387.

Stuart, E. W., Shimp, T. A., & Engle, R. W. (1987). Classical conditioning of consumer attitudes: Four experiments in an advertising context. *Journal of Consumer Research, 14*, 334-349.

Tom, G. (1995). Classical conditioning of unattended stimuli. *Psychology and Marketing, 12*, 79-87.

Van De Water, T. J. (1997). Psychology's entrepreneurs and the marketing of industrial psychology. *Journal of Applied Psychology, 82*, 486-499.

Van Houten, R., Rolider, A., Nau, P. A., Friedman, R., Becker, M., Chalodovsky, I., & Scherer, M. (1985). Large-scale reductions in speeding and accidents in Canada and Israel: A behavioral ecological perspective. *Journal of Applied Behavior Analysis, 18*, 87-93.

Wagner, J. L., & Winett, R. A. (1988). Prompting one low-fat, high fiber selection in a fast-food restaurant. *Journal of Applied Behavior Analysis, 21*, 179-185.

Watson, J. B. (1922, April 20). *The ideal executive.* Address presented to the graduating class of young executives, R. H. Macy Co. Typescript contained in the John Broadus Watson Papers, Manuscript Division, Library of Congress, Washington, D. C.

Werner, E. E., Mittelbach, G. G., & Hall, D. J. (1981). The role of foraging profitability and experience in habitat use by the bluegill sunfish. *Ecology, 62*, 116-125.

Welsh, H. B., Bernstein, D. J., & Luthans, F. (1992). Application of the Premack Principle of reinforcements to the quality performance of service employees. *Journal of Organizational Behavior Management, 13*, 9-32.

Welsh, H. B., Luthans, F., & Sommer, S. M. (1993). Managing Russian factory workers: The impact of U.S.-based behavioral and participative techniques. *Academy of Management Journal, 36*, 58-79.

Wikoff, M., Anderson, D. C., & Crowell, C. R. (1982). Behavior management in a factory setting: Increasing work efficiency. *Journal of Organizational Behavior Management, 4*, 97-127.

Wilkie, W. (1994). *Consumer behavior* (3rd ed.). New York, NY: Wiley.

Wilson, E. O. (1998). *Consilience: The Unity of Knowledge.* New York, NY: Random House.

Williams, M., Thyer, B. A., Bailey, J. S., & Harrison, D. F. (1989). Promoting safety belt use with traffic signs and prompters. *Journal of Applied Behavior Analysis, 22*, 71-76.

Winett, R. A. (1977). Promoting turning out lights in unoccupied rooms. *Journal of Environmental Systems, 1*, 237-241.

Winett, R. A., Hatcher, J. W., Fort, T. R., Leckliter, I. N., Love, S. Q., Riley, A. W., & Fishback, J. F. (1982). The effects of videotape modeling and daily feedback on residential electricity conservation, home temperature and humidity, perceived comport, and clothing worn: Winter and summer. *Journal of Applied Behavior Analysis, 15*, 381-402.

Winett, R. A., Kaiser, S., Haberkorn, G. (1977). The effects of monetary rebates and daily feedback on electricity conservation. *Journal of Environmental Systems, 6*, 329-341.

Winett, R. A., Kramer, K. D., Walker, W. B., Malone, S. W., & Lane, M. K. (1988). Modifying food purchases in supermarkets with modeling, feedback, and goal-setting procedures. *Journal of Applied Behavior Analysis, 21*, 73-80.

Winett, R. A., Leckliter, I. N., Chinn, D. E., Stahl, B., & Love, S. Q. (1985). Effects of television modeling on residential energy conservation. *Journal of Applied Behavior Analysis, 18*, 33-44.

Winett, R. A., Moore, J. F., Wagner, J. L., Hite, L. A., Leahy, M., Neubauer, T. E., Walberg, J. L., Walker, W. B., Lombard, D., Geller, E. S., & Mundy, L. L. (1991). Altering shoppers' supermarket purchases to fit nutritional guidelines: An interactive information system. *Journal of Applied Behavior Analysis, 24*, 95-105.

Winkler, R. C., & Winett, R. A. (1982). Behavioral interventions in resource conservation: A systems approach based on behavioral economics. *American Psychologist, 37*, 421-435.

Winterhalder, B. (1981). Foraging strategies in the boreal forest: An analysis of Cree hunting and gathering. In B. Winterhalder & E. Smith (Eds.), *Hunter-gatherer foraging strategies* (pp. 66-98). Chicago: University of Chicago Press.

Winters, L. C., & Wallace, W. H. (1970). On operant conditioning techniques. *Journal of Advertising Research, 10*, 39-45.

Witmer, J. F., & Geller, E. S. (1976). Facilitating paper recycling: Effects of prompts, raffles, and contests. *Journal of Applied Behavior Analysis, 9*, 315-322.

Wolf, A., Newman, D. Z., & Winters, L. C. (1969). Operant measures of interest as related to *ad lib* readership. *Journal of Advertising Research, 9*, 40-45.

Footnotes

1. This is not to say that employee behavior is not considered in business disciplines concerned with other intra-organizational functions such as accounting, finance, risk management, or operations management, but rather that "management" and "human resources" bear more directly on daily employee behavior than do these other disciplines. Indeed, many of the rules and principles of accounting and finance were developed to control behavior (see Hantula, 1992).

Discussion of Hantula

Bringing Systems Analysis to the Study of Consumer Behavior

Lori H. Miller

Western Michigan University

Consumer behavior can be understood in the context of a Total Performance System (Brethower, 1995; Dean & Ripley, 1997). This paper complements Hantula's review of the history of studies of consumer behavior with a systems analysis approach. It is necessary and possible to study the contingencies that control consumer behavior. Employing a consistent framework to organizations and consumer behavior will drive the ideas and notions of the study on this topic forward.

Using behavior analysis to understand and predict consumer behavior as well as viewing the consumer in the context of a system can help organizations improve elements of their own system to meet consumers' needs. As Hantula points out, advertising and promotion strategies continue to be developed with the goal of changing or shaping consumers' attitudes toward products or services in hopes that these attitudes will drive or influence purchases. For organizations to build on their responsiveness they can study consumers through the lens of systems analysis to understand and predict consumer behavior in the changing environment.

The Total Performance System

Brethower's model of the Total Performance System encompasses the perception that a healthy system contains seven components: 1) a mission, 2) inputs, 3) processes, 4) outputs, 5) receiving system, 6) receiving system feedback, and 7) processing system feedback. In essence, a healthy system must align as well as balance the load of each of these parts in order to grow in a positive direction.

Consumers are the receiving system for organizations that provide goods or services. The receiving system feedback is what drives the work within the organization. To clarify the role of total performance system here, lets look at consumer in the seven system components:

1) The mission of a consumer is to live a healthy, productive, and happy life.
2) Consumer inputs are information and prompts about a product or service. These are provided to consumers by organizations through outlets such as commercials on television, displays in stores, telephone, the Internet, magazine, newspapers, and other sources of communication.
3) The consumer process is decision-making. Decisions are made based on the inputs. Decisions are also made based on the learning history of the consumer.

4) The consumer output is the end of a purchase response such as paying money or trading something to obtain a good or service is a consumer.
5) The receiving system of consumer is the organization that receives the money for the product or service. The receiving system of consumer also includes the consumers themselves and others who are affected by the product or service.
6) Receiving system feedback of the consumer system is recognized by reactions from the consumers themselves or others in their environment in relation to the consumption of a product or service.
7) The processing system feedback for consumer behavior is based on the reinforcing effect of a product or service that was consumed. The consumer evaluates how the product or service somehow aligns with their mission.

Now lets look at the organization total performance system, specifically in relation to the consumer:

1) The mission of an organization is to continuously advance in their environment.
2) Inputs are supplies, materials, and labor/employees. These are all things that assist an organization to perform in alignment with their mission.
3) Processes in organizations are the production of the goods or services that will be available for the consumers.
4) Outputs are information, products, and services. Information can be fashioned by the organization in a way to direct the consumer purchase response.
5) The receiving system is the consumers. They are the ones who consume the output.
6) Receiving system feedback is customer feedback recognized by ways such as overall sales, repeat vs. one-time sales, comparison of competition's sales figures, and customer opinions.
7) Processing system feedback is the examination of internal processes. Are processes efficient and cost effective? Was the output delivered on time? Did it meet the customer's expectations? What can we do better next time?

Aligning the Consumer and the Organization Systems

Employing the systems framework assists in the analyses of consumer behavior and the development of strategies to influence purchase responses. For example, establishing operations and the contingencies responsible for maintaining the behavior supporting them focus business strategies such as marketing display and pricing. Displays and pricing influence buyer decisions, which characterize consumer processes. The link between the two total performance systems is further illustrated in Hantula's review of the three cycles of the study of consumer behavior.

The first cycle of the study of consumer behavior Hantula discusses is the Applied Analysis of Consumer Behavior. Behavior analysis is used as a tool. When consumer behaviors can ultimately be understood, the proper contingencies may be implemented.

The second cycle of the study of consumer behavior is the direct recording of the reinforcing effectiveness of information of a product or service, such as a commercial. This research allows for direct feedback from the receiving system. It is useful in the processing component of an organizational system because information on the reinforcing effectiveness of a product can direct processes in a meaningful direction.

The third cycle of the study of consumer behavior is the Behavioral Perspective Model and the Behavioral Ecology of Consumption. The Behavioral Perspective Model focuses on theoretical contingencies of consumption. This models consumer acquisition contingent on different levels of reinforcement. The Behavioral Ecology of Consumption approach views consumption as acquiring products and services altered by the consumer's options, time, environment, and space.

An interesting issue Hantula discusses is prey selection (as a part of the behavioral ecology model). Prey selection involves the consumer process of deciding what to do when faced with various products and deciding whether to accept or reject them. Decisions are altered by knowledge of how selection will maximize reinforcement. This knowledge can be controlled by the organization selling the product or service by supplying information that may include things such as timeliness of delivery, quality, location, etc.

All of these approaches to the study of consumer behavior complement each other in the understanding on the topic. By studying the contingencies that affect behavior, organizations can specifically design the process component of their system to adjust to these contingencies and place them in the proper context of the total performance system of the consumer.

For example, advertising focuses on the process of the construction of information to consumers about their goods or service. The following is a systems approach to this organizational process involving the central role of the consumer:

1) Mission: To influence the consumer to buy and use their products/services.
2) Input: Research and feedback. Mainly to understand consumer behavior in order to know what the reinforcers are for a targeted market.
3) Process: Development of marketing strategies based on research results of what reinforcers are for consumers
4) Output: advertising that appeal to the senses of the consumers. This will involve linking the product with reinforcers based on research results.
5) Receiving system: consumers (potential purchasers)
6) Receiving system feedback: customer sales
7) Processing system feedback: are marketing strategies working?

Conclusion

Effective organizations recognize the consumer's integral role in their successes. As Hantula discusses, the consumer plays a fundamental role within an organization because it is the consumer who drives the changes that happen inside the organization. Systems analysis simplifies the method of controlling the behavior of consumers "outside the box". The explorations in the field accentuate the necessity for the persons within organizational charts to work to create and maintain proper functions within their organizations in order to maintain a healthy system (Brethower, 1995), one that aligns with the consumer system.

References

Brethower, D. M. (1995). Specifying a human performance technology base. *Performance Improvement Quarterly, 8*(2), 17-39.

Dean, P. J., & Ripley, D.E. (1997). *Performance improvement pathfinders: Models for organizational learning systems.* Washington, DC: International Society for Performance Improvement.

Hantula, D., Di Clemente, D. F., & Rajala, A. K. (2001). Outside the box: The analysis of consumer behavior. In L. J. Hayes, J. Austin, R. Houmanfar, & M. C. Clayton (Eds.), *Organizational Change.* Reno, NV: Context Press.

Balanced Scorecards and Performance Scorecards: A Brief Background

John Austin

Western Michigan University

Performance management has long been recognized as an approach effective in addressing a wide variety of work issues. Daniels (1989) describes a set of procedures and analysis techniques based soundly in applied behavior analysis, and the other chapters in this book cover, in more detail, these applications of applied behavior analysis principles. One of the prerequisites to effectively using applied behavior analysis techniques is that practitioners must have accurate and timely performance-related data. A problem that modern organizations do not have is one of *collecting* these sorts of data. In most cases, organizations collect so many forms of performance data *automatically* and immediately, that managers' main problem is deciding which are the best data and determining how exactly to locate and handle these data.

Although there has been considerable (and growing) interest in systems-level views of organizational management (e.g., Krapfl & Gasporotto, 1982; Rummler & Brache, 1995), as opposed to the performer-level views that have been traditionally more closely embraced by performance management (e.g., see Bailey and Austin, this volume), few behavior analysts have worked on the issue of data management techniques in organizations. The current chapter describes a systems-level approach to utilizing many of these performance management tools and techniques through the use of performance scorecards.

Performance scorecards have some history of use in organizations. The most popular incarnation is likely represented by the recent work of Kaplan and Norton (1992), called the "Balanced scorecard" approach. The balanced scorecard is a measurement system that weighs several important measures of organizational performance and links these to the strategy and vision of the organization. Although companies must adapt balanced scorecard measures to their own vision and strategy, many argue that the scorecards should portray measures in at least four areas: customers, internal processes, financial, and learning and growth (Chow, Haddad, & Williamson, 1997). According to Hanson and Towle (January/February, 2000), 35% of respondents, to a recent survey on performance management in large organizations, reported that they were using or had plans to use balanced scorecards in their measurement systems. The balanced scorecard is a very popular topic of discussion in business journals and magazines, however, my literature search conducted for purposes of this article found no empirical research on the use of scorecards in organizations.

Another form of performance scorecard was described by Daniels (1989), and called the "performance matrix". In the case of the performance matrix, several important results or behaviors are listed and each given weights corresponding to their importance to the organization. Then, the current and goal levels of each performance are filled into the table, and several interim values are entered. The end result is a table of performance values that can be used as a log for performance during the next period of monitoring. When each new level of performance is recorded, scores are obtained for each result or behavior and then added to obtain a single total performance score.

What these approaches have in common, quite obviously, is that they allow managers and employees to record, summarize, and make sense of many performance measures at once. The issue of "data overload" is not entirely avoided by using this approach, however. In large organizations, when many performers are doing many different tasks at many different levels, the challenge may become to manage the scorecards themselves while making them individualized enough so that they have meaning to employees and managers throughout the organization. This chapter describes an approach developed by Abernathy and Associates whereby scorecards are "cascaded" from the top to the bottom of an organization. As opposed to having hundreds of unrelated scorecards throughout the organization, this cascading approach links important performance on the cards and allows the system to be more easily controlled. This chapter does not focus on the details of how to implement such a system. Instead, the goal of this chapter is to report the results of several different analyses of years of data from companies that used this approach to data and performance management. The chapter is important because it represents some of the only research I was able to locate on the effectiveness of scorecard-type approaches to managing performance in organizations.

An Analysis of Twelve Organizations' Total Performance Systems

William B. Abernathy
Abernathy & Associates

Overview and Scope of the Analyses

This chapter examines the effects of monthly performance scorecards and incentive pay on employee performance in a variety of organizations. Twelve organizations are examined with a combined 4,289 employees and 2,195 objective performance measures. Specific dimensions of scorecard design and administration are analyzed including the number of employees assigned to a scorecard; whether the employees are hourly or salaried; the number of measures in a scorecard; the type of measure; the measure base, goal, and priority weight; and how frequently the base, goal and priority weight are changed. Specific incentive pay issues examined with respect to employee performance improvement include the effects of incentive opportunity and incentive pay out magnitudes. The general conclusions are that, when improvements are observed, they are reached by promoting personal and small team measures and measures that employees can directly affect. However, the effects of incentive pay on employee performance appear to be significant only when the incentive pay out exceeds twenty percent of the employee's base pay. Finally, the data suggest that frequent changes to performance goals reduce performance improvement.

The first twelve months' results of twelve organizations' performance scorecard and incentive pay systems are analyzed below. All the organizations reported monthly performance scorecards through Abernathy & Associates' outsourced administration service. The twelve were selected from a total reporting group of thirty-five companies. The inclusion requirements were that the organization had reported 15 consecutive months and had a database in which the measure types were coded to allow for an analysis. Table 1 lists the organization type, number of employees, and the number of performance measures for each organization.

Six of the organizations experienced significant overall performance improvements, four yielded no significant change, and two experienced a decline in performance. The key variable clusters affecting performance change were found to be scorecard design and administrative variables, incentive pay variables, and organizational structure variables. A case is presented that the critical success variable is to ensure employees can directly influence the scorecard measures.

Each organization's performance scorecard system was developed using the method of 'cascading objectives'. An organizational 'strategic scorecard' was first

Company	Type	No. Employees	No. Measures
A	Manufacturing	286	179
B	Retail	62	61
C	Manufacturing	348	39
D	Banking	464	18
E	Publishing	66	54
F	Distribution	206	228
G	Banking	747	536
H	Banking	186	94
I	Distribution	99	56
J	Banking	1140	618
K	Distribution	148	75
L	Manufacturing	537	237
ALL		4289	2195

Table 1. Organization type, number of employees and the number of performance measures for each organization.

designed and served as the 'blueprint' for scorecards at successively lower levels of the organization. The strategic scorecard was carefully linked to the vision and strategy of each organization. A scorecard could be assigned to an individual, team, or department. Scorecard measures could relate to data from an individual performer, a team or group. Therefore, a given scorecard could consist of team measures, individual measures, or a combination of both. The basic format of the performance scorecards was common to all companies. In practice, each employee received a scorecard for the month's performance in the following month.

Scorecards all had the following characteristics:

Base – The base is the measure that represents zero (or the baseline level of performance) on the performance scale. Typically, this was defined as the current or minimally acceptable performance.

Goal – The goal is the level of performance that is desired by the organization. This measure is represented by 100% performance on the scorecard. So that they were challenging, yet attainable, the goals were defined as one standard deviation above the mean and were changed as required to achieve higher level goals.

Scale – Each scorecard had an eleven-interval scale that spanned from –20% to 100%. The last two intervals (representing 90% and 100% performance) were larger to increase the pay out as the performer neared the goal. The data were easily converted to a 'percent gain' using the formula [(actual – base) / (goal – base)] and then interpolated on the scale (performances were rounded down). The scale interval in which the percent gain fell was termed the "performance score".

Weight – Each performance measure was given a weighting percentage which represented how important that measure was, relative to the others and in light of the organization's strategic objectives. The sum of the percentage weights always sums to 100%.

Weighted Score – Each measure's performance score (i.e., the interval into which a particular level of performance falls for each measure) was multiplied by the weight of the measure to compute the measure's weighted score.

Performance Index – The weighted scores were summed to compute the overall scorecard performance index. The index percentage was multiplied by each month's incentive pay opportunity percentage to compute incentive pay outs.

Data Collection Procedures

For the current analysis, performance measures were restricted to only measures in which the formula and data remained constant over the 15-month study period. Performance data were collected monthly for a fifteen-month period. The first three months were excluded from the study due to typical inaccuracies in reporting and changes in scorecard parameters when the system is first introduced. This decision to improve the accuracy of the study data by excluding the first three months typically reduced the overall performance trend improvements, since performance in these months was often at its lowest level and improvements are most dramatic at this time.

The data for each performance measure were gathered from either direct export from the organization's internal databases, or from manually entered data collected by managers and supervisors. Each month's data were transmitted to Abernathy & Associates early in the next month. Data were verified through a series of audit reports and corrected as required. Employees received their scorecards and incentive payments in the third or fourth week of the following month.

A variety of variables were included in the current analysis; including the company type; employee characteristics (salaried vs. hourly); scorecard system complexity; scorecard complexity; percentage gains on scorecard measures, number of team measures; average weighting score per each measure; number of base (i.e., baseline), goal, and weight changes; guaranteed and total incentive opportunity as a percentage of monthly base pay; pay out amount; measure type; and performance trends. Table 2 lists and describes, in more detail, the variables used in the study analysis.

Variable	Description
Company	Companies are assigned an I.D. from A-L.
Employees / Scorecard	The ratio of employees to unique scorecards. The ratio is considered a measure of the organization's scorecard 'system complexity'.
Measures / Scorecard	The ratio of performance measures to unique scorecards. The ratio is considered a measure of 'scorecard complexity'.
Performance Index	The sum of the weighted measures percent gains on a scorecard. This index is the employee's score and partially or totally determines the employee's incentive payout.
Team / Individual	Team refers to measures to which two or more employees are assigned and receive the same score.
Average Weight	The average priority weighting assigned to a measure. Weightings on a scorecard sum to 100% and determine the measure's contribution to the overall performance index.
Base Changes	A measure's scorecard base is the scale value that equals zero percent gain. The number of changes to the base value over 12 months is reported.
Goal Changes	A measure's scorecard goal is the scale value that equals 100 percent gain. The number of changes to the goal value over 12 months is reported.
Weight Changes	The number of changes to the priority weight over 12 months is reported.
Hourly / Salaried	The exempt or non-exempt status of employees reporting on a measure.
Guaranteed Opportunity	The percentage of an employee's base pay that is a fixed or guaranteed incentive pay opportunity. This percentage is multiplied by the employee's scorecard Performance Index to compute the incentive payout for the month.
Total Opportunity	The percentage of an employee's base pay that represents the total incentive pay opportunity. This percentage is the sum of guaranteed opportunity plus profit-indexed opportunity.
Payout	The Actual Opportunity multiplied by the employee's assigned scorecard's Performance Index.
Measure Type	Measures are classified as Sales, Expense Control, Productivity, Regulatory Compliance, Quality, Customer Service and Projects
Score	The scorecard scale conversion for a measure's data.
Trend	The dependent variable for the study. All raw data were converted to z scores to allow for comparisons. The slope of the 12 month trend line was then computed and the sign adjusted to reflect whether the slope direction was an improvement (+) or a decline (-) in performance.

Table 2. Description of study variables.

Experimental Questions Addressed by the Analyses

A variety of issues were explored in the analyses I undertook. These issue fall into two broad categories: 1) Design and administration of the scorecards; and 2) Incentive pay issues. Although there is considerable writing on the topic of performance scorecards in organizations (especially when called "balanced scorecards"), there is little or no empirical research on the topic. The current analyses are exploratory in nature: I focused on the variables that I suspect are of interest and conceptual significance. There are many, and in the future, I will likely determine that some are not actually important, whereas others really are. These analyses represent the initial steps in determining which variables are valuable enough to further explore.

The scorecard design and administration issues in which I was interested included; 1) Does performance improvement differ among the types of performance measures (sales, customer service, quality, productivity, expense control, regulatory compliance, or projects)? 2) Do team or individual scorecards yield the most performance improvement? 3) Do hourly employees respond more to the system then salaried employees? 4) Does the complexity (employees per scorecard) of the system constrain improvements? 5) Does the complexity of the individual scorecards (measures per scorecard) constrain performance improvement? 6) Does the priority weight assigned to a measure affect performance improvement? 7) Does the level at which a measure's base or goal is set affect performance improvement?; and, 8) Do frequent changes in a measure's base, goal or weight affect improvement? The issues in which I was interested that related to incentive pay were as follows: 1) Does the level of incentive pay opportunity affect performance trend?; and 2) Does incentive pay out affect performance trend?

Results

The results that follow are divided into three sections: 1) Trend analyses for all companies; 2) Trend results for each individual company; and 3) Experimental questions addressed by the analyses. The reader should remember that the trend results represent overall effects of the scorecards on the performance indicators selected by each company. Furthermore, for the purpose of this study, these effects were converted to z-scores, to facilitate our comparisons of unit changes on different types of measures. Z-scores standardize unit changes and re-state them in terms of their number of standard deviations from the mean (Howell, 1997). So, for example, a z-score of +1.00 represents a value of one standard deviation above the mean. Clearly, in these analyses positive trends suggest improvement in each company's measures, whereas negative values represent corresponding declines.

Trend Analyses for All Companies

The trend analyses for all of the companies in the study are listed in Table 1, along with an indication of the statistical significance (a=.05; indicated as 'yes' or 'no') of each analysis. As stated above, positive trends indicate improvement[1] for that

Company	Number of Measures	Trend Mean	Trend S.D.	Annualized Trend %	95% Confidence Limit
A	179	+.0266	.1230	+31.92%	Yes
B	61	-.0026	.1048	-3.12%	Yes
C	39	+.0125	.1119	+15.00%	No
D	18	-.0251	.1415	-.30.12%	No
E	54	.0015	.1267	+1.80%	Yes
F	228	-.0013	.1120	-1.56%	No
G	536	.0383	.1128	+45.96%	Yes
H	94	+.0304	.1164	+36.48%	Yes
I	56	-.0106	.1211	-12.72%	Yes
J	618	-.0011	.1245	-1.32%	No
K	75	+.0279	.1246	+33.48%	Yes
L	237	+.0256	.1436	+30.72%	Yes
ALL	2195	.0158	.1226	+18.96%	Mixed
SIGNIFICANT	1292	.0276	.1223	+33.12%	Yes

Table 3. Summary of Performance Trends.

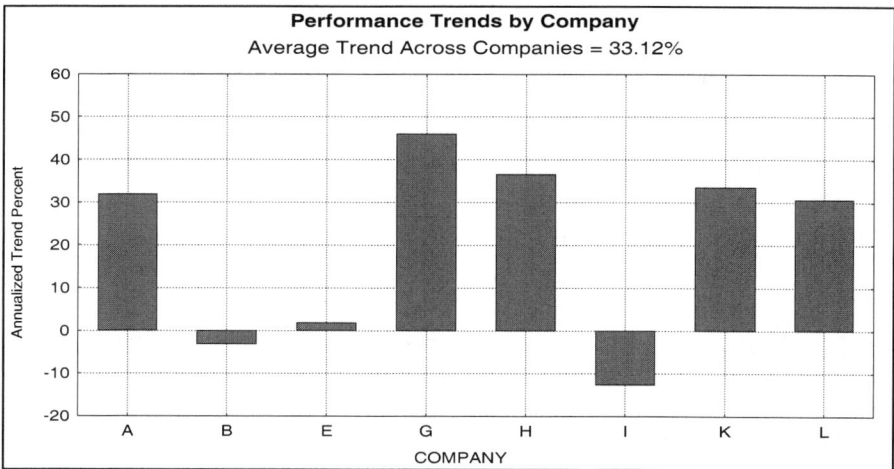

Figure 1. Summary of significant trends for each company. Annualized average improvement = 33.12%

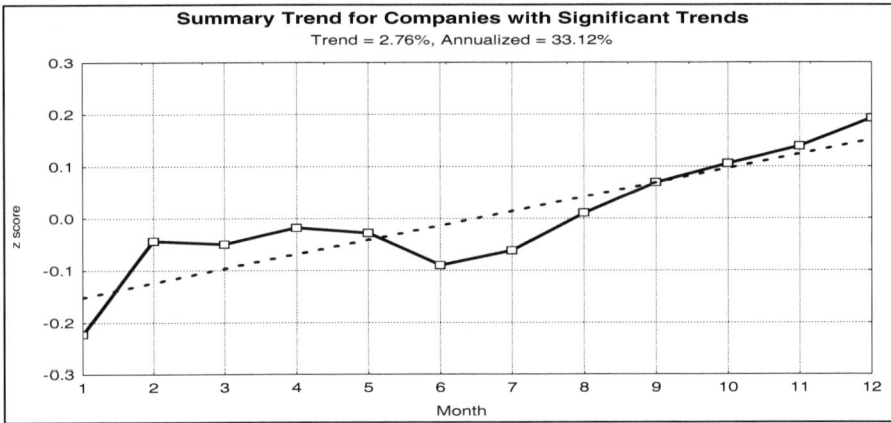

Figure 2. The overall trend of the eight companies with significant trends was +2.76 with an annualized trend of +33.12%.

company, on the measures they selected, over the 12-month study period. Of the 12 companies, 8 of these had significant positive or negative trends. Figure 1 is a graphic comparison of these eight companies' significant trends. Six of the companies experienced significant improvements, while two of the companies had significant declines in performance (i.e., negative trends). The 8 companies with significant trends were then subjected to additional trend analysis of their own, to determine the overall trend of companies who experienced significant change during their study period. Figure 2 represents the overall trend of the eight companies with significant trends (+.0276). That is, the average improvement trend was .0276 standard deviations per month over the 12-month period. One interpretation of the initial improvement in the first month is that the feedback focused employees on results for which they had a high degree of discretionary control. Changes in behavior (improvement plans) were implemented for measures that were easiest to improve.

Trend Results for Each Company

The overall performance trend for all twelve companies 2,195 measures and 4,289 employees was computed for months 1-12 (see Figure 3). The average trend (slope) was .0158, representing an improvement of .0158 standard deviations per month. However, as non-significant trends are included in this analysis, any interpretation should be viewed with caution.

Company A, a manufacturing company with 286 employees and 179 small team and individual performance measures, had a significant that averaged .0266 (see Figure 4). Through visual inspection, one can see that performance improvements begin in about the seventh month of scorecard operation. Company B, a retail firm with 62 employees and 61 small team and individual performance measures, had a significant and that averaged -.0026 (see Figure 5). However, I should note that the results are confounded by seasonal industry-related variables that alter the employees' opportunity to perform. Figure 6. Company C is in manufacturing, employs 348 employees, and had 39 small and large team performance measures. The trend was not significant, but averaged .0125, moving the desired direction (see Figure 6). Though the trend was not significant, visual inspection reveals a reduction in month-to-month variability in the months after the fifth month. Company D is in banking, they have 464 employees, and had 18 large team performance measures. The trend was not significant, but averaged –.0251, which is in the undesired direction (see Figure 7). In this case, there was an average of 26 employees assigned to each scorecard. As will be discussed, companies, such as this, that assigned the same scorecard and score to large numbers of employees did not improve as much as those companies with small team and personal scorecard measures. Company E, a publishing company with 66 employees, had 54 small team and individual performance measures. The trend was significant and averaged .0015 (see Figure 8). The large negative 'spike' in performance in month ten substantially reduced the overall improvement trend. Such a spike is typically due to variables outside direct control of employees (i.e., system or larger scale economic variables). Company F is in distribution with 206 employees and 228 small team and individual performance measures. The trend was not significant, and averaged -.0013 (see Figure 9). Though there was no significant improvement, beginning in month seven there was a reduction in month-to-month performance variability, which is often favorable. Company G, a retail banking company with 747 employees and 536 small team and individual performance measures. The trend was significant and averaged +.0383 (see Figure 10). The trend in this figure appears similar to the aggregate chart for all organizations. That is, inspection of the figure shows an initial improvement followed by an 'incubation period' that is followed by additional improvements. Company H is the operations area of Company G with 186 employees and 94 small team and individual performance measures. The trend was significant and averaged .0304 (see Figure 11). Again, this figure shows that performance improved in the initial months, followed by no improvement, and then improvement again in months 10-12. Company I, a distribution company with 99 employees and 56 small team and individual performance measures, had a significant trend that averaged –.0106 (see Figure 12). The Figure illustrates a cyclical trend suggestive of a seasonal issue that may restrict opportunity and override any employee performance improvements. Company J is in banking with 1,140 employees and 618 small team and individual performance measures. The performance trend was not significant, and averaged -.0011 (see Figure 13). A substantial improvement occurred in month two followed by a gradual decline. This result could be due to poor goal setting or a failure to provide on-going feedback and reinforcement after the program was launched. Company K is in distribution with 148 employees and 75 small team and individual performance measures. The trend was significant and averaged .0279 (see Figure 14). Company K also

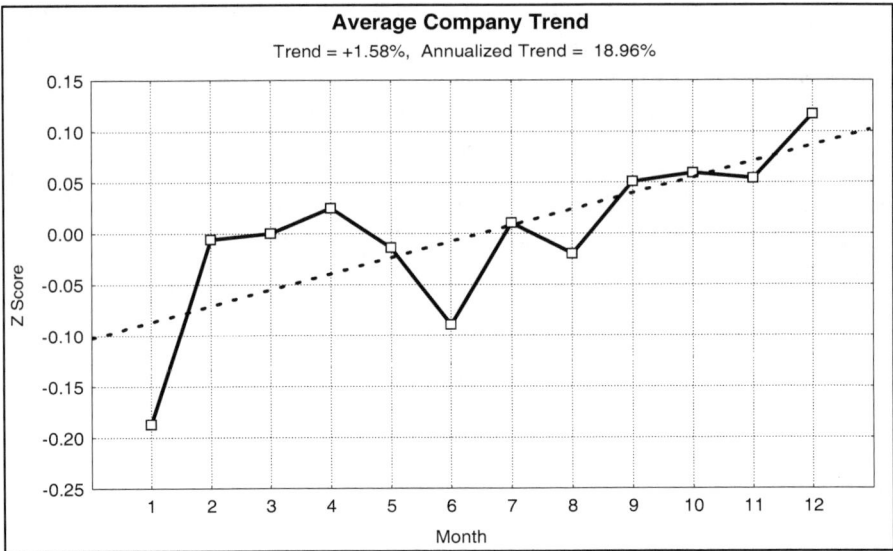

Figure 3. The overall performance trend for all twelve companies 2,195 measures and 4,289 employees was computed for months 1-12. The average trend (slope) was +1.58% with an annualized trend of +18.96%.

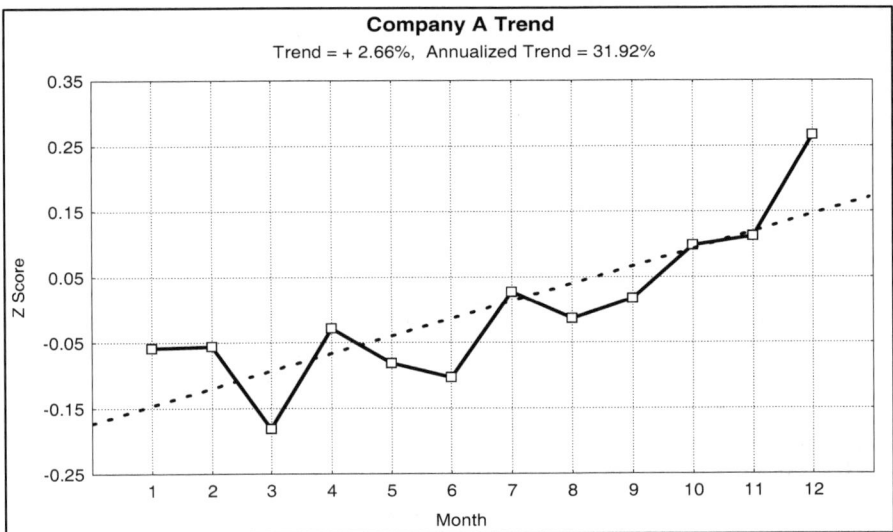

Figure 4. Company A is in manufacturing with 286 employees and 179 small team and individual performance measures. The trend was significant and averaged 2.66% with an annualized trend of +31.92%.

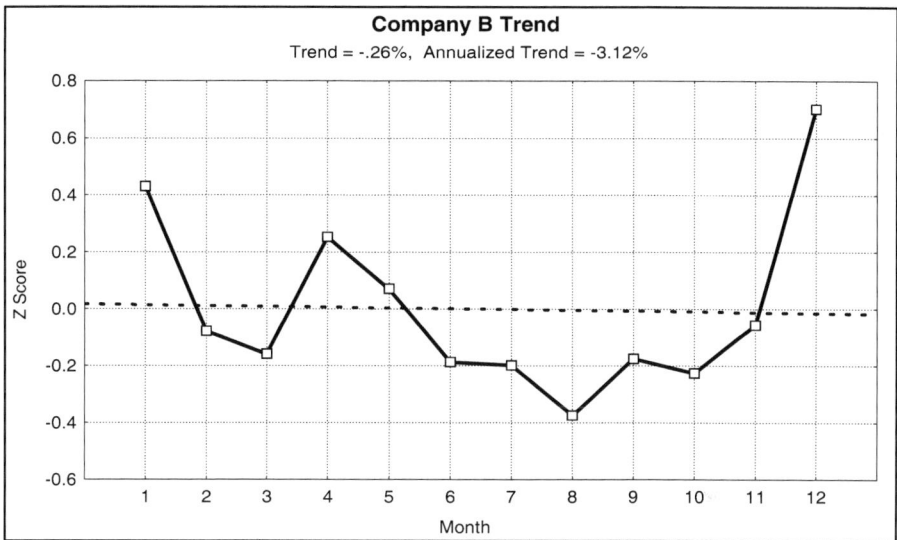

Figure 5. Company B is in retail with 62 employees and 61 small team and individual performance measures. The trend was significant and averaged -.26% with an annualized trend of –3.12%.

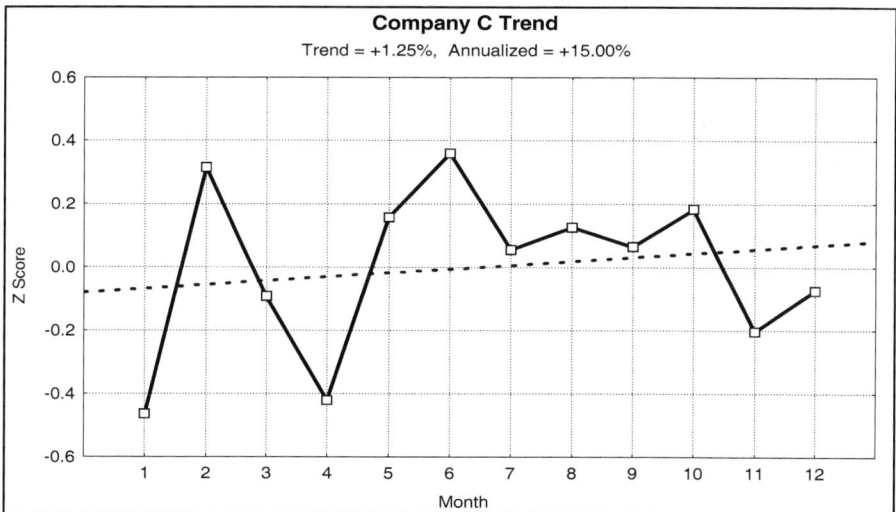

Figure 6. Company C is in manufacturing with 348 employees and 39 small and large team performance measures. The trend was not significant but averaged +1.25% with an annualized trend of +15.00%.

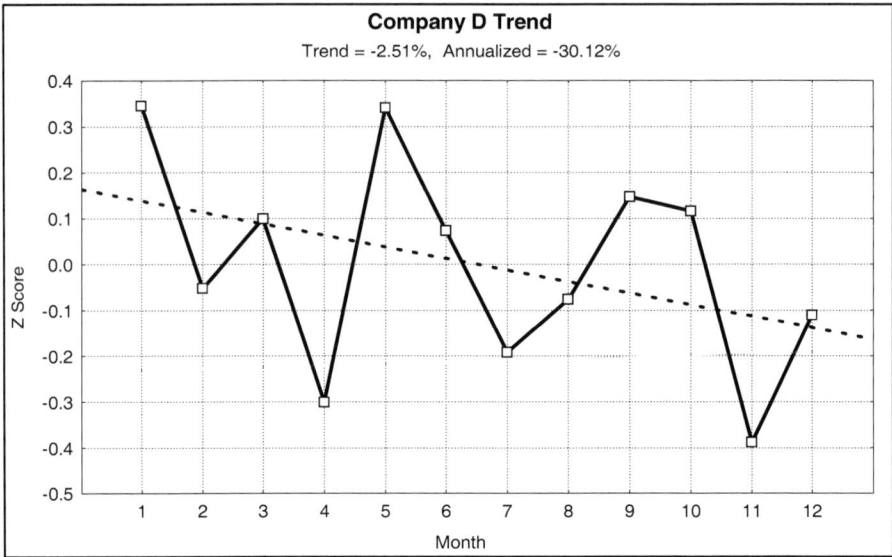

Figure 7. Company D is in banking with 464 employees and 18 large team performance measures. The trend was not significant but averaged –2.51% with an annualized trend of –30.12%.

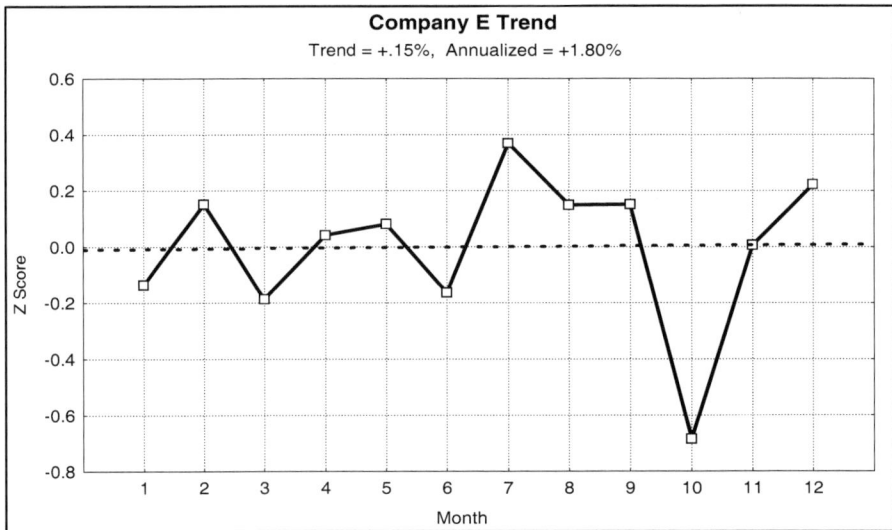

Figure 8. Company E is in publishing with 66 employees and 54 small team and individual performance measures. The trend was significant and averaged +.15% with an annualized trend of +1.80%.

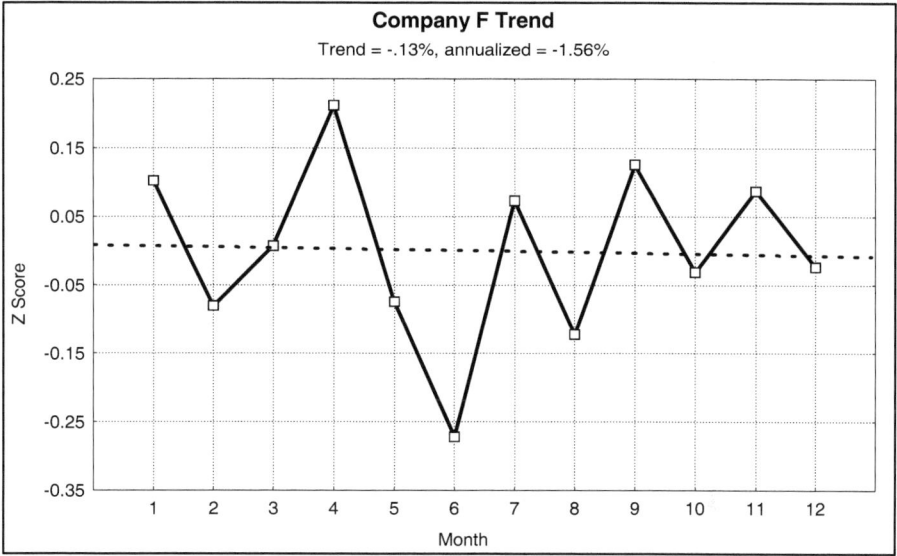

Figure 9. Company F is in distribution with 206 employees and 228 small team and individual performance measures. The trend was not significant but averaged -.13% with an annualized trend of –1.56%.

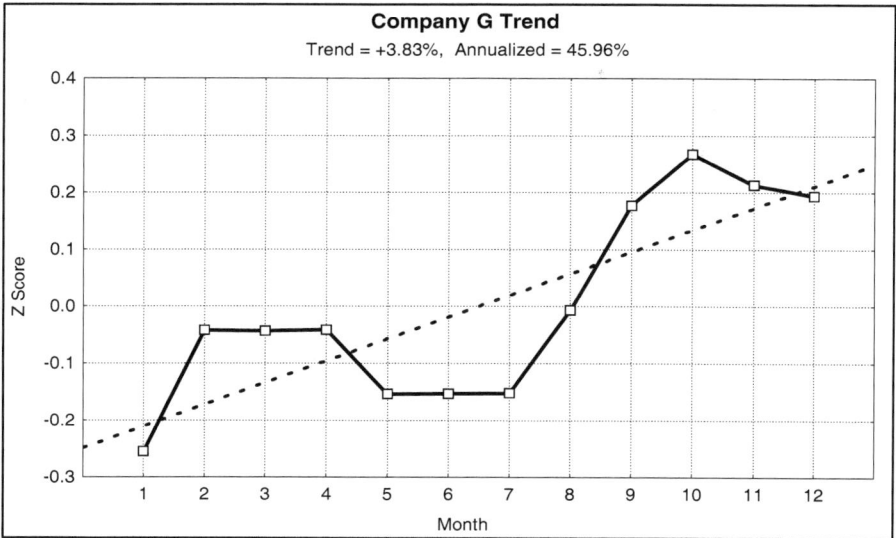

Figure 10. Company G is in retail banking with 747 employees and 536 small team and individual performance measures. The trend was significant and averaged +3.83% with an annualized trend of +45.96%.

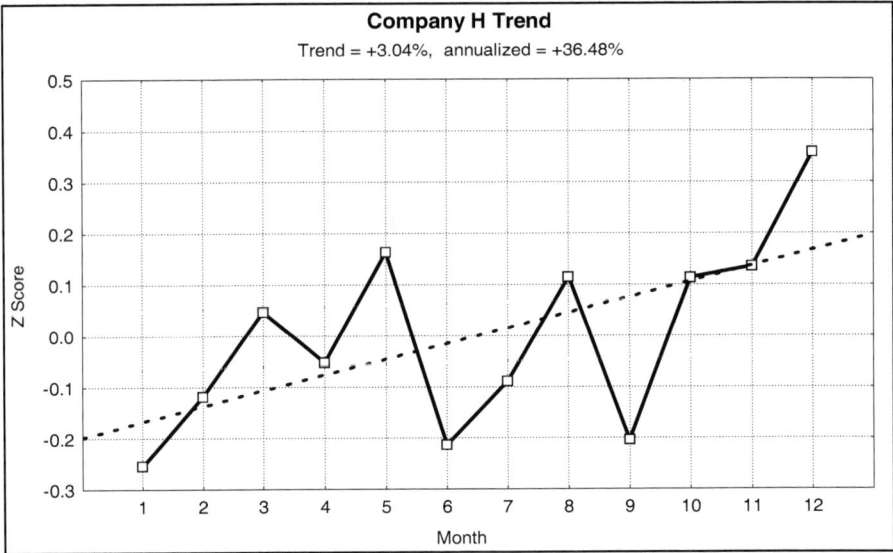

Figure 11. Company H is the operations area of Company G with 186 employees and 94 small team and individual performance measures. The trend was significant and averaged +3.04% with an annualized trend of +36.48%.

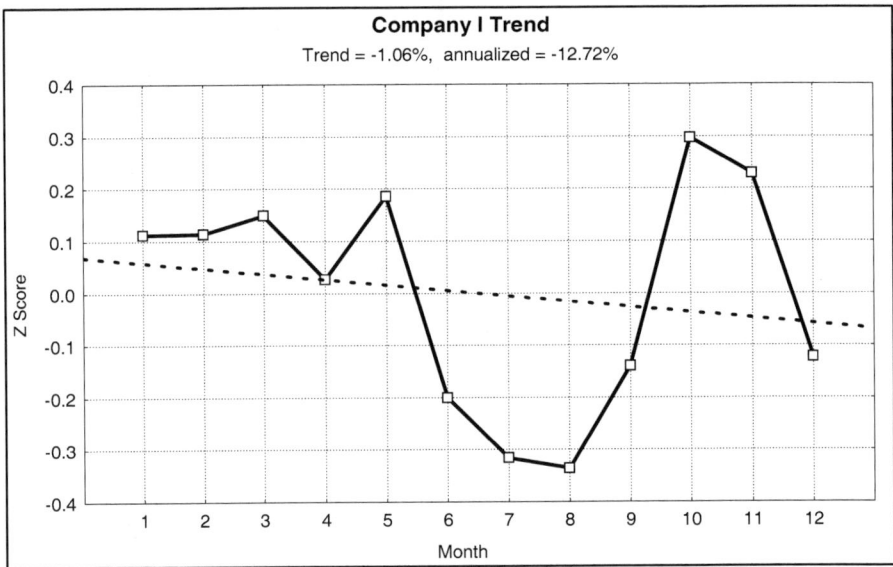

Figure 12. Company I is in distribution with 99 employees and 56 small team and individual performance measures. The trend was significant and averaged -1.06% with an annualized trend of –12.72%.

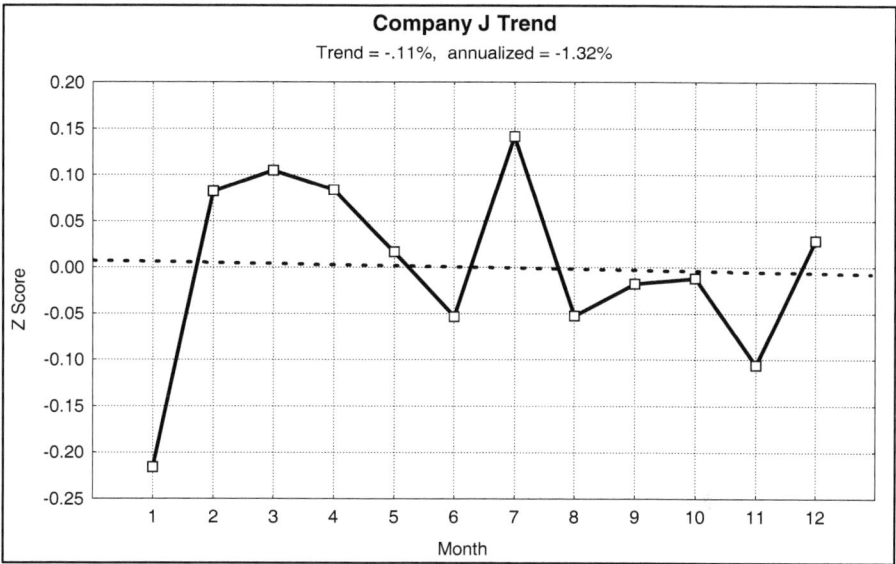

Figure 13. Company J is in banking with 1,140 employees and 618 small team and individual performance measures. The trend was not significant but averaged -.11% with an annualized trend of –1.32%.

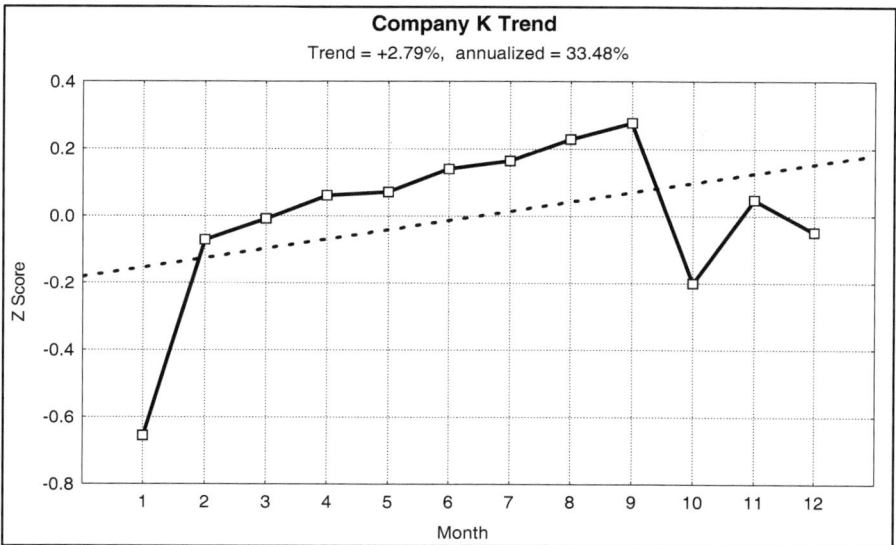

Figure 14. Company K is in distribution with 148 employees and 75 small team and individual performance measures. The trend was significant and averaged +2.79% with an annualized trend of +33.48%.

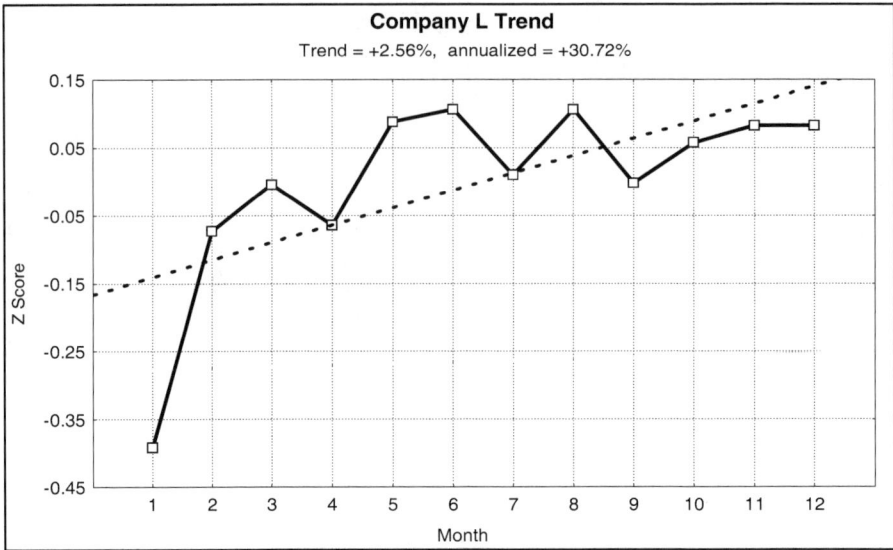

Figure 15. Company L is in manufacturing with 537 participating employees and 237 manager performance measures. The overall trend was +2.56% and the annualized trend was +30.72%.

experienced a substantial improvement in month two. However, modest improvement continued in the following months without the 'incubation period' experienced by other organizations. Finally, Company L is in manufacturing with 537 employees participating and 237 manager performance measures. The overall trend was .0256 (see Figure 15). This figure is of special interest since this was the only organization of the 12 in the study that did not award incentive payments for performance improvements. The initial improvement, similar in fashion to Company K, is followed by a smaller, but consistent improvement for the next four months.

Experimental Questions Addressed by the Analyses

Analysis of scorecard system design variables. I analyzed the variables to address 8 experimental questions related to scorecard system design administration. The results of these are below, organized by experimental question.

Question 1. Does performance improvement differ among the types of performance measures? When designing scorecard systems, organizations must select the measures that are most relevant to their organizational strategy and vision. I therefore encountered many types of measures in working with the diverse organizations reported in this study. From these measure, I developed seven different measure types to be considered in this analysis. These include: 1) expense control measures;

2) sales measures; 3) quality measures; 4) regulatory compliance measures; 5) productivity measures; 6) projects measures; and 7) customer service measures.

Table 4 and Figure 16 display the overall average trends for each measure type. An analysis of variance detected a significant (p= .0012) difference between the measure type means. Quality, regulatory compliance and customer service measures improved more than other types of measures. A possible explanation is that employees have more 'discretionary control' over these types of measures. For example, employees often have more direct influence on safe practices, on-time performance and accuracy. Expense control and productivity (staffing levels) tend to be more under the control of management than workers, although workers can create a productivity improvement opportunity through gains in efficiency and utilization. The modest gains in sales may be because sales feedback and commission plans were already in place in most cases, leaving little room for improvement when the study began. Project performance should have had higher gains if employee control is the underlying determinant. A possible explanation is that milestone setting affects gains as much as actual project behavior. Since formal project tracking was new to all clients, this may also account for these results.

Measure Type	Examples
Expense Control	Cost per unit, percent budget met, expense/revenue
Sales	Revenue, gross margin, cross-sell, referrals
Quality	Quality measures refers to internal quality and include internal customer satisfaction ratings, percentage on-time, percentage accurate, quality checklists
Regulatory Compliance	Safety, housekeeping and environmental checklists, recordable injuries, audits
Productivity	Labor expense per unit, units per labor hour
Projects	Percentage of project milestones met, percentage of days early/late, milestone quality rating

Measure Type	Trend %	Standard Deviation	Number of Measures
Expense Control	.75%	13.57%	326
Sales	.58%	12.18%	581
Quality	2.55%	11.20%	513
Regulatory Compliance	4.56%	13.54%	82
Productivity	.94%	12.20%	463
Projects	1.28%	12.50%	64
Customer Service	4.13%	11.80%	166
All	1.58%	12.26%	2,195

Table 4. Average trend for each measure type.

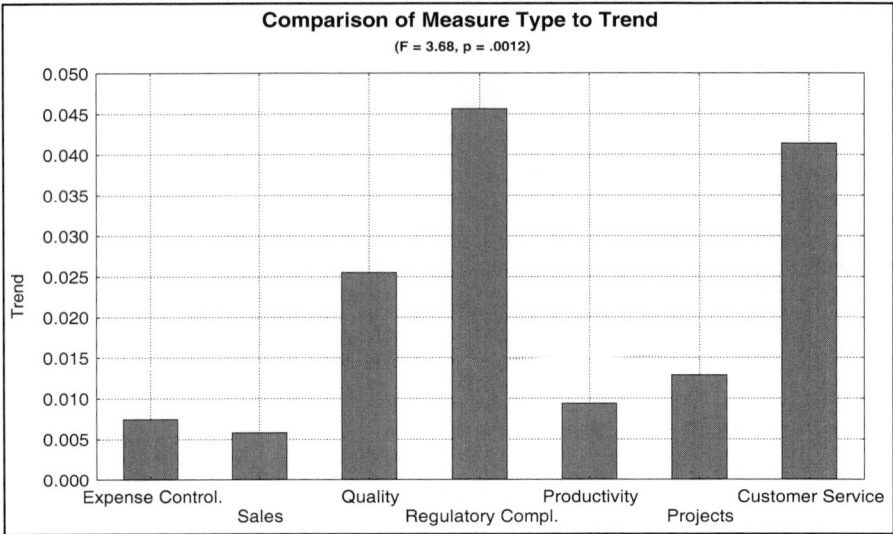

Figure 16. Average trend for each measure type. An ANOVA finds a significant (p=.0012) difference between the measure type means.

Customer Service   Customer service refers to external quality and includes customer satisfaction ratings, percentage on-time, percentage accurate, returns, account attrition

Question 2. Do team or individual scorecards yield the most performance improvement? The aggregate mean trend of all team measures (N=1,831) was .014 with a standard deviation of .1239. The mean of the 364 individual measures was .023 with a standard deviation of .1160. A t-test for independent samples yielded a p = .214 indicating no significant difference in the effects on performance of team versus individual measures. The lack of significance may, however, be due to unbalanced group sizes (1,831 vs. 364).

Deeper analyses revealed that team measures seem to yield better results for measure types where the team leader or manager has more discretionary control than the workers do. That is, team measures produce better performance on expense control and project measures than do individual scorecard measures. The team versus individual measures are viewed by measure type in Figure 17.

Question 3. Do hourly employees respond more to the system then salaried employees? The 1,210 salaried employee measures were compared to the 985 hourly employee measures. The salaried mean was .0036 with a standard deviation of .1186. The hourly employee mean was .0307 with a standard deviation of .1259. A t-test for independent samples yielded a significant result (p = .0000). This

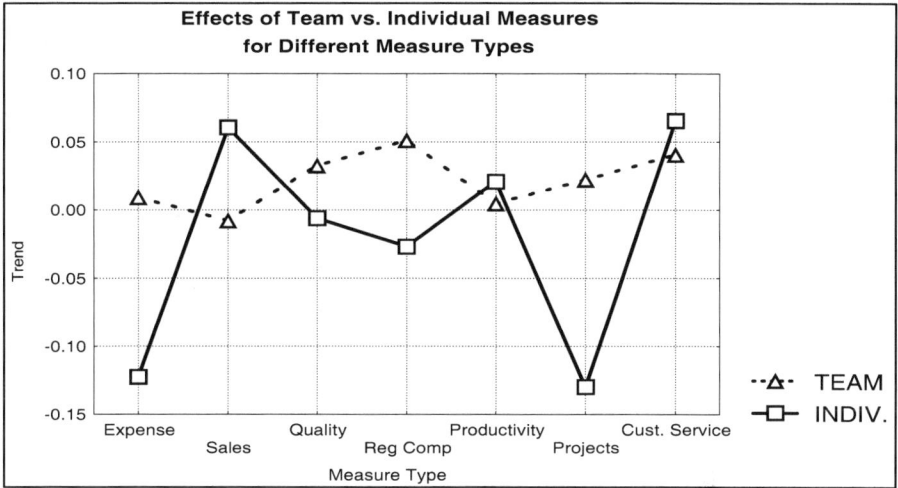

Figure 17.

difference is likely due to the fact that many salaried employees are managers. Manager measures are typically based on the performance of subordinates or the company and are therefore less under the direct control of the manager.

When the measure type is considered (see Figure 18), it appears that hourly employees perform better on all types except expense control and customer service. The lack of differences in expense control and customer service are likely due to the

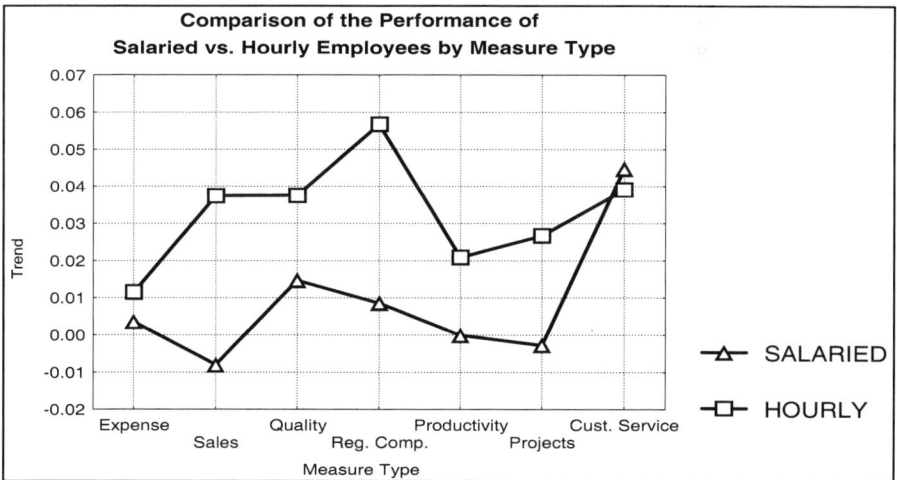

Figure 18.

fact that managers often have more control over expenses than do employees. The probable explanation for the lack of difference on customer service measures is the typical practice of using team or department customer survey data to measure this performance dimension and assigning both managers and hourly employees the survey score.

Question 4. Does the complexity (employees per scorecard) of the system constrain performance improvements? System complexity was computed as the number of employees divided by the number of scorecards. The most complex scorecard system will have one unique scorecard for each employee. The mean employees per scorecard across all companies was 2.24 with a standard deviation of 4.13. An F-test across values yielded a $p = .143$ which was not significant. Figure 19 graphically displays the trend analysis results. Performance trend appeared to remain consistent

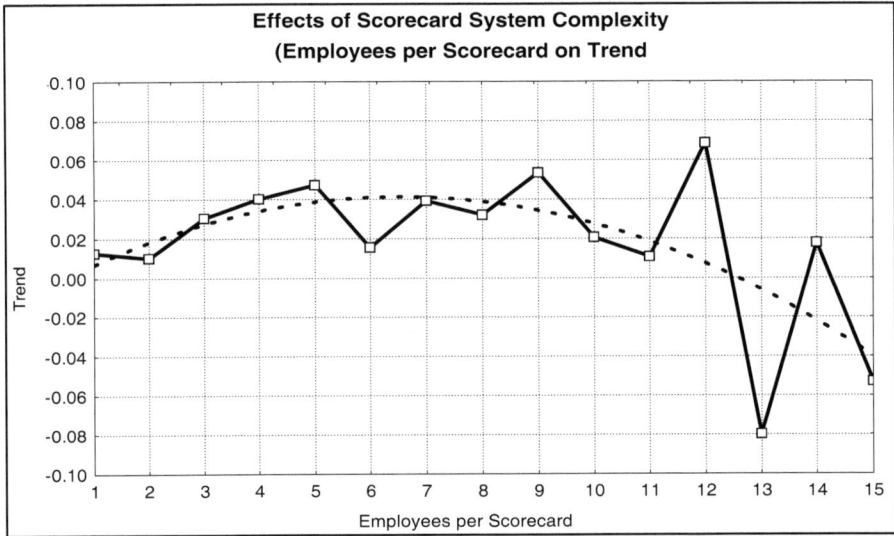

Figure 19.

for up to 12 employees per scorecard after which trend decreases and variability increases. This suggests that trends improve in scorecards as the complexity decreases, to a point (around 12 employees), at which the scorecards are too general and trends begin to decline.

Question 5. Does the complexity of the individual scorecards (measures per scorecard) constrain performance improvements? Scorecard complexity was computed by dividing the number of performance measures by the number of scorecards. The ratio is considered to be an indicator of the complexity of an organization's

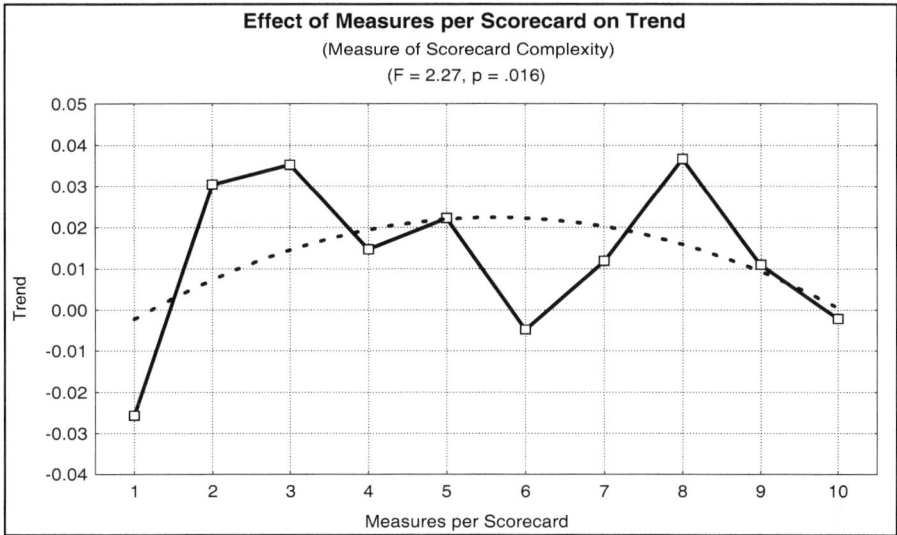

Figure 20.

individual scorecards with the simplest scorecard having only one measure. The mean of this indicator was 5.04 with a standard deviation of 1.48. The minimum scorecard measures was 1.00 while the maximum averaged 10.33. Figure 20 graphically displays the trend results. The likely explanation for such poor performance on single-measure scorecards is that these are often sales scorecards where feedback and incentives were already in place, or they are support group scorecards in which the performance of production employees is simply assigned to the support group.

It is common to find more measures at higher organizational levels due to increased span of control and accountabilities. Figure 21 displays the effects of measures per scorecard on trend for salaried (managers) vs. hourly employees. These results suggest that increasing the number of scorecard measures had different effects on these two groups. That is, increasing the number of scorecard measures for hourly employees tends to reduce performance improvement, whereas an increase in measures for salaried employees (ignoring the single-measure scorecards) has little effect. Again, this result may be explained by the more direct control hourly employees have over their assigned measures than do salaried managers or staff.

Question 6. Does the priority weight assigned to a measure affect performance improvement? The priority weight of any given measure can range from 0% to 100%. The weight determines both the relative contribution of the measure to the overall performance index of the scorecard, and the incentive pay out amount. The mean

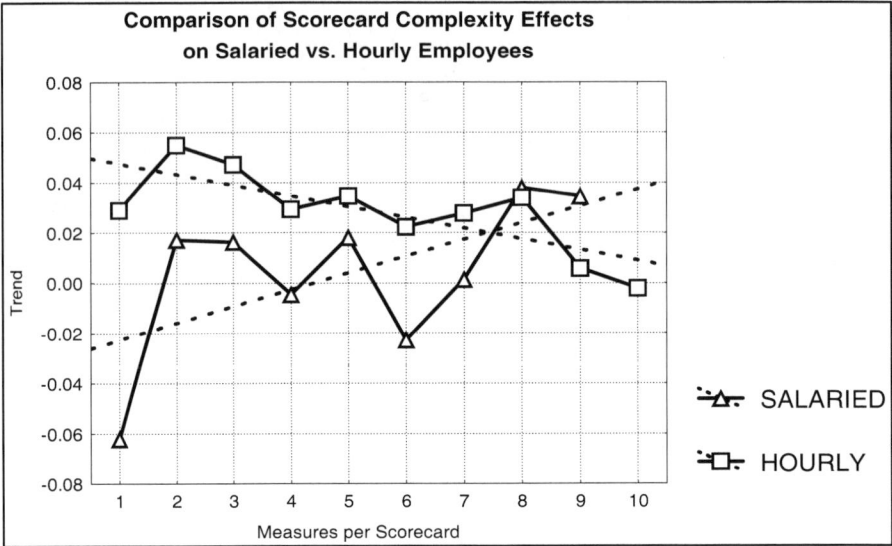

Figure 21.

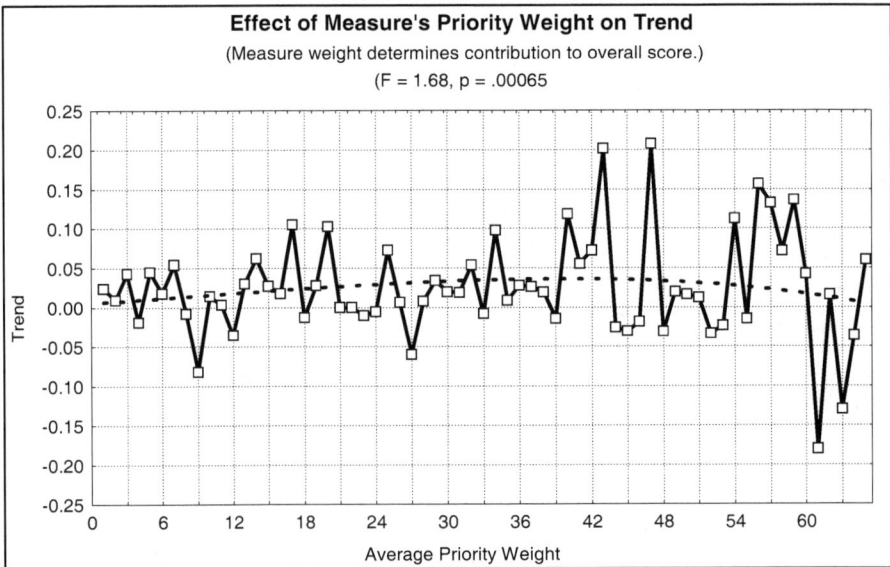

Figure 22.

weight was 22.84% per measure with a standard deviation of 14.50%. (range: 0 to 100%). The F-test yielded a significant effect with p = .00065, indicating there differences between the effects of at least some weight ranges. The fact that the mean weight was around 23% and the average measures per scorecard was about five, indicates that across all scorecards, measures tended to be evenly weighted (5 measures evenly weighted would each be weighted 20%). A review of Figure 22 suggests rather nominal effects on trend until the weight exceeds 40%. Weights larger than 40% appeared to drive increased variability in the trends but not necessarily improvement.

Question 7. Does the level at which a measure's base or goal is set affect performance improvement? Each scorecard score is computed as a percent gain, where [percent gain = (actual − base) / (goal −base)]. All of the scorecards in the study then interpolated this value on an eleven-point scale that typically ranged from −20% to

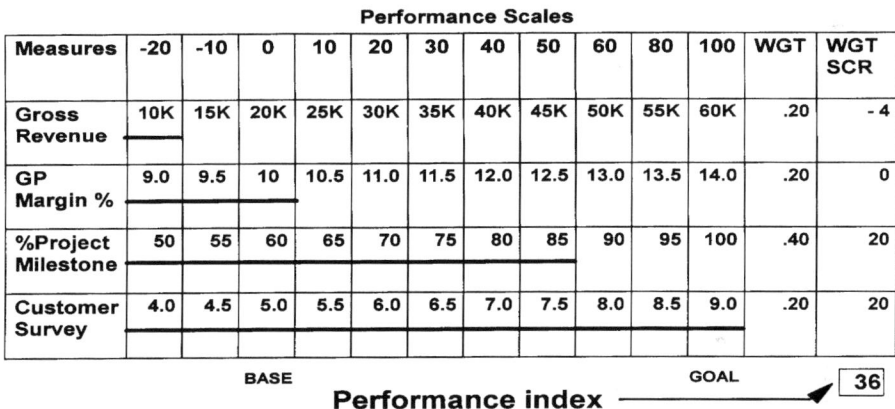

Performance Scales

Measures	-20	-10	0	10	20	30	40	50	60	80	100	WGT	WGT SCR
Gross Revenue	10K	15K	20K	25K	30K	35K	40K	45K	50K	55K	60K	.20	- 4
GP Margin %	9.0	9.5	10	10.5	11.0	11.5	12.0	12.5	13.0	13.5	14.0	.20	0
%Project Milestone	50	55	60	65	70	75	80	85	90	95	100	.40	20
Customer Survey	4.0	4.5	5.0	5.5	6.0	6.5	7.0	7.5	8.0	8.5	9.0	.20	20

BASE   GOAL   36

Performance index ⟶

Figure 23.

100% (i.e., -20 -10 0 10 20 30 40 50 60 80 100). All scorecards also have a partially accelerating scale in which the last two intervals are larger (see Figure 23 for an example). This feature increases pay outs as performance nears the goal performance.

The percent gain formula is applied to the raw performance data and the result is assigned the scale interval it falls in (all values are rounded down). Scorecard scores are, of course, affected by actual performance data, but also by changes in the measure's base and/or goal. That is, when the goal level is changed to a higher level, scorecard scores go down, given a constant level of job performance. The opposite effect occurs when the base level is raised.

The mean scorecard measure score was 56.92 with a standard deviation of 35.94. Therefore, approximately two-thirds of the individual measure scores fell between 19 and 93. A review of Figure 24 suggests that the variability in trend score

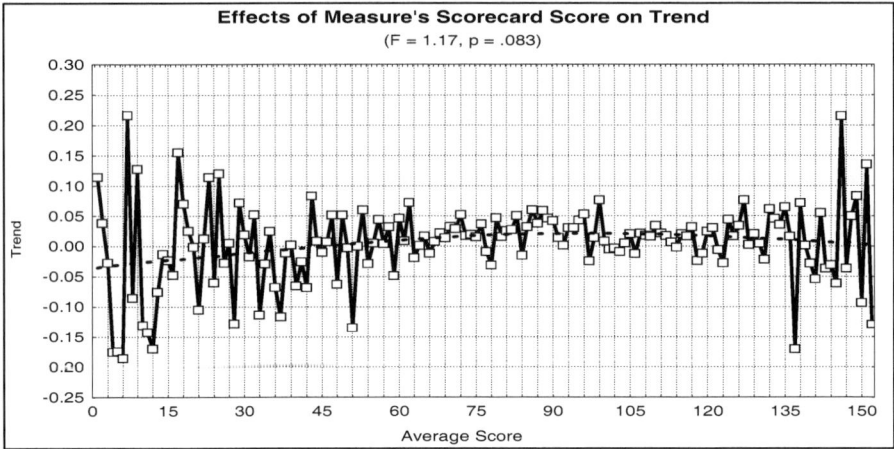

Figure 24.

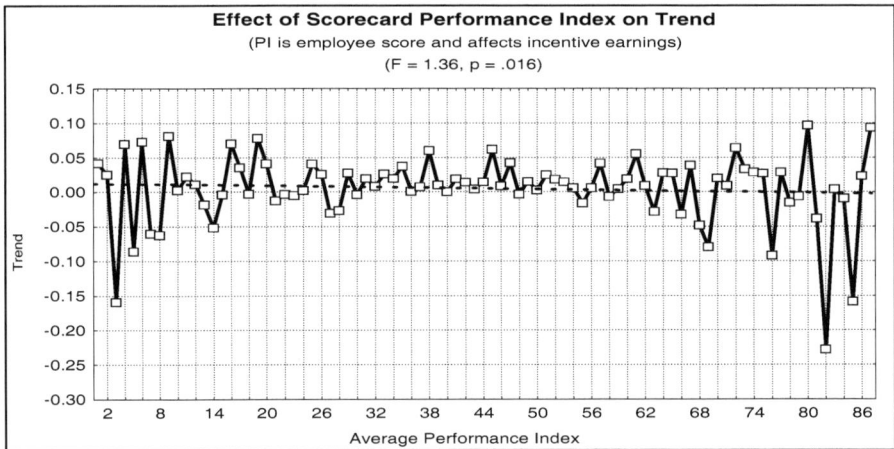

Figure 25.

increases substantially as scores fall below 30 or exceed 135. Low scores affect both social and cash reinforcement, whereas scores above 100% have no added value since, in most cases, the scale is capped at 100%.

As a related measure, I also examined the effects of performance index measures on trend. The performance index is the sum of the weighted scores on a scorecard. In most cases, the performance index ranges from 0% to 100%. The index determines how much of an available incentive opportunity the employee earns. For example, if an employee were eligible for an incentive that costs 10% of his base pay, and received a performance index score of 70%, the employee would earn 10%

x 70% or 7% of his base pay. The mean performance index was 45.89 with a standard deviation of 23.4. Therefore, two-thirds of the performance indices fell between 22 and 69. A review of Figure 25 suggests an effect similar to the individual measures scores, with trend variability increasing below about 20 and above 65. The effects of low and high performance indices are the same as scores with the exception that the performance index is the summary, and so directly affects social recognition and pay where individual scores can be offset by performances on other scorecard measures.

   Question 8. Do frequent changes in a measure's base, goal or weight affect performance improvement? Each scorecard measure has the parameters of base, goal, and priority weight. All measure definitions remained consistent over the study. The 'changes' studied were the number of times a *parameter* was altered in the twelve-month period. The mean for number of base changes per month was .285 (3.4 changes per year); the mean number of goal changes per month was .278 (3.3 changes per year); and the mean number of priority weight changes per month was .272 (3.3 changes per year). The similarity in these across the three measure parameters suggests that often two or more parameter changes were performed simultaneously (most likely base and goal changes were made at the same time). The F-tests for the effect of each change on trend were each non-significant (base changes: $p = .070$; goal changes: $p = .141$; and weight changes: $p = .293$). Visual inspection tells us that each trend had a negative slope, suggesting that companies that made more changes also saw lower levels of improvement from the scorecard process. This does not mean that changing the scorecard design is a bad idea, but rather that changes in scorecard design are associated with lower levels of improvement. It could be that companies that perform lower for some other set of

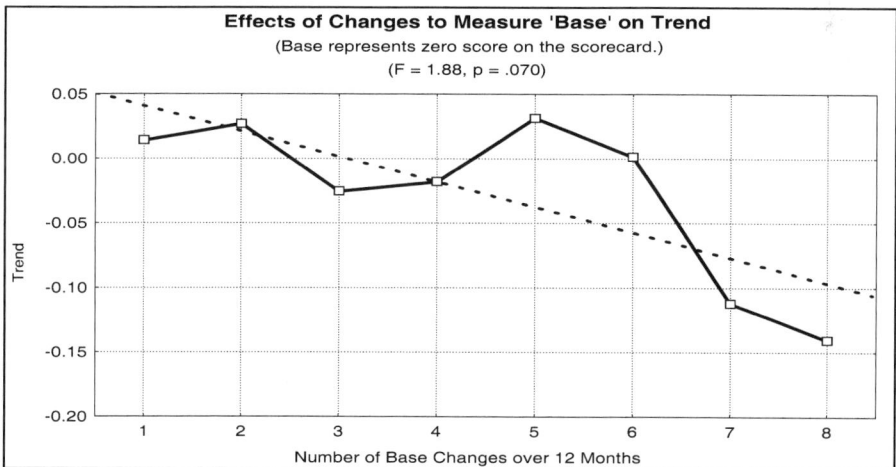

Figure 26. Changes to the Base.

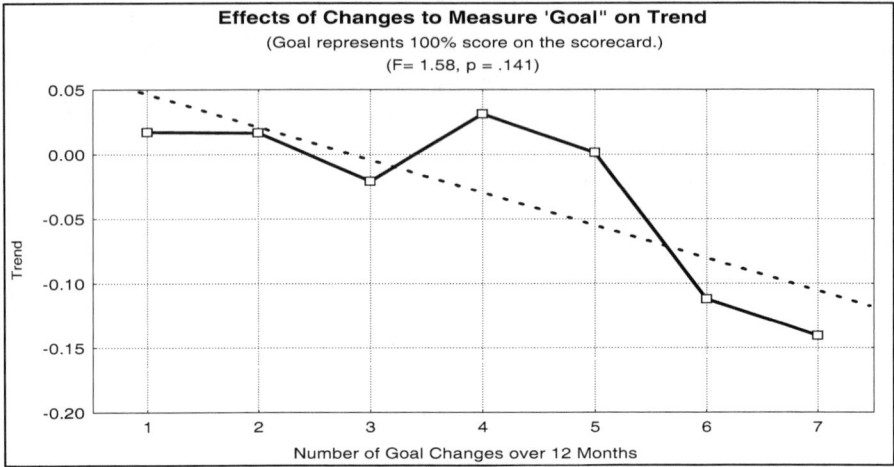

Figure 27. Changes to the Goal.

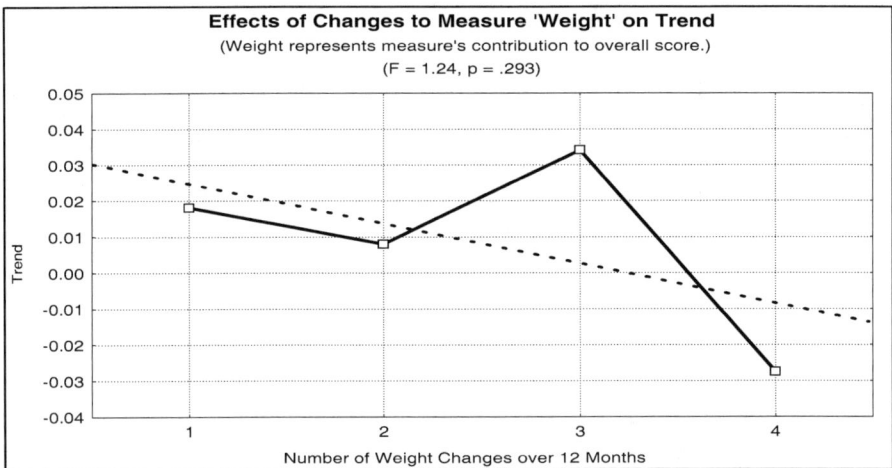

Figure 28. Changes to the Weight.

reasons also see the need to change the scorecard system, or any other of a multitude of explanations for the relationship are possible. See Figures 26 – 29 for graphic display of the results.

Analysis of incentive pay variables.

Question 9. Does the level of incentive pay opportunity affect performance trend? The first analysis I did to examine this question was to look at the effects of guaranteed incentive opportunity on performance trend. Each guaranteed incentive

Incentive Opportunity %	Measure Count	Percent of Total
0%	1,020	46.44%
0% – 10%	1,000	45.61%
11% – 20%	137	6.24%
21%-30%	21	.94%
31%- 40%	2	.09%
41%-50%	15	.68%
Average = 4.58%		
Std Dev = 6.03%, Max = 46%		100.00%

Table 5.

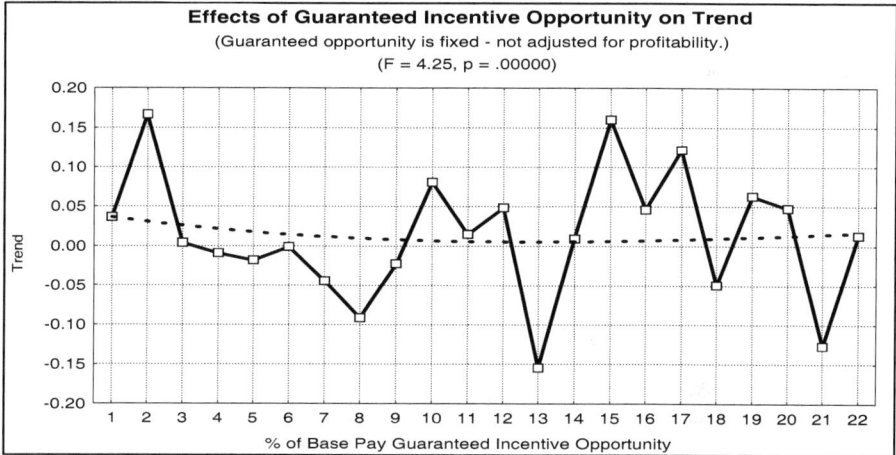

Figure 29.

Incentive Opportunity %	Measure Count	Percent of Total
0%	470	21.41%
0% – 10%	865	39.41%
11% – 20%	744	33.90%
21%-30%	76	3.46%
31%- 40%	21	.96%
41%-50%	4	.18%
51%-60%	9	.41%
61-70%	0	0.00%
71-80%	6	.27%
Average = 9.57%		
Std Dev = 8.0%, Max = 74%		100.00%

Table 6.

opportunity was the same each month for an entire year, and was not adjusted for company profitability or any other factors. 'Opportunity' represents the most an employee could potentially earn, if all possible incentive money was earned by the

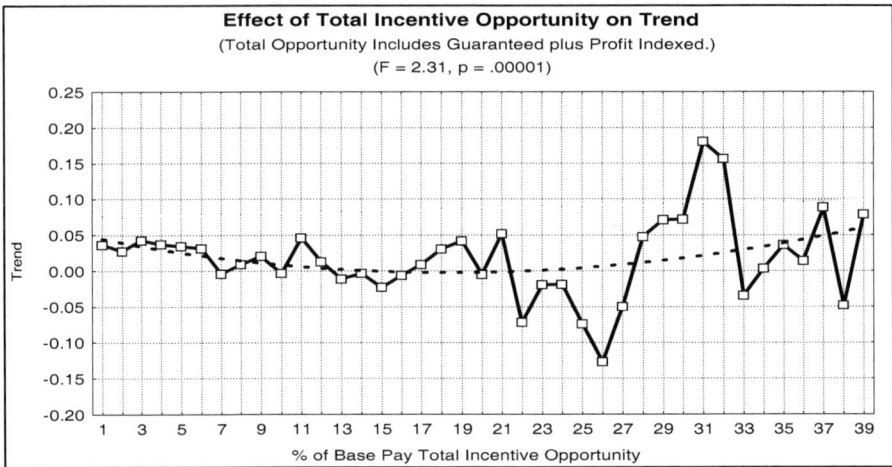

Figure 30.

individual. Incentive opportunity was multiplied by the employee's scorecard performance to determine the actual incentive pay out. Table 5 categorizes the number of measures for various levels of guaranteed incentive opportunity. Figure 29 compares guaranteed incentive pay opportunity to trend. There is an unexpected absence of any significant relationship between the level of guaranteed incentive opportunity and performance trend.

As a further level of analysis, I recognized that total incentive opportunity (shown in Figure 30) includes both guaranteed opportunity (shown in Figure 29) and profit-indexed opportunity. Profit-indexed opportunity varies each month depending on the profitability of the organization, whereas guaranteed incentive opportunity, as its name implies, remains the same each month. Table 6 categorizes the number of measures for various levels of total incentive opportunity.

Figure 30 compares average total incentive opportunity to performance trend. The trend line suggests that as total incentive opportunity increases above 29% of base pay, the performance trend increases. One interpretation of the results of Figures 29 and 30 is that incentive pay opportunity, without respect to actual payout, has little effect on performance.

Incentive Payout %	Measure Count	Percent of Total
0%	470	21.41%
0% – 10%	1386	63.14%
11% – 20%	293	13.36%
21%-30%	27	1.23%
31%- 40%	11	.50%
41%-50%	6	.36%
Average = 5.44%		
Std Dev = 5.54%, Max = 45%		100.00%

Table 7.

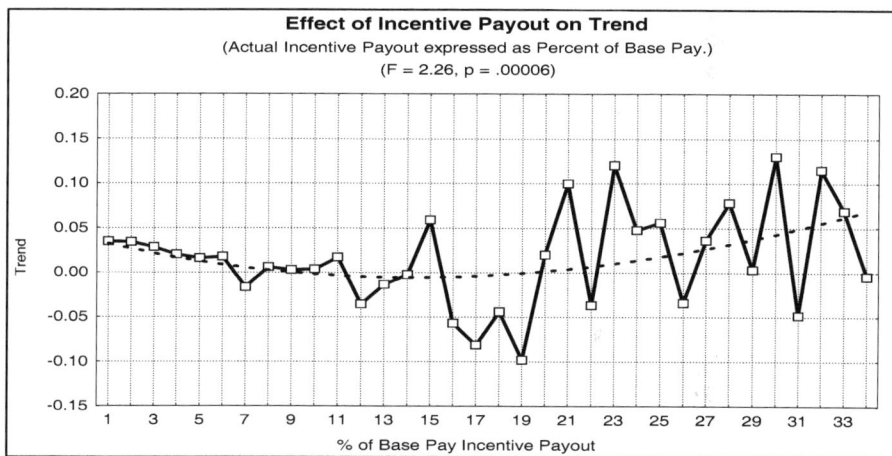

Figure 31.

Question 10. Does the level of incentive payout affect performance trend? Incentive pay out is computed as the employee's scorecard performance index multiplied by both guaranteed opportunity and profit-indexed opportunity for the month. The pay out represents the dollar amount that the employee earns, shown as a percentage of her base pay. Table 7 categorizes the number of measures for various levels of average incentive pay out. Figure 31 compares average incentive pay out percentage to the companies' performance trends. This Figure suggests that the level of pay out affects performance trend only when pay outs were above 20% of base pay or higher. This finding has significant implications since most discussions of the effects of incentive pay do not consider the actual amount paid.

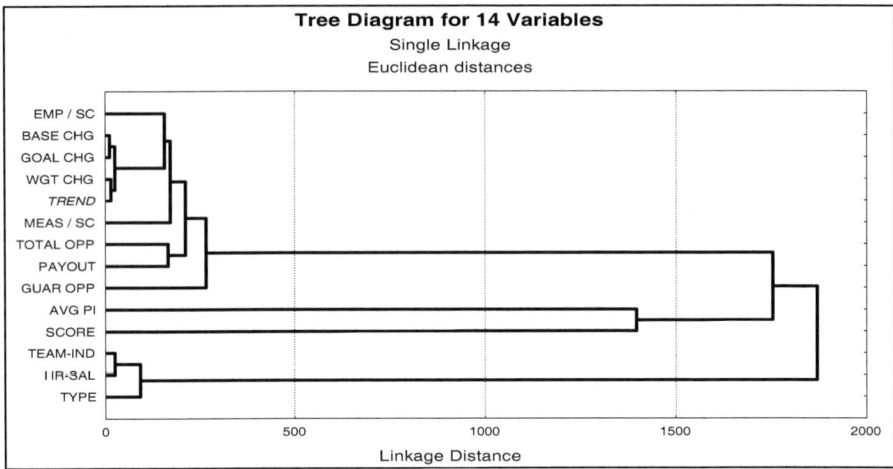

Tree Diagram for 14 Variables
Single Linkage
Euclidean distances

Figure 32.

Discussion

A cluster analysis (see Figure 32) was performed to determine if the variables could be logically grouped. Three groups of important variables were identified: 1) Scorecard design and administration variables; 2) Incentive pay out variables; and 3) Organization structure variables. Below are concluding comments on each of these conceptual domains.

Group I: Scorecard design and administrative variables. This set of variables includes employees / scorecard, base changes, goal changes, weight changes and measures per scorecard. These are considered 'scorecard design and administrative' variables.

The first three questions in this area (Experimental questions 1-3) compared performance trend to measure types, team versus individual measures, and hourly versus salaried employees. The general findings suggest that the more 'discretionary control' performers have over a measure, the greater the observed performance improvement. This finding supports the common view that individual and small team measures are more effective at prompting and reinforcing performance improvement than are larger group measures. Care should be taken in the development of the measurement system to ensure that participants can directly influence the measures selected, insofar as this is possible.

The next two questions (Experimental questions 4 and 5) explored the relationship of scorecard system complexity and individual scorecard measure complexity to performance trends. The results of these analyses suggest an 'optimal' system complexity of from three to twelve employees per scorecard. Performance trends tend to decline above or below this range. The optimal number of measures per scorecard is not clear, but the results tentatively suggest that hourly employees may be more negatively affected by high numbers of scorecard measures than are salaried employees.

Experimental questions 6 and 7 explored the relationship of specific measure parameters to performance trends. These parameters included the measure's priority weight, base and goal, and the overall scorecard performance index achieved by the employees. The priority weight of a measure appears to have little effect on performance until it is defined at 40% or more. At these levels, the variability in trend across weightings increases but there is no clear relationship to performance trend. This may be due to the confounding effect that high priority weights tend to be applied to more one-dimensional jobs like sales and production.

Similarly, a measure's base levels, goal levels and scorecard performance index do not have simple, linear relationships to performance trend. The variability in trend across the average measure score increases below 30 and above 135. Performance trend variability also increases when the scorecard's performance index falls outside a range of from about 20 to 65. These results suggest that more consistent performance improvement is achieved when bases and goals are assigned that produce scores that fall in the middle range of the scorecard scale. This may be due to low scores creating adverse social and monetary outcomes, whereas scores above 100% do not increase incentive pay outs because they are 'capped'. Further, scores well above 100% encourage management to increase the goal requirements.

The final experimental question in this category of variable (question 8) concerns scorecard administration. Does performance improve more when bases, goals and weights are frequently changed, or when these parameters remain relatively constant? The findings suggest that performance improvement is enhanced when parameters remain relatively constant – especially the bases and goals. The recommendation is to minimize the number of base and goal changes throughout the year. This finding may represent common sense, to some extent: Fewer major changes to any process enhance the chance that employees will understand it and engage in the behaviors related to the process (i.e., buy-in to the process).

Group II: Incentive pay variables. The second variable group includes incentive pay out, total incentive opportunity, guaranteed incentive opportunity, average performance index, and average score. These variables are considered the 'incentive pay' variables.

Experimental questions 9 and 10 explored the relationship between incentive opportunity and incentive pay out to performance trend. Though not a strong effect, it appears that the levels of both incentive opportunity and pay out affect performance trends. However, this relationship is not linear. Pay out magnitude appears to begin to increase performance trends at around 20% of base pay. Incentive pay can be expensive, and often reduces the performance system's flexibility with respect to parameter changes. Organizations considering incentive pay should only do so if the incentive opportunity will generate pay outs above 20% of base pay. Given this, the practice of indexing incentive pay opportunity to profitability is critical. Indexing incentive opportunity to profit ensures the 'affordability' of the incentives at higher pay out levels. That is, if incentives are linking to profit gains, the organization pays out money only when money is made beyond some standard.

Group III: Organizational structure variables. The third variable set includes team versus individual measures, hourly versus salaried, and measure type. These variables are considered the 'organizational structure' variables because the nature and set-up of the business determines, in part, whether measures can be defined for individuals, the hourly – salaried mix, and the type of measures employed. The results suggest that organizations able to define and track measures that are 'close to the individual', and that provide employees some discretion in how they achieve the goal will experience greater performance improvement than organizations that measure higher-level group indicators. There is little evidence that incentive pay opportunity or incentive payouts influence performance improvement unless these conditions are first met. If not, incentive pay and other performance management systems may be a poor investment. Organizations considering a performance improvement initiative should also include hourly employees, since this group showed the most performance improvement in the current analyses.

General Conclusions

Figure 33 displays the average trend improvement for all twelve companies, which was 2.76% a month or 33.12% annually. These companies employee groups ranged from 54 employees to 536 and represented industries including manufacturing, retail, publishing, distribution, and banking.

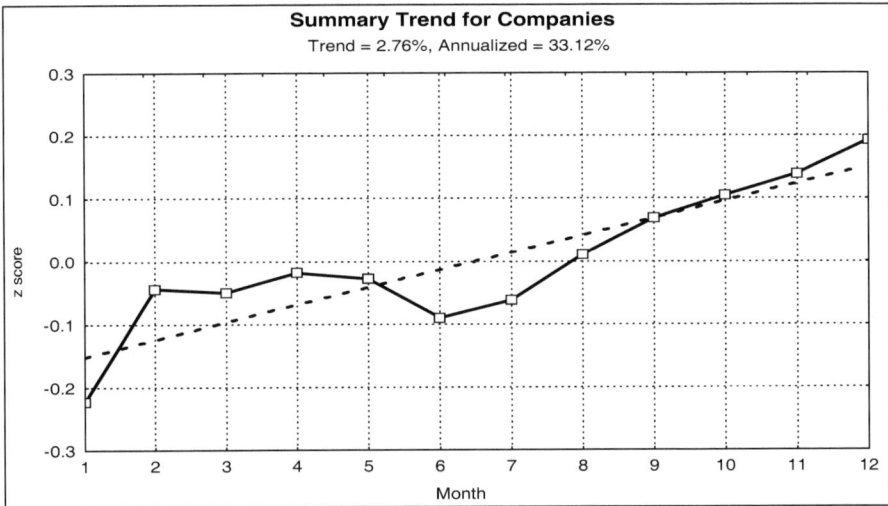

Figure 33. Average performance improvement for a sample of 2,195 scorecard measures. Average client improvement (33%) with an average 7% payout.

The most important implication of the study was the influence of the level of control employees had over their assigned performance measures. Individual measures produced more improvement than team measures, hourly employees improved more than salaried, more controllable measure types displayed more improvement, and a low number of changes in scorecard parameters increased improvement.

Surprisingly, only high levels of incentive pay appeared to have a relationship to performance improvement. Although it is speculative given the data in this study, I believe the relationship of measure controllability and incentive magnitude may be roughly analogous to Newton's general gravity principle. In non-behavioral language, the closer a measure is to an employee's personal control, the more the measure "attracts" the employee's interest. As the measure moves away from personal control, the incentive pay magnitude (and other consequences) required to produce an equivalent improvement must increase substantially.

Unfortunately, it is often impractical to measure critical organizational outcomes at the personal level. In these cases, "performance management" is required to bring the measure closer to the individual. Managers can bridge the gap between delayed, improbable consequences and behavior by pinpointing employee behaviors and outcomes that directly relate to scorecard measures. Managers can further enhance employee control through prompting, timely feedback, and working with employees to develop behavioral and process improvement plans. This assertion is confirmed by the fact that only one organization in the study (Company L) did not provide an incentive pay opportunity for its employees yet had the third highest overall improvement. Company L implemented significant process improvement and performance training for its managers prior to the introduction of the scorecard system. No other company in the study provided its managers these skills.

I chose to begin the analysis of these data with an examination of 'large' effects across a diverse population. Future studies will look at more specific relationships including the relationships of specific measure types (accuracy, timeliness, customer surveys, efficiency, utilization, prospecting, closing, etc.) to each other and to performance trends. In addition, a more detailed examination of the conditions under which incentive pay works best is underway as well as an investigation of performance management effects including feedback, manager behavior, and performance improvement planning activities.

Endnotes

1. Company A's results are from four small plants in four different locations. Company F's results are from two primary locations. Company G is the retail portion of a bank while company H is the 'back office' of the same bank. Company J represents a holding company consolidation of several smaller banks. Company L results are from six primary locations. Company L did not implement an incentive pay program. Only Company L provided formal performance management training to their supervisors and managers.

References

Chow, C. W., Haddad, K. M., & Williamson, J. E. (1997). Applying the balanced scorecard to small companies. *Management Accounting, 79*(2), 21-27.

Daniels, A. C. (1989). *Performance management.* Tucker, GA: Performance Management Publications.

Hanson, J., & Towle, G. (January/February, 2000). The balanced scorecard: Not just another fad. *Credit Union Executive Journal,* 12-16.

Howell, D. C. (1997). *Statistical methods for psychology* (4th ed.). Detroit, MI: Duxbury Press.

Kaplan, R. S., & Norton, D. P. (1992). The balanced scorecard: Measures that drive performance. *Harvard Business Review, 70*(1), 71-80.

Krapfl, J. E., & Gasparotto, G. (1982). Behavioral systems analysis. In L. W. Frederiksen (Ed.), *Handbook of organizational behavior management* (pp. 21-38). New York: Wiley-Interscience.

Rummler, G. A., & Brache, A. P. (1995). *Improving performance: How to manage the white space on the organizational chart.* San Francisco, CA: Jossey-Bass.

Discussion of Abernathy

Making Sense of Employee Compensation Strategies: Are we just in it for the money?

Mark R. Dixon
Southern Illinois University

Abernathy and Williams' paper in this volume is an important contribution to the organizational literature. Data from twelve organizations are presented to illustrate the role of many potential variables impacting performance. Z-score transformations allowed for standardized analyses of trend across companies. Abernathy & Williams' results yielded substantial positive performance changes in six organizations, no performance changes in four organizations, and negative performance changes in two organizations. Main variables that influenced performance were scorecard design, organizational and administrative structure variables, and incentive pay variables.

Abernathy and Williams' data also lend support for an individual based performance system and unit of analysis, at a time where group-based systems are growing in popularity (McAdams, 1996). Although the latter claims to align the employee and the organization on one common path, only the former can directly tie pay to individual controllable performance. This brings us to another important finding in Abernathy and William's data – controllability.

Employees with high levels of control over their performance measures performed better then employees with lower levels (Abernathy & Williams, this volume). This suggests that when perceptions of control are removed from the pay-for-performance system, potential improvements in performance are reduced. Similar research findings on the importance of personal control (or even perceived control) have been demonstrated in many areas, from gambling (Dixon, Hayes, & Ebbs, 1998), to sexual behavior (Reed, Taylor, & Kemeny, 1993). We may argue across disciplines whether to attribute these effects to constructs such as "social loafing" or "learned helplessness", or to observable events such as histories of reinforcement and punishment, yet consequences on behavior are the same. Until now, the knowledge of the relevancy of controllability in organizational contexts has been unknown. Abernathy and Williams' data suggest that it is of critical importance when designing an effective compensation system.

Another critical variable Abernathy and Williams found to predict success in the implementation of a compensation system was the pay structure of that organization's employees. Substantially larger performance increases were found for hourly employees when compared to salary employees. This finding may initially suggest that certain types of employees (i.e. entry level, lower income) find an incentive bonus more reinforcing than other types of employees (i.e. executive, high income). Yet, deviations from these findings might be expected if the magnitudes of bonuses or their percentages of base-salary were varied at the individual employee level.

In summary, Abernathy and Williams have shown all of us that simply giving employees the opportunity to earn extra money is not enough. Rather, the authors have provided professionals in the area of employee compensation with a number design characteristics to enhance the effectiveness of an implemented pay system. Addition-ally, they have provided researchers in employee compensation with a number of possible topics with which to further enhance compensation analysis. These topics may include, attempting to assess the competitive and cooperative contingencies structured within individual-based compensation systems, varying the degree of control over scorecard items' weights, designs and criterias, and creating hybrid wage structures beyond salary or hourly which may work optimally within a variable pay environment. While these research topics which fall directly from Abernathy and Williams' results, there are other lines of study also needing to be addressed.

A Research Agenda for Studying Compensation

A future research agenda in the area of compensation may include applying some of the rising applied behavior analytic technologies to organizational situations. One such technology is the stimulus preference/reinforcer assessment (e.g. DeLeon & Iwata, 1996). These assessments may lead to the discovery of different possible compensation options for different employees. For example, if desired performances have been attained, employees might be allowed to select from an array of items that might function as reinforcers (i.e. extra-day off, cash, free eye-exam). If total costs of these items were held constant, employees could benefit by matching "bonuses" to their individual needs. Providing employees with bonuses they tend to prefer, rather than what the organization assumes they prefer, may consequently result in higher levels of desired work behavior, and reduced turnover rates.

Another applied behavior analytic technology that might be generalized to the workplace is the use of noncontingent reinforcement (NCR). Here again, very substantial clinical advances have been made in the reduction of problem behaviors with greater easy of implementation then traditional response contingent interventions (Vollmer, Iwata, Zarcone, Smith, & Mazaleski, 1993). In an organizational setting this too may be a viable option, where it is very difficult to always deliver contingent responses to every employees' behavior. Many companies use this technology infor-mally when they have events such as free food, quarterly parties, and holiday bonuses. Although many boast of their successes (Branch, 1999), systematic investigations still need to be conducted.

In addition to current applied technologies, one may wish to examine the effects of varying the delay time to bonus delivery. Many companies deliver bonuses when it is convenient for them, often quarterly or annually. Yet, basic research findings on self-control and delayed reinforcement imply that this period of time can be a critical feature in resulting choice behavior (e.g. Richards, Zhang, Mitchell, & de Wit, 1999). If employees are given the choice between working "extra-hard" to attain a small bonus at the end of the day versus a larger bonus at the end of the year, many would prefer the more immediate option. Research examining employees' "indifference points", or at what delay they would prefer either option equally, may also enhance our knowledge of why some pay-for-performance plans succeed and others fail.

Lastly, and most importantly, future researchers must consider the role that rules and verbal behavior play in strengthening organizational behavior. Since pay-for-performance consequences are often delayed months at a time, rules emitted by employees and/or delivered by managers might be tracked. Differences across company successes with similar bonus plans may in fact be due to the types of rules that are controlling employee behavior. Research in this domain might take the form of varying the specificity of rules describing the behaviors needed to be emitted to earn bonuses, or selecting different means of delivering the rules (i.e. public posting; supervisor individually instructing each employee).

Conclusion

In conclusion, Abernathy and Williams have provided us with an excellent reference on the potential variables that may underlie an organization's success with its pay-for-performance system. The system generalizes across company size, is based on data, and yields extremely promising results.

References

Abernathy, W. B., & Williams, W. E. (2001). An analysis of the results and structure of twelve organizations' performance scorecard and incentive pay systems. In L. J. Hayes, J. Austin, R. Houmanfar, & M. C. Clayton (Eds.), *Organizational Change*. Reno, NV: Context Press.

Branch, S. (1999). The 100 best companies to work for in America. *Fortune, 139*(1), 118-144.

DeLeon, I. G., & Iwata, B. A. (1996). Evaluation of a multiple-stimulus presentation format for assessing reinforcer preferences. *Journal of Applied Behavior Analysis, 29*, 519-533.

Dixon, M. R., Hayes, L. J., & Ebbs, R. E. (1998). Engaging in illusionary control during repeated risk-taking. *Psychological Reports, 83*, 959-962.

McAdams, J. L. (1996). The reward plan advantage. San Francisco, CA: Jossey-Bass, Inc.

Reed, G. M., Taylor, S. E., & Kemeny, M. E. (1993). Perceived control and psychological adjustment in gay men with AIDS. *Journal of Applied Social Psychology, 23*, 791-824.

Richards, J. B., Zhang, L., Mitchell, S. H., & de Witt, H. (1999). Delay or probability discounting in a model of impulsive behavior: Effect of alcohol. *Journal of the Experimental Analysis of Behavior, 71*, 121-144.

Vollmer, T. R., Iwata, B. A., Zarcone, J. R., Smith, R. G., & Mazaleski, J. L. (1993). The role of attention in the treatment of attention-maintained self-injurious behavior: Noncontingent reinforcement and differential reinforcement of other behavior. *Journal of Applied Behavior Analysis, 26*, 9-21.

Service Review: Increasing Consumer Benefits by Linking Service Outcome Data to Direct-Care Staff Service Delivery and Decision-Making

W. Larry Williams
University of Nevada, Reno
Anne R. Cummings
Western Michigan University

An organizational level management strategy is described for establishing and maintaining consumer outcome related activities by direct care staff in a community residential service for persons with developmental disabilities. Overall service outcome data are presented for 25 consumers in three group homes over a four-year period. Individual consumer service objectives, training sessions, and consumer progress data were monitored over a two-year period in which a monthly review of outcome data was established by management and group home supervisors. All consumers received an increased number of training sessions and achieved more training objectives after introduction of the review practice. Further increases in rate of training and progress were observed when a standardized program decision form was introduced at the direct care level. A reversal of the management review for one group home, with a subsequent re-introduction of the arrangement allowed for a demonstration of the effect of the procedures. A theoretical analysis of the operating principles of the procedures is presented as well as suggestions for future research.

Increasing Consumer Benefits by Linking Service Outcome Data to Direct-Care Staff Service Delivery and Decision Making

Introduction

A defining feature of a behavior analysis approach to human service delivery has been its reliance upon the recording of empirical outcomes for the purposes of both assessment of service needs as well as the demonstration of the effectiveness of adopted service interventions to meet those needs. Indeed the major operating principle of any behavioral endeavour is that decisions about what to do next, must be governed by careful and timely scrutiny of the effects of what has or has not worked so far. In short, decisions must be data driven. A major frustration and challenge to applied behavior analysts in human services however, has been the lack of a widespread practice of data collection and data based decision making (Reid, Parsons, & Green, 1989; Riley & Fredrickson, 1983; Williams & Lloyd, 1992).

There are many reasons why outcome data do not affect programming decisions. Data are not collected; training or activity sessions are not conducted; activities are conducted but not using methods that allow for clear observation of progress on the part of the consumer over opportunities for learning or practice; data outcomes from activities are maintained but are not transferred to summaries that show actual performance over time; summaries exist but are not present when decisions are made. Unless the use of data summaries is an explicit objective-activity of the organization, with arrangements to increase and maintain it, the organization runs the risk of allowing consumer service related decisions to be superstitious (Reynolds, 1968).

Accurate data summaries of individual consumer community living skill progress are often maintained by direct service personnel as part of their regular participation in formal community living skill training and support for their consumers. The skills required to effectively teach or interact with consumers with respect to identified individual service plan learning or skill development goals may be acquired through training but require specific management arrangements to maintain in the natural working environment (Reid et al., 1989; Williams & Lloyd, 1992). Although applied behavioral interventions have provided numerous tools for staff and supervisory training, there is an increasing recognition of the need for staff performance methods operating at the organizational management level (Reid et al., 1989; Williams, 1995; Williams & Lloyd 1992; Wu & Williams, 1990).

The Total Performance Model (Brethower 1982) described a "general systems" diagram for organizations with internal and external three term information "loops". These essentially represented informational control or decision procedures at the individual department or sector level as well as for the organization as a whole. Brethower argued that in order to make effective decisions, senior managers/ directors needed to have as much information from as many areas of their organization as possible, and that this information was best gathered by having individual sectors receive and provide relevant information from and to other sectors and to the overall direction of the organization.

Total Performance Service Review (TPSR), an adaptation of the Brethower (1982) model is an organizational level practice that increases the probability of decision-making-in-the-presence-of-consumer-performance-summaries by direct care staff, and therefore the probability of consumer service related activities being conducted and being conducted effectively (see Figure 1). This paper describes the combined effects of an organization wide review of individual service outcome measures and a direct care level decision making procedure as a strategy to establish and maintain relevant staff service behaviors and subsequent consumer benefits.

Understanding the service review organizational chart: The adaptation of the Total Performance System (Brethower, 1982) for a human service situation is represented in figure one. Additionally, the Chart indicates the location of the "Service Review" process. Examination of the Chart reveals four different processing loops, each one consisting of input information (or job / work objectives), some form of job / work activity, and some form of tracking or monitoring how well the

TOTAL PERFORMANCE SERVICE REVIEW

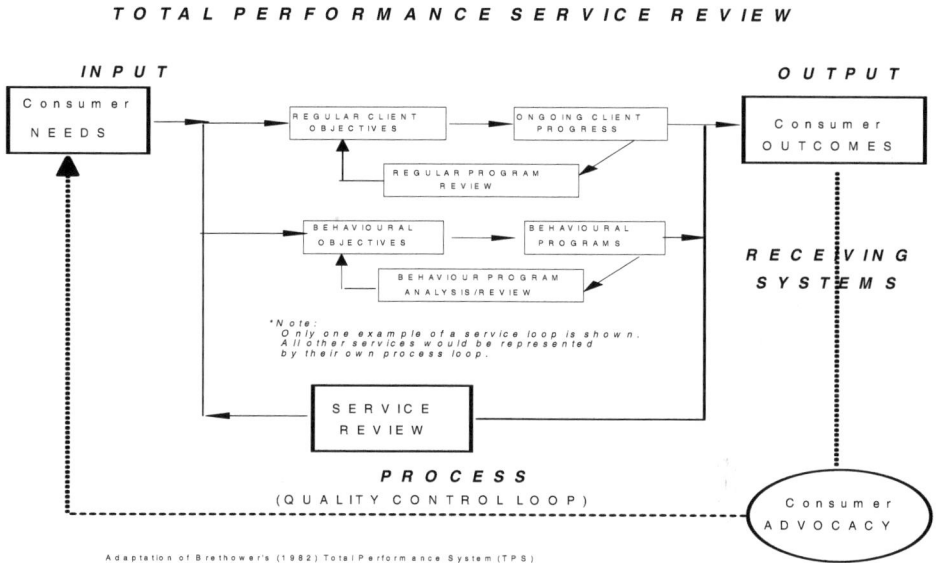

Figure 1. The Total Performance Service Review Process. Job inputs and outputs are analyzed at several levels of activity within the organization and the process is replicated at higher levels within the organization.

job activity is meeting the needs of the job objectives or requests. At the level of services for a given individual client, the "regular service objectives" could represent all or any one of a variety of services that an organization may provide for that client. The "ongoing consumer progress" box represents the results of the service activity that is provided on a regular basis for the client. The "regular program review" represents how the service provider monitors the application of the service for the client to assure that the service is of benefit for the client (as indicated by client progress). These three parts can represent one or all services provided for one client or all clients, depending on the level of analysis one wishes to conduct or review.

A second process loop is seen below the first and it represents specifically a behavioral clinical or training service. As in the previously described loop there are inputs or objectives, activities or services, and a regular monitoring of the effectiveness of those services. (Note that this activity is especially natural and common to any behavioral interventions). A third and more comprehensive loop is represented by the outside lines and their linking of consumer needs to consumer outcomes and the feedback of information on the adequacy of those outcomes to the organization. This feedback loop represents customer satisfaction. Note how the first two loops we described are contained within the larger consumer loop. Indeed, they *are the job or activity sector of the larger loop.*

The "Service Review" line represents a fourth process loop. This loop represents the overall monitoring of all activities related to all client service objectives within the organization. Like the consumer feedback loop, it encompasses all organizational activities and is the overall quality assurance or monitor function of the organization. Because of this feature, it allows for maintaining or improving lower level monitoring simply because it represents monitoring of that monitoring or an organizational quality assurance management system.

Setting and participants

The current application involved the operation of three group homes, part of a privately operated residential living system in Metropolitan Toronto. The homes were the residence at any one time over a four-year period for 25 developmentally delayed youth and young adults ranging in age from 9 to 28 years. They all were diagnosed as developmentally disabled requiring for the most part extensive or pervasive (Luckasson et al., 1993) levels of intensity of supports. Several of these consumers had additional psychopathological diagnoses. Many of the consumers also received some form of psychotropic medication at some time over the four years. The analysis of the management interventions was conducted for eighteen consumers who were followed over an initial two year period while group data for all twenty-five are presented over a four year period.

An initial needs analysis of the residential sector of the service agency was conducted with the executive director, program director and three supervisors (Williams & Murray 1993). Although this analysis is not directly necessary for the purposes of this chapter and will not be presented, in general terms it involved meeting every two weeks and assigning and reviewing information gathered by managers and supervisors. The activities concerned establishing what information was available and adequate to describe issues such as consumer service related goals and outcomes, staff skills related to these outcomes, estimates of the time distribution of staff and supervisors for activities either directly involving consumers, indirectly involving them, or activities which did not require their presence, as well as job satisfaction measures concerning what kinds and format of data were in place on consumer service plans,

This "service review team" was formed during the initial three month needs analysis and continued to meet approximately monthly for a year. During this time the authors (with assistance from colleagues) taught all staff specific service plan writing skills (Cummings et al., in press) followed by generalized behavioral teaching skills (Ducharme et al., 1993). The original purpose of the monthly team review meetings was to provide follow-up probe measures for these two teaching projects at one year and eighteen months respectively, as well as to analyse changes in overall consumer service benefits during one year of the "service review" practice. Specifically, the present analysis will describe the effects of management practices at the organizational and the individual residence level for data taking and analysis practices by direct care staff, on the extent to which consumer service activities were conducted and objectives were met.

Method

Service review procedures

The meeting. The major feature of the service review was an approximately 2 hour meeting of the site supervisors, the Program Director (chair of the meeting), at least one consultant (one or both of the authors) and the Executive Director. Meetings occurred every month, with the minutes taken in revolving order by the supervisors, and sent to all participants about a week before each meeting. The meeting agenda, always included site consumer progress updates (see below) as well as any operating or new behavioral issues that had arisen since the last meeting. Allotment of consultant's time in terms of visiting a given house for staff training or clinical consulting was also decided at these meetings as well as arrangements for meetings with supervisors in order to have access to consumer training progress data, observe training sessions, and provide suggestions for specific clinical interventions that might arise etc.

Consumer service outcome data. Each site was supplied with a three ring binder containing standardized "Service Review" graphs as well as a Site Outcome Summary "SOS" chart. Examples of these tools are presented in Figures 2 and 3.

These charts were filled in prior to the meeting and presented by each supervisor. Essentially the charts simply provided a standard format by which a graphical representation of any service plan or Individual Program Plan (IPP) related activity or goal could be maintained as a monthly summary. Supervisors and their staff maintained graphs for the IPP related activities of each consumer as well as any "clinical behavioral" interventions and medications in effect for a given consumer. The charts were designed to allow for percent or frequency correct responses during training sessions as well as to allow for indications of milestones in programs such as completion of a step in a task analyzed skill, changes in teaching strategies such as reinforcement requirements or instructional and prompt changes, or termination of one program and starting of another. Once the charts were completed, supervisors completed the "SOS" chart for all programs, across all consumers in their residence, by judging whether a given program's data indicated that the consumer was doing "better than", "worse than" or "the same as" (+ / - 5% of the last data point) their progress from the previous monthly review. For each program that was better than the last month, the supervisor filled in a square above the line for that month. "Worse than" and repeat "same as" programs resulted in that consumer's initials being entered in a square below the centre line (see Figure 3). The result was a "floating" histogram providing a visual indication of priority program issues for the next month (those items below the centre line). Thus, each service review meeting represented an opportunity for all managers to see what was actually happening at all sites, and to see the successes and problems of each site, negotiate the use of resources, as well as the best use of the consultants' time for attending to training and or clinical intervention needs.

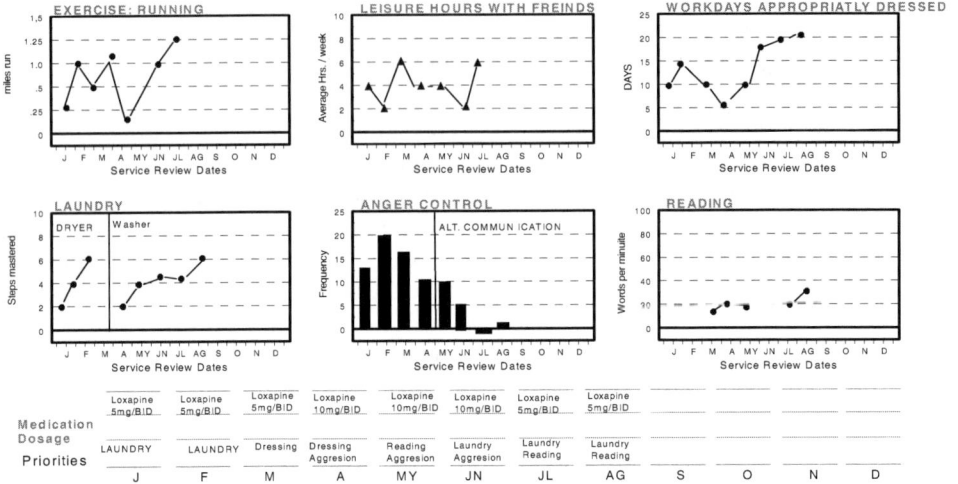

Figure 2. An example of the monthly consumer program progress chart incorporated to track consumer progress on several different training and community involvement activities.

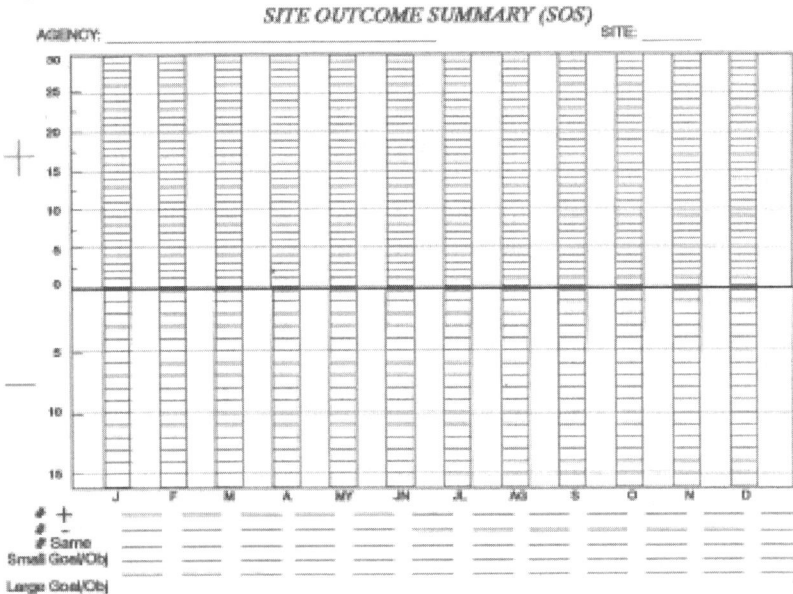

Figure 3. The Site Outcome Summary chart. Prepared by the supervisor each month by classifying all consumer programs as improved, the same as, or worse than last month, the next month's priorities are seen below the center line.

Staff skills data. Once taught a specific format for the form and content of written Individual Program Plans (Cummings et al., 1993), those criteria were simply adopted by the organization as those to follow when devising new programs for any consumer. All supervisors were trained in the original IPP writing program and were given scoring protocols to use for providing feedback to staff on all new IPPs written after the first six months.

In a similar fashion, supervisors and the program director had been trained in generalized individual community living teaching skills (Ducharme et al., in press). Supervisors had been asked to now regularly assist sessions or activities being conducted by staff in order to observe a few trials and provide feedback to staff to maintain or improve these skills.

Inter-observer agreement measures. The Program Director also periodically visited each site and observed staff conducting sessions, for the purposes of obtaining inter-observer agreement measures for consumer training session progress, collecting consumer performance data and evaluating the teaching skills of staff by observing them on several training trials and providing feedback to them on the spot. Occasionally a consultant also conducted such assessment scores together with the program director. For houses one, two and three respectively agreement measures on consumer progress data were taken on 35%, 32% & 38% of training sessions the first year, 37%, 35%, & 30% of training sessions the second year, and for 38%, 32% & 24% of sessions for the last two years. Agreement measures were calculated by dividing the total individual trial outcomes agreed upon by the total trials agreed and disagreed upon, and multiplying this fraction by 100. Agreement scores for consumer training sessions from houses one, two and three respectively were 88%, 92% & 87% for year one, 84%, 94% & 94% for year two, and 87%, 95%, & 84% for the last two years.

Linking regular staff data collection and review to overall organization product. During the first several meetings, the service review supervisory team focused on having each site be able to present complete " binders" with graphs and "SOS" sheets completed for all consumers. Once this outcome was obtained, discussions began to deal with the need for supervisors to observe their staff, and meet with them in order to establish performance goals and provide feedback. Finally, during the ninth monthly meeting a standardized activity tracking form was established at service review.

Beginning in the tenth month, although the program director continued to observe training sessions at the houses, the consultants stopped visiting each site to observe sessions and supervisors were asked to begin arranging observation times in order to evaluate staff teaching skills, as well as general "business relevant" aspects of their group home. These were to be maintained and reported as part of the regular service review report. Additionally, the consultants introduced an Individual Program Decision Form (see Table 1) to be used at weekly house programming meetings by staff at their individual sites when reviewing their individual consumer IPP programs (the individual, daily consumer program data from which monthly

DATE:_____   ATTENDANCE_____

CONSUMER _____   SITE:_____

PROGRAM / ACTIVITY _____   CURRENT : LEVEL
                                            CONDITION / MATERIALS
                                            % GOAL MET

PREVIOUS DECISION	COMPLETED Y / N	IMPLEMENTED Y / N		ON HOLD ( )
SINCE LAST REVIEW	BETTER ( )	WORSE ( )	SAME ( )	+ OR - 5%
TREND -LAST 3 REVIEWS	BEST THAN ( )	WORSE THAN ( )	SAME AS ( )	MEAN ( )
TREND LAST 6 REVIEWS	BEST THAN ( )	WORSE THAN ( )	SAME AS ( )	MEAN ( )
GRAPH	# SESSIONS ( )	DATA SUMMARY ( )	CURRENT ( )	DECISION BASED ON GRAPH ( )
DECISION	CONTINUE ( )	STOP PROGRAM ( )		
REVISE	PROCEDURE ( )	CONDITIONS ( )	GOAL ( )	OTHER ( )
INCREASE	SR+ ( )	SESSIONS ( )		
GENERALIZATION	TRAINERS ( )	LOCATION ( )		

ACTION / GOAL:	COMPLETION DATE WHO IS RESPONSIBLE?

_____   _____   _____
PRIMARY STAFF SIGNATURE   HOUSE SUPERVISOR   PROGRAM DIRECTOR

Table 1. The Individual Program Decision Form (IPDF).

service review summaries were derived). This form essentially prompted staff to review the data available on a given program and record what information was being drawn upon for weekly program maintenance or change decisions, as well as assign who would attempt training or program writing activities and estimated deadlines.

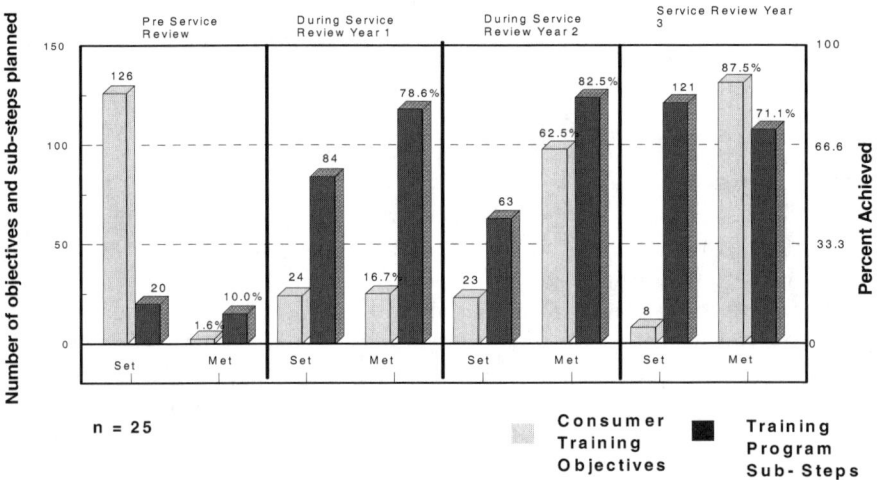

Figure 4. The frequency of consumer training objectives and their corresponding sub steps that were established by staff and the number that were attained before, during and after the service review practice was implemented.

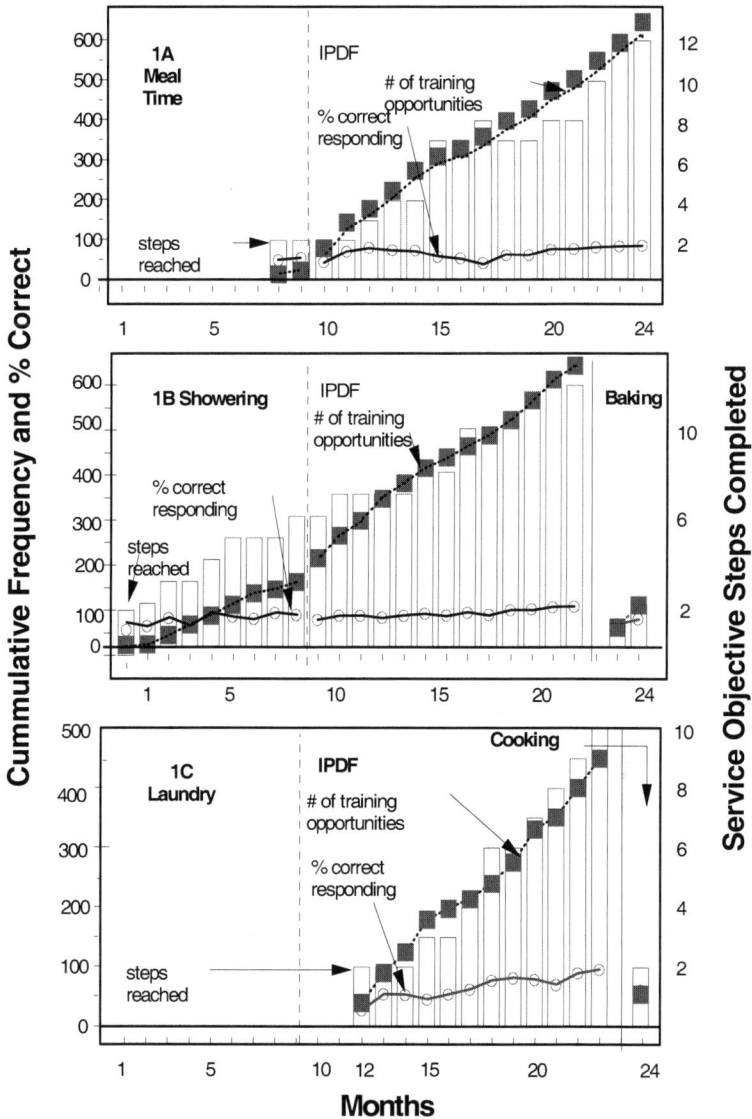

Figure 5. Cummulative frequency of training sessions, training sub steps achieved and percent correct responding for consumers 1A, 1B and 1C during 9 months of service review and after inclusion of the Individual Program Decision Forms (IPDF).

Results

Figure 4, shows the comparison of goals met by the consumers living in the three group homes in total, during the needs analysis phase, the staff training phase, the initial service review maintenance phase, the introduction of the IPD forms, and the following year, spanning a four year period. Clearly, there were more overall goals and component objectives met for these consumers as the review management procedures were implemented. Figures 5, 6, 7, & 8, show the cumulative frequency of training sessions conducted, the corresponding percent correct responding of the consumers in those sessions, as well as the number of program sub-objectives or "steps" mastered for each consumer, at each of two sites, during the immediate post staff training phase (9 months) and the 15 months after introduction of the "Individual Program Decision Forms" (IPDF). The progress data for all consumers show a clear increase in the rate of training sessions conducted with a corresponding increase in success achieved after introduction of the Individual Program Decision forms at the individual house level, as compared to performance rates with the organizational level monthly review meetings in effect before.

Whereas these data as a whole represent a replication of the intervention over twenty consumers, Figures 9 & 10 provide a demonstration of an unplanned reversal of the review procedures for the eight consumers of the third home, with a subsequent reintroduction of the procedures for seven of the consumers. (See consumers 3A-3F in Figure 9). This occurred as a result of an unplanned loss of the

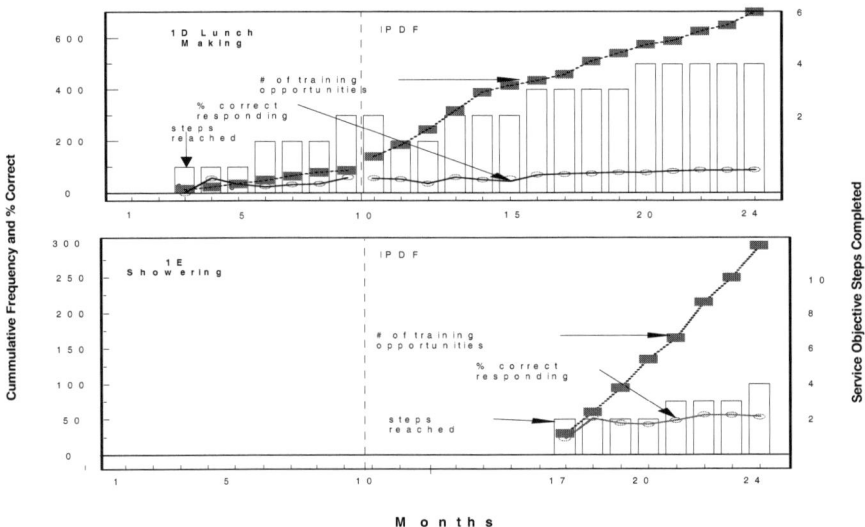

Figure 6. Cummulative frequency of training sessions, training sub steps achieved and percent correct responding for consumers 1D and 1E during 9 months of service review and after inclusion of the Individual Program Decision Forms (IPDF).

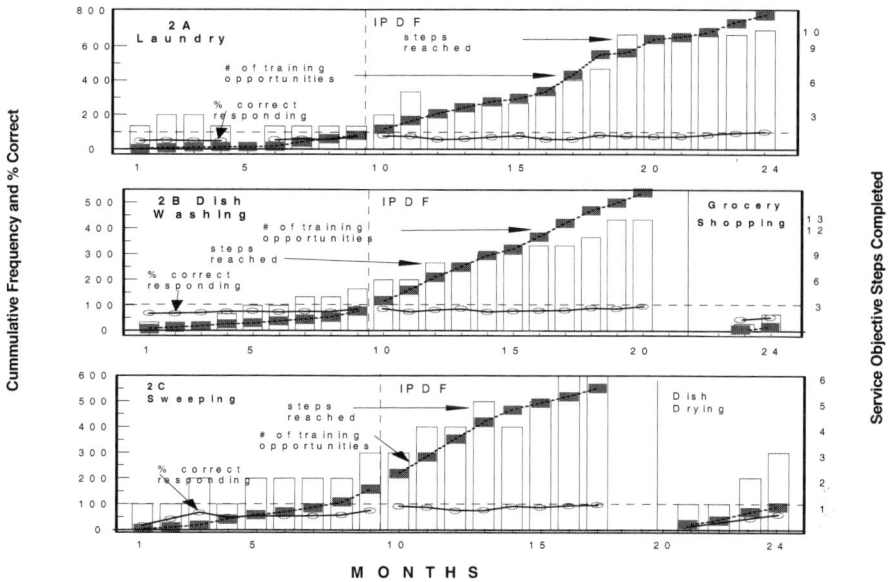

Figure 7. Cummulative frequency of training sessions, training sub steps achieved and percent correct responding for consumers 2A, 2B and 2C during 9 months of service review and after inclusion of the Individual Program Decision Forms (IPDF).

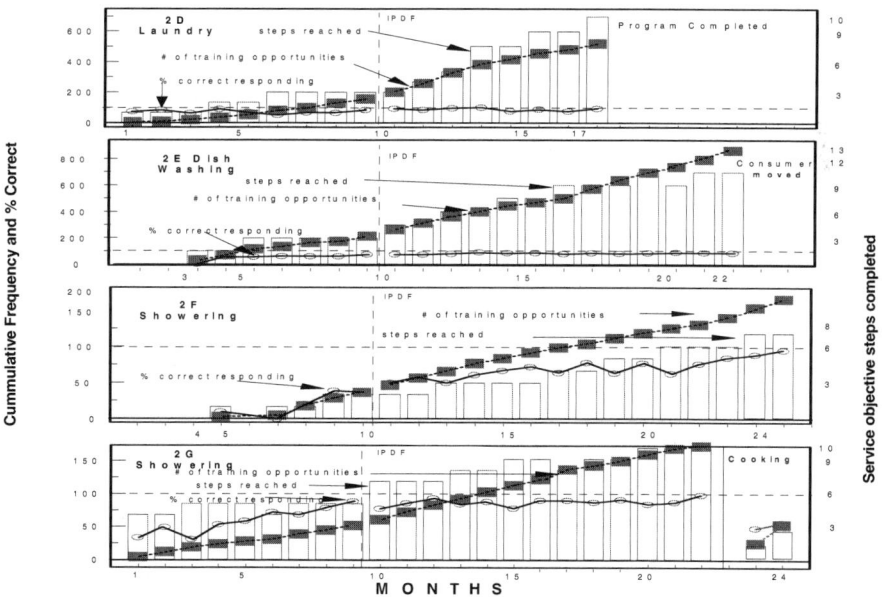

Figure 8. Cummulative frequency of training sessions, training sub steps achieved and percent correct responding for consumers 2D, 2E, 2F and 2G during 9 months of service review and after inclusion of the Individual Program Decision Forms (IPDF).

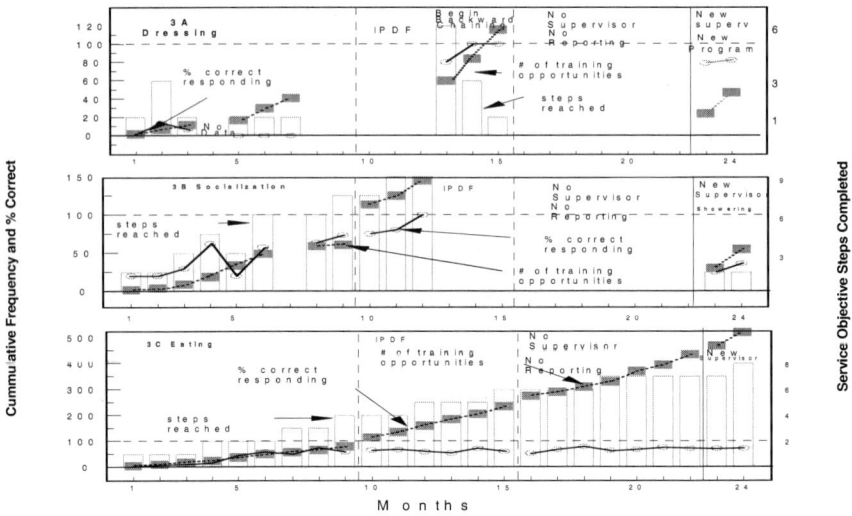

Figure 9. Cummulative frequency of training sessions, training sub steps achieved and percent correct responding for consumers 3A, 3B and 3C during 9 months of service review, 6 months of Service Review and the Individual Program Decision Forms (IPDF), 7 months of IDPF forms alone, and two months of Service Review plus the IPD forms.

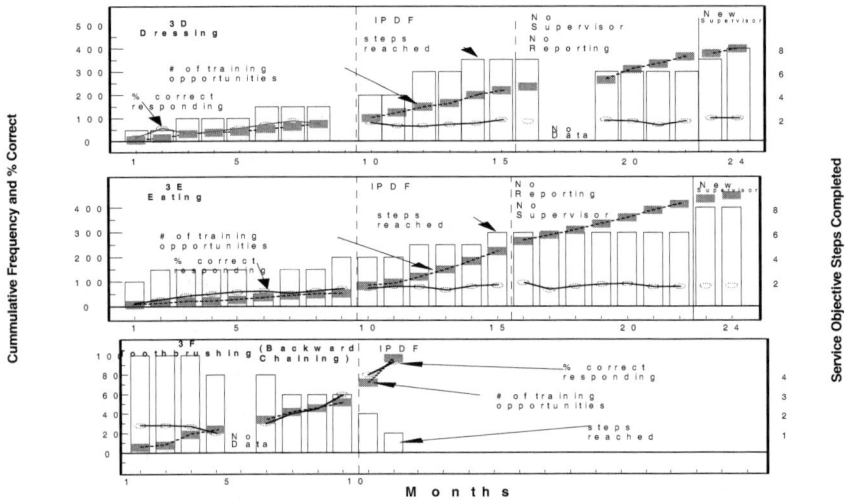

Figure 10. Cummulative frequency of training sessions, training sub steps achieved and percent correct responding for consumers 3D, 3E and 3F during 9 months of service review, 6 months of Service Review and the Individual Program Decision Forms (IPDF), 7 months of IPDF forms alone, and two months of Service Review plus the IPD forms.

supervisor and recruitment of a replacement supervisor over an eight-month period. During this time, a staff member from the residence would attend the monthly review meetings and present whatever training data were available. The program director, and occasionally a consultant continued to attend training sessions that were expected to be conducted and to collect inter-observer agreement on those sessions that were conducted in their presence. Some training was reported for 5 consumers indicating maintained training frequency progress (consumer 3E) and or a lowering in training frequency with a subsequent resumption in training session rate and improving performance (see consumers 3C, 3D, 3H, & 3G). For two consumers (3A & 3B) no data were presented as these consumers had completed a previous training objective, but new programs were not devised or implemented until a new supervisor was appointed and attended the monthly management review meetings.

These results may be compared to the frequency of training sessions and the corresponding progress of consumers for the other two residences as depicted in figures 5, 6, 7 & 8, which indicate a continued and accelerating progress on existing programs (all consumers except 2D & 2E who moved), with immediate transfer to new programs upon completion of an existing program (see consumers 1B, 1C, 2B, & 2C), or the start of new programming for a new consumer (1E).

Discussion

These results are important for several reasons. First, they provide a demonstration, replicated over twenty consumers, of the effectiveness of direct service prompting methods when combined with organizational level review of actual service outcomes. Second, they indicate (from the reversal of the management review via an assigned supervisor for home three) that although arranging for direct service decisions to be influenced by past service records, there is a need for a regular analysis of overall service priorities at the unit of service level (in this case each group home), in order to maintain or accelerate service activities and subsequent benefits for consumers. These findings are consistent with the current staff training literature (Reid et al.; 1989; Williams & Lloyd, 1992) which indicates that training of relevant direct care skills may be necessary but not sufficient for the actual application of such skills on a regular basis by direct care providers. Interestingly, the current findings also indicate that management practices, such as regular review of service outcome data, while they may serve to increase or maintain such activities that lead to the production of such data, can be enhanced when specific decision tools such as the IPD forms are introduced to guide such tasks.

While a more secure design could better isolate the relative effectiveness of organizational as opposed to individual variables for increasing consumer benefits, the current results are sufficient to show that such organizational level approaches can be powerful. Indeed, independent of the component causal variables in the present application, it is clear that training increased and became more efficient, an effect which would have to reflect training activity practices on the part of direct service staff that by definition were more efficient and therefore presumably less based on spurious or irrelevant information.

Related to the demonstrated effects is the nature of the improvements seen. The data presented represent overall goals and sub objectives. These were derived from the actual programs that were written and their format. Whereas the programs in place during the start of service review typically described major learning achievements for consumers such as learning to do their own laundry, or learning to operate the dishwasher with few, if any sub tasks or goals, the later programs were described in a task analysis format with criteria for completion of each step. This feature, while in place prior to the introduction of the IPD form may represent a confound in the increases observed in programming outcomes. However, an analysis of the outcomes over the two-year figures, reveals that individual training sessions and rate of correct responding occur at the individual program level, over a variety of programs and sub steps. Thus while still a possible variable in the overall effects observed, there is a demonstration of a change in learning outcomes over a range of meaningful and not superfluous objectives for these consumers. Thus, while future investigation may monitor the effects of service review on program quality or size, this issue does not seem to be of immediate concern.

Reynolds (1968) distinguished between "contingent" behavior and "dependent" behavior.

> An environmental event is said to be *dependent* on behaviour if the event must, by the nature of the situation, occur following the behavior. An environmental event is said to be *contingent* on behavior, if the event does in fact follow the behavior but need not do so. (1968, p. 31)

A behavior analytic model of service decision making (in practice at least in applied clinical and educational settings and the associated literature) clearly attempts to place decision or choice behavior of the educator, clinician, or manager under control of the most up to date information with respect to the effect of (presumed) causal variables on empirical dependent variables (usually a clinically or educationally important behavioral outcomes). While the basic and applied behavioral literature is replete with examples of appropriate decision making on the part of behavioral practitioners with respect to relevant measures of experimental or intervention manipulations, the wide spread establishment of this crucial practice, especially in human service delivery is still wanting.

Recent work by Goltz (1992) has indicated that decision-making behavior such as business or financial investment decisions can be largely affected by reinforcement schedules (intermittent reinforcement leads to increased resistance to extinction). Related to this is the work of Capaldi (1990; 1992) on "second order" schedules. Basically Capaldi has shown that units of individual behaviors (such as fixed ratio bursts) can themselves be viewed as units or "chunks" of performance which come under control of schedules of reinforcement at that level. It is possible to show that humans as other organisms can and do respond to outcomes that are related to larger units of "organized" behavior. Conducting community living skill activities and deciding to maintain, alter, or replace such activities may be viewed as "chunks" of community living care behavior that also are susceptible to the control of irrelevant or superstitious variables.

Direct service providers in human services may behave under control of consumer performance and changes in performance that are "perceived" but not real. This risk can be greatly reduced if formal consumer program / activity decisions are made in the presence of accurate record summaries that describe consumers' most current performance progress in terms of previously identified community living objectives for that consumer. An organizational level review of direct consumer service outcomes appears effective in implementing and maintaining relevant direct care staff performance, as well as for the timely distribution of resources and service emphasis.

The present demonstration indicates that such organizational level management arrangements may function as an "establishing operation" (Keller & Shoenfeld, 1950; Michael, 1993; Agnew, 1998), making salient for staff, the data summaries of their consumers' progress as a result of their training efforts. That is, although it is expected practice for direct care staff to conduct service training activities, this may not occur, it may occur at low rates, or in an inefficient manner. When data summaries, which can only be obtained when the activities they represent are completed (except in the case of outright falsification), are the subject of organizational management review, there is an increased probability of those activities being conducted, and being conducted correctly. The inclusion, however, of antecedent procedures or rules (such as the IPD forms) at the direct care level, that bring staff decisions about training under the relevant control of current and past performance, appear to be an effective method of increasing the efficiency of the overall enterprise.

Anecdotal evidence from the introduction of the service review procedures described here also indicate a much higher satisfaction and lower "turnover" rate in staff, as well as obvious advantages for the service provider in terms of the current and increasing demands for accountability in active treatment provision, and satisfaction of consumers and advocates. These outcomes, however, await formal systematic investigation. Further investigation into the variables of the service review method and service delivery may address such issues empirically. Independent variables such as the effects of automated timely data collection and summary methods, supervisory training in performance feedback and goal setting procedures, methods for improving consumer and advocate determination and evaluation of service outcomes, and replication of the service review procedures with different interdisciplinary groups would be useful future investigations.

References

Agnew, J. (1998). The establishing operation in organizational behavior management. *Journal of Organizational Behavior Management, 18*(1), 7-19.

Brethower, D. (1982) .The Total Performance System. In R. M. O'Brien, A. M. Dickinson, & M. P. Rosow (Eds.), *Industrial Behavior Modification*. New York, NY: Pergamon Press.

Capaldi, E. J., Miller, D. J., Alptekin, S., & Barry, K. (1990). Organized responding in instrumental learning: Chunks and superchunks. *Learning and Motivation, 21*, 415-433.

Capaldi, E. J. (1992). Levels of organized behavior in rats. In W. K. Honig & J. G. Fetterman (Eds.), *Cognitive aspects of stimulus control*. Hillsdale, NJ: Earlbaum.

Cummings, A., Williams, L. W., Meagher, S., Drummond, C., Bernicky, G., & Ducharme, J. (1993 May). Acquisition and Maintenance of generalized individual program plan writing skills by direct care staff.. Paper presented at the 19th annual convention of the Association for Behavior Analysis, Chicago, IL.

Ducharme, J. M., Williams, W. L., Cummings, A., Murray, P., & Spencer, T. (in press). General case quasi-pyramidal staff training to promote generalization of teaching skills in supervisory and direct-care staff. *Behavior Modification*.

Goltz, S. M. (1992). A sequential learning analysis of decisions in organizations to escalate investments despite continuing costs or losses. *Journal of Applied Behavior Analysis, 25*(3), 561-574.

Luckasson, R., Coulter, D. L., Polloway, E. A., Reiss, S., Schalock, R. L., Snell, M. E., Spitalnik, D. M., & Stark, J. A. (1992). *Mental Retardation: Definition, Classification, and Systems of Support*. Washington, DC: American Association on Mental Retardation.

Michael, J. (1993). *Concepts and Principles of Behavior Analysis*. Kalamazoo, MI: Society for the Advancement of Behavior Analysis.

Reynolds, G. S. (1968). *A primer of operant conditioning*. Glenview, IL: Scott Foresman and Company.

Reid, D. H., Parsons, M. B., & Green, C. W. (1989). *Staff Management in Human Services: Behavioral Research and Application,* Springfield, IL: Charles C. Thomas.

Riley, A. W., & Frederiksen, L. W. (1983). Organizational Behavior Management in human service settings: Problems and Prospects. *The Journal of Organizational Behavior Management, 5*(3/4), 3-16.

Williams, W. L. (1995) Dilemmas in the provision of clinical behavior analysis services in community settings: Individual vs. organizational variables. In H. Ayala-Velasquez and J. Urbina Soria (Eds.), *Current Fields of Application in Psychology*. Mexico City: National Autonomous University of Mexico.

Williams, W. L., & Lloyd, M. B. (1992). The necessity of managerial arrangements for the regular implementation of behavior analysis skills by supervisors and front line staff. *Developmental Disabilities Bulletin, 20*(1), 31-61.

Williams, W. L., & Murray, P. (1993, May). Service Review: A management procedure for establishing decision-making under control of service outcome data. Paper presented at the 19th Annual Association for Behavior Analysis Conference, Chicago, IL.

Wu, B., & Williams, W. L. (1990, May). Trends and a descriptive summary of thirty years of behavioral staff training research. Paper presented at the 16th annual meeting of the Association for Behavior Analysis, Nashville, TN.

Discussion of Williams

On the Benefits of Data-Driven Interventions

Matthew Normand
Western Michigan University

It is this author's opinion that Williams' chapter regarding Service Review should be used as an example of how to combine the data-driven technology of behavior analysis with a scientifically based theoretical analysis of the variables responsible for behavior change. Because of the detail with which Williams explained the intervention and data, one has the necessary information to make an informed analysis of the data on their own. Similar opportunities are often missing in published accounts of behavioral interventions, especially in organizational behavior management (OBM) (Normand, Bucklin, & Austin, in press). Without a fairly detailed functional analysis and subsequent data, it is impossible to make an informed decision about an intervention's utility in other settings. Without an understanding of the variables responsible for behavior change we are hindered in our ability to be effective behavior modifiers (Deitz, 1978). Additionally, without data to support our methods, the dissemination of our behavioral technology to those outside the field of behavior analysis is made more difficult.

Assessment

One refreshing aspect of Williams' chapter is his use of the Total Performance Service Review (TPSR), a variation on Brethower's (1982) Total Performance System (TPS) model. Rather than use the TPSR as an intervention, Williams used it as an assessment tool to decide which behaviors are of importance to the organization so that a functional analysis could be conducted on those targeted behaviors. Once the target behaviors were identified, it was possible to measure those behaviors individually and provide consequences for them. The TPSR is not an end in and of itself, but rather a means to an end. Simply identifying the various aspects of a system and then mapping them is not an intervention, it is only a first step.

Also important is that Williams continued to evaluate the system and intervention after the initial assessment. The assessment continued and strategies were altered according to the data, not anecdotal reports. This was accomplished not by just re-mapping the system but by collecting data on individual behaviors and making appropriate procedural changes based on that data.

Training

After the initial assessment was conducted and target behaviors identified, there was another important step taken; the staff were trained. Herein lies the focus of

Williams' intervention. What may seem like an obvious step is often times overlooked or poorly executed. It is important that the staff be trained specifically on the tasks they will be required to perform. Too often it is assumed that the staff should automatically "know what to do." The reality is that not only may they not understand what to do, but they probably don't understand why they are doing it. Although behavior management may seem simple and "obvious" to many people, it is a complex area requiring at least some minimal behavior analytic repertoire on the part of the practitioners. Without such a repertoire, the behavior of the staff members will probably experience a gradual topography shift that could be detrimental to the program. If the staff members are not aware of the mechanisms by which their behavior is affecting the consumers behavior then such a shift in topography may go uncorrected or even unnoticed.

For example, if a staff member does not know why it is important to provide consequences for a behavior immediately, the latency from behavior to consequence may increase. There is a considerable response-cost involved in immediately attending to the behavior of a consumer. It is much easier to take a more relaxed approach than to remain vigilant in one's observation of consumers' behaviors over extended periods of time. Without a clear understanding that the consequence must follow a behavior immediately to be most effective, it is understandable why a staff member may choose to deliver the programmed consequence at a more convenient time.

Response-cost

Williams has developed several worksheets that effectively display the data and are easy to use, thus minimizing response-cost. Minimizing response-cost in an applied setting (especially with direct-care staff) is important to the success of the intervention. Direct-care staff are often required to do many things in addition to attending to, and collecting data on, their consumers. Moreover, it is often the case that one staff member is responsible for several consumers at one time, thereby making it difficult to promptly provide consequences for, and take data on, the behavior of any one consumer.

Another important part of minimizing the response-cost for data collection is to specifically train staff to fill out the worksheets correctly. This was a primary focus of Williams' intervention. Initially, staff members were only required to present completed binders of worksheets ready for the monthly review sessions. The actual data were not important at that time and merely having and presenting them was reinforced. Eventually the actual data became the primary goal and behavior was gradually shaped toward its accurate collection and presentation. Another refreshing aspect of Williams' intervention was the use of inter-observer agreement measures to ensure that the data were collected correctly. The staff member's contact with reinforcers was maximized by breaking the task into small components and providing reinforcement for successive approximations to the target behavior.

Data

The use of feedback at the monthly review sessions also served some important purposes. First, the required data presentations necessitated that the data be collected. Making such data collection necessary thereby served as a means of insuring that the required behavior occurred on the part of the staff, unless they falsified the data outright. Data presentations also allowed people to see the progress of other treatment programs and compare their own progress with that of their peers. As a result, data presentation probably established the sight of one's own poor data (or lack of data) as an aversive consequence, thereby increasing those behaviors that would lead to improved data collection.

Suggestions

As good a job as Williams has done with the intervention and its reporting, there are still some areas that could be improved. First, I would have liked to have seen a more thorough description of the training given to staff members. This seems especially important given that it was the training at the organizational level that was the focus of the intervention. It was this training that ultimately effected performance at the consumer level.

Also, I am aware that Williams has a rather extensive table operationalizing the behaviors that were targeted throughout the intervention. Inclusion of these operational definitions would have been useful both in understanding the details of the intervention and in providing examples of how to operationalize target behaviors.

Summary

In summary, Williams has done an excellent job in both intervening and reporting on the intervention. I am especially impressed with his integration of the TPS model (Brethower, 1982) with Applied Behavior Analysis. In the current literature, it seems that often the TPS model is used at the expense of an intervention at the behavioral level, or vice versa. Williams' intervention is a nice example of the data-driven technology of behavior analysis at work. Such an approach removes much of the superstitious decision-making that is necessary when relying on anecdotal reports of an intervention's efficacy.

Finally, data-collection not only makes an assessment and intervention more efficient, but it also makes communicating with those outside the field easier. It is much more effective to show people what you are talking about than to try to explain it to them without empirical evidence. Without data, our analyses may seem like pure speculation to someone unfamiliar with behavior analysis, perhaps even to someone who is familiar with behavior analysis. The truth is, they should. An intervention that is not data-driven warrants suspicion form researchers and practitioners alike.

References

Brethower, D. (1982). The Total Performance System. In R. M. O'Brien, A. M. Dickinson, & M. P. Rosow (Eds.), *Industrial Behavior Modification*. New York, NY: Pergamon Press.

Deitz, S. M. (1978). Current status of applied behavior analysis: science versus technology. *American Psychologist, 33*, 805-814.

Normand, M., Bucklin, B., & Austin, J. (in press). The analysis of behavioral mechanisms in *JOBM*. *Journal of Organizational Behavior Management*.

Putting The Horse Before The Cart: Process-Driven Change[1]

Maria E. Malott
Malott & Associates

This chapter presents a method to battle the side effects of rigid organizational structures and the development of unsystematic processes. The chapter concludes: (a) The focus of organizational change should be on core processes. (b) We cannot change processes effectively without first understanding them. (c) Processes must drive structure changes. (d) Processes must drive technology acquisition. (e) Only with the active participation of the performers in the processes can effective improvement be made. (f) Change produces resistance. And (g) processes do not last unless maintenance strategies and structures are placed in the organization.

As an illustration I present a scenario of streamlining a particular process: producing an advertising flyer in a retail establishment. The same strategies illustrated here could be used to improve any process. I created a fictional story around a real case to protect the identity and confidentiality of a client organization[2].

Shoes For Sale[3]

Pete enjoyed reading his Sunday newspaper while drinking a cup of coffee. As the shoe buyer for *VEN, Inc.* he always first looked at the advertising flyer. Pete was astonished when he saw the hottest sport shoes, the Z-95's, on sale for only $60. The sale price should have been $75. There was an error printed in the weekly flyer again!

His annual bonus heavily relied on the profits made from the products he purchased. After bargaining, he was able to get a good deal on the price of the shoes. Pete was sure the Z-95's would attract a new crowd of customers to the stores. Competing stores were selling the same shoe for $80.

The chain of *VEN* stores sells clothes, shoes and accessories for children, babies and adults. The company grew from a small store Mr. Carl Pratt opened in 1957. Now the chain has 300 stores nationwide. Mr. Pratt himself never imagined his company would one day have 20,000 employees.

That Sunday for the first time the Z-95's appeared in the flyer nationwide. The same ad was printed in all markets of the entire chain. The ad took half of the first page on *VEN*'s weekly flyer. Pete estimated the cost of the error: $15 loss for each pair of shoes, 500 pairs of shoes on sale for each store and 300 stores in the chain. The estimated loss was $7,500 per store, $2,250,000 total!

Pete was furious. He called Eve, manager of the Advertisement Department. In a firm voice he asked ... *Did you read the newspaper? The Z-95's are practically being given away*. Eve had no clue.

At nine o'clock Monday morning, Pete received a meeting notice announcing a two o'clock meeting with a group of representatives from both the Advertising and

Buying Departments. The topic of discussion: Analyzing the quality of the ads in the weekly flyer. Requestor: Mr. Pratt.

Mr. Pratt started the meeting with his typical calm, yet firm, voice: *In the past six months we have had 18 significant errors in our weekly flyer. To date, the cost of these errors could have potentially been approximately four million dollars.*

Buying accused Advertising of being at fault for the misprints. Advertising blamed Buying for constantly providing them with incorrect information moments before deadlines. *What deadlines?* Screamed Eve! *You ignore all our commitments and expect us to work overtime to get the flyer out at your convenience.* The discussion escalated.

This was almost a daily problem. Processes across departments were messy. Departments did not communicate with each other regarding key issues of the business. And there were no clearly defined accountabilities or responsibilities.

Mr. Pratt was impressed with the success of his rapidly growing business in spite of the internal chaos. But things were changing. Competition was becoming fierce. In fact, in some of the markets *VEN* was losing money. Mr. Pratt knew that his company had to streamline processes now, before it was too late.

Understanding The Process

VEN's situation is typical. When tension is high, performers change processes without much thought. And when problems arise, departments point fingers at each other. All organizations are messy, the bigger the messier. Escape from this chaos requires streamlined processes. I will review a method that succeeded at streamlining a process in the middle of chaos. It generated a new process that reduced at least three times the number of tasks, the duration and the cost of the existing process.

Understanding a process takes effort, thought, and skill. Managers are busy dealing with the consequences of ineffective processes; usually they do not take the time and do not have the technical skills needed to streamline their processes. Performance-management specialists are needed to analyze and redesign problem processes by focusing on the crucial areas for improvement. However, the specialists can only succeed, if they have the support of the business units and work closely with those directly involved in the processes. As we will now see, performance-management specialists should look at the organization, the department, the process itself, and the performer. They should also look at the cost and benefits of possible solutions.

The Organization

To figure out how a process fits in the organization, we should study the organization structurally and functionally. We learn about the structure with the organizational chart. We learn about function by transforming the organizational chart into a functional one. A *Functional Organizational Chart* helps look at the organization as a process where each departments' products (outputs) serve as resources (inputs) for the other departments. The functional organizational chart should fit one page to help create a simple framework for analyzing the business (Figure 1).

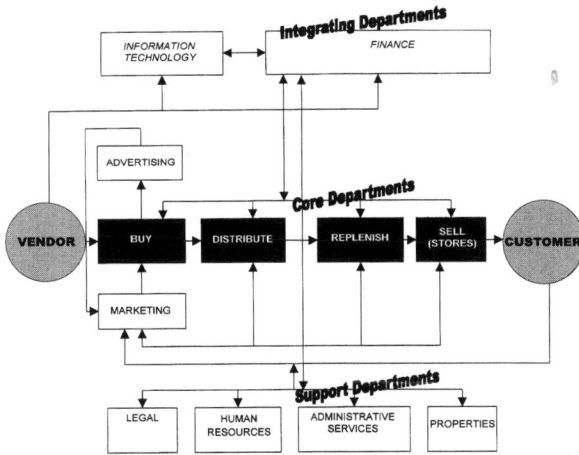

Figure 1. VEN's Functional Organizational Chart.

The retail operation is a throughput business: Vendors on one side and customers on the other. *VEN*'s job was to get merchandise from vendors to customers while achieving sales and margin goals. There are four core functions: buying, distributing, replenishing and selling. Each function corresponds to the *core departments*, the engine *of VEN,* the drivers of the business.

Core departments should work cooperatively. For instance, Distribution should ensure that all products arrive at the stores in time to fulfill merchandising and store needs. Replenishment should make sure that stores never run out of stock. Stores should display the merchandise according to shelf plans recommended by Buying.

Support departments should help core departments function effectively and efficiently. For instance, Marketing should study the market to assist buyers with their understanding of market trends and consumer needs. Advertising should analyze promotions of other retailers and propose competitive strategies. Human Resources should hire and effectively train qualified employees. *Integrating departments* (Finances and Information Technology) should receive and provide key financial and process information to all departments.

But *VEN* had the chaos typical of many organizations in all industries: manufacturing, service, communications and retail. All have the same functional problems. Every department acts as if it were a core department. Furthermore, core departments do not work cooperatively; support departments do not assist core departments; and integrating departments work independently. Departments lose sight of what they are supposed to do. They do not understand the importance of their function to critical issues of the business. As a result Buying and Stores have no support and must do much work that other departments should do for them.

They acquire too many responsibilities to do a good job and, therefore, are overwhelmed and ineffective.

The Department

In order to change a process effectively, we must understand the reporting line and structure of key departments involved in the process to be studied. The organizational chart helps us with this understanding. Buying and Advertising were the two main departments in the production of the weekly advertising flyer. The relationship between them was hurt by their ineffective relationship with other departments.

Figure 2 shows a sketch of the Buying Department Structure *at VEN*. Each box consists of a different type of job. Within each box there could be several people performing similar functions. The lines represent the reporting structure. The boxes in black consist of jobs from the Buying Department that participate in the process of the weekly advertising flyer: Managers, Buyers, Buyer Assistants, Advertising Coordinator and the Assistant to the Advertising Coordinator. A similar analysis should be done with the Advertising Department.

Figure 2 shows that the Buying Department made no sense. It had 24 different types of jobs and the reporting structure was cumbersome as well. For instance, the

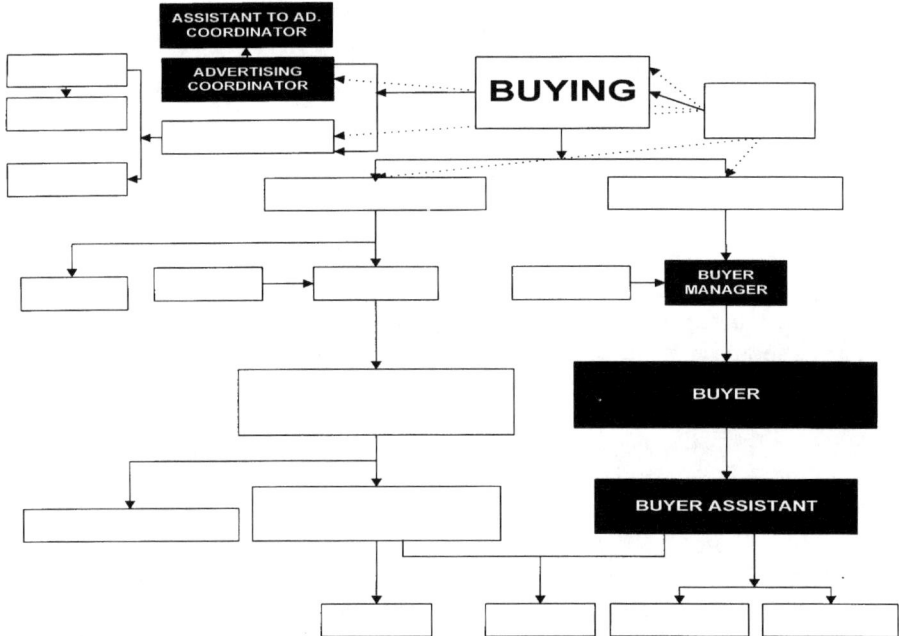

Figure 2. Buying department structure.

Advertising Coordinator's job was disconnected from the Managers and Buyers in the production of the weekly flyer.

When a department or a business has no systematic plan for growth, it typically develops long, disorganized ways of doing the jobs. Systematic growth requires analyses of the critical functions, identification of cost-effective processes to perform those functions, integration of processes with technology, and placement of the right people in the right functions. Functions must drive structure. Unfortunately, structure usually drives function.

The Process

We should study the process as a *Total Performance System* (Brethower, 1972). The analysis starts by asking, What is the process? What departments are involved? Where does the process begin and end? At *VEN*, the process was the one that produced the weekly advertising flyer. The departments involved were Advertising and Buying. The process began with the decision to advertise a product and ended when the flyer went to the printer.

The scope of the process is relative. We could have defined its scope beginning with the interaction with the vendor and ending when the customer received the flyer. In that case, we should include the processes taking place at the printer and at the newspaper distributors, given that the flyer was an insert in the Sunday newspapers.

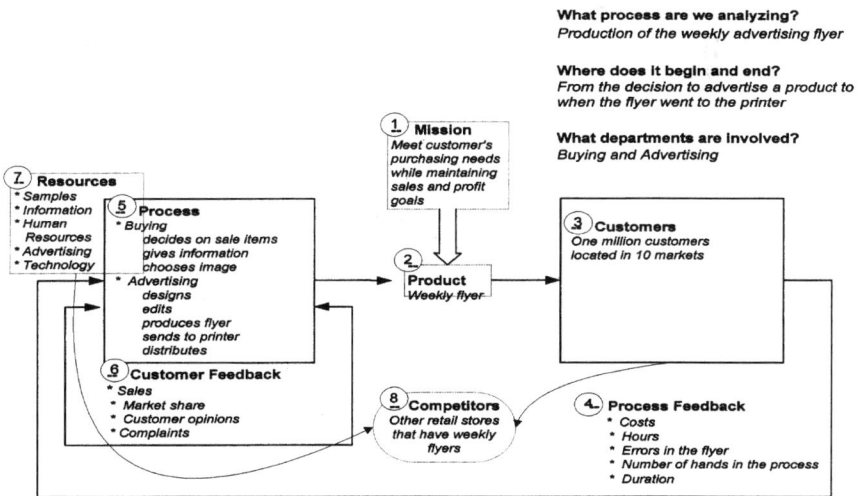

Figure 3. Total performance system.

Mission

Often organizations identify distinct goals for departments and processes. Soon we have too many goals, sometimes inconsistent with each other or with the overall mission of the business. *VEN*'s mission was satisfying customer-purchasing needs while meeting corporate sales and profit-margin goals. This should be the mission of Buying, Advertising, Human Resources, and every other department, and every process, like the production of the weekly advertising flyer.

Product

Processes and departments generate different products (outputs) that should all lead toward the same mission. However, products are often confused with mission. The product of the process we are studying was the weekly advertisement flyer. The three departments produced the equivalent of 260 flyer pages a year, five pages a week. On average, eight ads were printed per page. For 260 pages, 2,080 ads for specific products were advertised in the flyer among the three departments.

Customer

VEN divided its market into 10 segments. The markets were defined based on social, economical and demographic characteristics of the population. About 100,000 people per market received the flyer in the Sunday newspaper, totaling about one million customers.

Customer Feedback

Drucker (1986) said that what the people in the business think they know about the customer and market is more likely to be wrong than right; the only person who really knows is the customer. How do we know what the customer thought of the weekly flyer? How do we know if it made any difference?

Some crucial indicators could be actual sales increases of the advertised products, market share of Z-95's for *VEN* versus other retailers, and customer opinions regarding the offer and the presentation of the ad. There are various ways to collect the data, for instance, by checking sales from customers who received the flyer to see if the flyer indeed had an effect on sales. And focus groups can provide feedback from customers concerning the flyer.

Competition

Competition refers to retailers who pursue the same customer base. What type of flyers does the competition use? How do their flyers compare with *VEN*'s flyer? What processes do they use to produce their weekly flyer? In our case, the competition's flyers had more sophisticated layouts than *VEN*'s. The Buying and Advertising departments at *VEN* were developing unique and interesting layouts to compete effectively with other retailers' layouts.

Resources

In order to produce an ad, the following resources were needed: An image of the sale product (e.g., a picture of the Z-95's), detailed information about the sale (e.g., ad start and end date), the sale price and the theme of the sale (e.g., Christmas gifts), capable human resources (e.g., graphic designers); and technology (e.g., photo image software).

Advertising Flyer Process

In general, Buying was responsible for developing the overall advertising plan, including the specification of the advertised items, the sale price, the theme of the flyer, and the advertising schedule. Advertising was responsible for designing the flyer and sending it to the printer.

Task Analysis Guide

Processes cannot be analyzed in the abstract. It is important to study in detail what a representative group of buyers does to advertise a particular product in the flyer. For instance, how did Pete work with his Assistant and the Advertising Coordinator Assistant to obtain information that would help promote the Z-95's? What tasks were involved in Advertising to produce the final draft ready for the printer? I use the Task Analysis Guide shown in Figure 4 for a careful analysis of the tasks involved in the process.

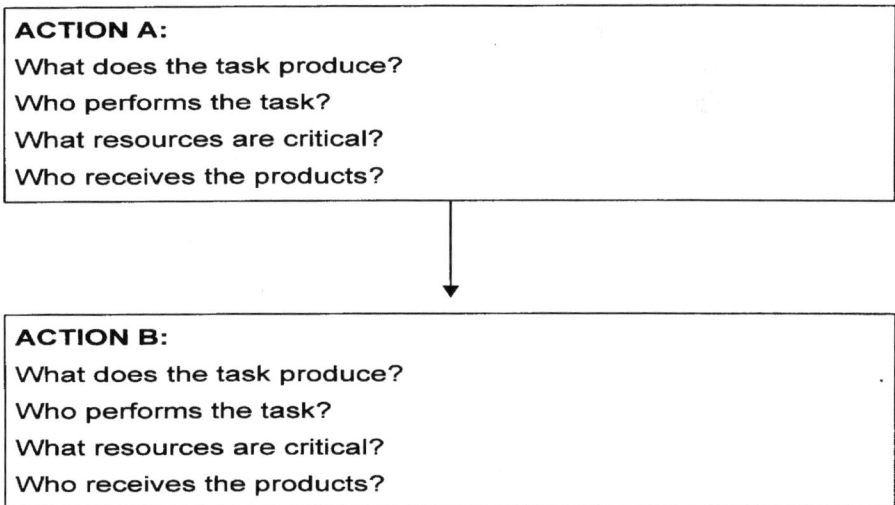

ACTION A:
What does the task produce?
Who performs the task?
What resources are critical?
Who receives the products?

ACTION B:
What does the task produce?
Who performs the task?
What resources are critical?
Who receives the products?

Figure 4. Task analysis guide.

Let's look at the analysis of two tasks: Task A was to produce the space guides by product line. Task B was to produce the space guides by buyer.

Task A: Production of Space Guides by Product Line

    What did the task produce? The space guides by product line for the upcoming week. The space guides specified the number of pages and the sequence of space assigned to each product line (i.e., accessories, clothes and shoes).

    Who performed the task? The Advertising Coordinator.

    What resources were critical? The flyer used for the same week of the previous year.

    Who received the products? The Buying Manager. The performer of Task B is the one who receives the product of Task A.

Task B: Production of Space Guides by Buyer

    What did the task produce? The space guides by buyer. The guides specified the dimensions of the space, the number of products to be advertised and the number of pages of the flyer.

    Who performed the task? The Buying Manager.

    What resources were critical? 1. The space guides by product line for the upcoming week. 2. Analysis of competitors' flyers. 3. Analysis of marketing trends.

    Who received the products? Each buyer.

By using the task analysis guide we can identify the process that Pete used in the Buying Department to promote the Z-95's. Each buyer at *VEN* used a different process to advertise merchandise in the weekly flyer. Processes tend to be inconsistent. This is typical.

Process Functional Analysis

From the Buying Department, the participants in the process were the Advertising Coordinator, Advertising Coordinator Assistant, the Buying Manager, the Buyer and the Buyer Assistant. Some of the tasks completed in the Buying Department were as follows:

1. Prepare the first draft of the space guides by product line for the upcoming flyer (Advertising Coordinator).
2. Prepare space guides by Buyer. (Buying Manager)
3. Prepare a proposal of products to place on ad. (Buyer)
4. Revise proposal of products to place in the ad and give feedback to the Buyer. (Buying Manager)
5. Make revisions based on the Buying Manager's comments. (Buyer)
6. Adjust space based on changes made by the Buyer and the Manager. (Advertising Coordinator)
7. Distribute the first draft of the space guides to all the buyers. (Advertising Coordinator Assistant)
8. Record relevant information about the product being advertised. For example, product number, size, quality, sales price and regular price. (Buyer Assistant)

Figure 5 is a graphic display of how each process within a department can be represented. It includes the first eight tasks performed by the Buying Department in the production of the weekly flyer.

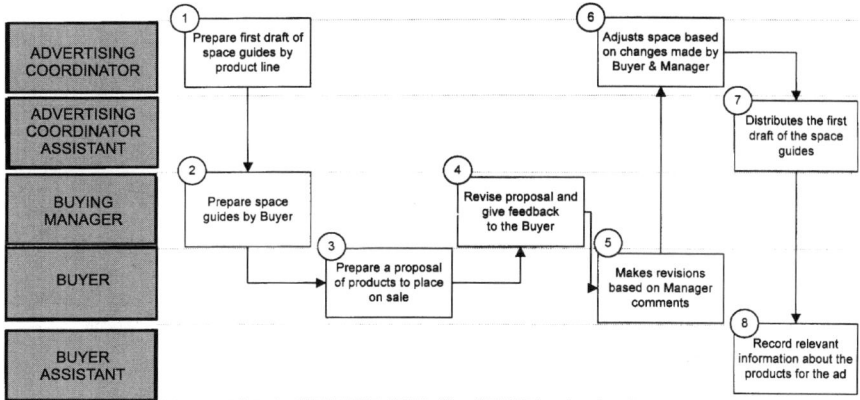

Figure 5. First eight tasks of the production of the flyer in the buying department.

In Figure 5, the boxes to the far left refer to the jobs of the performers involved in the process. Each rectangle corresponds to a specific action. The circled numbers refer to the sequence of the tasks. If we continue flowcharting the process of the weekly flyer as presented in Figure 5, and include all the transactions between Advertising and Buying, we will create a process map that looks like Figure 6, a functional analysis of the publication of the weekly flyer.

In Figure 6, the top boxes represent the five basic sub-processes the two departments carried out to produce the weekly flyer: 1. Create the space guides. 2. Decide on products to place on ad. 3. Generate the first draft. 4. Produce and review additional drafts. 5. Prepare the final version for the printer.

The boxes on the far left represent the performers involved in the process: the shaded boxes refer to the performers involved from the Buying Department; the non-shaded boxes represent the performers involved from the Advertising Department. Each numbered box consists of a task in the process. The numbers refer to the sequence of tasks.

Rather than the Buyer and the Assistant providing the needed information at once, they passed along partial and sometimes incorrect information. So they had to review the information again and again. Knowingly, Buying also provided partial and sometimes incorrect information to Advertising. Buying reviewed the first draft and made changes. Advertising incorporated the changes and created a second draft... and so forth. The process was repeated until the final draft was produced and approved by the Buyer.

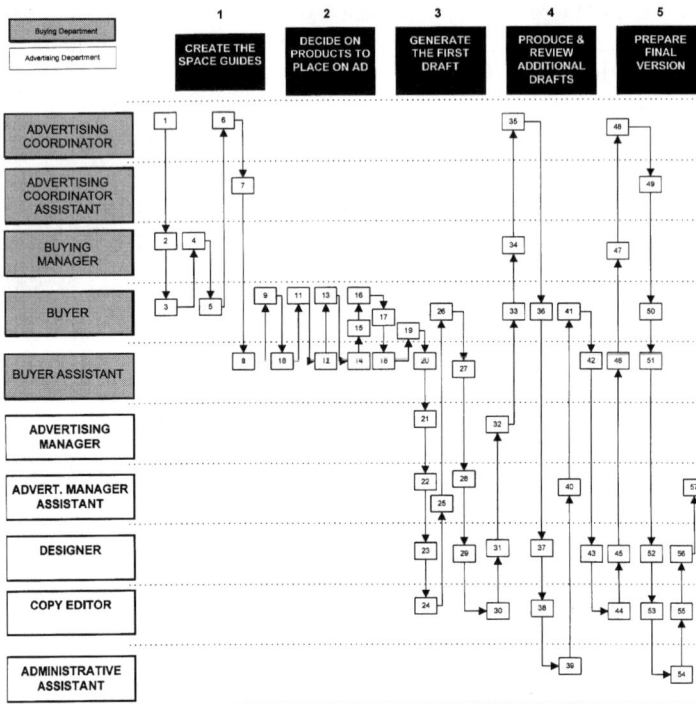

Figure 6. Process functional analysis: Publication of the weekly flyer.

The process of generating the weekly flyer was inefficient and error prone. On average three different drafts for each product were created each week. The buyers of accessories, shoes and women's clothing alone advertised a total of 2,080 products per year and therefore generated a total of 6,240 ad revisions. To complicate matters, each buyer customized their ads to a maximum of 10 different markets, so a Buyer and the Buyer Assistant could review up to 30 drafts of each product every week.

Process Feedback

By measuring the process we can determine if change is needed, persuade others, determine performance baseline, and establish the criteria for feedback to evaluate progress. Daniels (1994) said that management by common sense is not management at all. We would be better off basing our decisions on systematic, data-based information. Key measures of the process include the number of tasks involved in the process, the duration, the quality, the accuracy of the information, the number of work hours required, and the cost of producing the flyer.

Number of Tasks Within The Process

Advertising a product in the weekly flyer took an average of 57 tasks, varying from 52 in Accessories to 63 in Women's Clothing. Out of the 56 tasks performed to advertise shoes in the flyer, 29 were performed in the Buying Department and 27 in the Advertising Department.

Duration

Advertising and Buying took 25 business days to produce an ad for the weekly flyer. Women's Clothing and Accessories used an average of 22 workdays. Occasionally a senior manager requested adding a product to the flyer as an emergency. Interestingly, the process accommodated those exceptions and placed the product in the flyer within eight business days. There was a potential for improvement.

The slowness of the process created a significant problem. The price of the products was vulnerable to the changes based on competition. Initially, Pete decided to sell the Z-95's for $85, but the competition surprised him with a sale for $80. Two days before sending the final draft to the printer, Pete changed the price. He decided that an aggressive price would attract new clients to buy shoes at *VEN*. The Copy Editor in Advertising was confused because Pete changed the price of the product five times during the five weeks of the process. On one of the drafts, Pete himself made the mistake of putting the Z-95's on sale for $60—the sales price that ended up being printed in the flyer. No one spotted the error in the process, not Pete, nor his Assistant, nor the Designer, nor the Copy Editor.

Quality

A quality process is one that does not produce errors. There are two possible type of errors, publication errors and process errors. Publication errors ended up printed in the flyer. *VEN* had printed 18 significant errors in six months. Process errors occurred in the process and they often were caught and corrected before sending the flyer to the printer. If a process error was not caught, it would become a publication error.

Process errors consisted of a discrepancy between the original information at its source and the information at the destination. For example, an error was made when the price for the product provided by Buying did not correspond to the price entered in the *VEN* information data system. The Buyer's Assistant made an error when copying the regular price from the computer screen to the printed format that Advertising required. Another example of an error is that the Copy Editor in Advertising failed to incorporate the changes provided by the Buying Department.

There were process errors in three key stages: information generated from the Buying Department about the product, the creation of the first draft and the creation of the second draft. The process error varied between 21% to 32% by stage in the process. So if 2,080 ads for accessories, shoes and women's clothing were advertised a year in the flyer, between 487 and 666 of the information exchanged between Advertising and Buying concerning those product ads was incorrect or missing.

Work Hours

VEN invested 160 hours per month to advertise shoes in the flyer. Between Advertising and Buying, 40 hours a week were dedicated to prepare ads for shoes—

the equivalent of one full time employee. Women's clothing required more hours because there were more ads. The three lines of products required 487 hours each month. This represented the equivalent of more than three full time employees.

Cost

Advertising and Buying invested 5,844 hours of work per year (487 hours per month x 12 months) to advertise accessories, shoes and women's clothing in the weekly flyer. If the average cost per hour was $30, the cost per month would be $14,610 (487 hours a month x $30 an hour). The annual cost to produce the ads for accessories, shoes and women's clothing would be $175,320 ($14,610 per month x 12 months). If we consider *VEN*'s other six product lines, the annual labor cost invested in the production of the flyer would be $1,051,120 a year.

Aside from the labor cost, the cost of making an error should also be considered. In six months, *VEN* had the potential loss of four million dollars due to misprinted prices in the flyer. Occasionally when the publication error was caught early enough, *VEN* would correct the error at the registers in the stores. So customers were asked to pay a different price than that advertised in the flyer. Usually corrections were not a problem when the actual price was lower than the advertised price. But when the opposite happened and the actual price was higher than advertised, customers would get upset. It was a toss up between upsetting customers and taking the financial loses, neither of which was a winning situation.

A process should be measured before it is changed. By measuring we found clear evidence of the implications of the process. The process had too many steps, it lasted too long, it produced too many errors, it required too many hours of work and it cost too much. The process needed to be changed.

The Performer

Organizations should place performers in jobs that match their skills. They should also provide performers with the resources and tools they need to do their jobs well. Figure 7 is the Performance Engineering Guide, a variation of Gilbert's (1996) Behavior Engineering Model[5]. The guide categorizes the essential contributions from the organization and the performers' repertoire for maintaining expected performance.

Rather than offering the information and tools needed for a process, organizations typically spend a lot of energy in the blaming game. Performers blame management for not helping them do their job. Management blames performers for not caring or being motivated about their jobs. Blaming performers for the cause of ineffective processes when the organization fails to provide the basic rules, tools, and contingencies is victim blaming–those who suffer the consequences of a poorly engineered process are accused of being the cause of the problem. It is the responsibility of the business to facilitate the engineering of the right processes. It is the responsibility of the performer to proactively contribute to process improvement.

	Rules	Tools	Contingencies
Organization	Does it provide clear rules?	Does it provide the needed tools? (e.g., technology?)	- Does it provide the feedback or incentives to perform the job? - Are the feedback and incentives contingent on performance?
Performers' Repertoire	Do they understand the rules?	Have they the basic skills to use the tools? (e.g., are they able to use the available technology?)	Are the feedback or incentives of value to the performers?

Figure 7. Performer engineering guide.

Rules

The organization must provide clear and consistent performance rules. A rule is a verbal description of a behavioral contingency; it specifies the expected behavior, the occasion when it should occur and the consequences of that behavior. Instructions and prompts could be partial rules. They tell the performer about the expected behavior but do not necessarily specify the consequences. Training, if done right, should specify a set of relevant rules.

Here is an example of a rule for the buyer's behavior: If you provide incomplete advertising information (behavior), by the agreed day with Advertising (occasion), your ad will not be included in the weekly flyer (consequence). A behavioral contingency is the actual implementation of the rule. So when Pete gives incomplete information for his ad by the agreed day, Advertising in fact does not place that ad in the flyer.

However, specifying rules is not enough. Before concluding that there is a lack of motivation, be sure lack of understanding is not the cause of the problem. Telling, sending written documents and distributing handbooks are useless unless the performer understands clearly what has been asked and its implications. Organizations often fail to appreciate the need for verifying the performers' understanding of the rules.

Tools

Often, the performer needs tools to do the job, for instance, technology. Enabling technology must help performers implement processes. And the performer must have the skills to use the technology.

However, here are some words of caution. Organizations tend to look for quick fixes to solve process problems. A typical quick fix is to buy standard technology packages. More often than not standard packages do not solve process problems even when the performers have the skills to use the technology. This is because technology development is usually directed by experts in technology rather than by experts in core business processes. Key performers in core processes are so busy putting out fires because of ineffective processes that they don't spend time figuring out the right process before considering technology.

Technology should be developed after the performers responsible for implementing the process design the right process. However, technology is often acquired first. Processes become more cumbersome because performers have to do many unnecessary tasks for the core departments to cope with technology limitations. It becomes a vicious circle. Technology is acquired to fix business processes. Business processes become more ineffective. Then more technology is acquired to fix added inefficiencies, and so on... Technology is not the solution per se. The solution lies in process-driven technology development. That is, analyze the process first, then make technology serve that process.

Contingencies

Behavioral contingencies are at the heart of change. Process change is about specifying the behaviors of the performer, delegating responsibility, and implementing accountability. For instance, assume that we are analyzing the compliance behavior of the buyers. What happens when the product is placed in the weekly flyer in spite of the buyer's violating the rule of providing complete information by the deadline? In the future, the buyers will not comply with the rule about providing complete information on time.

If inadequate performance occurs, it is because the existing behavioral consequences maintain that performance. Completing all the information needed for the ad on time (behavior) might require more effort (aversive consequence). Actions that produce immediate aversive consequences are more likely postponed or not done. Why would the buyer go through the inconvenience now, if he/she can postpone the effort until later? Near the real deadline (the printer deadline), failure to provide incomplete information is more aversive than the effort that it takes to comply with the rule of providing information on time. Strict deadlines tend to control behavior effectively.

Performance management consists of engineering supplemental effective contingencies when natural contingencies do not support the desirable performance. (For details of such contingency management see Malott, 1992; Malott, Malott, & Shimamune, 1992; Malott, Whaley, & Malott, 1997). Designing a process that works involves building the effective behavioral contingencies when the existing ones fail to generate the expected behavior. For this to happen, process design must also include a process manager. The process manager is the one who controls the consequences and who manages the performance of those involved in the process. If contingencies for the desirable behaviors are not maintained, performance will not be maintained.

If we fail to deliver the consequences for the behavior specified in the rules, the rules will not control behavior. Consequences must be delivered consistently to obtain performers' compliance. However, in order for the contingencies to work, the consequence must be of value to the performer. Honest and consistent recognition by management tends to be of value, partly because such recognition is often paired with promotions and pay increases.

At *VEN* there was no question that the process of generating the weekly flyer needed change. There were no performance rules, feedback, incentives, accountability for errors, or consequences for quality outputs. In addition, the available technology did not facilitate the preparation of the flyer. Detailed revisions were postponed to the last moment; performers carried out redundant tasks; and the process took so long that original prices had to change often to react to competitors' ads.

Changing and Maintaining The Process

Organize Teams

Unfortunately organizations take change efforts too lightly and without much thought. In order to change a process effectively, I recommend the following change teams be put in place: Improvement Team, Strategic Team, and Ad Hoc Teams

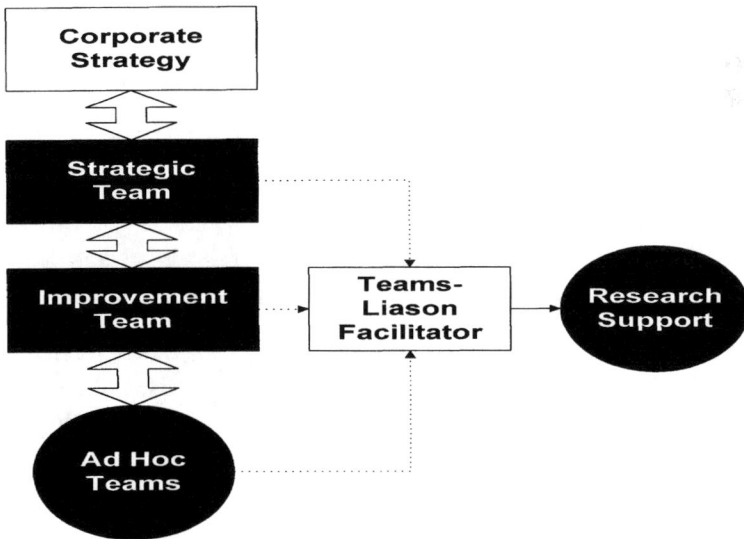

Figure 8. Change engine.

along with a Team-Liaison Facilitator. I refer to the teams and the facilitator as the *Change Engine* because together they proactively change the business. (See Figure 8.)

Improvement Team

The Improvement Team should include only representatives of the business units that need change. No one else will better understand the implications of the change. Too often businesses assign the task of process re-engineering to the wrong people. It is common to give the task to departments such as Information System, Training, Human Resources, or to outside consultants. The problem with this is that none of them understand the business process, nor would they have to live with the conclusions of their work.

Even when teams include performers of the process, management tends to assign members to teams regardless of their commitment. Performers usually feel that they can't refuse a management assignment and will participate marginally in the team effort.

Selecting the Improvement Team should be taken seriously. The Improvement Team should consist of no more than 12 people. Scheduling and coordination of team efforts can become time consuming with too many people on a team. Members of the Improvement Team should have the right skills, must be respected by their peers, must believe in the need for change and must want to be part of the effort. The members of the Improvement Team must be part of the change during process development, implementation and follow up.

Strategic Team

The top management of the business representing the departments involved in the process form the Strategic Team. Its role is to provide direction and guidance so process development aligns with the direction and ongoing initiatives of the organization. Management often assigns process change endeavors to teams and later does not support the change. The Strategic Team must understand the process change needed, must want the change, and must support the change initiative in the long-term.

Ad Hoc Teams

The Improvement Team will not have all the necessary knowledge and expertise to design a process that fits well in the organization. For instance, information about the technology and its limitations might be fundamental for the process development. Ad Hoc Teams should be assembled to study specific issues that affect the process. Members of the Ad Hoc Teams should not be part of the Improvement Team because process development becomes too hard to manage. Ad Hoc Teams should not be assembled ahead of time. They should result from needs of the Improvement Team.

Teams-Liaison Facilitator

A facilitator should serve as a liaison between the Improvement, Strategic and Ad Hoc Teams. The facilitator should have the following characteristics: (a) should not be part of any of the departments affected by the change to maintain objectivity; (b) must have expertise on process change; and (c) must understand how the process works and fits in the organization. The facilitator must have support to conduct the research for the background analysis needed by the teams.

At *VEN*, Mr. Pratt and the vice-presidents of Buying and Advertising formed the Strategic Team. The following people became part of the Improvement Team: From Buying, Pete and his assistant, the buyer of women's clothing, the buyer of accessories, the manager of the shoe buyers; from Advertising, Eve (Manager of the Advertising Department), a designer, a copy editor, and the administrative assistant. The Teams-Liaison Facilitator was a performance management expert.

Provide Direction

In representation of the Strategic Team, Mr. Pratt opened the first meeting of the Improvement Team explaining that the misprints in the flyer were signs that the process was not functioning well. Mr. Pratt asked the group to remove departmental walls and look at the process objectively.

The criteria for success were somewhat arbitrary. He himself had requested adding products to the flyer and he was able to get the changes into the flyer within eight days from ad break. In the emergency cases, they accomplished this doing less than 10 tasks. And he knew that the process could be almost error free.

Mr. Pratt gave the following challenges to the Improvement Team: *Can you design a process that...*
-Reduces duration from 25 business days to 8?
-Reduces the number of tasks from 57 to less than 10?
-Reduces the process error from 30% to 1%?
-*Maintains market flexibility?*
Furthermore, Mr. Pratt gave the Improvement Team the following rules:
-Lose departmental ownership.
-*Figure out the business process.*
-*Start with the end in mind.* (Start with how an ad looks in the flyer and work your process backwards. What do you absolutely need to produce that ad?)
-Question everything.
-Each person that does a task in the process must not do that same task more than once.
-*The process should be tested manually before adding technology solutions.*

The Improvement Team met for several weeks for half-day sessions. They created two Ad Hoc Teams to help them with designing the new process: Store personnel formed one Ad Hoc Team. It helped to figure out the type and timeliness of the information needed to prepare the advertised products for the sale at the stores. Information technology experts formed the other Ad Hoc Team. It helped them to understand that the current technology was too limited to serve the process well.

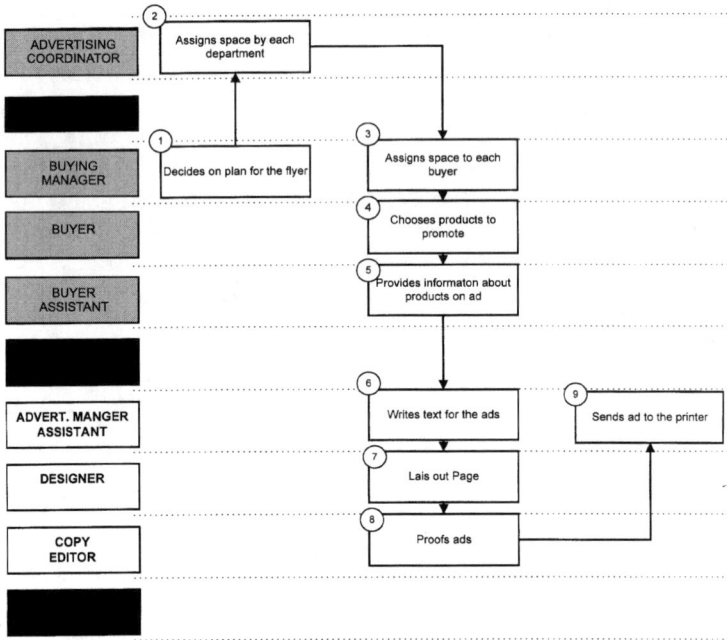

Figure 9. 9-step process for the publication of the weekly flyer.

Develop The New Process

After much discussion and research, the Improvement Team engineered a new process that included only nine tasks: (1) The Buying Manager decides the general plan of the flyer. (2) The Advertising Coordinator assigns space to each department. (3) The Buying Manager assigns space for each Buyer. (4) The Buyer chooses products to promote. (5) The Buyer Assistant provides information relevant to the products for promotion (for example, price and photograph identification number). (6) The Advertising Manager Assistant writes the text for the ad. (7) The Designer lays out for the weekly flyer. (8) The Copy Editor proofs the ads. (9) The Advertising Manager Assistant sends the final version to the printer. The process came to be known as the 9-Step Process. Figure 9 shows the functional analysis of the new process.

In the 9-Step Process, Buying completed the tasks it was supposed to and participated in the process once. After giving the information to Advertising, their role was done. Advertising did what it was supposed to do once before sending the final output to the printer. The process was more effective; it no longer included unnecessary revisions between the two departments. The new process included only 9 tasks, instead of the 57 in the original process. (See Figure 10.)

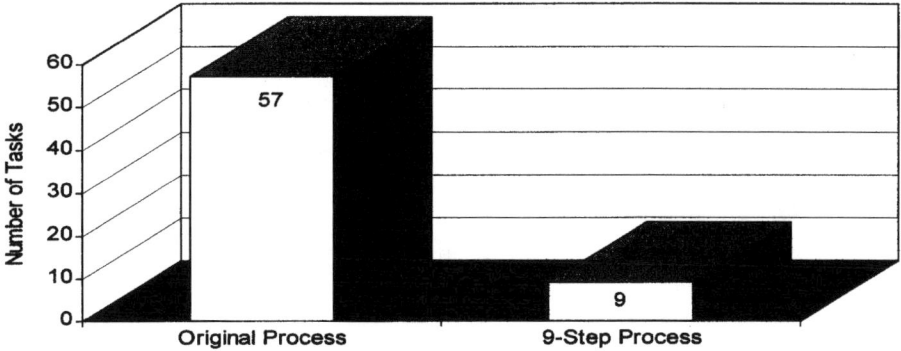

Figure 10. Number of steps in the production of the weekly flyer.

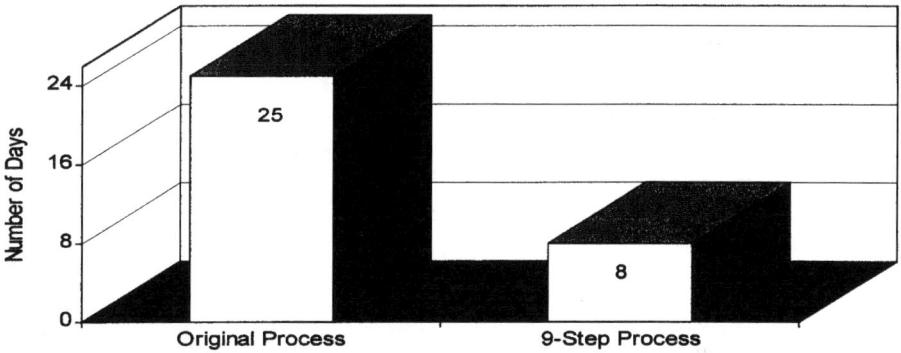

Figure 11. Number of business days to produce the weely flyer.

The number of workdays was reduced from 25 to 8. (See Figure 11.) In the 9-Step Process the involvement of two of the participants was no longer needed: the Assistant to the Advertising Coordinator and the Advertising Manager. They could use their time in other tasks of more value to the organization.

The process was tested for two months in the three product lines represented in the Improvement Team: accessories, shoes, and women's clothing. Errors in the process were also significantly reduced. Process errors went down from an average of 30% to less than 1%. Publication errors were also greatly reduced, not only the number of errors made, but also the impact of those errors. For instance, a typographical error in the ad had no financial impact as opposed to a mistake on the price of the product. Labor hours were reduced by 77%. The total labor cost was $1,051,120 a year across all product lines; so the labor saving produced by implementing the 9-Step Process was about $800,000 per year when the process was totally rolled out. The cost of developing the new process was about $100,000. This included the time invested by all the parties involved in the analysis and the development of the new process and the technology. This amounts to 12.5% of the potential savings in the first year alone. Savings will multiply by continuing to implement the process in years to come.

Rollout The New Process

Resistance To Change

As much as possible everyone should participate in the change process. However, in large organizations, it is too costly and practically impossible to get everyone directly involved in the change. New processes rollouts often meet much resistance. Most successful rollouts go through four phases: confusion, resistance, resignation, and endorsement.

Confusion

Performers try to figure out what the new process means to them. There is always confusion in the training no matter how clear the training aids might be. It is always safe to assume that half of the participants will not understand fully the implications of the new process on their jobs during the initial training until they actually have to use the process. Some strategies to minimize confusion are the following: (a) Educate the participants on the rational for the change and for the new process. (b) Have the participants explain the process to demonstrate they have a clear understanding. (c) Help performers incorporate the process when they go back to their jobs.

Resistance

Initially, it takes less work to keep doing things the way we have been doing them than to learn and incorporate into our work a new process, even if the new process is more efficient and effective. People resist change when they have to do something different. Goldratt (1990) pointed out that any change is a perceived threat to security and such perceived threat engender resistance.

Three things can be done to minimize resistance: (a) Management should provide consistent support. (b) New processes should be based on input from the performers directly affected by those changes because ultimately they would have to implement the changes. Sidley (1997) argues that letting the team figure out the solution is a way to have them buy into it. (c) The performers will more readily comply if management provides consistent support for the process changes.

Resignation

Resignation consists of the performers complying with the process in spite of their reservations. Here are some things that can be done to make it easier for the performers: (a) Components of the existing processes that work well should be kept, if they can be integrated into the new process. (b) The process should provide clear benefits to the performers. Radical changes fail, if they involve more work for the user. (c) Listen carefully to objections to the process. Minor adjustments might be needed and should be granted if the adjustments do not affect the integrity of the process. (d) Develop technology that supports the process before the roll out.

Endorsement

After the process is in place and the technology adjusted, the payoffs to all participants become clear. Then the performers endorse the process. After maintaining the new process, changes would cause resistance.

At *VEN* the process was implemented across all the product lines, with some initial resistance. A few performers not in the Improvement Team resented the change. But using the strategies mentioned in this section, eventually the process was accepted and endorsed. The major reason for resistance was that the existing technology did not support the most effective process. In the rollout, the technology was developed and incorporated into the process.

Maintain The New Progress

When organizations do manage to change processes, they often fail to maintain them. Maintenance is taken for granted. In order to maintain processes we need to build maintenance, audit performance and adjust the process to other changes.

Build Maintenance

Build the maintenance functions in the existing jobs in the organization. (See Langeland, Johnson, & Mawhinney, 1998 for long-term maintenance of a performance management intervention.) At *VEN*, the jobs involved in the process required the compliance with the rules of the process. For instance, the Buyer's Assistant job required that all the advertising information be provided to Advertising every Wednesday by 5 p.m. Failure to comply, would postpone the publication of the ad one week. Also responsibilities and accountability were clearly defined.

Audit Performance

Processes not audited weaken and eventually loose their integrity. At *VEN* the Improvement Team developed a feedback system so performers and departments knew every week how they were doing on process and errors in the printed advertisements. (See Abernathy, 1990, 1996 on how to design scorecard systems for business measures).

The auditing functions should reside outside of the audited units. If the auditor is affected by the auditing, the auditing becomes too biased. At *VEN* the auditing function remained in an independent performance management department.

Adjust Process

Adjust the processes to changes in technology, market, and other organizational changes, while maintaining the new process integrity. Processes that do not adjust die (Rummler, 1990). At *VEN* the team developed the technology after implementing a manual system first. When the members of the team were convinced that the manual system was effective, they developed the technology to serve the process.

The process change at *VEN* was a successful one. However, it would be naïve to conclude this chapter with the implication that the challenge was over. Process change is continuous. The process will need to be revised and improved in the years to come. Anticipate struggles as changes in performers and technology take place.

Conclusions

Often structures and technology acquisitions are done before organizations ever figure out their core business processes. Then performers have to do too many unnecessary activities to cope with the constraints of the structure and the limitations of technology. It is like putting the cart before the horse. In this chapter I argue that the performers responsible for implementing the process design the right process first.

Businesses should acknowledge that changing processes takes resources, time and perseverance. They need to formulate a strategy for change and house it in the organization. Change should be generated from the inside. Businesses should add a department designed to facilitate process change and to maintain auditing and troubleshooting. However, this function cannot be carried out successfully without the direct involvement of performers from the business units requiring change.

Management needs to decide what processes are worth changing, what processes they are willing to invest in years of development, and what processes they need to monitor over time in order to have a healthy business. Change should then be approached in a systematic way. The members of the change engine need to understand the business from the organization, department, process and performer level. Only then should they attempt to change processes, test them, roll them out, develop supporting technologies, and build the relevant maintenance.

By way of summary, consider the following job aid for process change (Figure 12). For each vantage point or level within an organization, there is a list of questions to guide in understanding the process change along with the tools needed to make that change.

Vantage	Questions	Tools
Organization	What is the mission of the organization? How is the organization structured? What are the core departments and their functions? What are the integrating departments and how do they work? How do support departments contribute to the core departments?	Organization chart Organization functional analysis
Department	What is the department's structure? What is the goal of each department? What are the functions within the department? What are the reporting lines?	Department's organization chart
Process	What is the process to be analyzed? Where does the process begin and end? What departments are involved? What jobs in the departments participate in the process? What is the product of the process? Who are the customers? What is the feedback from the customers? What resources are needed to produce the products? How is the process functioning? (process feedback) Who are the competitors? What are the specific tasks in the process? What tasks might be a challenge? What are the critical measures of the process? How do the department interact in the process?	Task analysis guide Process functional analysis Measure of volume, duration, timeliness, quality, and cost
Performer	What does the performer do in the process? Are there rules for the performer to participate in the process? Do the performers understand the rules? Do the performers have the necessary tools to do the jobs? Do the performers have the skills to use the tools? What are the contingencies in the process? Are the consequences for performance of value to the performer?	Performer engineering guide Contingency analysis
Change	How is the Strategic Team formed? Who participates in the Improvement Team? Who is the Team-Liaison Facilitator? Is there a need for Ad Hoc Teams? How does the new process improve the previous Process? How does the new process alter the contingencies for the performer? What technology is needed to maintain the process? How will the new process be tested?	Change engine
Maintenance	How will the performers receive ongoing feedback after the process is implemented? Whose responsibility will troubleshooting and enhancing the process be? What are the upcoming challenges and how should they be approached? How would technology be enhanced to keep up with continuing process improvements? How will we know the process is maintained?	Auditing system

Figure 12.

References

Abernathy, W. B. (1993). *How to design effective incentives plans.* Memphis, TN: Abernathy & Associates.

Abernathy, W. B. (1996). *The sin of wages.* Memphis, TN: Abernathy & Associates.

Brethower, D. (1972). *Behavioral Analysis in Business & Industry.* Kalamazoo, MI: Behaviordelia.

Daniels, A. C. (1994). *Bringing out the best in people.* New York: McGraw Hills.

Drucker, P. F. (1986). *Managing by results.* New York: Harper Business.

Gilbert, T. F. (1996). *Human Competence.* Washington, DC: International Society for Performance and Instruction

Goldratt, E. M. (1990). *Theories of Constraints.* New York: North River Press.

Langeland, K. L., Johnson, C. M., & Mawhinney, T. C. (1998). Improving Staff Performance in a Community Mental Health Setting: Job Analysis, Training, Goal Setting, Feedback, and Years of Data. *Journal of Organizational Behavior Management, 18*(1), 21-40.

Malott, M. E. (In press). *Paradox of change.* Veracruz University Press. Xalapa, Mexico.

Malott, R. W. (1992). A Theory of Rule-Governed Behavior and Organizational Behavior Management. *Journal of Organizational Behavior Management, 12*(2), 45-65.

Malott, R. W., Malott, M. E., & Shimamune, S. (1992). Comments on Rule-Governed Behavior. *Journal of Organizational Behavior Management, 12*(2), 91-101.

Malott, R. W. Whaley, D. L., & Malott, M. E. (1997). Elementary Principles of Behavior. Upper Saddle River, NJ: Prentice Hall.

Sidley, N. (1997). Some Things I've Learned About Changing Behavior in a Fortune 100 Company. *Journal of Organizational Behavior Management, 17*(2), 99-108.

Rummler, G. A., & Brache, A. P. (1995). *Improving performance: How to manage the white space on the organization chart.* San Francisco, CA: Jossey-Bass.

Footnotes

1 This article is a modification of a chapter of the Spanish edition of a book in process titled *Paradox of Change* by Maria E. Malott. The story *Shoes for Sale* is included in that book. Partial translation of this document was done by Alicia Alvero, a master's student from Western Michigan University.

2 The data used in this chapter are fictional. However, the proportion of change corresponds to reality.

3 The author thanks Dick Varnell (retail industry) for the opportunity to work in a similar project to the one described in this chapter. Special thanks to David Avery for assisting in the actual development and maintenance of the project.

4 Gilbert (1996) talked about motivation and motives in his Behavioral Engineering Model. I prefer to talk about contingencies and value of consequences. The terms motivation and motives are explanatory fictions and do not help with a clean analysis of performance.

Discussion of Malott

Distilling the Need for Process-Driven Change

Monica M. Garlock
University of Nevada, Reno

Maria Malott's chapter "Putting The Horse Before The Cart: Process-Driven Change" describing the organizational success she has had with the company in question was well prepared and exciting to follow. She enhanced her discussion on reducing the number of steps in a marketing process from an average of 57 to 9 by displaying a banner of all of the original steps across the *entire* back wall. A large number of steps for a process doesn't necessarily signify inefficiency. Any process could be complex and require numerous steps. The condition of this process, though, contained many redundant steps that required added time to complete. This banner clearly illustrated the complex intertwining of departments and truly represented a need to simplify the system. This topic represented an applied undertaking for the Nevada Conference on Organizational Change and was well received and sparked much discussion.

A significant part of this success story is the systematic approach across departments. Resolving an isolated problem in only one department would not be sufficient. The marketing *system* was analyzed. In Rummler's model, the overall organizational level must be examined first because it establishes the context for designing and improving the process and job levels of performance. This level is where the business is structured and managed to direct the organization in meeting its business objectives (Dean & Ripley, 1998).

The organization can be viewed as a system in which we consider inputs and outputs as well as conditions and processes. It serves as a model for considering ways to modify performance in the workplace. A systems-based model of organizational analysis helps bring out the impact that changes in one part of the workplace can have on the rest of the system. (Dean & Ripley, 1998). In this case, when efficiency on one part of the process was increased, redundant checking was reduced in another part of the process. All of the different departments had to work together to improve the marketing flier production and stay in line of the organization's overall goals of customer satisfaction and increasing profits by reducing costs of inefficiency.

Maria Malott's success with the company began with the identification of the then current state of the marketing process. This resulted in the banner contents to illustrate the urgency for change. This needs analysis identified the existing steps required, at the time, to generate and distribute a marketing newspaper flier for a major department store. The inadequacy of the system was evidenced gradually by the increasing length of time to prepare the flier and the increasing number of errors on the ads. These situations greatly amplified costs for the company. Improvement was a necessity. Over time, steps were repeated across departments to check for errors or changes in sales. This built up a degree of resentment across departments. Increased time was needed for all of the "double checking." Because of this added time, managers had to predict sale prices nine weeks in advance! They had to be able to predict competitors' behavior long before the competitors' environment contained the controlling variables that would influence their behavior. Management had to design an appropriate system that would work efficiently and be more effective.

By having the management work together to identify the appropriate and minimum number of people in the minimum number of departments to be involved in the generation of the newspaper ad, many steps were eliminated. Time and errors in production were reduced and, as a result, costs were lowered significantly. This is a true success story.

Most probably, the system grew to this stage based on contingencies of previous behavior. All of those steps were not designed in the system from the beginning, they were formed by the contingencies and the shaping of behavior of the employees in the various departments over time. For example, "Jane", in shoe sales, may have marked a certain shoe on sale at a certain price and, in the past, a mistake had been made when the preproduction flier had come back from the artist before printing. In order to eliminate this, she may request that she see the proof before and after the art department. She may also want to see it in the printer's "preprinting stage." This added extra steps.

Another set of steps could come about when, possibly at one time, a person in the sales department was a good proofreader so the step of showing the flier to him/her was added. When that person left that position, the step remained because historically, "We've always done that." This demonstrates how the system could have grown to the 57 steps.

When a system is established and changed because of its history of contingencies for behavior of employees, it can become inefficient and lose sight of its original, efficient, planned systematic approach based on business goals. What can be done in the future to help companies avoid this type of degrading of their systems?

Behavior analysts can be of service to set up these systems in the first place and to help companies avoid this degradation. With our understanding of system design, we can assist companies in the initial stages of development. True working systems are designed for long term use instead of using the entrepreneurial approach of "Let's see if this works." A good design includes avenues for maintenance, evaluation, feedback, and intentional modification of the system. We can be of more service than just becoming involved at the point of chaos to correct systems.

In the discussion period that followed the presentation, several topics were introduced for debate and clarification. One of these topics was "How did the employees respond to the change in the production steps?" Another topic for discussion was whether Malott and her team experienced much resistance to the changes that were implemented. Departments were giving up their second and third proofreading chances and final approvals of sales ads. This could make them less confident in their product since they had built up these redundancy checks to do just that. In business, there tends to be territorial blaming, distrust, and even sabotage of other departments. There was a degree of that in this story which is why the extra steps were added in the first place for "double checking" of the ad at each stage.

Malott mentioned she worked exclusively with the upper management of these departments so she had buy-in of all of the requested changes. Without this level of involvement, the system would not change. Since the system was instituting policy revisions which resulted in more accurate ads with shorter generation time and less work, people had little trouble accepting the changes. Although there was some initial resistance, the success of the new system was enjoyed by all involved. Buttons for the new nine-step process were produced for everyone which celebrated this major change in policy and efficiency.

Another topic that was raised during the conference concerning this presentation was "How does one measure the true costs of production?" Costs in this project were calculated by hours of eliminated work multiplied by a wage, in addition to, loss of profit due to printing errors of sale prices of merchandise in the fliers. This could give a ballpark figure but does not the cost also involve utilities to produce reruns of fliers, office space of unneeded work, price of redundant consumables, and amount of work that could have been done by the employees if they were not working so much on these fliers? How far does one go to measure the cost of an operating system?

Certainly a consultant would look more successful if he/she could add these costs in as savings for the company. But how does one put a dollar value on them? With the measurement and observation skills of a behavior analyst, a more accurate account of production costs may be identified. The most important reasons for identifying costs are to convince management of the need for change. This essentially tells management that the cost for the consultant and implementation will more than be paid for by the savings in correcting inefficient work. This is measured prior to the intervention. The other reason to analyze costs is to give management a measure of success of the changes in policy. This is measured after the intervention and shows the worth of the increased efficiency. One must find the balance of identifying minute costs compared to the cost of identification. If it costs more to calculate than to work inefficiently, one is looking too finely. It is important to have accurate numbers in an effective, timely manner.

This success story was significant in its size, degree of improvement, and the enthusiasm of the employees after a "job well done." It was presented in a straightforward, clear, and interesting fashion.

References

Dean, P. J., & Ripley, D. E. (1998). *Performance improvement pathfinders: Models for organizational learning systems.* Washington, DC: International Society for Performance Improvement.

Theoretical Issues in the Design of Self-Managed Work Teams

Cloyd Hyten
University of North Texas

In the early to mid-1990s I worked with a sociologist colleague of mine, Dale Yeatts, on a National Science Foundation grant to study differences between successful and unsuccessful self-managed work teams (SMWTs). We studied work teams in manufacturing, human services, and government agencies for several years, the results of which were described in our recent book (Yeatts & Hyten, 1998). I had been teaching organizational behavior management (OBM) classes for some time and I found it challenging to understand SMWTs from a behavior analytic perspective. Many aspects of SMWTs seemed to require adaptations of conventional OBM practices, and the philosophy underlying teams seemed to be quite different from that underlying the conventional OBM approach. Because we had written our book for a diverse audience, I did not have the chance to present a behavior analytic view of teams in that book, so I will try to do so in this chapter.

I found few references in the OBM literature to SMWTs or even to teamwork in general. Fewer still were references to employee involvement or empowerment strategies, a major trend in American business in the last decade. Boyett and Conn (1995) see involvement strategies as essential components of complete performance management systems, but they appear to be the exception. Some prominent behavior analysts (e.g., Daniels, 1994) question the utility of work teams and some like Hopkins (quoted in Daniels, 1994, p. 134) are very skeptical of the trend to empower workers. Why is there such indifference, or even resistance, toward team ideas in OBM? Clearly, Daniels (1994) is worried that teams are another empty management trend in the never-ending search for a miracle cure for performance problems, and that is certainly a legitimate concern. However, I believe that there are more fundamental reasons for this stance toward teams and that these reasons are problematic for the continued development of OBM.

Applied Behavior Analysis and OBM

The fact that OBM developed, in large part, from earlier work in applied behavior analysis means that OBM adopted some of the approach toward its subject matter from the kind of approach typical of applied behavior analysis. Applied behavior analysis got its start working with dependent, low-thinking clients, typically mentally retarded individuals or children. The therapist assumed the role of the dispenser of reinforcement, increasing those behaviors deemed appropriate by a parent or a teacher or an administrator, and decreasing those behaviors deemed inappropriate. It was not commonplace to ascertain what the client wanted to do, nor was that possible in many cases. Given the dependent client population, it is not surprising that applied behavior analysis adopted this rather paternalistic (therapist-knows-best), low-involvement intervention model.

Although many desirable features of applied behavior analysis (such as pin-pointing and an emphasis on measurement) were transferred to OBM, some undesirable features also became part of that legacy. OBM adopted a strikingly similar model of intervention even though the employee populations were of normal intelligence and quite capable of acting independently. In OBM, it is the consultant and management that most often determine what the required behaviors are to reach certain goals, and OBM consultants teach supervisors and other first-line managers to dispense reinforcement for the desired behaviors. It appears that little consideration goes into soliciting employee input about operational goals, or ways to achieve them. In OBM texts such as Daniels (1989), employee input seems mainly limited to identification of desired consequences for use in reinforcement systems controlled by management. There is practically nothing in OBM models regarding ways to empower employees or of making jobs more intrinsically interesting. So, most OBM models simply suggest ways to make managers more effective in managing the behavior of those under them rather than re-thinking the role of employees and the role of management. Thus, conventional OBM models preserve and even amplify paternalistic, management-knows-best management roles.

Given this intervention model in OBM, it is not surprising that work team concepts (or other radical departures from traditional hierarchical management systems) did not spring forth from OBM theorists or practitioners. This suggests that our models may be stifling some variations and innovations that may be effective as well as attractive to the business community. However, from listening to convention presentations it is apparent that practitioners of OBM find themselves consulting more often in team-based environments these days, or in other management systems that encourage employee involvement. Because these consultants appear to be reasonably successful in operating there, it may be more the case that our ways of talking about OBM are traditional and paternalistic rather than the actual practices of consultants. Therefore, we need more discussion of our models and their theoretical components to keep them from lagging too far behind useful practices in the field. I will discuss some concepts that may be useful in understanding SMWT environments, so that team environments are appreciated for their particular features, yet understandable in behavioral terms.

Self-Managed Work Teams

What are SMWTs?

There are many types of groups variously called "teams" and within types there are degrees of those teams. For example, steering teams are often formed to decide policy issues or project implementation, but they may be little more than a temporary committee. Self-managed work teams are a particular form of work team. SMWTs are typically permanent groups responsible for performing and managing technical tasks that result in some product or service deliverable to an internal or external customer (Yeatts & Hyten, 1998). A high degree of interdependence characterizes the work of team members, and the team is typically held accountable as a group for their performance.

As the self-managed prefix indicates, SMWTs also manage themselves at least to some extent. This means that they may be responsible for such things as monitoring their own performance, troubleshooting, scheduling work, hiring team members, securing resources, identifying training needs, communicating with customers, and improving their performance. Particular leadership responsibilities, such as team leader or person in charge of scheduling or safety (sometimes called starpoints reflecting a non-hierarchical position of special responsibility), are usually rotated so that all team members develop multiple leadership skills. Of course, there are still management personnel that oversee a number of teams and fulfill a number of responsibilities such as communicating management expectations to the teams, monitoring team development, and assisting the team when it needs some resource that requires management approval.

Why SMWTs?

Work teams have become widespread in American business in the 1990s as global competition has forced management of many corporations to look for ways to reduce costs and increase performance and flexibility (Mohrman, Cohen, & Mohrman, 1995; Orsburn, Moran, Musselwhite, & Zenger, 1990; Yeatts, Hipskind, & Barnes, 1994). SMWTs can reduce management overhead costs because the positions of supervisors are typically eliminated or reduced in number while changed in function. Some supervisors are re-assigned as regular team members, while others are selected as coaches or as managers overseeing many teams. This is part of a larger trend in the business sector toward leaner, flatter organizations with fewer management layers. Organizations also hope that teams will give them a more flexible workforce, one that is able to adapt quickly to changing work demands or customer needs. They also are attracted to teams by the potential for improved performance brought about by better work processes discovered by teams, more collaboration rather than competition within the organization, better decision-making by employees, and a more involved workforce.

Of course, whether these extolled benefits really do occur in actual practice is difficult to ascertain because so many variables affect team development and team performance. This means that the effectiveness of teams can be obscured by poor management support, poor access to needed training, and a host of other problems that can sabotage any large-scale intervention. Those pro and con teams can each find studies supporting their arguments that teams are or are not effective, though the weight of studies clearly favors teams (for a review see Guzzo & Dickson, 1996). What is clear is that teams are a reality in many organizations, and thus OBM practitioners should be comfortable with teams and should be able to help them improve performance. Furthermore, SMWTs are actually very interesting to study because they are so behaviorally complex and present so many challenges to successful implementation and maintenance.

The Complexity of Teams

Teams require a special set of behaviors in order to function well. Those behaviors include all of those things necessary for working together as a group: communicating well, getting along with team members, participating in team meetings and so on. For many employees, these are new behaviors and thus some training, coaching, feedback and reinforcement are necessary. Besides the social skills essential for teaming, what makes teams complex are the multitude of factors that affect team performance. These include such things as the team design, work processes used by the team, customer requirements, individual charactcristics of the team members, and the large set of factors included in the organizational environment. Yeatts and Hyten (1998) describe a model that includes these many factors and discusses them in more detail than can be provided here. For the purposes of this chapter, my interests focus on those components within the organizational environment that make up the motivation system for SMWTs.

The Motivation System for Teams

The motivation system consists of these elements:

- Formal Reward Programs- Most large organizations have some form of recognition programs in place, and some have compensation systems that have reward mechanisms.

- Formal Punishment Policies- Including contingencies for disciplinary actions and termination.

- Informal Consequences by Management- This includes management's reactions to ideas generated by the team as well as reactions to team performance.

- Informal Peer Consequences- Daily reactions to peer behavior and job performance.

- Reinforcement Systems Outside Work- They may interact with reinforcement systems at work to affect work motivation.

- Automatic Consequences of Work- Including automatic reinforcers and punishers built into or established as part of the natural work flow.

- Establishing Operations- Those events that modulate the functions for the various consequences above.

The elements of the motivation system are the same in work team environments and in traditionally managed environments, but the relative strength of the elements can be different in work team environments. If what I have described as the motivation system truly operates as a system, changes in the relative strength or operation of one element can change other elements. This means that the functioning of the motivation system might be quite different in work team environments than in traditionally managed environments. Before proceeding to a more specific analysis of how motivation might be different in work team environments I wish to first clarify how I am using the concepts automatic reinforcement and establishing operations.

The concept of automatic reinforcement (and automatic punishment) is used here to mean that aspects of working on or completing a job contribute to the strengthening or weakening of the behavior involved. Examples might include instances where successfully machining a defect-free part is an event that strengthens the behavior of operating the machine, or where participating in a productive team meeting increases the likelihood of attending and contributing to future team meetings. Some of these things are often subsumed under the heading of "pride of workmanship" but that seems to make it a static property of an individual's personality rather than a dynamic function of certain behavioral outcomes.

Automatic reinforcement is an important concept but one that has been poorly articulated in behavior analysis (Vaughan & Michael, 1982). It may or may not be isomorphic with the popular conception of "intrinsic rewards" depending on the definition of that term; however, I believe that there is substantial overlap between the phenomena to which these two concepts refer. Based on Skinner's many uses of the term, Vaughan and Michael (1982) defined automatic reinforcement as simply a natural result of behavior that strengthens that behavior without the deliberate mediation of another person. They argued, as have others (e.g., Donahoe & Palmer, 1994; Sundberg, Michael, Partington, & Sundberg, 1996) that it is an essential concept for understanding and interpreting complex behavior. Recently, it has also been used extensively in interpretations of functional analyses of problematic behavior such as self-injury (e.g., Iwata et al., 1994; Thompson, Fisher, Piazza, & Kuhn, 1998).

Vaughan and Michael's definition has one problem: its use of the phrase "without the deliberate mediation of another person" seems to exclude all forms of social mediation from participating in automatic reinforcement. I believe it is proper to identify automatic reinforcement as something not delivered deliberately by another person, but what about the establishing operation? Are not the automatic reinforcing functions of many things established by other people? Surely, most of the automatic consequences provided by work have functions that were socially established, so there is an important kind of social mediation involved. For definitional purposes here, I will describe automatic reinforcement in the following manner: automatic reinforcement (with the exception of things producing pleasurable or painful physiological stimulation) by work-related events is socially established (by the culture in general or by what people in that work environment say or do). It is a dynamic function that can be increased or decreased. It can be a very durable function: some things that we learned to love to do in our youth (e.g., reading, solo sports) we continue to do for the rest of our lives. Little is known about the variables affecting the durability of automatic reinforcement, but I suspect that it may require other events (such as recognition) as "booster shots" to be sustained over very long time periods.

My definition of establishing operations (EO) is broader than that of Michael (1982; 1993), who articulated the modern form of this concept that has come to be accepted by most behavior analysts (Chase & Hyten, 1985). Michael (1982) defined an EO as an event that a) momentarily alters the effectiveness of a consequent stimulus as a reinforcer or punisher, b) evokes or inhibits behavior that has been consequated by those events in the past.

The major problem I have with this concept as stated by Michael is that it limits EOs to events that momentarily, that is temporarily, affect consequence functions. I believe that many important things have relatively enduring effects on consequence functions, and that these should be recognized as EOs. In fact, many real-world examples discussed as EOs in conformity with Michael's definition appear, upon close inspection, to be instances of things with long-lasting or even permanent effects on functions. Recently, Agnew (1998) discussed the utility of Michael's EO concept to OBM; however, most of her examples of EOs are things that may have longer time spans of effect on consequence functions. For example, she discussed the use of sports heroes to endorse sports shoes in TV commercials as increasing the value of the advertised shoes. That effect may endure for years beyond the original exposure to the advertising. The same is true for the interpretation of performance goals as EOs that she discussed. A goal may establish or enhance the reinforcing effectiveness of praise or feedback for months or even years. So, the expanded definition of EO I am using in this paper includes events that have any timeframe of action, from momentary to permanent, on the functions of consequences. Expanding the timeframe of action has major ramifications for the EO concept, but discussing them would take us far afield. I will leave that discussion for another venue.

SMWTs and Motivation

Most components of typical SMWT implementations are antecedents, as are most organizational changes. Behavior analysts often discount the effects of antecedents as if all antecedents were simply discriminative stimuli (S^Ds), such as prompts or cues. These things, when thought of as S^Ds, rely on consequences for their sustained effectiveness and therefore consequences are emphasized as being relatively more important for changing behavior. However, though the things I will discuss are antecedents in the sense that they are elements of the kickoff or rollout of teams, they are not simply S^Ds. They may have other antecedent effects, from enabling new team behaviors to motivating behaviors as EOs.

Empowerment

Empowerment is a defining feature of self-management. Teams are allowed to have more control over their work; at a minimum that includes greater authority for a certain scope of decision-making along with the enhanced responsibility that necessarily entails. Empowerment tactics usually make explicit at team startup the scope of this empowerment together with a prompt to engage in such behaviors. The scope of empowerment (just what teams can do and not do on their own) varies considerably from organization to organization, and it changes within an organization as teams develop and are granted more autonomy. For a successful implementation, it is necessary to establish supporting elements such as management awareness/acceptance of such a new practice on the part of teams. Thus, empowerment tactics enable and encourage teams to behave in a more autonomous fashion.

This greater authority means that team members often have more input, control, and intellectual challenge in their job than they would have under a traditionally managed system. What is the effect of this empowerment on the motivation of team members? Empowerment may often act as an EO in creating or enhancing the effectiveness of automatic reinforcers derived from the work itself. As one manufacturing team member told me, "Before we had teams, I used to start working at the whistle and shut my brain off, but now I have to do a lot more thinking." Most of the dozens of team members I have interviewed reported that the empowerment they were granted made their jobs more challenging and desirable. In fact, teams are often so excited by the prospect of empowerment that it has to be granted in stages, lest they get drunk with their own power and let their inexperience with decision-making get them in trouble.

The notion that empowerment can make work more reinforcing is hardly new. Such ideas were a component of several schools of organizational thought, including the human relations movement, the participative management movement, and sociotechnical systems theories that contributed ideas later incorporated in SMWTs (Hackman & Oldham, 1976; 1980; Katzell & Thompson, 1990; Lawler, 1986; 1992; Manz & Sims, 1987; 1989; see Yeatts & Hyten, 1998 for a review). If empowerment can boost the automatic reinforcing properties of work, it is unfortunate that it has received so little attention in OBM. Surely it would be desirable if workers can become more motivated to work effectively without relying on the addition of more artificial, high-management-overhead, and sources of reinforcement. This is not to say that empowerment strategies have no costs associated with them, for they certainly do. At the very least, empowerment should be a strategy worth considering in any performance improvement effort.

Increased Business Knowledge

SMWT implementations often include an education component that focuses on increasing team member understanding of the organization's business (e.g., how we stay competitive enough to bid for contracts) and even of the entire industry (e.g., what the economic forecast is for defense-related industries in the next 5 years). Such education is necessary for several reasons. Team performance is often measured by new metrics integrated with higher levels in the organization, such as matrixes or scorecards that include elements critical to the success of the team as well as the entire organization. An example of one of those metrics might be labor costs. Team members have to understand the importance of things like labor costs so they can see why they need to be kept in check and to search for ways to reduce them. Without such an understanding, a comprehensive measurement system might appear to be confusing and valueless. An improved understanding of the business is also essential in order to understand group compensation system like gainsharing (see Belcher, 1991) that return some of the money saved by performance improvements to individuals. Without such an understanding, gainsharing pay may seem like an entitlement or something dispensed at management's whim. If this were to happen, any motivational possibilities of the gainsharing pay would be lost.

For many team members, especially those making the transition from more traditionally managed work environments, learning about the business as a whole may be the first time they see the "big picture" of how their job affects the entire company. Rather than viewing their job narrowly as what they have to do to get through each day, team members may now see how important their performance is to everyone downstream of them and to the success of the organization. With the value of their work more apparent to them, the properties of work associated with success may acquire automatic reinforcing functions or existing functions may be enhanced. To the extent this is true, we may say that the education about the business functioned as an EO for the automatic reinforcing properties of work itself. This may not be the only EO effect of such education. The effectiveness of performance feedback, in the form of measurement data or comments from team members or management, may also be strengthened as reinforcers for successful working. Thus, a training component, often thought of as a simple antecedent, may have complex motivating functions that include several EOs.

Increased Customer Contact

Another common component of SMWT implementations is more frequent and direct contact with customers. This may include external customers as well as "internal customers" of the team, such as downstream teams or other recipients of the team's products or services within the organization. Increased customer contact is consistent with the idea of SMWTs because it means the team accepts the responsibility of interacting with its customers instead of that contact being handled by management. This is an added burden to the team but it should lead to better service because customer communications are not being delayed or filtered by layers of management above the level of the team. For example, a production team might contact the team leader of a downstream team to coordinate the production schedule of a special order to prevent an unexpected bottlenecking problem that might occur with increased production. I have spoken with teams that had direct phone contacts with external customers, sometimes even site visits, to discuss problems that customer had with a product of the team. This enabled the team to figure out the cause of these problems and solve it without substantial involvement of management.

Because the team has increased contact with its customers, team members can better see how their performance affects particular people- people with names and faces. This close connection with a distinctly non-anonymous customer can increase the value of doing good work to the team members. If they do a shoddy job, team members may hear about it from someone they know to some extent. Thus, increased customer contact can also be an EO boosting the automatic reinforcing function of good work. I have seen service teams that had close contact with external customers go out of their way (e.g., put in extra hours) to fulfill a customer request in a timely fashion because team members knew how important the service was to the particular customer.

Training in Team Interpersonal Skills

Successful teaming requires fairly sophisticated interpersonal skills to be able to handle team meetings with their problem-solving activities, new leadership responsibilities, the inevitable interpersonal conflicts, and the need to provide regular feedback to peers. For this reason, most team implementations require team members to participate in various forms of training to provide or enhance those interpersonal skills. If the training is effective, team members will acquire skills that enable them to minimize or get past a lot of the interpersonal difficulties common in workplaces of all kinds, but especially problematic in team environments.

This reduction in the aversive interpersonal aspects of the work environment directly affects the Informal Peer Consequences element of the motivation system. It means that such training can have an EO effect in that the aversive or positive functions of peer comments are modulated following training. For example, the normal aversive functions of criticism may be neutralized if the person criticizing does so skillfully and the recipient has been taught to accept such criticism. Such effects of interpersonal skills training on the social environment of the team workplace can result indirectly in boosting the automatic reinforcing functions of work. The automatic reinforcing functions are enhanced simply by virtue of diminishing some of the "demotivators" (Spitzer, 1995) that can override these functions in other circumstances. I have heard team members report that training in listening and conflict resolution even generalized to dealing with their family members more effectively, so there appears to be little doubt that there are effective kinds of training being used currently.

Interestingly, the EO concept may suggest a useful result of what otherwise would seem to be training activities of rather questionable value to the workplace. For example, it has been common for teams in many organizations to be exposed to "experiential training" activities like ropes courses (group activities involving physical challenges like climbing across elevated ropes). I certainly was skeptical of such activities designed to "build trust" or enhance "team spirit," but that was because I could not see any real skills being imparted that would generalize to job performance. Looking at it from an establishing operations viewpoint, these pleasant experiences may have useful EO effects if they alter the social functioning of team members so that, say, the value of peer opinions is enhanced following such training experiences. In this regard, these activities may share EO functions with related activities such as "icebreaking" activities often used at the beginning of workshops to make the audience members more comfortable with each other and more receptive to the workshop leader's talk.

Constraints on the Motivating Effects of SMWTs

Many of the components of SMWT implementations can boost the automatic reinforcing functions of successful work, but this effect depends on several factors:

Nature of the team environment. If the team environment enables more control over work and input about the work than previous work environments team members have experienced, then the team environment is truly a more empowered environment and we may expect that automatic reinforcement will be enhanced for many team members. It is possible that some team environments represent **less** autonomy than prior work environments, or that the positive effects of autonomy are compromised by other factors, so the effect on automatic reinforcement will be negligible or the opposite of that described above.

There is some evidence suggesting that several dimensions of team environments interact with autonomy and job motivation. Survey research of knowledge worker teams by Janz, Colquitt, and Noe (1997) found that the positive correlation between elements of autonomy and self-reported job motivation could be reduced somewhat when there are high degrees of interdependence in the team's task. This is presumably because the high task interdependence required more complicated planning and coordination, which took away some of the fun of having the greater autonomy over task planning or decision-making. Janz et al. (1997) also showed that the stage of team development interacts with job motivation and effective team processes. Although one must be cautious in mapping the findings of self-report studies to a behavioral framework, this study suggests that some team environment configurations can moderate the motivational effects normally enhanced by teaming.

Team member preferences. Do team members like or dislike the components that make up the team environment? Not everyone enjoys more responsibility in their work. I have had some team members tell me that they missed the old days when they could go complain about a co-worker to their supervisor, for example. In one discussion with team members on the third shift in a manufacturing plant, these late-nighters indicated that they didn't like the hassle involved in teaming and would rather just be left alone to run their machines. Some teams handled transitions from a traditionally-managed organization by placing the former supervisor on the team as a "regular" team member. The former supervisor saw this as a demotion and was none too thrilled at the whole new team environment. In other cases, the transition to teams was accompanied by a general status leveling between teams and lower levels of management. Some managers didn't like these changes and left the company.

Non-automatic consequences for new team behaviors. In particular, it is critical that the managers who interact with the team reinforce new team behaviors. That is, when managers approve of team ideas, or approve requested resources, the teaming behaviors are likely to be strengthened. This will also have an effect on the automatic reinforcement provided by working in the team environment. I have seen teams whose excitement and innovations were quashed by unsupportive middle management. These teams were full of demoralized people who no longer felt that teaming was worth the effort. Empowerment can quickly lose its luster if accepting more control over your work ultimately leads to management rejection of your ideas. I am suggesting that socially-mediated consequences can interact with automatic consequences, indeed even override them under certain circumstances. This is only one kind of interaction between different consequences in the motivation system. In the next section I will discuss consequence interactions more broadly.

Motivation System Interactions

There are interesting kinds of interactions possible between elements of the motivation system. Let us examine a rather common scenario. Company X has a traditional, hierarchically managed structure. There is little employee empowerment and the work is inherently tedious, but there is some bonus compensation available to employees for achieving goals. In this work environment, parts of the motivation system are in conflict. The work itself possesses automatic consequences that are aversive, but the bonus pay (or other formal rewards) has behavior-strengthening functions acting in the opposite direction. This is a common, though hardly pleasant, motivational environment. The function of the formal rewards is to add to the benefits side (along with salary or wages) of a very close cost/benefit ratio just enough to keep the employee there and working. People in this situation continuously feel the urge to escape because of the aversive nature of their job, but that is overridden (if only just) by the salary and formal reward structure.

If the level of automatic reinforcement from the work itself were high, we would have a very different scenario. In that case, more parts of the motivation system would be aligned. If this were to happen, another question would be raised. Would the effects of other (non-automatic) reinforcers such as recognition or bonus money be **amplified** because they are now working in the same direction as the automatic consequences, or would they be **reduced** because they are less necessary? There is yet a third interaction possibility. There may be no effects on some other reinforcers because they stand in an independent relation to automatic consequences. This could occur because different consequences affect different behaviors (e.g., working hard, staying with the company, making good work decisions, getting along with peers), and these behavior-consequence units may be functionally separate. These three interaction possibilities are consistent with the types of reinforcer interactions described in the field of behavioral economics.

Behavioral Economic Interactions

Behavioral economics classifies interactions between reinforcers on a continuum (Green & Freed, 1993; Hursh, 1984). Because certain economic factors can

modulate the effectiveness of a consequence as a reinforcer, these valued consequences are usually referred to more generically as commodities. Furthermore, the
focus in behavioral economic analyses is more on consumption of those commodities rather than on response rate changes, the usual metric of reinforcement
effectiveness. However, response output of some form is required to consume the
reinforcing commodity, so there is a relationship between consumption and
reinforcing effectiveness. At one end point of the continuum is perfect *substitutability*. If two commodities are substitutable, as consumption of one commodity
increases, consumption of the other decreases. For example, I might read fewer
experimental journal articles from journal A if I have been reading more experimental articles from journal B. At the midpoint on the continuum there is *independence*,
or no interactive effects of consumption of one commodity on the other. At the
other endpoint is perfect *complementarity*. A complementary relation holds between
two commodities when increased consumption of one commodity causes increased
consumption of the other (or a tandem decrease). Think of the relation between
consumption of pizza and your favorite beverage.

According to a behavioral economic analysis, if formal recognition and money
are complementary with the kind of automatic reinforcement occurring in SMWTs,
then the effects of recognition and money will be amplified when the level of
automatic reinforcement is high. If they are independent, there will be no interaction
between levels of automatic reinforcement and other reinforcers. If other reinforcers
are substitutable for automatic reinforcers, then the higher the level of automatic
reinforcement, the less effective those other reinforcers will be.

Behavioral economics describes these interaction possibilities well, and provides quantitative methods to analyze such interactions, but there is no a priori
method to determine the nature of the interaction between reinforcers without
examining their effects under certain changing circumstances. For any given
organizational environment, reinforcer interactions may fall anywhere on the
continuum. Relations like substitutability are not properties of the reinforcer, they
are properties of the interaction between reinforcers. Furthermore, Green and Freed
(1993) point out that substitutability and complementarity are likely contextually
determined, meaning that other environmental factors may modulate reinforcer
interactions, perhaps even on a momentary basis. This suggests that economic
interactions between elements of the motivation system in an organization may be
quite dynamic.

A common finding in behavioral economic analyses is that reinforcing effectiveness, as expressed by the demand for the reinforcer, changes as a function of
variables that make up the price of that reinforcer (see, e.g., Tustin, 1994).
Interestingly, behavioral economics predicts that response requirements (construed
here as an element of price) required to obtain a given reinforcer will modulate its
reinforcing effectiveness, and therefore modulate the effectiveness of reinforcers
with which the given reinforcer interacts. For example, if the response requirement
for a team bonus increased (as when performance goals increase) the effectiveness

of the bonus might decrease; and if automatic reinforcers from the work itself were complementary, then their effectiveness would also diminish. Under these circumstances, the effectiveness of any substitutable reinforcer would increase. If those substitutable reinforcers were derived from goofing off or nonproductive socializing with peers, we would have a full-blown motivational problem on our hands. Because of these effects, price changes qualify as complex forms of establishing operations: they modulate the reinforcing effectiveness of several different interacting consequences.

Issues of reinforcer interaction in OBM (and much of applied behavior analysis) are usually dealt with by reference to the phenomena described by the "matching law" (Davison & McCarthy, 1988; Herrnstein, 1961; Mawhinney & Gowen, 1991; McDowell, 1988; Redmon & Lockwood, 1987). The matching law describes a pattern of choice in which the organism allocates behavior (or time) toward a particular choice (activity) in proportion to the relative amount of reinforcement obtained from that activity. One of the most touted effects of matching is that if one alternative choice provides increasing levels of reinforcement relative to that available from other alternatives, increasingly more behavior will be allocated toward it and less to the other alternatives. However, this relationship can only hold when the sources of reinforcement available from the alternatives are substitutable (as when they are qualitatively similar). The matching relationship does not hold when the reinforcers are independent. When the reinforcers are complementary, increasing reinforcement from one source will cause more behavior to be allocated to both alternatives! Although there are added parameters in some versions of the matching law that can cope with qualitatively different reinforcers (see McDowell, 1989), the most well-known effects predicted by the matching law are limited to situations involving choice between substitutable reinforcers.

Because organizational environments contain such qualitatively diverse consequences, perhaps behavioral economics can provide a more comprehensive framework for understanding behavior allocation and reinforcer effectiveness in these settings. Of course, the same caveats apply to behavioral economics that were suggested by Poling and Foster (1993) in examining the matching law as a useful conceptual framework for organizational analyses. In particular, matching analyses and behavioral economic analyses largely stem from research involving direct-acting contingencies of reinforcement, and little is known about how they pertain to the kinds of contingencies involving rule-governed behavior that are prevalent in organizational environments. Behavioral economic analyses have been extended to deal with complex human behavior problems such as drug abuse (Green & Bickel, 1996), which surely involve the rule-governed behavior of adults, so there is at least some indication that behavioral economics may be a broadly useful approach.

Based on the analysis outlined above, it may be useful to think of the motivation system in an organization as consisting of *contingency networks*. These networks are comprised of multiple four-term (EO, other evocative antecedents, behavior, consequences) contingencies that have interacting consequences. The nature of the consequence interactions is surely complex and dynamic, and it is probably affected by a multitude of factors including such things as the structure of the contingencies themselves, organizational changes, and even the stage of team development. Conceiving of the motivation system as a contingency network should prevent anyone from thinking that elements of the motivation system are simply parallel channels, each having its own linear, additive effect on work-related behavior (as suggested by common usages of balance of consequence types of ABC analyses). Instead, the many performance contingencies operating in an organization may influence each other as well as the behavior directly involved in each of them.

Extrinsic (Non-automatic) Rewards

If automatic reinforcement is enhanced in SMWTs, is there still a need for the consequences provided by other sources such as formal reward programs or by informal interactions with peers or managers? There are multiple reasons for retaining additional sources of reinforcement in team environments. If the individual behavior of team members were dominated by automatic reinforcement, you would have a group of employees who would show some of the properties of autism. They would have no need to care what their peers thought, and they would not have any vision beyond their job. These are hardly the ideal features of a team member! While amplifying automatic reinforcement supplied by work is a good idea, other sources of reinforcement are needed for balance and proper direction. Team-based organizations need a mix of extrinsic consequences targeted at rewarding accomplishments and reinforcing behaviors at three different levels:

· Individual Performer Level- Individuals can sometimes feel that their efforts are obscured by the team, so they need for their contributions to be recognized and rewarded somehow. In my observations of teams, this was most often handled by the team itself, usually through recognition, but sometimes through differential splits of team bonus money.

· Team Level- Rewards should be available for the accomplishments of the team, in order to reinforce team-related behaviors such as effective decision-making and collaboration. Retaining only individual reward programs after the transition to teams may encourage and reinforce individual efforts that are detrimental to effective team functioning.

· Suprateam Level- Teams must act in ways that help, not hurt, the performance of other teams in the organization. Many organizations find that they need to have reward programs focused on the accomplishments of multiple teams, departments, or even the whole plant, in order to promote interteam cooperation. Typical examples include gainsharing programs.

Extrinsic rewards are also valuable in team environments because they have multiple functions. Such rewards can have important informational and social functions that are sometimes ignored in OBM analyses. Management-delivered rewards can support communications about what is valued in the organization. Rewards for team accomplishments are necessary to indicate how serious management is about team goals and the entire team process. This is especially important in situations in which team members are skeptical of management's sincerity regarding empowerment and self-management. Extrinsic rewards can also strengthen the social bonds between management and team members or between peers in a peer-mediated reward program. It should be no surprise that people are more inclined to like people who deliver rewards to them, and this may translate into other behaviors such as attending to, agreeing with, and supporting the actions of the other person.

OBM analyses have traditionally focused on the performance-strengthening functions of extrinsic rewards. However, in recent years the analysis of these functions has expanded beyond simple reinforcement effects usually described in introductory texts. Malott (1989; 1992) contrasted direct-acting and indirect-acting contingencies. Direct-acting contingencies affect behavior through the direct influence of an immediate consequence. Indirect-acting contingencies involve consequences too delayed to directly affect the behaviors that produce them, and therefore require a rule (stated to the person or self-formulated) describing the relation between behavior and delayed consequence to be effective. According to this formulation, most contingencies in organizations are indirect-acting. All monetary compensation programs such as performance pay or gainsharing fit this description, as do most formal recognition programs.

Extrinsic rewards are crucial elements of indirect-acting contingencies. Malott's analysis of indirect-acting contingencies states that rules function as establishing operations for more immediate reinforcers, some of which are automatic in nature, that actually provide the mechanism maintaining all of the behaviors involved in producing the long-term consequence. For example, in taking a college course, the final grade is too remote to directly reinforce studying behavior during the semester; instead, a rule describing the relation between studying and doing well on quizzes on the ultimate final grade alters the reinforcing value of mastering material in the short term. As long as the delayed consequences eventually occur, the EO effect of rules describing them will be maintained. If the predicted or promised delayed reward does not occur, the rules will be inaccurate and will lose their ability to establish the reinforcing effectiveness of doing a good job. The whole indirect-acting contingency would then collapse, and the performance strengthening function would be lost. Thus, extrinsic rewards are critical to the durability of EOs created by rules describing the contingency.

It is also possible that extrinsic rewards can function directly as establishing operations enhancing the automatic reinforcers of work without the mediation of rules. Recognition from management or a peer for quality work may boost the automatic reinforcing properties of high-quality workmanship on a day-to-day basis. This may be a simple direct effect, or it may be an instance of the same processes involved in indirect-acting contingencies, but with the reward as the starting point rather than some antecedent such as a goal statement serving to initiate the process. In either case, extrinsic rewards are affecting work-related automatic reinforcement.

Additional Parameters of Reinforcement

The parameters that modulate the effectiveness of a reinforcement contingency are usually identified as immediacy of consequence delivery, value/size of the consequence, and the probability of the occurrence of the consequence. Those parameters have proven to be important for many kinds of reinforcers across many situations and species. However, because so little is known about automatic reinforcement or about consequences participating in indirect-acting contingencies, it is worth discussing whether there might be additional parameters affecting these contingencies.

Establishing Operations and Automatic Reinforcement

In the case of automatic reinforcement, immediacy and probability are essentially "built in" to the contingency. As a writer, when I write what I think is a terrific sentence, the effect is relatively immediate and certain. The remaining parameter of value remains more of a variable element, and that points to the importance of establishing operations. It appears that the EO that creates the reinforcing value of good work is the most critical parameter for automatic reinforcement. Earlier, I described several elements of SMWT implementations that may well serve as EOs to enhance the reinforcing value of work, but there are probably countless events that could also serve this function. Different events may have their own characteristics as an EO. For example, some EO effects may be short-lived whereas others may be longer lasting. Some EO effects may produce large changes in reinforcing value whereas others may only increment or decrement reinforcing value slightly. Agnew (1998) has argued for increased use of the EO concept in OBM and I concur with her recommendations. Further study of establishing operations in their many forms would contribute much to our science and to our applied technology.

Understandable Indirect-Acting Contingencies

Historically, most behavior analysts downplayed the role of understanding the contingency (in the sense of being able to describe it) in modulating the effectiveness of the contingency because the contingencies being discussed were implicitly thought to be operating in a direct-acting fashion. In the case of nonhuman subjects this was undoubtedly true. However, an indirect-acting contingency cannot function to strengthen behavior unless the person involved can follow the rule describing the necessary behaviors and the delayed outcome. Thus, how well a contingency is understood becomes a critical parameter of indirect-acting contingencies.

In some team settings I studied, multiple bonus contingencies were in effect for team performance, only a fraction of which were understood. Team members were not clear what they had to do or how much they would get for a given level of accomplishment. Clearly specified performance requirements and consequence magnitudes would seem to be essential for the desired motivational effects of such contingencies. Otherwise, important consequences like bonus money will appear to be dispensed in an arbitrary fashion. As Yeatts and Hyten (1998) pointed out, in such circumstances employees often suspect favoritism on the part of management and hostility may be the end result instead of greater work motivation.

Line of Sight in Indirect-Acting Contingencies

For an indirect-acting contingency to be effective, the person involved must not only understand the contingency, but must also believe their efforts will have a significant impact on the outcomes tied to the delayed reward. This perception of controllability is referred to as *line of sight*. In groups such as SMWTs, many other people's efforts (or lack thereof) can dilute the impact of any individual's efforts. Thus, the larger the team the less control any one individual has on the team's aggregate performance. In suprateam contingencies, such as gainsharing, the aggregate performance of many teams may be tied to bonus money paid to individuals derived from cost savings across the large group. Line of sight will become worse the larger that group. Therefore, the size of a team or any group participating in a group contingency will be one of the many factors determining the effectiveness of that group contingency (Zenger & Marshall, 1995).

Organizational stability may affect the two parameters of contingency understandability and line of sight. In a stable organizational environment, one in which the day-to-day work changes little for example, it may be easy to determine the causal relation between your work accomplishments and important delayed consequences. The greater the rate of changes in the work environment (in terms of people, products, processes, policy changes and the like) the more "noise" there is between behavior and delayed outcomes. In such circumstances it would be harder for people to understand how an indirect-acting contingency works and to see how they can control the outcomes. This suggests that team-based organizations with highly dynamic environments must take steps to ensure that team members continue to understand the operations of any indirect-acting contingencies for them to remain effective over long periods of time.

Conclusions

Work teams of all kinds are interesting variants from traditional, hierarchically managed organizational environments. Although many forms of self-managed or self-directed work teams have become popular in the last decade, it will take many more years of assessment before we know whether they can be successful variants over the long haul. In the meantime, those in OBM should be comfortable analyzing or operating in team-based environments. The fact that team ideas originated in a different theoretical tradition does not mean they cannot be understood in a behavioral framework. Terms like empowerment are not standard behavioral jargon, but if you examine how such tactics are implemented and how people behave in these systems they will make "behavioral sense." Behavioral theories should be able to describe what is going on in those situations and do so in such a way that useful predictions or ideas are generated.

I have attempted in this chapter to make behavioral sense out of SMWTs. I have suggested that many features of typical SMWT implementations affect the automatic reinforcing properties of work itself. Such effects may influence other elements in what can be called the motivation system. The motivation system has a complicated structure- contingency networks- with complex interactions between the elements and multiple effects on behavior. My analysis of motivation systems could probably apply to many organizational environments as it is just the application of a behavioral systems theory to motivation. I have used several key behavioral concepts in this analysis: automatic reinforcement, establishing operations, indirect-acting contingencies, and behavioral economics for the study of reinforcer interactions. These concepts have been used rarely in OBM analyses to date, but I believe they are essential for a more sophisticated understanding of work teams in particular and motivation in general.

References

Agnew, J. L. (1998). The establishing operation in organizational behavior management. *Journal of Organizational Behavior Management, 18(1),* 7-19.

Belcher, J. G. (1991). *Gainsharing.* Houston: Gulf.

Boyett, J. H., & Conn, H. P. (1995). Maximum performance management: How to manage and compensate people to meet world competition. Lakewood, CO: Glenbridge.

Chase, P. N., & Hyten, C. (1985). A historical and pedagogical note on establishing operations. *The Behavior Analyst, 8,* 121-122.

Daniels, A. C. (1989). *Performance management: Improving quality and productivity through positive reinforcement.* Tucker, GA: Performance Management.

Daniels, A. C. (1994). *Bringing out the best in people: How to apply the astonishing power of positive reinforcement.* New York: McGraw-Hill.

Davison, M., & McCarthy, D. (1988). The matching law: A research review. Hillsdale, NJ: Lawrence Erlbaum.

Donahoe, J. W., & Palmer, D. C. (1994). *Learning and complex behavior.* Boston: Allyn and Bacon.

Green, L., & Bickel, W. (1996). *Advances in behavioral economics, Vol. 3: Substance use and abuse.* Greenwich, CT: Ablex.

Green, L., & Freed, D. E. (1993). The substitutability of reinforcers. *Journal of the Experimental Analysis of Behavior, 60,* 141-158.

Guzzo, R. A., & Dickson, M. W. (1996). Teams in organizations: Recent research on performance and effectiveness. *Annual Review of Psychology, 47,* 307-338.

Hackman, J. R., & Oldham, G. R. (1976). Motivation through the design of work: Test of a theory. *Organizational Behavior and Human Performance, 16,* 250-279.

Hackman, J. R., & Oldham, G. R. (1980). *Work redesign.* Reading, MA: Addison-Wesley.

Herrnstein, R. J. (1961). Relative and absolute strength of response as a function of frequency of reinforcement. *Journal of the Experimental Analysis of Behavior, 4,* 267-272.

Hursh, S. R. (1984). Behavioral economics. *Journal of the Experimental Analysis of Behavior, 42,* 435-452.

Iwata, B. A., Pace, G. M., Dorsey, M. F., Zarcone, J. R., Vollmer, T. R., Smith, R. G., Rodgers, T. A., Lerman, D. C., Shore, B. A., Mazaleski, J. L., Goh, H.-L., Cowdery, G. E., Kalsher, M. J., McCosh, K. C., & Willis, K. D. (1994). The functions of self-injurious behavior: An experimental-epidemiological analysis. *Journal of Applied Behavior Analysis, 27,* 215-240.

Janz, B. D., Colquitt, J. A., & Noe, R. A. (1997). Knowledge worker team effectiveness: The role of autonomy, interdependence, team development, and contextual support variables. *Personnel Psychology, 50(4),* 877-904.

Katzell, R. A., & Thompson, D. E. (1990). Work motivation: Theory and practice. *American Psychologist, 45(2),* 144-153.

Lawler, E. E., (1986). High-involvement management. San Francisco: Jossey-Bass.

Lawler, E. E., (1992). *The ultimate advantage: Creating the high involvement organization.* San Francisco: Jossey-Bass.

Malott, R. W. (1989). The achievement of evasive goals: Control by rules describing indirect-acting contingencies. In S. C. Hayes (Ed.), *Rule-governed behavior: Cognition, contingencies, and instructional control* (pp. 269-322). New York: Plenum.

Malott, R. W. (1992). A theory of rule-governed behavior and organizational behavior management. *Journal of Organizational Behavior Management, 12,* 45-65.

Manz, C. C., & Sims, H. P. (1987). Leading workers to lead themselves: The external leadership of self-managing work teams. *Administrative Science Quarterly, 32,* 106-128.

Manz, C. C., & Sims, H. P. (1989). *Superleadership.* New York: Prentice-Hall.

Mawhinney, T. C., & Gowen, C. R. (1991). Gainsharing and the law of effect as the matching law: A theoretical framework. *Journal of Organizational Behavior Management, 11,* 61-75.

McDowell, J. J. (1988). Matching theory in natural human environments. *The Behavior Analyst, 11,* 95-109.

McDowell, J. J. (1989). Two modern developments in matching theory. *The Behavior Analyst, 12,* 153-166.

Michael, J. (1982). Distinguishing between discriminative and motivational functions of stimuli. *Journal of the Experimental Analysis of Behavior, 37,* 149-155.

Michael, J. (1993). Establishing operations. *The Behavior Analyst, 16,* 191-206.

Mohrman, S. A., Cohen, S., & Mohrman, A. M., Jr. (1995). *Designing team-based organizations: New forms for knowledge work.* San Francisco: Jossey-Bass.

Orsburn, J., Moran, L., Musselwhite, E., Zenger, J. H., & Perrin, C. (1990). *Self-directed work teams: The new American challenge.* Burr Ridge, IL: Irwin.

Poling, A., & Foster, M. (1993). The matching law and organizational behavior management revisited. *Journal of Organizational Behavior Management, 14(1),* 83-97.

Redmon, W. K., & Lockwood, K. (1987). The matching law and organizational behavior. *Journal of Organizational Behavior Management, 8*, 57-72.

Spitzer, D. R. (1995). *Supermotivation*: A blueprint for energizing your organization from top to bottom. New York: Amacom.

Sundberg, M. L., Michael, J, Partington, J. W., & Sundberg, C. A. (1996). The role of automatic reinforcement in early language acquisition. *Analysis of Verbal Behavior, 13*, 21-37.

Thompson, R. H., Fisher, W. W., Piazza, C. C., & Kuhn, D. E. (1998). The evaluation and treatment of aggression maintained by attention and automatic reinforcement. *Journal of Applied Behavior Analysis, 31*, 103-116.

Tustin, D. R. Preference for reinforcers under varying schedule arrangements: A behavioral economic analysis. *Journal of Applied Behavior Analysis, 27*, 597-606.

Vaughan, M. E., & Michael, J. L. (1982). Automatic reinforcement: An important but ignored concept. *Behaviorism, 10(2)*, 217-227.

Yeatts, D. E., & Hyten, C. (1998). *High-performing self-managed work teams: A comparison of theory to practice*. Thousand Oaks, CA: Sage.

Yeatts, D. E., Hipskind, M., & Barnes, D. (1994, July/August). Lessons learned from self-managed work teams. *Business Horizons*, pp. 1-8.

Zenger, T. R., & Marshall, C. R. (1995). Group-based plans: An empirical test of the relationships among size, incentive, intensity, and performance. In *Academy of Management Journal, best papers proceedings* (pp. 161-165). New Brunswick, NJ: Academy of Management.

Discussion of Hyten

The Value of Additional Complexity and the Reality of Self-Managed Work Teams

Laurie Larwood

University of Nevada, Reno

Professor Hyten must be commended for taking on the complex and exceptionally important topic of work teams. Historically, American notions of management centered on mechanistic models in which managers were concerned only with affecting the behavior of individuals in such a manner as to enhance their performance. Little effort was spent considering the possibility that people are often members of a group with which they interact. Only recently have the concepts of "team work" and "work teams" come to be topics of immediate concern among managers, as managers have suddenly become conscious of the potential and heretofore ignored explanatory and predictive power of group processes. Despite the newly acknowledged importance of the teams, however, to this point the great bulk of accumulated research and knowledge has been gathered only about the way in which individuals function in the working environment.

Aside from historical trends, a second reason for the relatively small amount of research and thinking that has taken place concerning teams is that this work is complex. It adds new variables to the mix for consideration and is more difficult to conceptualize and test. With that acknowledged, there is little reason to take issue with the detailed examination of the topic supplied by Professor Hyten. It fits gracefully into a largely untapped category of thinking; his work is both theoretically and practically important. Unquestionably it will stimulate further critical thinking and research on issues related to work team performance.

There are, however, some reasons to question the framework on which Professor Hyten concepts of "self-managed work teams" (SMWTs) rest. By questioning them, I do not intend to undermine the thinking that Professor Hyten has provided. That work stands. Nevertheless, his work is most clearly applicable within the bounds of a system which has been idealized and simplified. Additional complexity should be added to the mix if the model is to be seen as broadly relevant for explaining day-to-day team behavior.

In particular, Professor Hyten appears to have posited certain conditions for an SMWT in order to simplify his analysis. Unfortunately, in this case organizations and work teams are seldom so ideal, and the differences distinguishing the model and the world may be of substantial importance. Professor Hyten defines an SMWT in terms of four key characteristics: 1. a permanent group, 2. responsible for performing and managing technical tasks that result in product/service to some customer, 3. interdependent and group accountable, and 4. an entity with responsibilities which are typically rotated.

Considering the first characteristics, no group is permanent, but the assumption of permanence can be interpreted to mean that the group has been stable for some time before the period considered, and that no interruptions are scheduled or seem likely to distract the group participants. With respect to the fourth characteristic, responsibilities are indeed rotated in some real SMWTs, while in others they are not. Unpredictable rotation can add complexity to the analysis Professor Hyten has made, but these effects seem likely to be temporary until the system settles into a repetitive pattern and team members have fully developed their expertise. As with permanence, any difficulty with this assumption is likely to be transitory.

In contrast, however, the assumptions dealing with interdependence, accountability and responsibility seem more problematic. These portions of the definition mirror what the members of workplace SMWTs are told in practice, but are at variance conceptually with self-management. To be blunt, any work group that is held responsible and accountable for a particular activity, product, or other result is not fully independent, and thus not completely self-managed. This is, of course, premeditated in the stipulation that SMWTs are interdependent.

What is the problem? Managers would assert that the definition is realistic and that Professor Hyten's later analysis provides an excellent service in showing how the SMWT can perform in this condition. The difficulty lies in the fact that the SMWT operates in a far more complex environment than is suggested here. Team members are subject to stimuli and contingencies originating from the intended sources, but also from a series of unintended ones. These come from other team members, from other teams, from the customers, and of course from the supervisor.

The missing piece to the model rests on two added assumptions. First, telling group members that theirs is a self-managed work team creates an inherent conflict. On the one side members are informed that they are to self-manage, while on the other they are nonetheless held responsible and accountable. Individuals in the workplace are accustomed to this conflict, as it is basic to their interaction with their supervisor. Moreover, few members seriously believe that "self-managed" means "independent." By itself, the effect of the first assumption is probably a trivial problem for Hyten's SMWT model.

The second assumption is that a group interaction takes place which is enhanced (or more properly exacerbated) by the information that the team is self-managed. The "team" is, of course, an ephemeral construct. In the process of enacting it, however, effort must be undertaken by team members in order to assure that the product of the team is something different from the mere sum of the efforts of isolated individuals. The difference between teams and summed performance is the sought-after purpose for creating the SMWT. To the extent that a team process occurs, members might be said to be subject to reinforcers from the activities of team creation, unique from those otherwise experienced. Once created, the work team, and the individuals making it up, must somehow make the decisions for which the team is given both freedom and responsibility. This results in a different dynamic, one in which the relationship of responsibility to self-management must be discovered. Group accountability is not a simple problem. Similarly, as a result of the team process, supervision is unlikely to be directed in the same manner: Some of it turns to the team, addressing team behavior and product as separate elements.

As a consequence, these complications suggest that the "team" becomes a functioning entity for practical purposes, although individuals remain in the picture at the same time. Perhaps these added considerations are best conceived as a layering to Hyten's model. Although I would view them as essential to a close understanding of what takes place, the original model remains correct when examined on its own terms.

Finding Our Place in a Constructed Future

Linda J. Hayes
University of Nevada, Reno

My aim in this chapter is to direct our attention to the future, as articulated by futurists, for the purpose of assessing the preparation of behavior science to participate in it. In as much as the future is a probabilistic domain, it is necessary to examine futurists' claims as to its likely character, and to evaluate the coherence of their arguments in this regard. Having done so, we may examine the capacity of behavior science, as currently formulated, to contribute to its unfolding.

In making this analysis, I will be taking the position that the most significant and pervasive feature of the massive societal transformation said to be underway is the transition from mechanism to systems theory. I will argue, further, that neither futurists nor behavior analysts appear to be fully informed as to the nature of this theory or its implications. Finally, I will suggest that the future is, in essence, an aspect of the present circumstance. As such, systems theory is not so much something that behavior scientists will necessarily adopt when the future arrives, but rather something that they cannot afford to overlook in the immediate present.

Let me begin, then, by recounting the claims of futurist scholars as to the future of our society.

The Future in Futurist Perspective

The pace of change in society has increased enormously, and rather abruptly, over the past few decades. In fact, many scholars are suggesting that the latter third of twentieth century may be viewed as a period of fundamental transformation of the modern world (Ray, 1993; Brutoco, 1993; Ferguson, 1993; Zukov, 1993). Our society is said to be undergoing a "paradigm shift"[1], defined as "a profound change in the thoughts, perceptions, and values that form a particular vision of reality" (Capra, 1982, p. 30).

Transformations of so great a magnitude as to be described as a societal paradigm shift are observed only when societal conditions come to be configured in such a way that the continuation of the society they describe is threatened.[2] The scientific and industrial revolutions of the past centuries are widely believed to have produced just such a configuration of conditions (Harman, 1993; Harmon & Horman, 1993; Capra, 1982, p. 31; Capra, 1993; Henderson, 1993). While undeniable benefits to society have been forthcoming from the social and economic practices characteristic of these historical movements, along with them have come problems of gigantic proportions. The planet has become a dangerous place to live – no longer merely because of the impending doom of modern weapons of mass destruction – but also because of its contamination with hazardous waste, its man-

---

[1] See Kuhn (1970) for an extensive discussion of paradigms and paradigm shifts.
[2] Presumably, if a fundamental transformation is not observed under these conditions, what is observed is the degradation of a particular society.

made climate change, its pervasive degradation. Coupled with these conditions are uncontrolled population growth, chronic poverty, and hunger. In short, the global ecosystem, upon which the further evolution of life on earth depends, is at stake (Capra, 1982, p. 23; Gauntlett, 1993; Maynard & Mehrtens, 1993). The current transformation of societal practices shows a realization of the catastrophic proportions of this situation.

Capra (1982, p. 31) contends that a paradigm shift, such as the one underway, is not a unique circumstance in societal history. It is, rather, a phase of a much larger process of cyclical change in value systems observed in all manifestations of culture (Sorokin, 1937- 41).[3] Still, however, Capra (see also Zukov, 1993; Henderson, 1993) claims that the societal transformation currently underway "may well be more dramatic than any of the proceeding ones, because the rate of change in our age is faster than ever before, because the changes are more extensive, involving the entire globe, and because several major transitions are coinciding" (1982, pp. 32-33).

Major Coinciding Transitions

In proclaiming the unusually dramatic character of the present societal transformation, Capra (1982, p. 29-31) notes three coinciding transitions, one having to do with material conditions, one with philosophical views, and one with social relations. These transitions are described below.

Material Conditions. The first of these transitions is that from exhaustible fossil fuels to renewable solar energy, a shift that will involve radical changes in global economic and political systems (Capra, 1982, p. 30). The depletion of the world's supply of fossil fuels, occurring over the course of a relatively short period of unqualified growth, accelerated production, and excessive consumption, is being accompanied by certain adjustments in our understanding of cultural practices and their likely outcomes. For example, it is no longer possible to believe that unlimited material progress will be achieved through economic and technological develop-ment (Capra, 1993). Similarly, it is no longer profitable to view societal life as a competitive struggle for existence (Zukov, 1993; Henderson, 1993).

More specifically, in the economy of old paradigm, life was viewed as a struggle for power, necessitating manipulation and domination over nature. The outcome of this struggle, if successful, was wealth, defined solely in terms of financial assets (Maynard & Mertins, 1993). The society profited from a short-sighted exploitation of limited resources (Osterberg, 1993), and promoted excessive consumption via planned obsolescence, advertising pressure, and the creation of "artificial needs" (Ferguson, 1993).

The society of new paradigm is much more sensitive to the long-term ecological and human costs of such a strategy. The new paradigm embraces a more organic or Taoistic view of work and wealth (Joba, Bryant, & Ray, 1993). It emphasizes cooperation with nature, and conceptualizes wealth as intellectual capital and social accounting, in additional to financial rewards to stockholders. Sustainable levels of

---

[3] It is also possible that this process of cyclical change is a phase of an even larger pattern of change about which no such rhymic fluctuations are occurring, or have yet to have had opportunity for detection.

consumption are appropriate to this view, achieved by way of conservation, keeping and recycling of resources, as well as by promoting innovation and invention to serve "authentic needs" (Ferguson, 1993).

In summary, the new paradigm constitutes a commitment to the creation of what has come to be called a "sustainable society", defined by Lester Brown of the *World Watch Institute* as "one that satisfies its needs without diminishing the prospects of future generations" (as cited in Capra, 1993, p. 234). As Zukov (1993) explains, we are experiencing the shift from an economy based on scarcity and oriented toward exploitation, to one based on abundance and oriented toward contribution – a shift "from maximal extraction from the environment – human and nonhuman – to maximal contribution" (p. x).

Social Relations. The second transition focuses on a change in social relations, namely, the decline of patriarchy and its various conceptual implications. A patriarchy may be understood as a social system "in which men – by force, direct pressure, or through ritual, tradition, law and language, customs, etiquette, education and the division of labor – determine what part women shall or shall not play and in which the female is everywhere subsumed under the male" (Rich, 1977).

The patriarchal character of societal organization is difficult to recognize because it is so all-pervasive: As Capra (1982, p. 28) points out, patriarchy has prevailed in Western civilization and its precursors, as well as in most other civilizations, for at least three thousand years. As such, our most basic ideas about human nature and our relation to the universe are formulated in terms of this doctrine. Indeed, it has been so universally accepted that it is taken to be not just a particular doctrine but, instead, to constitute the "law of nature" itself. For purposes of exposition, however, patriarchal doctrine is recognizable in a number of interrelated themes, namely ownership, hierarchy, and domination (Zukov, 1993).

Until recently, patriarchy has never been openly challenged. This situation is now changing. Attention to the domination of a perspective historically associated with men has been drawn by Feminism, one of the strongest cultural currents of our time. While this movement has played out in the public domain as a gender conflict, it is not adequately depicted as such in the present context. The current paradigm shift is not one in which women will become equal to or surpass their male counterparts in more adequate or successful adoption of the societal views historically associated with men. Neither is it properly understood as the emergence of a matriarchy. Rather, the eastern polarity of the yin and yang more closely depicts the shift in social relations underway at the present time.

Eastern sages have articulated this polarity as a unity of opposites, one pole representing self-assertion, the other integration. Self-assertion, or yang behavior, is displayed in demanding, aggressive and expansive action predicated on linear, casual thinking. In opposition, integration is furthered by yin behavior, which is predicated on field-theoretical assumptions. Yin behavior is responsive, cooperative and intuitive, as well as shows sensitivity towards and awareness of one's surrounds (Capra, 1982, pp. 43-44). Neither operates effectively in the absence of the other. Rather, both yin and yang behaviors are necessary for harmonious social and ecological relations. The Feminist movement represents a restoration of balance in societal organization and understanding, a circumstance Capra believes "will have a profound effect on our future evolution" (1982, p. 30).

To summarize the transitions occurring with respect to material conditions and social relations, futurists claim that the "Age of Information", culminating out of the scientific and industrial practices of past centuries reached a point at which conditions were ripe for change. Society is, thereby, entering a new age, the "Age of Light" (Henderson, 1991, 1988), as reflected in the shift from expansion to conservation, from competition to cooperation, from quantity to quality, and from domination to partnership (Capra, 1993).

Philosophical Views. The third transition, intimately related to the other two, represents a shift in the dominant philosophical perspective of culture from one of mechanism to that of systems theory. This transition is articulated in both ontological and epistemological terms. From an ontological perspective, the realistic and reductionistic view of the universe as a mechanical system, composed of elementary building blocks, is being replaced by a more holistic perspective. In this new perspective, everything is assumed to be interrelated with everything else, their interrelations, further, constituting the *subject* of analysis (Capra, 1993; Harman & Hormann, 1993; Zukov, 1993; Henderson, 1993).

In epistemological terms, the shift to systems theory may be observed in the current challenge to scientific method as the only valid approach to knowing (Hayes, 1997). Other ways of knowing, while as yet somewhat vaguely defined, are coming to be seen as having equal, if not greater, value. For example, Zukov (1993) appeals to the concept of "intuition"; Henderson (1993) to "soul" or "spirituality"; and Capra (1982, 1993) and Hayes (1997a) to a kind of "mysticism", as valid means of knowing.

I will return to these characterizations of knowing. For now, however, we may simply acknowledge that the philosophical views of the new paradigm reflect what has come to be called systems theory, in contrast to the mechanistic theories of the old paradigm. As previously indicated, a paradigm shift occurs when societal conditions come to be configured in such a way that the continuation of the society they describe is threatened. More conceptually, a paradigm shift occurs when the philosophy of the old paradigm is no longer able to describe events in accordance with our experience of them. The philosophical ideas of the old paradigm have reached a stage at which their limitations, and the severity of those limitations, have become apparent. They are no longer workable.

Accelerating Pace of Change

Capra (1993) further suggests that the current societal transformation may be more dramatic than any of the proceeding ones because the pace of change is so much greater now than in previous eras. Hence, at this juncture, we may consider the pace of change itself, along with its sources and implications.

Information Access and Scholarship

As has been documented elsewhere, (e.g., Davis, 1987; Toffler, 1980) the accelerated pace of change in our age is a function of the development and dissemination of information technologies. The possibility of access to information, in the form of descriptions and depictions of others' experiences, expands an individual's scope of contact with the world far beyond what would be possible to experience directly in a single lifetime (Skinner, 1969, p. 141). Information technologies have expanded the scope of that contact to global dimensions. Moreover, they have made vast amounts of information available in near-instantaneous time.

One outcome of immediate access to vast amounts of information has been a shift in emphasis in scholarship. At the turn of the century, it was still possible for an individual scholar to demonstrate expertise in multiple domains of knowledge. In other words, Renaissance thinkers, while in diminishing numbers, were still among us. However, as the quantity of scientific information grew rapidly over the next several decades, and the time required to access and manipulate it remained unchanged, scholarship of this sort was no longer possible to accomplish. Accordingly, scholarship became increasingly specialized, focusing on ever more restricted domains and encompassing significantly less ground than that of even a single historical discipline. This narrowing of focus occurred in all of the sciences, and to a degree commensurate with the quantities of scientific knowledge produced by them. As such, the trend toward disciplinary subdivision has been most pronounced in the most well established and productive of the basic sciences. It has also been apparent in our own science of behavior. It was over these decades that applied behavior analysts lost contact with the basic science of behavior, basic scientists likewise with the applied domain, and both of them with the philosophy of behaviorism, let alone with the discipline of psychology as a whole.

Evidence of this change in the character of scholarship can be found in the rather cumbersome mismatch of structural and functional units on most university campuses. While traditional academic departments still constitute the principle structural units, the functional units are comprised of academic programs representing subdivisions of these traditional disciplines, often sharing with other subdivisions nothing more than their organization as a structural unit.

In more recent times, the trend toward specialization in scholarly pursuits has begun to reverse, as seen in the rise of interdisciplinary programs on university campuses across the country. While many of these programs originated as collaborative efforts among collections of specialized scholars dealing with overlapping subject matters, they no longer depend on collaborations of this sort. On the contrary, we are witnessing a revival of the Renaissance thinker in our society. That is to say, it is once again possible for individual scholars to demonstrate competence in multiple domains of knowledge, a circumstance made possible by immediate access to enormous quantities of information heretofore unavailable.

Skepticism concerning the new scholarship. A certain amount of skepticism prevails with respect to the quality of this new scholarship. One theme poses doubt concerning the adequacy of the scholarly repertoires developed; the other is directed at the adequacy of its source. With regard to the repertoires of the new scholars, the view prevails that while these repertoires may be extraordinarily broad in scope, they lack precision. The new scholars are said to lack the depth of understanding characteristic of the repertoires of the old scholars. The criticism levied against the source takes the form of assertions that the Internet is full of junk and misinformation.

Both of these criticisms have some legitimacy, but only in so far as the new scholarship is unlike the old. It is, in fact, very likely the case that the depth of understanding of any one discipline on the part of an interdisciplinary information worker is more shallow than that of a print specialist of an earlier day. It is also the case that the same standards of quality assurance that have regulated print media do not prevail for the electronic distribution of information. Neither of these criticisms is worth making, however. The new scholarship is part and parcel of the massive transition currently underway and it cannot be avoided. It's too late for these sorts of criticisms. The revolution has already happened.

Furthermore, depth of understanding is no longer necessary to acquire as a potential repertoire in the sense that Skinner (1974) has formulated this construction. Whatever depth may be required in coming to terms with a particular subject matter is immediately available. The locus of potential, in other words, is no longer the individual scholar. It is the source of information. It is the source that possesses the repertoire, in other words. As such, cumulative personal knowledge, of the sort once needed for problem solving in a given field of study, is no longer needed. It is available *as needed,* and instantaneously so. Hence, the depth of understanding of the new scholar's repertoire is not an issue of needed concern.

It is also not useful to say that the scholarship of the present day is superficial – that today's Internet scholar is somehow less adequate than the Renaissance scholar of an earlier day. Quite the contrary, today's scholar has access to much more information than had even been accumulated by all of yesterday's Renaissance scholars put together. In short, scholarship is no longer the province of those whose lifetimes have been spent laboriously thumbing through rapidly deteriorating printed works pulled from the dusty shelves of over-stuffed libraries. Scholarship has become a matter of how facile one is at accessing immediately available information, a circumstance that ought to be producing a massive restructuring of university curricula more rapidly than appears to be occurring.

Skepticism concerning the source of information. Secondly, the argument that the source is unreliable is to overlook the fact that this circumstance applies to all information media. Print media do not embody truth anymore than electronic sources. I say this for two reasons, first the concept of correspondence-based truth is vacuous (Hayes, 1993). Secondly, if pragmatic truth is at issue, it is evaluated in terms of its usefulness. Utility is a relative issue, though – one requiring multiple examples and non-examples for its evaluation. Immediate access to enormous quantities of examples and non-examples, made possible by information technologies, is most surely an advantage in assessing the relative truth of any particular bit of information. That is to say, the new technologies make judgements as to the quality of information much easier to make.

The adequacy of electronic sources of information poses a threat to print scholarship, however. To suggest that the limitations imposed by the time required to access information from print sources are sufficient to reduce the value of such information has the effect of undermining the entire scientific enterprise. Irrational confidence in these sources serves to nullify this claim. That is to say, it may well be that confidence we have developed with regard to print sources is a function of the limited number of sources any given scholar has been able to contact in a lifetime. Similarly, it seems likely that rigidity of scientific method, with which our own science is burdened, evolves as an antidote to relatively limited opportunities to contact multiple exemplars as to their relative utility. The latter circumstance implies a confusion of scientific rigor, which is essential to scientific development, with methodological rigidity, which has the opposite effect (Kantor, 1970). In short, critics of the Internet, as a superior source of information, protest too loudly. In summary, there is no cause for concern about the source of information upon which the new scholar operates.

Opportunities for communication. The scholars of the new age are not merely passive recipients of information. The new technologies enable previously unheard-of possibilities for participation. The sources are alive. In other words, it is not merely an issue of *information access* that the new technologies afford. It is *communication* among information workers.

The combination of information access and reciprocity of information exchange has meant that ours is becoming an ever more verbal existence. While almost all human behavior is verbal to some degree, this being the distinguishing characteristic of human behavior (Hayes & Hayes, 1992), this aspect of human action has become its dominant feature in recent times. Increasing numbers of people are spending increasing proportions of their waking hours engaged, not only in verbal behavior as a concomitant of other forms of activity, but as their primary form of activity. They have become "information workers", spending all of their productive hours, as well as much of their recreational time, in front of computers. The characterization of the present societal configuration as "The Age of Information" acknowledges this aspect of our societal circumstance, along with the rapid and massive societal change produced and predicted by it.

Implications of an Increasingly Verbal Society

The characteristics and implications of an increasingly verbal existence are both exceedingly difficult to describe and beyond the scope of the present chapter. Nonetheless, some discussion of the implications of this circumstance and its relevance to changing material conditions, social relations, and philosophical views, seems warranted.

Verbal interaction is the means by which we are able to contact things and events in their absence, including such things as are absent by virtue of their separation in time and space, their existence configuring by way of logical operations, their extraordinarily small or large size, and even their non-existence (Parrott, 1984). In short, our contact with such things as are not immediately available for non-instrumental observation depends on verbal activity, and its written and graphical products.

Verbal interaction is also the means by which complexities may be captured in symbolic form for ease of handling, and for conjoining with other complexities, in taking account of vast amounts of data. Complexities of this magnitude are not able to be contacted, much less comprehended, in the absence of verbal interaction. Quite simply, in the absence of this type of action, our orientation to our world is limited to our contacts with things and events of the immediate present.

Language is not only the means by which we may make contact with things and events in their absence, and in so doing, comprehend complexities of enormous scope, it is the basis of all deliberate modifications of the natural world. In other words, culture is configured by language, and the elaboration of culture is a matter of how prevalent is language in the culture at large, and how dominant is this type of activity in the repertoires of its individual members.

The evolution of an extraordinarily verbal culture in a relatively short period of time, as an outcome of the advent and expansion of information technologies, cannot help but draw into consideration a culture's historical problem solving strategies. That is to say, it becomes necessary to address the manner in which its new-found complexity may be understood and managed. Inevitably, the culture's overarching philosophical perspective, namely mechanistic determinism, is held up to scrutiny; and in the unfolding of the new societal context, it is found wanting. More specifically, when the subject to understand becomes vast arrays of verbally confronted things and events, along with their patterns of simultaneous interaction, mechanistic thinking is ill-suited to the task of making it comprehensible. Mechanistic thinking structures events in series, on a linear temporal plane; and the matrix of events to be structured do not have this character. They comprise, instead, ever-expanding, multi-factor, fields of interaction.

The above analysis suggests that the relation between the material, social and philosophical conditions of a culture is one of mutuality of influence, such that changes in one are accompanied by changes in the others. The pace of this change is thereby quickened by transformations in any of these circumstances. At the present time in our culture, we are experiencing an explosion of verbal activity, and our increasingly verbal existence may be understood to be at the heart of the societal transition currently underway.

The analyses to follow are based on this understanding, albeit somewhat ill developed at this point. For present purposes we may simply acknowledge that society has changed radically of late, that the pace of change is ever quickening, and that verbal action is both a source and a medium of these changes.

Critical Analysis of Futurist Logic

While Capra (1993) and others describe the transitions occurring with respect to material conditions, social relations and philosophical views as *coinciding*, their concurrence at this time is by no means a coincidence – at least such would not be concluded from the perspective of systems theory. From a systems perspective, as indicted above, massive changes in ecological and economic circumstances, entailing massive changes in our practices with respect to them, would not be expected to occur in a context of ill-suited social practices and contradictory philosophical understandings. On the contrary, the decline of patriarchy, coupled with the transition to systems theory, bespeak of our *immersion* in a changed ecological and economic circumstance. In other words, these three transitions have emerged in concert with one another – as interdependent aspects of the societal paradigm shift already in progress.

Systems theory problems. The confusion in this regard relates to the issue of systems theory in particular. It is not completely clear that futurist thinking, as cited previously, reflects the fundamental character of this theory. Underlying this theory is a number of inviolable premises upon which futurists appear to vacillate improperly. In the first place, systems theory assumes that everything is interrelated with everything else; and further, that these interrelations constitute the *subject* of analysis. Implied by this premise is a reformulation of the concept of causality. More specifically, the dichotomy of cause and effect, which is absolutely fundamental to mechanistic thinking, is abandoned by systems theory. In place of this construction is the view that causal knowledge is knowledge of the factors participating in an event field, along with their organization or pattern of interrelation (Kantor, 1950, p. 157).

As such, systems theorists demonstrate expert treatment of their subject matter by incorporating an increasingly large number of factors and their interrelations into their accounts. This is quite unlike the practices of their mechanistic counterparts, whose aim, instead, is to isolate as small a number of factors as possible, for the purpose of assigning them independent causal, or dependent effect, status.

Secondly, mechanistic theory promotes an understanding of events in terms of their temporal relations, wherein causes and effects are nominated in irreversible succession. Systems theory, by contrast, focuses on the simultaneous concurrence of factors, promoting an understanding of events primarily in terms of their spatial arrangements.

So enormous are these differences, and so contrary to mechanistic views as to the nature of scientific knowledge and the means by which it is accumulated, that systems theorists are obliged to challenge scientific method, arguing that it is not the only valid approach to knowing.

Their alternative, described variously as "intuition", "spirituality", and "mysticism," among other such terms, lacks precision, however. Even more troubling, these conceptualizations of knowing appear to imply free construction. That is, they appear to represent products of constructional activity that are neither built up from confrontations with things and events of the natural world, nor are continuous with them.

Meta-science solutions. Another, more palatable, interpretation, while not explicit in the works of these scholars, is possible to make of these views, though. It seems likely that what these scholars are referring to is a kind of knowledge achieved as an outcome of an elaborate series of legitimate, logical abstracting and generalizing operations, which are common to all scientific enterprises (Kantor, 1945, pp. 26-27). Such practices eventuate in highly abstract concepts, which are valuable outcomes for science provided that they sustain a continuity with descriptions of observed things and events. In any given science, series of abstracting and generalizing operations proceed without restraint so long as the abstractions achieved continue to be useful in the articulation of laws and principles (Kantor, 1950, pp. 20-21), and, in general, provide for a more effective orientation of the system builder to the things and events originally observed.

In the present case, the science at issue is not any one, but rather many sciences in interdisciplinary relation. As such, the processes of abstracting and generalizing adopted by futurists pick up at a latter point. Specifically, they begin with the most abstract concepts developed in these specific sciences, and produce conceptual products of even greater abstraction, and importantly, of inordinately greater scope. Futurist scholars are working at a meta-scientific level, in other words. As a way of distinguishing the outcomes of logical operations at the meta-scientific level from those produced at the level of the specific sciences, and as a way of drawing attention to them, meta-scientific knowing comes to be described as "intuition", among other more provocative terms.

As I see it, provocation is an unnecessary tactic if, indeed, meta-scientific knowing emerges without a break in continuity with descriptions of the things and events making up the confrontable subject matters of the specialized sciences. In short, if the aim of futurist thinkers is to comment on a kind of knowing that, though unlike disciplinary scientific knowing, is not itself anti-scientific, then terms less objectionable to scientific sensibilities would have been more appropriate choices.

Cautions. The deliberate selection of objectionable terms thereby raises concern. Specifically, we may wonder if the requisite continuity between abstract constructions and original observations is being sustained in futurist thinking; and, further, we may ask if the series of abstracting and generalizing operations undertaken by futurists have proceeded beyond the point at which their products have scientific meaning or utility. There is a danger, in other words, that meta-scientific thinking on the parts of futurists is becoming absolutistic and universalistic, both of which imply mechanistic suppositions.

Tendencies in this regard are common among philosophers with little or no training in naturalistic psychology, wherein the available alternative on this theme is cultural tradition. In this tradition, the human organism is endowed with transcendental powers of reason and will which serve to overcome the uncertainties of human existence. One of the uncertainties of the human existence is, of course, the future; and it is the future that futurists believe they are describing in their treatises.

The Future in Behavior Analytic Perspective

As a behavior scientist, operating upon a foundation of systems theory, I do not believe that it is possible to describe something that has yet to unfold. Predicting the future is not antithetical to behavior science, however. On the contrary, prediction is one of the stated aims of the enterprise (Skinner, 1953, p. 18). Indeed, events of both the past and the future figure prominently in causal explanations of observed happenings. I believe that my disagreement with radical behaviorists on this issue bespeaks of our operating on different philosophical foundations. As I see it, Radical Behaviorism is not an instance of systems theory. It is, rather, one of mechanistic determinism.

Mechanistic determinism is not an insignificant foundation for the operational branch of any science, including the science of behavior. Causal constructions, grounded in linear time, are particularly serviceable, and thereby common, at the investigative level of most sciences. However, when mechanistic thinking is expanded out of this domain to that of postulation, where definitions and premises are articulated, it inevitably keeps unwitting company with dualism. To the extent that behavior science distinguishes itself from conventional psychology on the basis of its rejection of dualism, this alliance is problematic.

In the present section, my aim is to substantiate these claims. In doing so, I will suggest that the causal constructions characteristic of behavior science are indicative of its adherence to mechanistic philosophy. I will also suggest that such constructions are inevitable when events are conceptualized as occurring on a linear temporal plane, and that these premises comport with dualistic notions.

We turn, then, to this analysis and its implications for what it means to talk about the future.

A Linear Conception of Time

As ordinarily conceived, time is understood as a metric by which is measured the irreversible succession of events constituting our universe. Time is the means by which this succession is construed in the broadest of senses.

The beginning and the end. The linear structure of this concept cannot help but engender consideration of its beginning and ending, as succession necessarily entails boundary conditions of this sort. Conceptualizing the beginning and ending of time presents a difficulty, however, in that neither is possible of direct experience on the part of any one. From the standpoint of any one's experience, there has never been a time in which the events of this succession were not ongoing, nor could there be a time in which they were not. In other words, in any one's experience there has been no beginning – we have always been here and it has never been any time other than now.

The end, likewise, is not possible of direct experience since this experience would require a continuation beyond the end of experience from which standpoint the end could be seen as such, and to see it as such is itself experience. Hence, to conceptualize the beginning and ending of time, as demanded by the linear structure of this concept, it becomes necessary to postulate something "not of experience" to complete the analysis.

Historically, the most often postulated something "not of experience" has been a deity of sorts. Only a deity seems capable of the sort of timeless-spaceless conceptualization required to solve the problems of the beginning and the end of time. And, more specifically with regard to the beginning, it is only a deity who seems capable of creating something out of nothing, as the beginning of time conceptualized as the onset of the event succession, implies.

The story of creation is not merely a solution to the problem of origin, though. The assumption of a first cause in the configuration of the universe is inevitably coupled with the end or destination toward which the succession of events is proceeding. A beginning implies an end and, as just argued, the end, like the beginning, is realizable only on the part of something "not of experience." It is thereby necessary to assume that the end will occur when the succession of events has reached its destination – a point known only to one who has both seen the end at the beginning, and who will continue to prevail beyond the end so as to recognize its achievement. It is only a deity who seems capable of fulfilling this analytical requirement.

Means of progressing from beginning to end. In postulating an end to the succession of events, as required by the postulation of its beginning, there comes an obligation to characterize the succession itself. The succession of events is not held to be aimless, in other words. It is assumed to proceed to an end – a destiny conceived at the time of its beginning – and which constitutes its purpose or *raison d'être*. A characterization of the means by which one event follows another to the end foreseen in the beginning inevitably follows. More than one answer to this question has been proposed in the history of thought. As formulated in behavior science, however, this analytical requirement has been fulfilled by the concept of causality: The succession of events is put into motion by a first cause, after which each event in succession causes the next until the end it reached.

In summary, the conceptualization of time as a measure of an irreversible succession of events makes it necessary to postulate both its beginning and its end. Because these points are inconceivable from the standpoint of any one's experience, they are held to constitute aspects of the experience of something other than ourselves. A deity is thereby assumed to set the events in motion toward a predetermined end, on a pattern of linear causality, measured in time.

A linear conception of time, wherever invoked, identifies the system in which this conceptualization operates as a dualistic one. Hence, behaviorism, despite its purported rejection of dualism is, at the most fundamental level, thoroughly dualistic. Behaviorists are particularly wary of the implications of dualistic premises for scientific and philosophical understandings. Hence, I am assuming that behaviorists, more than any other group of intellectual workers, may find some value in an alternative, non-dualistic philosophical formulation, in which time is conceptualized in a non-linear fashion.

Preliminaries to a Discussion of Non-linear Time

Pursuant to a formulation of non-linear time are certain clarifications, the first having to do with the standpoint from which the characterization of psychological phenomena must be made; the second, with the manner in which psychological phenomena must be characterized so as to fit within such a formulation.

Standpoint of Analysis

A linear conception of time, as we have been discussing, is experienced from the standpoint of an observer of events (Parrott, 1986).[3] By way of contrast, non-linear time is experienced in the role of a participant in those events. The latter perspective raises an insurmountable difficulty when one's aim is not merely to experience non-linear time but also to describe it, as I aim to do in the following section. Nonetheless, I will proceed, recognizing that some inconsistency in what I will say is inevitable.

Psychological Phenomena

Absence of substantive structure. A non-dualistic formulation of psychological phenomena requires that they be conceptualized as *events* as opposed to things, as we ordinarily understand these terms. More specifically, a psychological event is an interrelation of actions arising, simultaneously, from organismic and environmental sources. To put it another way, a psychological event is a function obtaining between responding and stimulating – a function embedded in an event field comprised of many other factors. Understood in this manner, a psychological event has no substantive or material structure.

The absence of substantive structure characteristic of psychological events does not relegate them to the category of the "non-natural." Neither are such events assumed possible of acquiring substance by way of their participation in fields in which substantive events are also participating. This is to say, from the present perspective, a psychological event is not possible of being located in, based on, reduced to, or otherwise interpreted as a physical, chemical, biological, or any other type of *thing*. To repeat, psychological phenomena are not things. They are events.

Having no substantive structure does not imply that psychological events are devoid of other properties. On the contrary, psychological events are distinguished from other event types on the basis of their corrigibility, their complexity, and their contextual operation.

Corrigibility and complexity. The corrigibility and complexity of psychological events go hand in hand. Psychological functions, that is, respondings with respect to stimulatings, evolve over repeated occurrences in such a way that they become increasingly complex. This complexity reflects the cumulative entailment of previous configurations in each new configuration of a given function. To reiterate a psychological function is a process of change – an evolution in which is entailed its history, and through which it thereby becomes increasingly complex.

Contextual operation. The isolation of insubstantial functions from their substantive sources permits a conceptualization of events that is not limited to the participation of functions inherent in the structural properties of immediately present object sources. Let me explain.

---

[3] L. J. Hayes is formerly known as L. J. Parrott.

Psychological events are always ongoing in an event field comprised of many other factors. As such, responding with respect to stimulating arising from one source object is always ongoing in spatio-temporal proximity to responding with respect to stimulating arising from another source. This proximity of functions permits substitutions of responding and stimulating (Kantor, 1924, p. 296), by which is meant that responding with respect to one source object is able to be actualized by the presence of another, and vice versa. To put it another way, the stimulation arising from object A may transfer to object B and thereby be available by way of the presence of object B.

Moreover, this availability is independent of the presence of object A in a given event field. In short, the transfer of insubstantial stimulus functions from one source object to another, occurring under conditions in which two or more functions are occurring in proximity, is the means by which we are able to respond to stimuli in their absence. It is also one of the principle means by which psychological functions become increasingly complex over repeated occurrences. In other words, once established, substitute stimulus functions continue to be entailed in the ongoing event configuration.

Further Clarification of Psychological Phenomena

A somewhat more radical approach to the issue of event characterization is required for an understanding of non-linear time. What is required for this purpose is not merely a distinction between functions and their object sources but, instead, the elimination of the sources as objects. In more familiar terms, a reconsideration of the concept of form is required for the present analysis (Hayes, 1997b).

Ordinarily, we conceptualize objects as having two sorts of properties: formal and functional. The formal properties of objects are regarded as inherent in those objects, whereby they are held to prevail independently of our interactions with them. The functional properties, conversely, are thought to be engendered in our interactions with them, and their prevalence is thereby dependent upon such interactions. This distinction is taken to be real in behavior science as evidenced by the fact that common functional properties are routinely attributed to common formal properties in this science.

From the present perspective, however, the formal properties of objects are *also* engendered in our interactions with them. We know that an object is heavy when we have difficulty lifting it, in other words. Accordingly, form may be understood as a reification of function – one that has served to give substantive characteristics to the background in which the insubstantial functions of the psychological sort are ongoing. As such, form is not an independent construct. It is derived from function, and this derivation is ill suited to an understanding on non-linear time. In the discussion of non-linear time to follow, therefore, we will be speaking only of psychological functions – only of *events* – and, moreover, we will be speaking of them from the standpoint of a *participant* in them.

The Future in Systems Theory Perspective

My strategy in attempting elucidate the meaning of non-linear time, as implied by systems theory, will be to reveal it through a stripping away of dependent constructions entailed in the conceptualization of linear time.

Event Plurality

The irreversible succession of events, of which linear time is construed as a measure, implies a plurality of events, as well as a means by which one event may be distinguished from another. From the standpoint of any one's experience, though, their participation in the event field is continuous, not discrete. No one's experience includes even a momentary discontinuity such as to suggest a plurality of events. Likewise, no one's experience includes a beginning of his or her participation, nor does anyone's include its ending. On the contrary, the event field in which any one is participating – that is, any one's participation – is continuously ongoing. There is only one event field in our experience – the one in which we are continuously participating. We are always right here and it is always right now.

Event Succession

If there is no plurality of events, then there can be no succession of them. The event field is more aptly construed as a continuous process of evolution wherein a pattern of interaction is becoming increasingly complex. Each "new" configuration entails the "previous" configuration such that the past does not "go by." The past is not "left behind" as a new event unfolds, as is suggested by the concept of succession. Instead, the past continues to prevail as an aspect of the ever-expanding complexity of the ever-present configuration of the singular event field (Hayes, 1992).

Causality

Turning to the construct of causality, recall that this construct is invoked in mechanistic formulations as the means by which one event produces the next in the purposeful succession of events, beginning with a first cause and continuing, event by event, until the end of events is reached. If, however, no plurality of events is experienced, and thereby no succession of them, there is no need to invoke a force by which one event of this plurality succeeds another. In other words, the concept of causality is superfluous in a non-dualistic formulation.

In summary, from the standpoint of an event participant, a plurality of events and their succession do not characterize our experience. There is, as such, no need for a concept of causality through which the succession of events may be seen to have purpose. More to the point, if there is only one event field, there is nothing to be measured in linear time. These are all constructions derived from our experience in our role as *observers*, for the purpose of *explaining* our experience. Ironically, they construe our experience in such a way that we are forced to invent something "not of experience" by which to explain it. In other words, there would be no need to appeal to a deity to account for the beginning of experience had we recognized that there is only one event and it has had no beginning. And there would be no need to appeal to a deity's foresight of the end, toward which the succession of events is proceeding, had we recognized that the one event in which we are participating is never ending.

Non-linear Time Defined

What this analysis suggests for the concept of non-linear time, as a characterization of the experience of participating in the continuously ongoing present, is that non-linear time is not really a time concept at all. It is, rather, a spatial conception. More specifically, it is a way of speaking about the ever-increasing complexity of the singular event field. Generally speaking, the more elaborate the action stimulated by current stimuli and those historically associated with them, the greater the number of "previous presents" may be assumed to have accumulated in that evolution of function. From this perspective, "memories" are not best described as old or new – of long or short term. They are, rather, more aptly described as thick or thin. Thick memories are relatively elaborate responses with respect to current stimulation, suggesting an evolution of many "previous presents." Thin memories are relatively simple responses stimulated by those same conditions, suggesting evolutions of functions involving few "previous presents."

Talk of the Past and Future

We turn now to what it means to talk of the past and the future.

Speaking of the Past. As may be obvious from what from what I have said so far, we do not experience the past as the past, but instead only as an aspect of the present circumstance (Hayes, 1992). It is in the complexity of this circumstance, which is continuously increasing, that we find what we ordinarily think of as the past, and what is operating when we speak of the past. The presence of the past in the present is what is implied in suggesting that the present is continuously ongoing. For analytical purposes, we might say that speaking of the past is "reactive" in that it occurs on the basis of existing functions of stimuli, most of which are substitutive in character, to use Kantor's (1924, p. 296) term.

Speaking of the future. Talk of the future may be understood similarly. In as much as the future has yet to unfold, our talk about the future can have the character only of the present circumstance. In other words, talk of the future is a description of what is already ongoing. It cannot describe that which is not yet subject to description.

Unlike talk of the past, however, talk of the future is "constructive" as well as reactive. By this I mean to suggest that, in addition to its occurrence on the basis of existing and primarily substitutive functions of stimuli, it appears also to be a process by which such functions are established. Talk about the future entails acts of abstracting, generalizing, and relating through which is constructed a substitutive and novel configuration of the event field. The scope of that configuration may be very narrow, as when a scientist predicts the occurrence of relatively trivial events; or it may be very broad, as when a futurist predicts a societal paradigm shift.

Operating in accordance with both existing and established substitute functions, talk of the future may also exhibit a less organized pattern than talk of either the past or the present. It is this aspect of future talk that gives it the appearance of novelty, and it would seem that the greater the scope of the event configuration constructed, the less patterned or more novel it becomes.

Despite these analytical distinctions, however, in the final analysis, talk of the future is not about the future. It is about the continuously ongoing event field. What we are doing when we speak of the future is making more and more elaborate descriptions of the present circumstance. Hence, we do not actually "predict" event configurations but rather describe the event configuration that is already ongoing. The probabilities we assign to future events, therefore, are not properties of those events but rather of our ongoing beliefs about them. Likewise, the goals we set are descriptions of "goals" we are already accomplishing. And the premises we adopt on the grounds of their utility are premises we already hold.

Utility. The concept of utility deserves a brief further comment. The utility of a description is able to be assessed only in a future event. Utility is an issue of how verbal action will operate in the future. Because the future has yet to arrive, though, the utility of some bit of verbal action must be evaluated in the ongoing event. However, the ongoing event, in and of itself, has no utility, and this is the only event available for analysis. From the standpoint of the present perspective, then, the construct of utility, like causality, is superfluous. We do not change the world by our actions; our actions are merely aspects of a change that is already underway.

Summary

In summary, I have argued that a linear conception of time comports with a dualistic philosophical formulation, and that both are evident in behaviorism despite its purported rejection of dualism. An alternative interpretation of time was suggested as a means of engendering a non-dualistic philosophical foundation upon which psychological events might be formulated. Required for this analysis was a characterization of psychological phenomena as functions operating in an event field, and the adoption of the perspective of a participant in that field for the purposes of description. The concept of non-linear time, achieved by way of these premises, was shown to be a spatial metaphor referring to the ever-increasing complexity of the evolving event field. Finally, I have suggested that talk of the past and future merely appear to suggest the possibility of control and prediction. Instead, they amount to more and more elaborate descriptions of the present circumstance.

Making Sense of Futurists' Claims

We return, now, to the claims of futurists, namely, that we are in the midst of a societal paradigm shift, and consider each of their claims in the context of the analysis just made of talking about the future.

Claims about Material Conditions

The transition from exhaustible fossil fuels to renewable solar energy is undeniable. The depletion of the world's supply of fossil fuels is not a claim about the future. It is a well-documented fact about the current circumstance. That it will entail radical changes in global economic and political systems, on the other hand, appears to be a description of circumstances as yet to unfold, that is, a description of the future. However, the interrelation of economic and political conditions with material conditions is not a description of circumstances as yet to unfold. It is, rather, a description of current circumstances in the manner of systems theory, in which everything is assumed to be related to everything else. How, precisely, economic and political conditions will configure with changes in material conditions – a future event of enormous complexity – can be neither described, nor accurately predicted. Nonetheless a change in any aspect of an integrated field implies a changed field (Kantor, 1950, p. 157). Hence there is no reason to doubt that the ongoing transition in material conditions is being accompanied by changes in economic and political circumstances. The latter are just more difficult to observe and document by ordinary methods of science, as a result of their inordinate complexity and breadth of scope.

Claims about Social Relations

As for the claim that our society is witnessing a decline of patriarchy, there is no shortage of evidence on this matter in current circumstances. From a systems perspective, it is antithetical to suggest that societal circumstances would not be reconfigured as women, embodying different anthropological and sociological histories, participate in them in growing numbers. Neither is it a comment on the future to characterize the perspectives of women in accordance with their historical circumstances.

To suggest, however, that women's yin characteristics of responsiveness, cooperation, intuitiveness, and sensitivity will remain intact, such as to balance the demanding, aggressive, and expansive characteristics of yang behavior, is questionable. This formulation of the future suggests an additive relation among the events participating in a field of interaction. Such relations are not in keeping with systems theory, however. From a systems perspective, "Causal changes in any field constitute a rearrangement in the simultaneous coexistence of factors in a unique pattern" (Kantor, 1950, p. 157). Hence to characterize the integration of yin and yang behaviors as one of balance and harmony is a questionable claim about the future formulated on a mechanistic plan..

To reiterate, that changes in societal conditions are occurring with increased participation of women in them is undeniable. Precisely how these changes will be manifested is not known nor can it be predicted with any accuracy, however. Hence, the claims of futurists in this regard are misdirected from a systems perspective.

Claims about Philosophical Views

With regard to the transition from mechanistic philosophy to systems theory, this claim also pertains not to future circumstances but to the current situation. Systems theory is fully ensconced in all of the basic sciences, including physics, chemistry, astronomy, and to a lesser extent, biology – at least at the level of postulation. It is also increasingly being adapted to fit the complexities of events characteristic of a number of social sciences and professional disciplines, including education, medicine, nursing, economics, and business, to name only a few. By contrast, mechanistic thinking thrives only in specific operational and technological circumstances, in which it is generally regarded as an analytic tool, as opposed to a philosophic foundation.

Moreover, the rapid growth of interdisciplinary sciences may be taken as evidence of the transition to systems theory, as it is only on the basis of this philosophic foundation that interdisciplinary work is of any consequence. By contrast, mechanistic logic obstructs effective interdisciplinary relations. More specifically, from a mechanistic perspective, the only relations one science may have with another are either to be reduced to the other, or to be relegated to effect status with respect to the other. As an example of the former, mechanistic logic fosters psychology's attempt to obliterate the independent sciences of sociology and anthropology on the grounds that their unique subject matters, of group action and cultural practices, may be interpreted as collections of individual behaviors. Relegation to effect status is illustrated in the mechanistic premise that psychological events are the effects of biological causes. It is only when the legitimate subject matters of the various specialized sciences are sustained intact as participants in complex fields of interaction, as postulated in systems theory, that consequential interdisciplinary work may be achieved. Systems theory is ideally suited to this task which, no doubt, explains its increasing prevalence on the emerging intellectual landscape.

Transition to Systems Theory in Behavior Science

The fact that behavior science has made so little progress toward systems theory, in the face of rather rapid changes in this direction in other basic sciences and applied disciplines, begs the question as to why this should be so. A plausible answer to this question may be gleaned from consideration of a number of inhibiting conditions peculiar to, or at least prevailing for, behavior science.

Inhibiting Conditions

Operational origins. System building in science necessarily takes place between two boundary conditions: the things and events of the natural world, and cultural traditions as to how that world is understood. Between these two boundaries, interrelated postulational and investigative sub-systems develop, the former alert to the vagaries and ineptitudes of cultural tradition, the latter in contact with the matrix of things and events. Neither of these sub-systems develops adequately in the absence of the other, as postulates constructed without regard to confrontable things and events are vacuous, and things and events interpreted in keeping with cultural tradition fail to adequately orient scientists to their world.

While all natural scientists recognize the value of keeping close to their observations of the world, not all appreciate the role of philosophy in assuring adequate treatment of those observations (see Parrott, 1986, for further discussion of this issue). In many sciences, particularly social sciences, postulation, that is, the construction of definitions and premises, is neglected in favor of investigation. This pattern may be attributed, at least in part, to the historical disservice of conventional mentalistic philosophy to science. While it has been important for science to abandon conventional philosophy in their system building efforts, overgeneralization to philosophy itself has led to inadequate postulational system building in many sciences.

The science of behavior fits this pattern. The philosophy of radical behaviorism grew out of its operational or investigative domain, which continues to constitute the principle source of its categorical concepts and premises. The definitional and assumptive products of system building by behavior analysts are not adequately articulated or organized, however. Even the most central of these concepts, namely response and stimulus, lack articulation and hence commonality of usage among proponents of radical behaviorism, as well as for the same proponent across different areas of study, is not found. My point is, simply, that the philosophy of Radical Behaviorism has not yet reached the fully postulational stage of its development (Parrott, 1986).

The fact that behavior science has not abandoned mechanistic logic in favor of contemporary systems theory is not, thereby, properly construed as "resistance to change". Resistance to change occurs when one is unduly wedded to the way things are. I don't believe radical behaviorists are sufficiently oriented to the way things are to be so tightly wedded to them. The issue is not one of resistance to systems theory. It is one of ignorance as to the nature and value of postulation of *any* sort in science. Radical behaviorists have taken an anti-philosophical stance, and it has prevented them from noticing or being impacted by the changes in philosophical views already in place in other sciences, and in the culture at large. In sum, radical behaviorism remains an operational system, and operational systems are, by definition, mechanistic is character.

Powerful technology. The stagnation of radical behaviorism at a philosophical level is also plausibly attributed to the extraordinary power of the technological products produced under its auspices. No other psychological system has developed technologies as powerful. Naturally enough, the technologies that were developed in this field emerged in concert with mechanistic determinism.

One outcome of this circumstance has been to foster the claim that since the purpose of science is to solve society's problems, the science of behavior, in having fulfilled this purpose exceptionally well, is beyond reproof. This, too, is a misunderstanding. In the first place, the exploitation of scientific products for social purposes does not constitute the only, nor even the most important, aim of applied science and technology. A more significant aim is the verification of scientific products (Kantor, 1958, p 158).

Secondly, it is not at the level of technology that systems theory has its most significant role to play, although even at this level, systems theory may be of service. For example, a systems approach might have prevented behavior science from having been crippled by mechanistic thinking at the operational or investigative level. Among the problems resulting from this alliance may be included: its unparalleled orthodoxy of method, circumscription of research to those problems able to accommodated by existing apparatus, and coverage of less than the full range of psychological events on the grounds of inconsistent logic as to the requirement of truth by agreement. (See Kantor, 1970, for other such issues.)

Isolationism. Finally, behavior scientists have a pursued a course of isolationism as a consequence of their initial lack of acceptance by the larger psychological community. One outcome of this course of action has been the development of an unusually high level of certainty and self-assurance among behavior analysts as compared to their counterparts in other sciences. In as much as science is the department of intellectual life that addresses itself to that which is unknown or unclear, and is thereby problematic, evangelism is not a particularly attractive characteristic for a scientist to cultivate, however. Certainty of this sort, both as an attitude and as an aim, is fostered by mechanistic thinking. That is to say, mechanism implies opportunity to achieve absolute truth and universal application. Systems theory makes no such claims. Quite the contrary, absolutism and universality are explicitly denied by systems theorists, adopting instead a specificity logic (Kantor, 1945, pp. 168-169).

Summary and Conclusions

My aim in this chapter has been to address the future of our society and our science. I began by examining futurists' claims that our society is undergoing a paradigm shift, involving massive transitions in material, social, and philosophical conditions, each characterized as having enormous implications for the future of society. This transformation of our society was also claimed to be occurring at an extraordinarily rapid pace, due to the advent and expansion of information technologies, a circumstance held to magnify even further the implications of the other changes said to be taking place.

I argued that the most significant of these changes was the shift in philosophical views from mechanism to systems theory, and that this transition was inevitable in view of the vast quantities of information to which our society now has ready access. Making sense of the multi-factorial, ever-expanding, fields of simultaneous interactions, which have become our new subject matter, is a task for which mechanism, with its emphasis on causality and its linear structure, is not well suited.

Whether or not futurists were operating in full accord with systems theory in characterizing the future of our society was questioned, however. Something short of full postulation characterizes much of this work, as exemplified in additive claims about the incorporation of new factors into integrated fields. It seems reasonable, as well, to be cautious about futurists' claims concerning the acquisition of knowledge, in that they suggest a search for absolute and universal truth.

Likewise, the philosophical foundations of radical behaviorism were drawn into question as to their workability with respect to making sense of our newly conceptualized subject matter. I concluded that radical behaviorism has yet to evolve out of the investigative stage of its development into a fully postulational system of science; and further, that as an investigative system, radical behaviorism inevitably operates against a background of mechanistic philosophy.

Having made these analyses, I proceeded to address the future from the perspective of a genuine systems theory, wherein time was formulated in non-linear terms, and the concepts of causality and utility were found to be superfluous. From this perspective, "talk about the future", in as much as the future is unavailable as a referent, does not refer to the future, calling into question the concept of prediction. Instead, talk about the future amounts to elaborate descriptions of the continuously ongoing, and ever more complex, singular event field in which we are all participating.

By way of conclusion, the fact that a great many, meta-scientific, interdisciplinary information workers are talking about a societal paradigm shift is evidence that our society is in the midst of such a change. Hence, it is in the interests of behavior analysts to examine their readiness to participate in its unfolding, particularly as it relates to the most significant of these transitions, namely the transition to systems theory. Moreover, it would serve behavior analysts to do so rapidly, given the pace of change our society is experiencing.

References

Brutoco, R. (1993). Sculpting a new business paradigm. In M. Ray & A. Rinzler (Eds.), *The new paradigm in business: Emerging strategies for leadership and organizational change.* New York: G. P. Putnam's Sons.

Capra, F. (1982). *The turning point.* New York: Bantum.

Capra, F. (1993). A systems approach to the emerging paradigm. In M. Ray & A. Rinzler (Eds.), *The new paradigm in business: Emerging strategies for leadership and organizational change.* New York: G. P. Putnam's Sons.

Davis, S. M. (1987). *Future perfect.* New York: Addison-Wesley.

Ferguson, M. (1980). *The acquarian conspiracy.* Los Angeles: Tarcher.

Ferguson, M. (1993). The transformation of values and vocations. In M. Ray & A. Rinzler (Eds.), *The new paradigm in business: Emerging strategies for leadership and organizational change* (pp. 28-34). New York: G. P. Putnam's Sons.

Gauntlett, S. (1993). The shifting paradigm of environmental management. In M. Ray & A. Rinzler (Eds.), *The new paradigm in business: Emerging strategies for leadership and organizational change.* New York: G. P. Putnam's Sons.

Harman, W. (1993). Approaching the millennium: Business as vehicle for global transformation. In M. Ray & A. Rinzler (Eds.), *The new paradigm in business: Emerging strategies for leadership and organizational change.* New York: G. P. Putnam's Sons.

Harmon, W., & Horman, J. (1993). The breakdown of the old paradigm. In M. Ray & A. Rinzler (Eds.), *The new paradigm in business: Emerging strategies for leadership and organizational change.* New York: G. P. Putnam's Sons.

Hayes, L. J. (1992). The psychological present. *The Behavior Analyst*, 15, 139-146.

Hayes, L. J. (1993). Reality and truth. In S. C. Hayes, L. J. Hayes, H. W. Reese, & T. Sarbin (Eds.), *Varieties of scientific contextualism* (pp. 35-44). Reno, NV: Context Press.

Hayes, L. J. (1996). Listening with understanding and speaking with meaning. *The Journal of the Experimental Analysis of Behavior, 65,* 282-283.

Hayes, L. J. (1997a). Scientific knowing in psychological perspective. In L. J. Hayes & P. M. Ghezzi (Eds.), *Investigations in behavioral epistemology* (pp. 123-141). Reno, NV: Context Press.

Hayes, L. J. (1997b). Understanding mysticism. *The Psychological Record, 47,* 573-596.

Hayes, S. C., & Hayes, L. J. (1992). Verbal relations and the evolution of behavior analysis. *The American Psychologist, 47,* 1383-1395.

Henderson, H. (1993). The age of light. In M. Ray & A. Rinzler (Eds.), *The new paradigm in business: Emerging strategies for leadership and organizational change.* New York: G. P. Putnam's Sons.

Joba, C., Maynard, H. B., & Ray, M. (1993). Competition, cooperation, and co-creation: Insights from the World Business Academy. In M. Ray & A. Rinzler (Eds.), *The new paradigm in business: Emerging strategies for leadership and organizational change.* New York: G. P. Putnam's Sons.

Kantor, J. R. (1924). *Principles of psychology,* Vol. I. Bloomington, IN: The Principia Press.

Kantor, J. R. (1945). *Psychology and logic,* Vol. I. Bloomington, IN: The Principia Press.

Kantor, J. R. (1950). *Psychology and logic,* Vol. II. Bloomington, IN: The Principia Press.

Kantor, J. R. (1958). *Interbehavioral psychology.* Bloomington, IN: The Principia Press.

Kantor, J. R. (1970). An analysis of the experimental analysis of behavior. *Journal of the Experimental Analysis of Behavior, 13,* 101-108.

Kuhn, T. (1970). *The structure of scientific revolutions.* Chicago: University of Chicago Press.

Maynard, H. B., & Mehrtens, S. E. (1993). Redefinitions of corporate wealth. In M. Ray & A. Rinzler (Eds.), *The new paradigm in business: Emerging strategies for leadership and organizational change.* New York: G. P. Putnam's Sons.

Parrott, L. J (1986). The role of postulation in the analysis of inapparent events. In H. W. Reese & L. J. Parrott (Eds.), *Behavior Science: Philosophical, methodological, and empirical advances.* Hillsdale, NJ: Erlbaum.

Parrott, L. J. (1984). Listening and understanding. *The Behavior Analyst, 7,* 29-39.

Ray, M. (1993). What is the new paradigm in business? In M. Ray & A. Rinzler (Eds.), *The new paradigm in business: Emerging strategies for leadership and organizational change.* New York: G. P. Putnam's Sons.

Skinner, B. F. (1953). *Science and human behavior.* New York: McMillan.

Skinner, B. F. (1969). *Contingencies of reinforcement.* New York: Appleton-Century-Crofts.

Skinner, B. F. (1974). *About behaviorism.* New York: Knopf.

Sorokin, P. A. (1937-41). *Social and cultural dynamics* (4 volumes). New York: American Book Company.

Toffler, A. (1980). *The third wave.* New York: William Morrow.

Zukov, G. (1993). Evolution and business. In M. Ray & A. Rinzler (Eds.), *The new paradigm in business: Emerging strategies for leadership and organizational change.* New York: G. P. Putnam's Sons.

Discussion of Hayes

Systems Theory for the Information Age

Kenneth W. Hunter, Jr.
University of Nevada, Reno

Dr. Hayes' paper begins with an exposition on the future, drawing heavily on the thinking of noted futurists like Capra. It is proposed by the futurists that we are in the midst of a societal paradigm shift of monumental proportions, perhaps even more significant than that which occurred during the industrial revolution. Dr. Hayes describes the futurist's perspective that the current societal paradigm shift has global dimensions, further characterized by a rapid rate of change on many fronts simultaneously.

The futurists lay out a set of global problems and their anticipated consequences, most prominent of which is the depletion of fossil fuels. I do not personally agree that fossil fuel depletion is the most important driver of societal change, and I certainly do not agree that renewable solar energy will satisfy any significant proportion of our global energy needs in the next decade. However, I do concur with the idea that changes are occurring that require society to look differently at itself, and in the spirit of Gaia, a philosophy that views the world as a complex, interconnected biotic and abiotic system, to pay particular attention to preserving the fragile green and blue planet on which we reside.

The two principal aims of Dr. Hayes' paper are both driven by this notion of a societal paradigm shift. She first elaborates on the idea that to properly construct the unfolding of a societal future, we must abandon past deterministic theories and embrace modern systems theory. She then proposes to more specifically examine the discipline of behavior analysis from a systems theory perspective. In the first section of the paper it seems as though Dr. Hayes supports the futurist position, but in the second part of the paper she takes exception to the futurists use of deterministic logic to define causes for their societal paradigm shift.

One of the curious notions presented by Dr. Hayes is her refusal to believe that the future can be predicted or even verbalized, suggesting that we are strictly limited to the "now". I certainly cannot dispute her philosophical position in that the future unfolds as it becomes the present, and there is no way we can predict the future with absolute certainly. However, I find it satisfying and indeed useful to read and talk about past events, to discuss the impact of these past events on the present, and to muse about such things as the way the past and present may influence future events. There are always too many antecedent contingencies in the present to predict the exact nature of the future, but knowledge of the past and present can yield valuable predictive information about future events. This is especially true, I believe, in the discipline of behavior analysis.

Dr. Hayes chooses to describe in some detail two coinciding transitions that are contributing to the proposed paradigm shift; systems theory and declining patriarchy. I found this to be a rather curious combination. Regarding systems theory she states that, "systems theory is replacing mechanical determinism as the dominant philosophical perspective in our society." I wonder what actual evidence exists for that statement, particularly since most of society operates without the benefit of knowing whether its actions are based on determinism or systems theory. Nevertheless, the notion of a systems theory in which strict causal relationships give way to broadly interconnected relationships between the parts of a greater whole is a well accepted operational concept. Modern systems theory, in which the whole can do new things that the individual parts cannot, is a very powerful concept perhaps descending from gestalt or holistic philosophies (or even mysticism, as Dr. Hayes proposes). I find it to be a very powerful concept.

Dr. Hayes mentions the decline of patriarchy as another of the major transitions occurring in and perhaps contributing to the societal paradigm shift. While one cannot deny the historic existence of patriarchy in most human societies, and while it is easy to agree that patriarchy is declining in many of those same societies, it is difficult to quantify the importance of the phenomenon to the proposed societal paradigm shift of today. She does not suggest that the decline in patriarchy will inevitably lead to a rise in matriarchy, but rather she describes the relationship using the eastern philosophic concept of yin and yang. In the spirit of yin and yang, the feminist movement will not come to dominate, but will help achieve a balance in societal organization.

As Dr. Hayes closes the first part of her paper and prepares to offer an "alternative interpretation" in the next section, I was left with the feeling that the complex issues that are thought to be driving this present societal paradigm shift had been oversimplified. In particular, the notion that society is completely aware of the rapid degradation of the earth's ecosystems and the precarious environmental consequences of human actions (and inactions), ignores the documented liaise-faire attitudes of many humans about the future. Paradigm shift or not, it is probably incorrect to assume that most members of society are aware of the reality of finite resources and infinite needs, nor is it correct to assume that even if they knew it would make a difference in their attitudes or actions. It may be that most members of society have little interest in the global future of the planet, or little need for futurists. However, I believe that substantial changes in society can arise through the efforts of a relatively small number of individuals who understand the challenges and bring to bear logical solutions such as those offered through a systems theory approach.

In the next section of her paper, Dr. Hayes embarks on an alternative account of societal transformation, first by throwing a wet blanket over the futurists. Interestingly, while the futurists may seem to embrace the idea of systems theory, their desire to attribute specific causes to the proposed societal paradigm shift (i.e., depletion of fossil fuels) actually smacks of blatant determinism. Dr. Hayes notes this conundrum, and moves forward with the idea of *change* as the currency of systems theory. More specifically, she notes that "culture is verbal action, verbal action culture", and so to understand the rate of cultural change we must understand verbal action.

If one equates verbal action with information exchange, then I agree completely with the notion that information availability through technological advances is changing our culture. Indeed, with very little effort just about anyone can experience sensory overload just sitting at their personal computer in their own home. And I also concur with Dr. Hayes about the way information access has led to the evolution of a new kind of Renaissance thinker. It is simply impossible for an individual to have comprehensive factual knowledge of a multiplicity of fields since no single individual can digest that much information. Sub-specialization in a discipline is the only way for most scholars who desire to master a subject. However, it may be that we are seeing the emergence of a new scholar, one that can utilize modern information technology to supplement the inadequate storage capacity of the cerebral cortex. Today's Renaissance scholar uses his or her brain for integration and synthesis, and relies more heavily on information technology for retrieving and storing factual information (computers handle long term memory, scholars simply need adequate RAM to process it!). This of course, will manifest itself in the way we structure our organizations, particularly in academia. The boundaries between colleges, schools, and departments need not be torn down, but they need to become porous. This porosity will minimize the historic barriers between disciplines and encourage work in interdisciplinary domains where, I believe, new discoveries occur more rapidly.

Dr. Hayes draws our attention to the adequacy of the information that is so readily available. When so much information can be accessed so rapidly, how can we be assured of its accuracy? My own notion about this is somewhat elitist perhaps, but after all I am a product of the academy. The internet should be viewed not as a source of information, but as a portal to a huge variety of sources of information. For example, if a scholar uses the internet to gain access to an on-line database of articles from archival scientific journals that are sponsored by professional academic societies and rigorously peer-reviewed, that source of information is no different than that obtained in a university library. Indeed, it is the same information. If a scholar obtains information from a personal or commercial website, that information should be viewed in the context of its source. Scholar beware.

Dr. Hayes further notes, quite appropriately, that information in the modern era is not disseminated in one direction (i.e., you read the author's book), but thanks to the miracles of information technology, the receiver of information can often interact with the purveyor of the information. Such communication is at the heart of the information age, and its nature is consistent with and supportive of a systems theoretical approach. Indeed, the facile communication made available through advances in information technology promises to strengthen the whole that represents our complex society by better establishing interconnections between its myriad parts.